SANDRA GUSTAFSON'S

CHEAP
SLEEPS IN
LONDON

The London Program
University of Notre Dame
Notre Dame, IN 46556-5639

FOURTH EDITION

**A Traveler's Guide to the
Best-Kept Secrets**

CHRONICLE BOOKS
SAN FRANCISCO

Printed in the United States of America

FOURTH EDITION

ISSN: 1074-5033
ISBN: 0-8118-1832-2

Book design: Words & Deeds
Author photograph: Marv Summers

Distributed in Canada by
Raincoast Books
8680 Cambie Street
Vancouver, B.C. V6P 6M9

10 9 8 7 6 5 4 3 2 1

Chronicle Books
85 Second Street
San Francisco, CA 94105

www.chroniclebooks.com

With heartfelt thanks to Marion Fujimoto, whose gracious help and support on the home front made this book possible.

Contents

To the Reader

Go where we may, rest where we will,
Eternal London haunts us still.
—Thomas Moore, Rhymes on the Road, *c. 1820*

When a man is tired of London, he is tired of life; for there is
in London all that life can afford.
—Dr. Johnson

The British hold a unique place in the hearts of Americans, for we are bound together and influenced in our daily lives by ancestral ties; shared language, laws, literature, customs, and traditions; and strong social and religious values. When we look back, most of us began our lifetime love affair with London as children, listening to nursery rhymes, singing songs, reading about the royal family, and pretending to be a part of it all. For many of us reared in the English-speaking world, a trip to London is like coming home.

Intriguing, invigorating, exciting, London is full of fascinating contrasts. Whether you are making your first or twentieth visit, whatever you are looking for is here: history, tradition, pomp and pageantry, the bright lights of the theater, wonderful music and famous art, fine shopping, and food from around the globe.

London is host to more than 25 million visitors every year from more than forty countries, and the hotel occupancy rate reflects this: It runs at almost 90 percent and is so inadequate that the London Tourist Board is targeting ten thousand additional rooms to be ready by the year 2000, and another five thousand by 2004. To make Cheap Sleeping matters even worse, the cost of a London hotel room has increased 60 percent over the last ten years and shows no signs of backsliding. London now has the unfortunate reputation as being one of the most expensive cities in the world to visit, listed in the top five with the highest per diem rates, right up there with Tokyo and ahead of New York City.

Many of London's top hotels can easily charge over $500 per night with breakfast and VAT (at 17½ percent) extra. The most expensive room in town, the Royal Suite at the Lanesborough on Hyde Park, will set you back a mere £4,112 *per night,* personalized business cards and stationery included, breakfast extra. At the other end of the spectrum, a campsite on the outskirts of town costs £4.

And even though travelers are learning that bigger hotels with fancy price tags are not necessarily better, the sad fact is that to many Americans, so-called budget accommodations in London are not "cheap." The average London budget hotel runs from £60 to £90 per night for two and offers little in the way of Ye Olde English charm—even less when it comes to space. Travelers who want their money's worth must be creative and remember not to be intimidated by the first quoted price . . . always try to negotiate. To trim costs, look for weekend packages, off-season rates, and, in small places, offer to pay cash instead of using a credit card. In many hotels, children sharing their parents' room sleep free or for half price. If your stay will be a week or longer, negotiate the seventh night and get it free.

In small mum-and-pop operations, don't look for many frills except on the lamp shades and curtains. Most have ten or twelve rooms done in a combination of styles and colors. The bathrooms are down the hall or, in an effort to please American guests, an airless portable unit has been wedged into a corner of the already small room, and the price increased to cover the "improvement." Despite these drawbacks and others, you will usually be treated as a welcome family guest by your hosts. The owner will call you by name, take your phone messages, and collect your mail. On your next visit, you won't have to tell him how to fix your bacon and eggs, and you will get your same room if you request it.

It is important that you know that this revised and updated fourth edition of *Cheap Sleeps in London* is *not* about where to find the cheapest beds in London. It *is* about where to find the best value for your money so you can spend it wisely. Whatever reason you have for visiting London, and whatever your budget may be, I hope *Cheap Sleeps in London* will hold the key for a more enjoyable stay, and make it easier for you to plan the best possible trip.

None of the listings in this or any of the books in the Cheap Eats/ Cheap Sleeps series that I write can be bought or solicited. I do *all* of the research and legwork, and for every edition, personally check and recheck every hotel and shop listed. Nothing is ever automatically "in." If I like the hotel, whether it be a tried-and-true listing or a new one, I consider it. If I find it dirty, unfriendly, overpriced, or otherwise unacceptable, it is out, no matter how great it used to be, how cheap it is, or how many others think it is good. Because I do all the hotel inspecting myself, I can offer candid, firsthand appraisals that give you in-depth, inside information, telling you when to leave your expectations at the door, or when to get ready for a Big Splurge stay in a lovely hotel you will want to return to again and again.

My primary guidelines, of course, are value for money and cleanliness, followed by location and management attitude. All Cheap Sleeps in London, except for the campsites and one or two youth hostels, are located within the Circle Line on the London Underground (tube), which means you will never be more than a thirty-minute tube ride from your hotel into central London. There is no reason to stay far from the action just to save a few pounds. You will quickly spend the difference on extra tube and bus fares, not to mention valuable vacation time and energy spent commuting to all the places you want to see. Think about it . . . do you really want to leave your lodging early in the morning and not be able to go back and rest or freshen up for dinner because it takes too much time in transit? If you are a woman, do you want to curtail evenings at the theater or attending concerts because it is not safe to ride out to the "burbs" late at night on the tube, never mind the walk from the tube stop to the door of your Cheap Sleep in the dark? I also expect hotel management to be helpful and friendly. In budget Cheap Sleeping digs, you cannot expect uniformed porters to carry your bags to rooms vying for a spread in *Architectural Digest,* but you can expect and insist on a clean room in a hospitable place.

During my research in London, I visited hundreds of hotels and other accommodation alternatives, finally narrowing the selection to include everything from bunks in dorms to tent pitch sites, family-run B&Bs, full-service apartments, rooms in private homes, and small antique-filled boutique hotels you will never forget. Some fall into the Big Splurge category, for those with higher expectations and more flexible budgets; others are utilitarian; and still more are just plain cheap and cheerful. When looking at hotels, I tried to consider your needs and anticipate possible disasters lurking in corners that could bring grief and inconvenience. I have ridden in elevators that were short prison sentences, and have felt as though I were on an Outward Bound course as I climbed twisting stairways and groped my way down gloomy hallways. I checked out the hall toilets, showers, and bathtubs; noted the condition of the shower curtains (if there were any); felt the toilet tissue (i.e., No. 1 sandpaper, waxed, or soft) and examined the towels; opened closets and dresser drawers; and bounced on beds and looked under them. I also checked on smoking versus nonsmoking policies. Did the hotel have rooms or floors specifically set aside for nonsmokers, or did the policy consist of the maid opening the window and spraying the room an hour before a guest's arrival? I dealt with rude owners, indifferent managers, and strange cleaning staff. I found dustballs under the beds, floods in the hallways, food hidden under mattresses, mice in the kitchens, and mold in many bathrooms. I walked more than 480 miles, wore out my shoes and an umbrella, and took notes seven days a week for three and a half months, rain or shine. Endurance was a necessity, not an option, but I loved every minute of it because my job *never* seems like work.

Wherever your dreams may take you, if you remember to always travel with a smile, lots of patience, and above all a positive attitude, your trip will be successful. May your weather be fair and your time rewarding. With *Cheap Sleeps* in hand, your money should be well spent. If, at the end of your trip, you return home pleased and satisfied that it was good based on my recommendations, then I have done my job well. Thank you for endorsing my efforts, and I wish you good luck and a safe and wonderful journey.

General Information

Economy is making the most of life. The love of economy is the root of all virtue.
—*George Bernard Shaw*

The good traveler has the gift of surprise.
—*W. Somerset Maugham*

TIPS FOR CHEAP SLEEPS IN LONDON

1. Know thyself. When booking a hotel room, what matters most to you? A view? Smoking versus nonsmoking? Quiet? Closet space? Charm? Convenience? Type of bed? Bathroom facilities? Consider your interests, habits, physical condition and needs, and sense of aesthetics. Is the hotel room a retreat, or merely a place to take a fast shower and spend the night? In other words . . . what is *your* bottom line of acceptance?

2. Unless you are a nomad backpacker who does not care where you lay your head, do not even consider arriving in London without confirmed hotel reservations. Why waste precious vacation time standing in lines at tourist offices or railway stations hoping to land something in your price range, only to wind up spending more money for accommodations in a marginal location because nothing else is available?

3. The cheapest room will be one in the back of the hotel, without private facilities. No matter where it is located, a room with a double bed and a shower will cost less than a room with twin beds and a bathtub.

4. In lower-priced hotels and B&Bs with a combination of rooms with and without private toilet and bathing facilities, you will save money and gain precious space if you reserve a room *without* a private toilet and shower or bathtub. Many of these "private" bathrooms are often little more than airless portable units squeezed into a corner of the room. In most cases, the hall facilities are far superior.

5. If you are susceptible to cold and visit London during winter, ask whether your room will be heated continuously or if the central heating will be turned off at certain times during the day and night, leaving you in icy discomfort. One hotelier told me his simple policy on this: "I turn the heat on when I think it should be, not when you think it should be." Conversely, if you go in summer, a room facing the front of the hotel may have the best

view, but if you open the window for air, you may get an overdose of noise, exhaust fumes, and dirt from passing traffic.

6. From a security standpoint, try to stay at least one floor above ground level.

7. To get the best hotel price, go in the off-season from November through March.

8. You would be surprised at the discounts you can get if only you ask. For instance, ask that the price of breakfast be deducted from your room rate; inquire about special weekend or holiday rates; if your children share your room, do they stay free? If you stay a week or more in a small B&B or offer to pay in cash, chances are you can get a price break. If you book through a toll-free 800 number from the States, these operators are seldom authorized to grant discounts. While it always pays to ask if they can reserve special rate deals, you usually have to speak directly with the hotel to do that. Also, if one 800 operator says the hotel in question is fully booked, wait a while and call back. Cancellations happen as often as reservations.

9. Another way to save money is to find a package combining your airfare with your hotel stay.

10. *Always* inspect the room before you check in.

11. Upon arrival, review the rates and what they include. Don't wait until the end of your stay; checkout time is not when you want to discover the rates did not include the VAT ($17\frac{1}{2}$ percent value-added tax) or those huge breakfasts you enjoyed every morning.

12. Be sure you understand the house rules. How late will someone be at the desk to let you in or to take telephone messages? When is checkout time, and can you store luggage at the hotel if your flight leaves later in the day? If you have an early morning flight, can you get a cup of tea or coffee and a roll before the hotel breakfast is served?

13. When calling home, beware of using the hotel telephone before inquiring about their surcharges. Use AT&T USA Direct, MCI, or Sprint, or buy a BT telephone card in London and place your call from a pay phone. Surcharges in hotels can run as high as 100 percent of the cost of the call. (See "Staying in Touch," page 24).

14. Seriously consider buying cancellation and trip-interruption insurance. British law states that hotel cancellations less than forty-eight hours prior to arrival can result in a two-night room charge. If the room can be relet, this may not apply, but who wants to take a chance? If you have prepaid a large portion of your trip, especially if you have rented a flat and paid a big chunk in advance, you are crazy not to buy cancellation insurance. London hoteliers and

flat managers, especially independents, are merciless when it comes to refunds. Their policy is very simple: no refunds. Period.

15. If you plan to stay in youth hostels or bunk in large dorm rooms in some of the college and university accommodations, invest in the best lock you can find for the locker you will be assigned. Wear a money belt, leave nothing of value in your room (even if you are just taking a quick shower down the hall), don't flash cash or jewelry, and lock up all valuables and important papers in the hotel safe.

16. Do your own laundry or take it to the neighborhood laundromat. If you wash clothes in your hotel room, please be considerate and do not let your things drip-dry onto the carpeting.

17. Always carry traveler's checks. If you have to pay your hotel bill in British sterling cash and your ATM limits won't cover it, take your traveler's checks and change them at a Marks & Spencer exchange office (best rates, no commission, accepts all types, open daily). The rates at the hotel will not be in your favor, nor will they be at the many Chequepoint or other exchange offices you will pass (see "Money Matters," page 17).

18. If you receive unacceptable service at your hotel, complain to the owner or highest person in charge, not to the desk clerk, who has no authority to make changes and may not report your complaint to higher-ups for fear of losing his or her job. If the situation cannot be resolved to your satisfaction, report your problem to the London Tourist Board. Then let me know (see "Readers' Comments," page 317). I cannot be your go-between, but I want to know if an entry of mine does not live up to your expectations. I will personally report all complaints and compliments to the management on my next visit to inspect that hotel.

One Last Recommendation: My final tip has nothing to do with London: it is about a marvelous bed-and-breakfast in Inverness, Scotland, which I must tell you about even though it's a long way from the British capital. If I could figure out a way to do it, I would experience a bit of heaven on earth by moving permanently to Dunain Park Hotel. This wonderful Scottish hotel is set amid gentle rolling green lawns and gardens overlooking the Inverness Valley. It is owned and personally run by Edward and Ann Nicol, who are ably assisted by Alex at the desk and two important permanent guests . . . Laddie and Lassie, the black dogs who had the good sense to be adopted by the Nicol family. Ann is a noted gourmet cook, and every meal you will enjoy here will reflect her talent and expertise. Edward is the official host, always on red alert to make sure everyone's needs are met.

Dunain Park looks and feels like the Nicols' own home because it is, with their many lovely antiques, paintings, family photos, and collectibles lovingly displayed throughout. The bedrooms are all spacious, tastefully furnished with comfortable sitting areas, cable television, views over the hills, and huge Italian marble–lined baths. The formal dining room shines in the morning light as you gently ease into a filling breakfast, cooked to your order. In the evening this serves as the stage set for Ann's exceptional dinners and dessert buffet. Just one of her many lovely touches is the tray of coffee and homemade sweets set out in the sitting room for guests to help themselves to after dinner. During the day, in addition to walking on the grounds, you can work off some of those delicious calories by doing laps in their heated indoor swimming pool. Only a mile away is the charming town of Inverness, beautifully situated on the River Ness and the perfect starting point for exploring the Scottish Highlands, strolling the banks of Loch Ness, or just meandering around town, appreciating its friendly atmosphere. You can visit Dunain Park Hotel any time of year, but two of my favorite times to go are during the Christmas holidays, when it is beautifully decorated and special meals are served, and again in summer, when the days are long and the heather is on the hills. Whenever you go, please give them my warmest regards and don't forget to say hello to Laddie and Lassie as well. Dunain Park Hotel, Inverness, Scotland IV3 8JN; tel: 01463-230512; fax: 01463-224532; email: Dunainparkhotel@btInternet.com. All of the rates, which are moderate when you see that they include dinner, bed, and breakfast, are quoted on request and change according to the time of year.

WHEN TO GO

A vacation is what you take when you can no longer take what you've been taking.
—*Early Wilson*

For most of us a trip to London is not a spur-of-the-moment decision made one day and acted on the next. It is usually part of a carefully planned vacation anticipated for some time. If you are really serious about having the most economical trip possible, you must plan to go during the low season. Low season for both airline fares and hotel rates generally runs between November and March, with the week around the Christmas and New Year's holidays excepted. The weather can be cold, damp, and rainy, but on the plus side, tickets to your favorite show will be easier to get, and you will not have to face crowds in the museums. If you are a shopper, don't forget the January sales, when prices are slashed to their lowest point of the year.

High season runs from April to October, with the big influx from June through August. In August you will share your London vacation with fellow travelers from around the world but very few Londoners, because most of them have escaped to the country for their summer holidays. Also, during summer, hotel prices will be at their peak. If there is a heat wave, you will swelter because few hotels have any sort of air-conditioning other than a fan, if you are lucky enough to snag one of the few the hotel *may* have on hand. Fall is my favorite time in London. The weather is nice, the colors are magnificent, and the tourists are few. As Christmas approaches, London becomes a fairyland of lights, and the beautifully decorated stores are filled with tempting presents.

HOLIDAYS

Public holidays in England—other than the universal ones of Christmas, New Year's, and Easter—are referred to as "bank holidays" because the banks are closed. It used to be that everything else was closed as well, but now you will find major stores and many shops open for five or six hours. Museums have their own bank holiday closing schedules; call ahead to check on openings.

New Year's Day	January 1
Good Friday	Friday before Easter
Easter Sunday	Varies
Easter Monday	Monday after Easter
May Day bank holiday	First Monday in May
Spring bank holiday	Last Monday in May
Summer bank holiday	Last Monday in August
Christmas Day	December 25
Boxing Day	December 26

LONDON CALENDAR OF EVENTS

The following calendar is a mere starting point. For detailed information, consult the weekly guides *Time Out in London,* or *What's On,* available at all London news kiosks.

January: Charles I Commemoration. Last Sunday in January marks the anniversary of the 1649 execution of King Charles.

February: Gerrard Street in Chinatown celebrates Chinese New Year. Dates are based on the lunar calendar.

March: The Easter Parade in Battersea Park includes floats and marching bands; wear your Easter bonnet and join the parade.

April: Late April, London Marathon Race (tel: 020-7620-4117). Also, the boat race between the eight-man rowing sculls of Cambridge and Oxford is on the first Saturday in April. The race is along the Thames from Putney to Mortlake.

May: Chelsea Flower Show, an international floral spectacle that defies description. For ticket information, write Shows Department, Royal Horticultural Society, Vincent Square, London SW1P 2PE; tel: 020-7630-7422; fax: 020-7630-6060.

June: June is a busy month. The Derby at Epsom Racecourse in Surrey, along with Royal Ascot, a four-day event in Berkshire, that is as well known for its fashion attendees, glamorous outfits, and outrageous hats as it is for its actual horse races (Derby Day: 01371-470-047; Royal Ascot: 01344-622-211). Another June event (the second weekend of the month) is Trooping the Colour, the official birthday celebration of the queen, which represents the ultimate in pomp and pageantry. For tickets, you *must* apply in writing between January and the end of February, enclosing an International Reply Coupon. You can ask for free, unlimited tickets to the first rehearsal, pay around £8 to attend the second rehearsal, or pay £15 for the actual day of the event and be limited to three tickets. Tel: 020-7414-2279 or 020-7414-2479. Send your application, with an International Reply Coupon, to Headquarters, Household Division, Horse Guards, Trooping the Colour, Whitehall, SW1A 2AX. Also in June: Wimbledon Tennis Tournament (tel: 020-8946-2244) and the Henley Royal Regatta (tel: 0149-157-2153).

July: Royal Tournament, at Earl's Court Exhibition Center, Warwick Road (tel: 020-7244-0371), a fabulous display of British athletic and military skills, and the Henley Royal Regatta in Oxfordshire (tel: 01491-572-153).

August: The Notting Hill Carnival, Ladbroke Grove, the largest street festival in Europe (tel: 020-8964-0544).

September: Chelsea Antiques Fair (tel: 0144-482-514).

November: State Opening of Parliament (can vary, sometimes in late October). The ceremony is not open to the public, but you can stand on the parade route and see the royal procession. Also in November is The Lord Mayor's Procession and Show, The City, a parade celebrating the inauguration of the new lord mayor, who rides in a gilded coach from Guildhall to the Royal Courts of Justice, usually on the second Saturday in November.

CLIMATE

When two Englishmen meet, their first talk is of the weather.
—*Dr. Johnson,* The Idler, *1758*

London's Average Daytime Temperatures and Rainfall

	Jan.	Feb.	Mar.	Apr.	May	June	July	Aug.	Sept.	Oct.	Nov.	Dec.
Temp (°C/F)	6/43	6/43	8/46	10/50	13/55	16/61	19/66	19/66	16/61	13/55	9/48	7/45
Rainfall (inches)	1.8	1.2	1.7	1.5	1.9	1.8	1.8	1.7	1.6	2.2	1.8	1.5
Hours of Sunshine	2	2.5	3.3	5.3	6.3	6.2	6.7	6.6	5.0	3.5	2.3	1.5

Day after day the weather reports on the radio and "telly" will be one or a combination of the following: fine but frosty; scattered clouds; possible showers interspersed with sunny periods; blustery. British weather is generally mild, but impossible to predict. To be safe, never leave the hotel without an umbrella and sunglasses.

Before leaving for London, you may want to call the *USA Today* weather hot line (900-370-USAT), which gives you the weather forecast for 490 cities worldwide.

WHAT TO WEAR

On a long journey, even a straw weighs heavy.
—Spanish proverb

If you accept only one piece of advice from me on packing, let it be this: *Travel light.* Take half as many clothes as you think you will need and twice as much money. You will thank me. Porters are almost relics of the past, especially in airports and train stations. They don't exist in any of the B&Bs I know about, and most of the time, neither do elevators. Dragging heavy bags up and down stairs in a B&B or tube station is no fun. Keep in mind you are going to London, not Pluto, so you will be able to wash, throw out, or buy more while you are there.

We all know comfortable, well-broken-in shoes are musts on everyone's list. So is an umbrella, the collapsible kind you can tuck into a purse or tote bag. Other essentials include sweaters for layering, a folding hat, and a raincoat with a zip-out lining. London is a rather formal city, where you see men in the supermarkets on a Saturday afternoon or a Sunday properly dressed in a coat and tie. Short shorts, halter tops, and other vacation-resort-style wear are inappropriate here, no matter how high the thermometer climbs in August.

Leave your diamonds, emeralds, gold bracelets, and other valuables at home. If you do bring something of value and are not wearing it, put it in the hotel safe. Don't hide it in your room, because hotel thieves know about every hiding place you can think of, and probably some you cannot.

MONEY MATTERS

Nothing is certain in London but expense.
—William Shenstone, remark quoted in Isaac
D'Israeli, Curiosities of Literature, *1791–93*

It doesn't seem to cost a lot of money to go away.
—Lewis Carroll, Alice in Wonderland

While cash never goes out of style, it isn't smart to travel with big wads of it. If you carry traveler's checks, charge on your credit cards, and use ATMs, you will have the money game down pat. Be sure to carry a few of your own personal checks. If you suddenly run out of money, you can use them to get cash advances, provided the credit cards you have allow that.

Always arrive in London with a few pounds in your pocket. True, you may pay something to get these pounds before you leave home, but it will be a welcome investment against standing in long lines at the airport, where currency exchange rates are definitely *not* in your favor. Some U.S. banks can supply foreign currency if you order it ahead. It is just as easy to contact one of the following companies that specialize in foreign currency orders.

American Express: 800-221-7282. Cash or traveler's checks in foreign currencies are a mere toll-free phone call away for American Express cardholders. If you have a green card, the commission on it is 1 percent. Gold and platinum cardholders pay no commission.

Capital Foreign Exchange: 888-842-0880 (toll-free). There is a flat fee ($10) to mail any amount of foreign cash or traveler's checks to your home.

Thomas Cook: Call 800-CURRENCY. You can order foreign cash or dollar traveler's checks to be sent, or picked up at a branch near you. The cost is $4.50 for transactions under $450, 1 percent for any amount above that. Thomas Cook foreign denomination traveler's checks are issued commission free and can be converted back into U.S. dollars at no additional fee.

Currency Exchange

Traveler's Checks: You usually get a better exchange rate for traveler's checks than you will for cash. I found the best rates at Marks & Spencer, commission-free exchange offices. Not only are their rates the best in town, they accept any brand of check and stay open during the week until at least 6 P.M., and on Sunday from noon to 6 P.M.

In London, American Express traveler's checks are the most widely accepted. Cardholders can order traveler's checks by phone (800-221-7282). Checks can also be purchased through many banks, in which case there is a 1 percent service fee unless you maintain a minimum balance. If you are a member of the Automobile Club of America, American Express traveler's checks are available free to you. In London, American Express traveler's checks can be cashed commission free at any of their offices throughout the city. For the office most convenient to you, consult the telephone directory; otherwise use one of these central American Express office locations: 6 Haymarket (tube: Piccadilly); 78 Brompton Road, almost across from Harrods (tube: Knightsbridge); 102 Victoria Street (tube: Victoria Station); 231–233 Regent Street in London House (tube: Oxford Circus); 40 Great Russell Street, near the British Museum (tube: Russell Square). Offices are generally open Mon–Fri 9 A.M.–5:30 P.M. and Sat 9 A.M.–noon. Call 0800-52-13-13 in the U.K. for further information when in London.

MasterCard traveler's checks can be cashed commission free at any Thomas Cook office in London. Of course, Thomas Cook (tel: 800-CURRENCY or toll-free in London 0800-96-47-67) traveler's checks can also be cashed commission free at any of their London offices. The MasterCard toll-free number in England is 0800-62-21-02; in the United States 800-223-7373.

Visa traveler's checks issued from a Barclay's Bank can be cashed commission free at most Barclay's Banks in London. Visa's toll-free U.S. number: 800-227-6811.

Many U.S. banks and credit unions offer courtesy traveler's checks for their customers. The American Automobile Association also offers them. Check before you get them, however, to make sure they are not some offbeat brand that will cost you time and money to convert in London. American Express, Thomas Cook/MasterCard, Thomas Cook, and Barclay's/Visa will cash their own traveler's checks without commission, but you must handle the transactions in one of their own offices. Your next best rate of exchange will be at a London bank. Banking hours are Mon–Fri 9 A.M.–4 P.M. Banks are closed weekends, holidays, and often in the afternoon before a holiday and sometimes the day after. After banks, exchange rates go from bad to worse: hotel, airport, and money changers. Chequepoint and other exchange businesses have offices throughout London. They have long hours, but their rates are *very* deceptive, even if they say they take no commission. The exchange rate may seem in your favor, but it never is. Someone is making money on the deal and it is *not* you. Avoid these places unless you are desperate.

Credit Cards

For the most part, I recommend using a credit card. The benefits are many. It is the safest way to spend because it eliminates carrying large sums of cash that must be obtained by standing in long lines to convert money. You have a record of your purchases, and best of all, you often get delayed billing of from four to six weeks after your purchases, whereas if you pay cash, the money is gone immediately. With a credit card, the money stays in your bank account, hopefully drawing interest, until you need it to pay your final bill. Credit card companies get wholesale exchange rates, passing this along to their customers. The credit card company will give you their best rate on the day of processing your bill, not on the day of purchase, and that can also work to your advantage.

Furthermore, with American Express, MasterCard, and Visa, you can get an instant cash advance in local currency *if* your card is tied to your bank account. Associated British banks will also give you cash advances as large as your remaining credit line. *Be careful,* the interest begins the moment you touch the money and it is usually prime plus $12\frac{1}{2}$ percent. These three major credit cards also work in some ATMs. The cards will require a four-digit PIN (contact your credit card company for details on obtaining one). Finally, MasterCard and Visa are known in the U.K. as EuroCard or Access and Carte Bleu or BarclayCard, respectively.

Lost or stolen credit cards: Heaven forbid that this will happen, but if it does, don't panic. Report the loss immediately to one of the following twenty-four-hour hot lines and then notify the police.

American Express: toll-free in London (0800-89-23-23) or from the U.S. (800-233-5432). Collect calls are accepted in the U.S. at 336-393-1111.

Diners Club: toll-free in London (0800-460-800) or in the U.S. (800-234-6377). Collect calls are accepted at 702-797-5532 in the U.S. For more information, visit their website at www.dinersclubus.com.

MasterCard: toll-free in London (0800-96-47-67) or in the U.S. (800-307-7309). Collect calls are accepted at 314-542-7111 in the U.S. For further information, contact the MasterCard website at www.mastercard.com.

Visa: toll-free in London (0800-89-17-25) or in the U.S. (800-336-8472). Collect in the U.S. at 410-581-9994.

Getting Money from Home

Having funds sent to you abroad can be complicated, costly, and fraught with peril. Consider this option *only* when every other possibility has been exhausted. Instead, use your American Express, Diners Club, MasterCard, or Visa to get cash, either by writing a personal check and presenting your card, or by going to a bank that gives cash advances for whatever card you are carrying.

American Express: Cardholders can get fast money, without commission, by writing personal checks (remember, I told you to bring some along). Green cardholders can write a check for $1,000 every twenty-one days; gold cardholders can get $5,000 every twenty-one days; and platinum members can write a check for $10,000 every twenty-one days . . . all provided there are funds in your bank account to cover the check. For more information on this lifesaving service and more, contact American Express Global Assist at 1-800-333-2639.

Diners Club: For any Diners Club cardholder, a cash advance of $500 a day or $1,000 a week is easy. Just present the card and a picture ID at any Eurochange bank and that's it.

MasterCard or Visa: Available through banks displaying these card signs. There are additional costs for the advance ranging up to 10 percent.

Western Union: Call 0800-833-833 in London and be prepared to pay a commission of 10 percent.

ATMs

What did we ever do before ATMs? These electronic wonders of convenience are now available in Britain, provided your bank belongs to one of the London networks. Before you race to the nearest London ATM and punch in your stateside PIN (personal identification number), there are some things you should know. For openers, commissions and fees could cost you up to 10 percent of the transaction. ATMs abroad may not always function, thanks to clogged computer lines, which means you will have to find another ATM or come back to that one. Your PIN also may not work. If your PIN is a word, learn the number equivalent, because some British ATM keypads show only numbers. Also, if your PIN is more than three or four digits, it may not work. If your ATM card displays the Cirrus or Plus logo, you are in business, but call your bank for a listing of corresponding London banks to check on the usability of your PIN and for limits on the frequency and amounts of withdrawals.

Many times you can use a credit card in London ATMs if your card company is tied in with a British bank. Check with the issuing bank and remember to have your card coded with a PIN. Because interest rates begin to accrue the minute of your withdrawal, consider this option carefully. It could cost you more than it is worth in interest and service fees.

Tipping

How much is too much, and what is enough? Americans are known as big tippers, but the British are funny sometimes about money, so you have to be cautious not to overdo your tipping.

Hairdressers	10 to 15 percent of the bill; £1 to £2 for shampoo person
Hat and coat checkers in the theater	50p per item
Hotels	A tough call. If the owner is helping you with your bags, a tip will offend. If his son or an employee carries them, then a small gratuity of £1 per bag might be appreciated.
Porters	£1 to £1.50 per bag, depending on how heavy and how far carried
Restaurants	*Only* tip if the service is *not* included. The VAT will be included. If the service is not included, tip 15 percent; *never* tip the barman at a pub.
Taxi drivers	10 to 15 percent
Washroom attendants	Leave 20p to 50p in their saucers, depending on what they do for you.

SAFETY AND SECURITY

London is safer than many large cities, and violent crime is rare. Generally, assaults are in the nature of handbag snatchers and pickpockets along Oxford and Regent streets; in Knightsbridge around Harrods; in crowded street markets such as Portobello Road and Petticoat Lane; and in the airports. The tube stations are also targeted areas, especially late at night. Thieves work in pairs . . . one creates a diversion, the other grabs your purse, wallet, or bags. If you follow these basic commonsense rules, you should be safe:

1. Use the hotel safe, and request a room above the ground level.

2. Put your money and valuables in a money belt worn inside your clothing, either around your waist or in a necklace money holder under your shirt.

3. If you are carrying a purse, wear it crosswise across your body with the opening against your body.

4. Do not leave belongings or coats beside, under, or on the back of your chair. Put your purse in your lap, not between your feet.

5. Leave expensive jewelry and furs at home.

6. Don't travel alone or walk down dark streets or through parks of any size late at night.

7. Women alone should avoid the tube at night, carry a loud whistle, and not be afraid to use it.

8. Never flash cash or credit cards.

9. Photocopy your passport; leave a list of your credit card numbers with someone at home in case the cards are lost or stolen. Also make a note of the telephone numbers on the back of your card to call if you have a problem. For a lost passport, you have to prove who you are, and a photocopy will do the trick. While you are photocopying your passport, copy any other papers crucial to a safe and sane trip and return home (air and rail tickets, medical data, etc.). Also, take at least four extra passport-size color photos, which will be necessary if you have to replace a passport.

10. Try to let someone know where you are going and when you will be back, especially late at night.

11. Call 999 in an emergency.

DISCOUNTS

Senior Citizen Discounts

Sometimes it pays to get older, especially if you are traveling. Significant savings are available to seniors as young as fifty. Interested? Read on.

Many airlines, including British Airways, offer special discounts on their regular airfares. British Airways also offers senior citizen discounts on a range of their tours within the country to those sixty or older, and to any companions traveling with them who are fifty or older.

Men who are sixty-five and women who are sixty qualify for some worthwhile discounts on train travel within the U.K. You may be able to save up to one-third on some fares and pay half price for off-peak Cheap Day Return Tickets. To purchase train tickets in London, it is easier to do so at mainline railway stations (Victoria, Euston, Charing Cross, King's Cross, St. Pancras, or Waterloo) than it is to unearth a rail-appointed travel agency (see page 30 for more on British rail travel).

Very often seniors can get reduced entry tickets to many London attractions, theaters, and at the movies. Always ask, and have your passport handy for proof; you never know where and when you will get lucky and get in for less. Usually these bargains are not advertised; *you must ask.*

NOTE: Senior citizens, unfortunately, are called old-age pensioners (OAPs) in Britain, so if the term *senior citizen* doesn't work, try OAP.

Student and Teacher Discounts

Youth and old age do have their privileges, and reduced travel expenses is one of the more interesting ones.

If you can prove you are a degree-seeking student in a secondary or postsecondary school and are over twelve, your best travel investment will be the International Student Identity Card (ISIC). With this card you will have access to more than eight thousand discounts on transportation, accommodations, and cultural events. You must always present the card to get the discount. Always ask about a discount even if none is mentioned. Because of bogus ISICs, many airlines and some other places now require other proof of student identity. To be on the safe side, carry with you a signed letter from your registrar attesting to your student status and stamped with the school seal, and carry your school ID card. If you buy your card in the States, you will get limited accident, medical, hospital, and medical evacuation insurance, and access to a toll-free hot line for help in medical, legal, and financial emergencies abroad. When you apply for the card, ask for a copy of the International Student Identity Card Handbook, which lists some of the discounts by country. The card is valid from September to December of the following year, and the cost is $18. To order the card using a credit card, call 800-255-1999. Several budget travel organizations also sell the card. See below.

The International Teacher Identity Card (ITIC) offers similar discounts, including the medical insurance. The cost is $18 and you can call the above 800 number and order it by credit card, or contact one of the budget travel organizations listed below.

If you are under twenty-six and not a student, you can still get some discounts. The Federation of International Youth Travel Organizations (FIYTO) issues a discount card to those under twenty-six and not students. It is known as the GO 25 Card. It costs $18, is valid for one year, and offers many of the same discounts and benefits as the ISIC. Most of the budget travel organizations listed below sell the card. To apply, you will need proof of birth date and a passport-size photo.

Budget Travel Organizations

The following list of budget travel companies offer discounted flights for students and young persons, rail passes, ISIC and ITIC discount cards, hostel memberships, travel guides, and general budget know-how based on firsthand experience.

Campus Travel: Specializes in cheap fares for students inside and outside the U.K. 52 Grosvenor Gardens, SW1, tel: 020-7730-2101 or 020-7730-8111; Internet: www.campustravel.co.uk; tube: Victoria;

hours Mon–Fri 9 A.M.–6 P.M., Sat 10 A.M.–4 P.M. Other offices: UCL Union 25, Gordon Square, WC1, tel: 020-7383-5337; 14 Southampton Street, WC2; tel: 020-7836-3343; 174 Kensington High Street, W8; tel: 020-7938-2188.

Council Travel: This full-service travel agency specializes in student, youth, and budget travel. They have more than fifty offices around the world and sell the ISIC, GO 25, and ITIC cards. In London they are at 28A Poland Street, W1, tube: Oxford Circus, open generally Mon–Fri 9 A.M.–6 P.M., Sat 10 A.M.–5 P.M.; tel: 800-226-8624. In London, call 020-7437-7767.

Educational Travel Centre: This budget travel agency has a free pamphlet, *Taking Off;* tel: 800-747-5551.

International Student Exchange Flights (ISE): Offers budget flights, Eurail passes, and sells all the student and teacher discount cards; tel: 800-225-7000.

Let's Go Travel: Offers a complete line of budget travel deals, student and teacher discount cards, maps, books, and travel gear. Call or write for a catalog; tel: 800-5-LETS GO.

STA Travel: A student and youth travel organization with a hundred offices worldwide and fourteen in the United States. In London, 6 Wright's Lane, W8; tube: High Street Kensington; tel: 020-7437-7767.

STAYING IN TOUCH

Mail

Have everything sent airmail. Surface may be cheaper, but it takes up to nine weeks for surface mail to reach its destination. Allow seven to ten days for an airmail letter or postcard.

Receiving Mail: If, for some reason, you don't want mail to arrive for you at your hotel address in London, there are two other reliable alternatives.

You can receive mail sent from home via *poste restante* at the Trafalgar Square Post Office. They will hold mail for one month and you must present a picture ID to pick it up. Have your correspondent write on the envelope your name, with the last name underlined or in capital letters, and the words "Poste Restante" and "Hold for 30 days" on the left side of the envelope, and send the mail to you at this address: Post Office, 24–28 William IV Street, London, WC2N 4DL. Be sure to bring a photo ID when you come to pick it up.

You can also pick up your mail at the American Express office at 6 Haymarket, London, SW1Y 4BS (tel: 020-7930-4411; tube: Piccadilly Circus). The envelope should be addressed to you, with your name in capital letters and "client letter service" boldly written on it. Mail will be held for thirty days free of charge for cardholders; others pay a small fee. After that it is by arrangement and there will be a fee for everyone.

Sending Mail: Stamps are sold at all post offices, large supermarkets, and from newsagents.

Sending Packages: Frankly speaking, sending packages from any place abroad can be a terrific headache. There are size and weight limitations, but these are minor when you see how much the postage on a box will cost, even for surface. Try not to do it. Somehow, stuff it into your luggage and if necessary pay for an extra bag on the airline, let the store mail it for you, or just leave it behind.

Telephone

As of April 22, 2000, all telephone numbers in greater London changed to eight-digit numbers. Thank goodness the change is a simple formula to remember. All numbers that were preceded by 0171 (e.g., 0171-123-4567) changed to 020-7 plus the existing seven digits (e.g., 020-7-123-4567). If you are in London, dialing another number within London, you do not use the 020 area code, you just need the eight-digit number. If you are outside of London, perhaps in Manchester, you will need to use the 020 area code plus the eight-digit number. Numbers preceded by 0181 (normally outside central London) are now 020-8 plus the existing seven digits. Example: 0181-987-6543 is now reached by dialing 020-8-987-6543. Again, you will only need to use the 020 area code if you are dialing into or out of its covered area. British Telecom has set up a toll-free hot line to deal with this; you can reach them at 0800-731-0202.

Calling the U.K. from Abroad: To call the U.K. from the United States, dial 011-44, the area code, and the number. London has two area codes: 0207 for inner London, and 0208 for outer. From the United States, drop the zero off the area code (example: 011-44-207-000-0000).

Calling from the U.K. Abroad: If you pick up the phone in your hotel and make an international call through the hotel operator, you could be charged an astronomical 100 percent surcharge. To simplify calling home and avoid the hotel surcharges, buy a prepaid telephone card, available at most newsstands and post offices, or utilize the services of one of the following long-distance carriers: AT&T, MCI, or Sprint. To access a U.S. operator from Great Britain, dial AT&T USA Direct, 080-089-0011, or Sprint's 080-089-877. To get a calling card, which you must have to call through one of these companies, call one of the following 800 numbers before you leave on your trip: AT&T USA Direct 800-874-4000; MCI Call USA 800-444-4444; or Sprint Express 800-793-1153.

The cheapest time to call home is between 8 P.M. and 8 A.M. Monday through Friday, and all day Saturday and Sunday.

Calls Made within Britain: There are three kinds of phones in Britain: those that accept only coins; BT (British Telecom) phonecards; or BT phonecards *and* credit cards.

The coin-operated phone booths are few and far between. They accept all but 1p coins and are inconvenient in that you have to have a pocketful of change, and the phones do not make change, so if you insert more than you use, tough luck.

BT phonecards are a much smarter way to go. You can buy them from post offices or news kiosks displaying the green-and-white phonecard sign. These cards come in values of £2, £4, £10, and more, and can be used to make a call around the corner or across the globe.

The credit card phone call is self-explanatory: the cost of the call is charged against your credit card account.

For long-distance calls within Britain, dial the area code, which begins with a zero, followed by the number.

London numbers are prefixed by 0207 for inner London and 0208 for the suburbs. If you are calling from inside the same zone, you don't need to use them. If you are calling from one zone to another, you do. Drop the zero *only* when calling London from abroad.

There is no such thing as a free call (other than toll-free and some operator information calls) in Britain. All calls fall into three rate periods: lowest, Mon–Fri 6 P.M.–8 A.M. and all day Sat and Sun; mid-range, Mon–Fri 8 A.M.–9 A.M. and 1–6 P.M.; and most expensive, Mon–Fri 9 A.M.–1 P.M.

TRANSPORTATION

Getting into London from the Airport

Gatwick, Heathrow, and Stansted airports all serve London. Heathrow is the world's busiest airport, with more than 56 million passengers transiting it every year. Gatwick is an also-ran with a mere 32 million passengers.

Heathrow: In a cab from Heathrow to London, prepare to spend £45–55, a charge for each bag, and a 10 to 15 percent tip. If there are several of you, it makes sense; otherwise it is an expensive way to start your London sojourn. One of the easiest ways to go is to use the fast-rail link, London Heathrow Express, which takes you to Paddington Station. The trip takes less than thirty minutes each way. A one-way ticket costs £10 for express class or £20 for first class. Children under five ride free, and those between five and fifteen pay half price. There are no senior discounts. Trains leave every fifteen minutes and run from 5:30 A.M.–11:30 P.M. When you return to Heathrow this way, nine airlines have check-in desks operating at Paddington, so you can check all your baggage here and never worry about it until you arrive at your destination. If you plan to turn in VAT forms, please allow time at Heathrow because as yet there are no facilities at Paddington for this. For further information, telephone London Heathrow Express at 0845-600-1515, or check their website at www.heathrowexpress.co.uk.

If you want the luxury of being met at the airport, call Airbus Hotel Shuttle at 020-8400-6656. With at least a forty-eight-hour advance notice to book your seat, they will meet your plane, put your luggage on their bus, and drive you to your hotel. When you leave London, they will pick you up from your hotel and take you back to Heathrow and charge you £15 each way. Credit card bookings can be made from 7 A.M.–6:30 P.M. by phone (020-8400-6656) or by email (book@airbus.co.uk).

A cheaper choice is to take the Piccadilly Line tube, which takes about one hour to central London and costs under £5 each way. Trains run from 5:30 A.M.–11:30 P.M. and leave from Terminals 1, 2, 3, and 4. The other option is the Airbus A1 or A2 (which also operates the Airbus Hotel Shuttle), with direct service to and from all four terminals. The A1 takes about an hour and goes to and from Victoria Coach Station with stops along the way at Earl's Court tube, Hyde Park Corner, and Harrods. It's up to you to get to where you want to be from the drop-off point. The same goes for the A2, which takes ninety minutes and goes to and from Woburn Place on Russell Square, with stops at Euston, Baker Street, Marble Arch, Queensway, and Notting Hill Gate tubes, and the Kensington Hilton Hotel. Buses run daily every thirty minutes from 7 A.M.–8:30 P.M. Tickets cost £7 one way, £12 return, less if you are a senior; tel: 020-8759-4321. For left luggage call 020-8745-5301 (Terminal 1), 020-8759-3344 (Terminal 2), 020-8745-4599 (Terminal 3), and 020-8745-7460 (Terminal 4).

Gatwick: Gatwick is farther out than Heathrow, but the Gatwick Express train into Victoria Station is a breeze. It runs twenty-four hours, every day, every fifteen minutes, except between 1:30 A.M.–4:30 A.M., when it runs every hour. Tickets cost around £10 for one way, £22 roundtrip. The trip takes between thirty and forty-five minutes to Victoria Station, where you can either hail a cab or get on the tube. You can also take a bus called Flightline 777. The trip takes at least seventy minutes and costs £8. These buses bound for Victoria Coach Station leave from Gatwick's North Terminal hourly from 5:30 A.M.–8 P.M. daily. Taking a taxi from Gatwick is prohibitive, upwards of £65, plus tip and baggage fees.

If you are flying British Airways, departing passengers leave from London Gatwick Airport. Ticketholders can check in at Victoria Station, which eliminates dragging luggage from London to the airport. You must arrive at the British Airways check-in desk at least two hours before departure to get your seat assignment, check baggage, and purchase Gatwick Express train tickets. Trains leave for the airport every fifteen minutes. Once there, you walk to your gate and board the plane. It is a breeze, and oh so convenient; tel: 01293-535-353. For left luggage, call 01293-502-214 (South Terminal) and 01293-502-013 (North Terminal).

Stansted: The best way to get from Stansted Airport into London is to take the Stansted Express train (0345-484-950) to Liverpool Street Station. The trip takes about forty-five minutes. Trains run Mon–Sat every thirty minutes from 8 A.M.–8 P.M., and every hour from 6–8 A.M. and 8 P.M.–midnight. On Sunday, they run every thirty minutes 8 A.M.–11 P.M.

Tickets cost around £12 one way. A taxi will be at least £50, plus tip and baggage fees; tel: 01279-680-500. For lost luggage, call 01279-663-213.

London Transportation

The Tube and Double-Decker Buses: Call London Travel Information, an invaluable twenty-four-hour information line for London bus and tube travel; tel: 020-7222-1234. Their offices are located in the following stations: Euston, Heathrow Airport, King's Cross, Liverpool Street, Oxford Circus, Piccadilly Circus, St. James's Park, and Victoria. Hours are generally daily 8 A.M.–5:30 P.M.

An essential investment, of course, is the *A–Z London Street Map.* This booklet will tell you more than you will ever need to know, and it will save you time and confusion when you don't know how to get from the Tate Gallery to Buckingham Palace. This booklet also has an Underground map.

The cheapest and fastest way to get around London is to master the Underground (tube) and bus systems. The tube will be faster, but the bus is much more scenic and fun. The view of London from the top of a red double-decker bus is unbeatable. Bus stops are marked with two kinds of signs: the compulsory stop, which has a white background, and the request stop, which is red. At the first, the bus will automatically stop; at the request stop, you have to flag it down. On a double-decker, the conductor will collect your fare from you. On the single-driver buses (no conductor), you will pay as you enter. To get off, ring the bell as you approach your stop. If you are not sure as to your stop, ask the driver to tell you. The most scenic bus routes in London are the following:

Bus 11: From King's Road to St. Paul's Cathedral

Bus 12: From Bayswater to the Houses of Parliament and Westminster Bridge

Bus 19: From Sloane Square to Piccadilly Circus, Bloomsbury to Islington

Bus 88: Oxford Circus to the Tate Gallery

To save money on both the tube and the bus, buy a Travel Card, which allows you to ride for less money than you would spend for single-fare tickets. Depending on the type of card you buy, it will be good for one to thirty days and can be purchased at any tube station. Travel Cards are sold by the zones. Most visitors need only a card for Zone 1, central London. You will need a passport-size color photo for the thirty-day Travel Card. Bring your own, or hope there is a photo booth in the tube station.

Taxis: Black cabs are as famous in London as red double-decker buses, but more expensive. The taxi drivers are reliable, know their way around, and have strictly enforced codes of conduct. Many enforce a no-smoking policy. Traditional London taxis are called black cabs, even though they may now be painted garish colors. Every licensed black cab has a "For Hire" sign and a white license plate on the back stating how many passengers it will carry. Drivers of black cabs must pass a complicated test called "The Knowledge" to prove they know where every street is and the shortest way to get to it. The qualification takes three years to achieve, and 30 percent fail. Hotels and main tourist areas have taxi stands, but you can also flag one down. If the yellow "For Hire" sign is on, the cab is available. Many cabbies turn the sign off at night in order to pass up undesirable-looking fares, so it pays to flag at night even if the sign is off. To pay, you must get out of the cab (rain or shine) and pay through the window. Tip the cabbie from 10 to 15 percent depending on your mood and his attitude and speed in getting you to your destination. There will be an extra charge for baggage. If you want to be assured of a taxi at a specific time, call a twenty-four-hour radio taxi. You will pay from the minute the driver gets the call, but you will avoid the worry of being late because you could not get a taxi during rush hour or at some odd hour. Radio Taxis (020-7272-0272) and Dial a Cab (020-7253-5000) are twenty-four-hour call services for black cabs.

Any complaints or inquiries about black cabs should be made to the Public Carriage Office; tel: 020-7230-1631/2. If you have a complaint, be sure you also have the number of the cab, which should be displayed both inside the cab and on the back plate. For lost property, call 020-7833-0996, Mon–Fri 9 A.M.–4 P.M.

Mini-cabs: Mini-cabs are not black cabs; they are ordinary cars available for hire by telephone. They cannot be hailed in the street because it is illegal. Over long distances, these cabs are usually cheaper than black taxis, but the drivers are unlicensed, untrained, and often uninsured, not to mention unreliable. If you do use one, always discuss price when you book and confirm it with the driver. Often, concierges use them if you ask for transportation to the airport. There is usually a kickback from the company to the concierge, but it is built into the price and you will never know what it is. Addison Lee, one of the more reliable mini-cab companies, is open twenty-four hours a day; tel: 020-7387-8888.

Driving Your Own Car or a Rental Car: In London! What for? Driving in London is hazardous to your health. It is a hair-raising experience and only for the very, very brave or foolish. The British drive on the opposite side of the road, which means having to retrain yourself to look in the opposite direction (and, obviously, to drive on the other side of the road). Parking is impossible. There is never any parking within walking distance of where you want to be, unless it is an expensive car park. Petrol (gasoline) is sky-high. But if you insist, check with your airline for a fly-drive package. Otherwise, shop the major car rental companies carefully *before* you leave home, because rates and deals vary greatly. If you wait until you arrive to make rental arrangements, you will be very put off by the prices and all the tacked-on charges.

Walking: One of the best ways to experience London is on foot. You can venture forth with the express purpose of wandering and seeing what you can along the way. Don't worry about getting lost; you can always jump on a bus or hail a cab if you get too far from your base. I think one of the best ways to learn about London is to go on a guided walking tour. On these two-hour tours, you will be guided by well-informed leaders to any number of interesting places you would probably not discover on your own. You can peek into the haunts of Shakespeare, Dickens, and Sherlock Holmes. You can explore the inner workings of legal London and sit in on an actual trial at Old Bailey, go on a late-night pub crawl, or see where Jack the Ripper stalked his prey. You will probably see brochures on these walking tours at your hotel; please try to make enough time to go on at least one. One of the best walking tour companies is called the Original London Walks. If you need more information, you can contact them directly; tel: 020-7624-3978/794-1764/911-0285; fax: 020-7625-1932; email: london@walks.com or london.walks@ bogo.co.uk; Internet: www. london.walks.com. For further information, consult the weekly *Time Out* guide or *What's On,* both available at news dealers.

Leaving London

Trains: All of Britain is joined by excellent rail links. The question now is . . . do you want to use this mode of transportation? Unfortunately, British Rail as we knew and loved it has been privatized. The railways are now independent train companies, which have turned train travel into what can be a nightmare of long delays, late departures and arrivals, and dirty, unkempt trains. Just to prove my point . . . on a return trip at Christmastime from Inverness to London, my train was two hours late in leaving, during which time all passengers were advised to wait outside, in 20-degree weather, beside the appropriate train track because the train would be arriving any minute. Once on board, we encountered further delays along the way, had engine failure (forcing those of us who had paid extra to have a straight-through trip to change twice, schlepping our own luggage because there were no porters), and learned there would be no toilets in service because the train had run out of water! And never mind heat—there was none of that either. This train trip from hell was so horrible that just before arrival (five hours late) into London, train officials boarded the train and passed out vouchers for free trips on future journeys.

If you plan to do much train travel, by all means look into a British Rail Pass, available for purchase *only* in the United States. There are different types of passes, issued for both first- and second-class travel and for specific time periods: the BritRail Pass for Britain only; Brit Rail Pass + Ireland; Brit Rail Pass + Southeast; Freedom of Scotland Travel pass. The passes are available for periods of four, eight, fifteen, and twenty-two days per month for consecutive or nonconsecutive travel. For more information, contact British Rail in the U.S. at 800-677-8585, your travel agent, or visit their website at www.raileurope.com.

If you do not have a British Rail Pass, you can purchase train tickets in London, but you *must* do it at one of the railway stations because rail tickets are no longer sold through travel agencies or from a central office in London. The special fares, deals, and prices are numerous. Always ask for the best price because there are lots of ways to save. For instance, if you are over sixty, it may pay you to invest £18 in a Senior Citizen Rail Card, which entitles you to ride the rails for a year for at least one-third less than regular ticket prices. (Also see "Senior Citizen Discounts," page 22.) Youthful travelers (sixteen to twenty-six) can participate in a similar program. For these and other money-saving fares, restrictions always apply. For information on your particular trip, call the National Rail Enquiry Service's twenty-four-hour information line at 0345-48-49-50. The railway stations in London are Charing Cross, Liverpool, Victoria, Waterloo, Euston, St. Pancras, King's Cross, Marylebone, and Paddington. All have tube stops.

Bus: Even riding the bus from one point to another in Britain is expensive, and it can seem to take forever. Travelers no longer have much choice of competing services. The two principal agents are National Express (0990-808-080), which goes to destinations all over England, Scotland, and Wales, and Eurolines (01582-404-511), which goes to the continent.

Rental Cars: Once you are out of London, driving is easier. Traffic is not what it is in the States; drivers are actually courteous, and roads are well marked. Car rental costs vary greatly, so shop around and make arrangements before you leave home to get the best prices. Gasoline (petrol) is expensive. If there are two or three in your group, driving may be more economical (and much nicer) than buying separate train tickets.

HELPFUL HINTS

1. *Insurance:* Check with your homeowner's policy and see if it covers you in any way when you are traveling. Consider adding a floater policy for the duration of your trip. *Medical insurance:* Even though all British are eligible for free medical care, visitors are not. Check with your health-care plan to see what, if any, coverage you will have and seriously consider taking out a supplemental policy to cover your trip. Trust me. The small amount you spend will be nothing compared to a foreign medical emergency with *you* picking up the tab.

2. Carry a copy of your prescriptions plus a letter from your physician giving the generic names of the drugs you take. American brands may not be available.

3. Look first to the *right* when crossing the street.

4. British current is 240 volts AC. If you are bringing a hair dryer, hair curler, or electric razor, you will need both a transformer and an adapter that will plug into the British wall socket and convert it to 110 volts AC, the standard in the United States.

5. What's happening? To find out the latest word on films, theaters, concerts, shows and exhibitions, museums and galleries, and much, much more, buy the weekly publications *Time Out* or *What's On* from any corner newsstand.

6. If you will be in London for more than a day or two, you will need to have a copy of the *A–Z London Street Map* (pronounced "a" to "zed"). I like the super-scale version of this detailed street map because it is possible to read the fine print without a high-powered magnifying glass. You can buy the map in book or foldout form. It is a purchase that never goes out of date or style and will save you time and anxiety when you can't get from points A to B because you are going in the wrong direction.

7. Disabled visitors to London should invest in the best book possible on the subject: *Access in London* (Irwin Press), by Gordon Couch, William Forrester, and Justin Irwin. It costs £8 in London and is worth every pence for the amount of detailed information included.

8. Whatever you want to know about your trip to London can undoubtedly be found on the Internet. Websites for Cheap Sleeps hotels and Cheap Chic shops have been provided in this book if they are available for the hotel, or appropriate for the shop. Here are a few of interest.

Buckingham Palace: www.royal.gov.uk

London Tourist Board: www.LondonTown.com

Prince Charles: www.princeofwales.gov.uk

The Telegraph (daily newspaper): www.telegraph.co.uk

PRACTICAL INFORMATION: WHERE TO FIND WHAT YOU WANT WHEN YOU NEED IT

American Embassy
24 Grosvenor Square, London W1
Tube: Bond Street
Tel: 020-7499-9000
Consular hours: Mon–Fri 8:30 A.M.–5:30 P.M.

American Express

6 Haymarket, London W1
Tube: Piccadilly Circus
Tel: 020-7930-4411
For locations of other offices, see "Money Matters," page 17.

British Tourist Authority (U.S. office)

551 Fifth Avenue, Suite 701
New York, NY 10019
Tel: 212-986-2266; 800-452-2748 (toll-free from the U.S.)
Fax: 212-986-1188
Internet: www.visitbritain.com
Branches: Chicago, Los Angeles, Atlanta

British Tourist Authority (London office)

Visit Britain Center
1 Lower Regent Street, London SW1
Tube: Piccadilly Circus
Tel: 020-7808-3808, 020-8846-9000
Hours: Mon–Fri 9 A.M.–6:30 P.M., Sat–Sun 10 A.M.–4 P.M.
The British Tourist Authority has information on all parts of Britain, including books, maps, gifts, theater and hotel bookings, and a travel agency.

The City of London Information Center

St. Paul's Churchyard, London EC4
Tube: St. Paul's
Tel: 020-7606-3030
Information and advice with emphasis on the City of London. Ask for the monthly *Diary of Events,* listing a wide variety of free entertainment in London.

London Regional Transport

Tel: 020-7222-1234 (twenty-four-hour hot line), 020-7222-1200 (recorded information)
Tube: Offices located at Euston, Heathrow Airport, Victoria, King's Cross, Oxford Circus, Piccadilly Circus, Liverpool, St. James's Park
These offices have information on London transportation via tube and bus and the Docklands Light Railway. They also provide information for disabled travelers, places of interest, guided tours, and free maps.

London Tourist Board

Victoria Station Forecourt, London SW1
Tube: Victoria
Tel: 020-7932-2000

Other offices: Heathrow Airport, Tower of London, Liverpool Street Station, Waterloo

For what is happening in London, call Visitorcall, a recorded service with different lines providing information on what to see and do: 020-7971-0027.

Telephone Numbers

Emergency Services: Ambulance, Fire, Police	999
Inner London area code	020-7
Outer London area code	020-8
Toll-free prefix within the U.K.	0800
Operator Services	
Operator	100
London Directory Inquiries	192
International Inquiries	153
International Operator	155
Airports	
Heathrow	020-8759-4321
Gatwick	01293-535-353
London City	020-7646-0000
Stansted	01279-680-500
Dental Care	
Emergency	020-7955-2186
Hospitals (twenty-four-hour emergency)	
Westminster Hospital, Horseferry Road, SW1; tube: Pimlico	020-7746-8000
Royal London Hospital, Whitechapel Road, E1; tube: Whitechapel	020-7377-7000
Doctor—SOS Doctors	020-7603-3332
Information for Travelers with Disabilities	020-7275-8485
Pharmacies (Chemists)	
Bliss Chemist, 5 Marble Arch, W1; tube: Marble Arch; daily 9 A.M.–midnight	020-7723-6116
Boots, 302 Regent Street, W1; tube: Oxford Circus; Mon–Fri 8 A.M.–7 P.M., Sat 9 A.M.–6 P.M.	020-7637-9418
Boots, tube: Piccadilly Circus; Mon–Sat 8:30 A.M.–10 P.M., Sun 10 A.M.–9 P.M.	020-7734-6126
Boots, 75 Queensway; tube: Queensway or Bayswater; Mon–Sat 9 A.M.–10 P.M., Sun 5 P.M.–10 P.M.	020-7229-9266

Lost or Stolen Items
  Report the loss or theft to police and then call:
  Lost at the airport
  Heathrow: 020-8745-7727
  Gatwick: 01293-535-353
  Stansted: 01297-680-500
  Lost on bus or tube   020-7486-2496
  Lost on railways. (Lost property is held for
  seven days at the rail station where it was
  found, and then is taken to Waterloo Lost
  Property.)
  Charing Cross   020-7922-6061
  Euston Station   020-7922-6477
  King's Cross   020-7922-9081
  Liverpool Street   020-7922-9158
  London Bridge   020-7922-6135
  Paddington   020-7313-1514
  St. Pancras   020-7922-6478
  Victoria   020-7922-9887
  Waterloo   020-7401-7861
  Lost on taxi   020-7883-0996
Time   123
  (note: daylight savings time is from the last
  Sunday in March to the last Sunday in
  October)   0891-200-821
                                               (national)
Weather   020-7388-7575
                                               (London)

If you cannot find what you need from
other resources, call Scoot, a business
directory service that provides telephone
numbers and addresses by type, not name,
throughout the U.K. The call and the
information are free.   0800-192-192

INTERNATIONAL WEIGHTS, MEASURES, AND TEMPERATURES

Temperature

To convert Celsius to Fahrenheit, multiply by 1.8 and add 32.
To convert Fahrenheit to Celsius, subtract 32 and multiply by .56.

Length, Distance & Area	Multiply
Inches to centimeters	by 2.54
Centimeters to inches	by 0.39
Feet to meters	by 0.30
Meters to feet	by 3.28
Yards to meters	by 0.91
Meters to yards	by 1.09
Miles to kilometers	by 1.61
Kilometers to miles	by 0.62

Weight

1 gram = .04 ounce
10 grams = .4 ounce
1 kilogram (kg) = 2.2 pounds
A British ton = 2,240 pounds
A U.S. ton = 2,000 pounds

Volume	Multiply
U.S. gallons to liters	by 3.79
Liters to U.S. gallons	by 0.26

5 Imperial gallons = 6 U.S. gallons
A liter is slightly more than a U.S. quart.

How to Use Cheap Sleeps in London

The advantage of a hotel is that it is a refuge from homelife.
—*George Bernard Shaw*

CROWN CLASSIFICATIONS

Hotels in Great Britain are not controlled by a government rating system, as they are in many other countries. The British Tourist Board operates a voluntary registration and optional grading system for all tourist accommodations, from the Ritz down to the grubbiest B&B. Note the words *voluntary* and *optional*. Many good hotels refuse to take part in this classification system because it does not mean that quality, cleanliness, or value go along with the rated hotel. In fact, many hotels in London displaying two and three crowns are filthy, without redeeming decoration or friendly management. They may have the required number of lights by the bed, or the right number of toilets and showers in order to qualify for a certain number of crowns, but there it stops. A word to the wise is to consider the crowns but not bank on them. *Cheap Sleeps in London* ignores them altogether.

ACCOMMODATIONS

In London, the hotel day begins and ends at noon. If you overstay (without prior arrangement), you will probably be charged the price of an extra day. If you leave earlier than your reservation ending date, you could be charged for the nights not stayed, and if you cancel altogether less than forty-eight hours before arrival, the law says you are liable to pay for two nights. These instances are rare, but they do happen, and you don't want to have these hassles. If your flight is leaving later in the afternoon, most hotels will keep your luggage in a safe place and let you use the lobby. If your flight arrives early in the morning, your room may not be ready for immediate occupancy. Most hotels will try their best to let you into your room as soon as possible, but if you absolutely *must* have the room early in the morning, you should consider booking it for the night before. You will pay for an unoccupied room, but it will be yours from the minute you arrive.

The lobby or reception area of a hotel is usually one of the most attractive parts of the building both because first impressions are important, and because this is where the owner and manager spend their day.

When you arrive at your hotel (especially in a B&B), ask to see your room. This is a normal and expected practice. After approving the accommodation, reconfirm the rate, making sure there are no hidden extras.

RESERVATIONS, DEPOSITS, AND CANCELLATIONS

Reservations

Are reservations necessary? Absolutely! Confirmed reservations are essential to the success of any trip to London or any other world capital if you want to be in charge of how much you spend. With the electronic age, it is easy to telephone, fax, or email reservation requests and in most cases to guarantee them with a credit card. In some small budget hotels and B&Bs, you may be asked to guarantee your room with an international money order in pounds (see "Deposits," page 39).

No matter how you make your reservation, the following points should be included in your inquiry:

1. The dates of stay, time of arrival (including flight number), and number of persons in your party. Tell the hotel you are a reader of *Cheap Sleeps in London* because you might get a discount or a better room.

2. The size and type of room you need: double or twin, with or without private facilities, quiet, with a view, nonsmoking, and so on.

3. The rates: Determine what the nightly rate will be and whether or not the VAT (value-added tax of 17½ percent) is included as well as what sort of breakfast the hotel serves. This is the time to negotiate any rate discounts.

4. The kind of deposit required and the form of payment.

5. *Important:* Request that the hotel send you a confirmation of your reservation and the amount of deposit, and carry this with you to the registration desk when you check in. This avoids a multitude of snafus when you arrive, such as having the desk clerk tell you that you have no reservation, or that it is "lost." Believe me, this happens more often than you would think.

6. Just as important as No. 5 is this: Always send a fax (and keep a copy) confirming *your* end of the reservation, noting the date and time of your call, the name of the person with whom you spoke, and the particulars of your reservation, spelling out the rates and any discounts that may have been given. Take this with you, along with the hotel's confirmation.

Now that you are convinced reservations are necessary, what is the best way to make them? A few suggestions follow on the best ways to make London hotel reservations.

Email: This is a quick way to nail down hotel reservation particulars. While you may not want to put your credit card number in an email message, you can fax it after you have made your arrangements. Whenever a hotel has an email or Internet address, it is provided with the listing.

Faxing: This is another easy way to reserve. It is also the best way to confirm. To send a fax message to London from the United States, dial 011-44 plus the hotel fax number, minus the first zero.

Telephone: When you consider the cost of a phone call to London, it is nothing in comparison to the cost of the trip . . . and the convenience is wonderful. It allows you to wheel and deal, sorting out the reservation so it is in your best interest. *Always* make the call during the hotel's weekday business hours (London is six hours ahead of eastern standard time and nine hours ahead of Pacific). That avoids talking to a night clerk who has no authority to negotiate rates or to offer you a deal. Before calling, write down all your requests and questions. Be sure to ask for a confirmation fax from the hotel and follow up your call with the same. To dial London direct from the United States, dial 011-44 plus the number of the hotel, minus the first zero.

Letter: In this day of electronics, why anyone would resort to letter writing for reservation purposes is a mystery to me. Many hotels let reservation letters stack up and deal with them later when they have time, which is usually never. Transatlantic mail can take as long as two weeks one way, and if there is a strike, who knows how long the letter could be in transit. When you consider the entire cost of your trip against the cost, convenience, and speed of email, a fax, or a telephone call, the letter option is way behind the times and woefully inadequate.

Deposits

After accepting your reservation, most hotels require at least a one-night deposit, more if you are renting a flat. This is smart insurance for both parties. The easiest way to handle all deposits is with a credit card. If the hotel does not accept credit cards, and many budget B&Bs do not, there are other ways of sending the deposit, none of which are particularly convenient or cost-free. Sending your personal check to these little establishments is not an option; they want the money in pounds sterling. Call American Express at 800-926-9400 for more information on sending a money gram, which is a direct wire service to a bank or office in London that will accept them. Or, if you prefer sending a money order, call 800-999-9660 Mon–Fri 6:30 A.M.–6 P.M., Sat 7 A.M.–3 P.M., mountain standard time. The benefit here is not time, but you can mail it and save a hefty wiring fee. This service is available to anyone. Another company handling foreign money matters is Thomas Cook. Contact them at 800-CURRENCY for information about money drafts and so on.

Cancellations

If you need to cancel or to cut your stay short, for *any* reason, be prepared for some anxious moments when it comes to getting back any prepaid money. When you reserve a hotel room or flat, you are entering into a legally binding contract with the proprietor of the establishment. This means that if you have to cancel or leave early, the proprietor may be entitled to compensation if he cannot re-let your room or flat. If a deposit has been paid, count on forfeiting it if you cancel at the last minute. This whole area has the potential of creating many Maalox moments, so know the hotel, B&B, or flat rental cancellation policy *before* you go, and before you tie up a big chunk of your vacation money.

As I have stressed throughout *Cheap Sleeps in London,* the best way to circumvent this cancellation nightmare is to buy cancellation and/or trip-interruption insurance before you leave home. Your travel agent or the American Automobile Association can advise you on companies that deal in this insurance. Some apartment-letting services also have cancellation policies you can take out. My advice is to compare several policy plans before investing. If you only have a one-night deposit invested, it is probably not worth it; but if you have a half-month deposit on a flat, it certainly is.

RATES: PAYING THE BILL

All hotels in Britain are required by law to plainly display their minimum and maximum overnight rates. The price must include service, and may or may not include VAT (value-added tax of $17\frac{1}{2}$ percent, and rising). Depending on the economy and the state of tourism, London hotel rates usually increase from 2 to 10 percent every year, around April. The rates quoted in *Cheap Sleeps in London* were correct at press time, but please allow for the chance of a yearly increase.

When reserving, *always* ask for a discount and be ready to negotiate the rates. Many hotels offer low seasonal rates, and you would be surprised at the tremendous discounts the high-end hotels will give. All it takes is for *you* to *ask.* Many times, the hotel won't mention them unless you do. All rates given in *Cheap Sleeps in London* are for the full price and do not reflect special discounts or discount time periods. Where these are available, they are noted. But, and this is important, even if no discounts are mentioned, that does not mean they will not be available.

Every hotel listed gives credit card information. In most Cheap Sleeps, payment is required to secure your first night. Few lower-priced hotels take any sort of credit cards. They accept only cash up front in British pounds. Hotel exchange rates are terrible, no matter what the front desk may claim. If you are paying your bill in cash, change your money into pounds *before* checkout time (see "Money Matters," page 17). Be sure to go over your bill carefully and get a receipt marked "paid in full."

HOTEL BREAKFASTS

All London hotels and private B&Bs serve either a Continental breakfast or a full English breakfast. The meal is usually included in the room price, but if you are trying to save as much money as possible, ask that the cost of the breakfast—per person—be deducted from your hotel rate. This per-day deduction must be arranged *before* check-in. The hotel will probably not allow you to eat there one morning and somewhere else another. You will have to make up your mind and stick to it.

Unfortunately, London hoteliers are very reluctant to deduct breakfast, and many will not, period. It is a big moneymaker. Actually, a full English breakfast enables many to skip lunch and to save money that way. A full English breakfast has many interpretations, anything from the addition of an egg and a slice of bacon to the regular Continental breakfast of toast and marmalade to a full-blown meal of hot or cold cereal, eggs any style, meats, beans, toast, fried bread, mushrooms, tomatoes, and all the tea and coffee you can drink. Many hotels and B&Bs pride themselves on their generous home-cooked breakfasts, a tradition in England. The smaller hotels and B&Bs seldom vary their breakfast menus, so after two or three mornings of this cholesterol festival, many of us yearn for just a simple piece of fruit and a bagel.

BIG SPLURGES

Some of the hotel listings fall into the Big Splurge category. They are higher priced due to their amenities, ambience, service, and overall appeal, but they still represent the best values in their class. These are hotels to consider if your budget is more flexible, if you are celebrating a special occasion, or if you want better facilities but prefer a less formal atmosphere than at the big hotels, along with their intimidatingly high prices. See the index of Big Splurges, page 313, for a complete list.

FACILITIES/ROOMS WITH AND WITHOUT BATHS

Each *Cheap Sleeps in London* listing gives the number of rooms and whether they have private baths, and if so, how many. This information appears below the establishment's address. At the end of each listing a brief summary describes hotel facilities. The better the hotel, the more services offered, and usually the higher its room rates. Check each listing for those amenities you consider essential for a comfortable stay. For a complete list of hotels with nonsmoking rooms, see page 313.

MAPS

Every postal code covered in *Cheap Sleeps in London* has a corresponding map listing all of the hotels and Cheap Chic establishments within that area. Each hotel's map key number is repeated in the text; it appears in parentheses to the right of the hotel name. Establishments located outside the boundaries of these maps have been given no number.

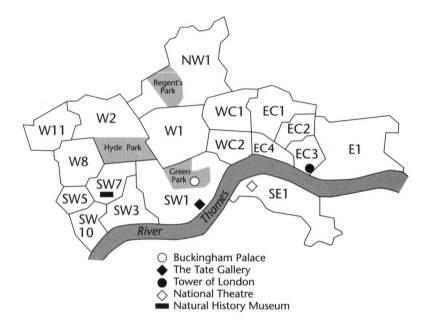

NW1

Regent's
Park

W2   WC1   EC1

W11   W1   EC2

W8   Hyde Park   WC2   EC4   EC3   E1

SW7   Green
Park

SW5   SW1   Thames   SE1

SW3

SW
10   River

○ Buckingham Palace
◆ The Tate Gallery
● Tower of London
◇ National Theatre
▬ Natural History Museum

Hotel Listings by Postal Code

London is far more difficult to see properly than any other place. London is a riddle. . . .

—G. K. Chesterton, All Things Considered, *1908*

London is chaos incorporated.

—George Mikes, Down with Everybody, *1951*

London is one of the largest cities in the world. With more than 610 square miles of area and seven million inhabitants in the metropolitan area, it is twice the size of Paris or New York City. Originally, London was a collection of small villages. In a sense, it still is, each "village" having its own unique character and atmosphere.

One of the great allures of visiting London is that you can never see it all. There is always one more pub, a special museum, or a historic street or neighborhood left to explore. It is beyond the scope of *Cheap Sleeps in London* to go into detail about all of the sight-seeing possibilities that await you. The following sketches of the highlights, organized by postal code, are designed to give you a quick idea of what is around your hotel. For the best in-depth description of what to see in London, the green Michelin *Tourist Guide to London* is a must.

As Paris is divided into arrondissements, London is divided into postal codes. You will see them included in all street addresses and on most street signs. Knowing one postal code from another is important when booking your hotel accommodations. The letters, which stand for compass directions with reference to the central district, start with W1 and then are divided into WC and EC for West Central and East Central, NW and SW for North West and South West, and so on. All districts bordering on the central districts are numbered with a one (1) and continue to increase in number as they get farther from the center. If you see W8, you know you are not in the heart of Piccadilly in the West End; SE10 tells you the address is well into the tourist boonies. All hotel and shop listings in *Cheap Sleeps in London* provide the postal code and are arranged accordingly. This system parallels the arrangement of the restaurants in *Cheap Eats in London.* If you are staying in SW1 and are trying to decide where to eat dinner close to your hotel, refer to the SW1 section in *Cheap Eats in London* for a listing of nearby restaurants.

W1

The West End: Mayfair, St. James's, Piccadilly, Soho, Marylebone, and Marble Arch

I like to walk down Bond Street, thinking of all the things I don't want.
—Logan Pearsall Smith, Afterthoughts, *1931*

The postal code West One (W1) corresponds to the West End, the area filled with department stores, theaters, shops, pubs, restaurants, and nightlife.

Mayfair and St. James's, which are west of Regent Street and north of Piccadilly, are characterized by gentlemen's clubs, expensive shops, plush hotels, royal residences, and parks. The tailoring standards of the world are defined on Savile Row, and the finest (and most expensive) shopping is found along Jermyn, South Molton, and New and Old Bond streets. St. James's Park and Green Park offer good views of Buckingham Palace. If you see the royal standard (flag) flying at Buckingham Palace, you will know the queen is in residence.

Piccadilly is London's equivalent of Times Square, with incessant traffic, crowds, bright lights, noise, and general confusion for the uninitiated. Piccadilly Circus isn't actually a circus anymore, but it seems like one with six traffic-clogged main roads spiraling from it.

The word *Soho* comes from the hunting call "so-ho." Its use as a place name seems to be associated with the area's former popularity as a location for fox and hare hunting. Today, Soho is full of character and characters, and the type of hunting has changed dramatically. For centuries this area has been home for immigrants and refugees, who opened a cosmopolitan mix of shops, restaurants, bars, pubs, and sleazy sex and strip joints. Bustling by day and exciting by night, this is London's center of entertainment and nightlife of all types. Here are the West End theaters, a great selection of cinemas, hundreds of restaurants catering to every taste and budget, and Chinatown, which hums until the wee hours, drawing many after-theater diners and other night owls.

Marylebone is a residential area with many lovely squares. Doctors offices line Harley Street, and all Sherlock Holmes fans know about 221-B Baker Street. If you are in Marylebone (pronounced MAR-lee-bun), you will be able to visit the Planetarium and stand in the interminable queue for Madame Tussaud's Wax Museum.

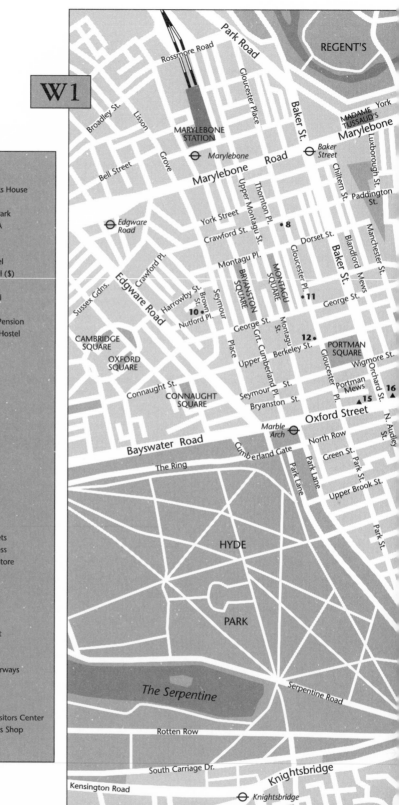

HOTELS in W1

OTHER OPTIONS

($) indicates a Big Splurge

GEORGIAN HOUSE HOTEL (8)
87 Gloucester Place, W1
19 rooms, all with shower or bath and toilet

TELEPHONE
020-7935-2211/7486-3151

FAX
020-7486-7535

EMAIL
info@georgianhotel
.demon.co.uk

INTERNET
www.accommodata.co.uk/
061095.htm
www.smoothhound.co.uk/
hotels/georgian.html

TUBE
Baker Street

CREDIT CARDS
AE, MC, V

For one of the best Cheap Sleeping values near Baker Street and within walking distance of Oxford Street and Regent's Park, the Georgian House Hotel receives my vote of confidence. It is obvious from first glance that owners Sam Popat and Nick Damji continue to spend time, money, and effort to maintain the consistently high standards of their spotless hotel. The identically decorated bedrooms, which are repainted yearly, are done in rich tapestries of gold and green. Good lighting, luggage racks, and individually controlled central heating add to their allure. So do new beds every three years, double-glazed windows where possible (it is a listed building and some things cannot be altered), and a London information packet. The bathrooms are exceptionally nice, with heated towel racks and collapsible laundry lines, so handy for those quick overnight drying needs. However, note that only nine of the rooms have an in-room bathroom; the other ten rooms have access to their own adjacent, private bathroom. The only real drawbacks are the ground-floor rooms, which open directly onto the street, and some of the back rooms, which face a wall. Naturally, these back rooms are quiet, and the opposing wall has been painted and potted plants positioned in an effort to break the monotonous view. A few rooms have bathrooms outside, but these are never shared with any other rooms. Best bets, in my opinion, are streetside rooms from the second floor up, especially No. 5, which has two floor-to-ceiling windows, twin beds, and a corner area for stashing luggage, or No. 19 on the back, with twin beds, a view, and its own private bathroom just next to it.

The breakfast room, also decorated in golds and greens, has a mirrored section that gives the room depth. Your morning breakfast buffet includes ham, cheese, hard-boiled eggs, fruit juices, cereals, toast, jam, and coffee or tea.

A final bonus point that really puts this hotel at the top of its class is that it has a lift to all floors.

FACILITIES AND SERVICES: Central heat, direct-dial phones, hair dryer and iron available, lift, office safe, TV, tea and coffeemakers, fax for guests Mon–Fri 8 A.M.–5 P.M.; desk open for reservations 7 A.M.–10:30 P.M.

HALLAM HOTEL (3)
12 Hallam Street, W1
25 rooms, all with shower or bath and toilet

New Zealanders Grant and David Baker own the friendly Hallam, which is just far enough from the crowded central part of London to make it a good choice for those who want a reasonably quiet stay. Situated immediately behind the BBC Broadcasting House, it is only a ten-minute walk to Oxford Circus, with all the neon lights and glitz the West End has to offer. The hotel was completely redone in the early 1990s. The rooms are alike, with attractive built-in mahogany furniture, soft green carpeting, and matching peach floral bedspreads and drapes. Room sizes range from minuscule singles known as "cabins," which are nothing more than a built-in bed squeezed into a five-by-ten-foot space, to large twins with ample closets and nice window seats. For solo travelers, No. 23, or "The Crow's Nest," is

RATES
Single £70–80; double £85–95; triple £95–105; family room £110–120; English breakfast buffet included

TELEPHONE
020-7580-1166
FAX
020-7323-4527
TUBE
Great Portland Street
CREDIT CARDS
AE, DC, MC, V
RATES
Single £90; double £105; English breakfast included

an attractive top-floor choice with a tub bath and a commanding view of the British Telecom Tower. Number 8, a front-facing compact double, might be noisy for some, and so might No. 13, a good-size single also on the front. A view is exchanged for peace and quiet in No. 6, a twin on the back. A plus for most will be the nonsmoking rooms, a rarity in London. Breakfast is served in a garden atrium on tables set with starched cloths and flowers. Good lighting makes the morning papers easy to read and the nonsmoking policy here pleases all but a few.

FACILITIES AND SERVICES: Central heat, fans on request for the top-floor rooms, direct-dial phones, hair dryer, lift, minibar, office safe, TV, tea and coffeemakers, 24-hour desk

HART HOUSE HOTEL (12)
51 Gloucester Place, W1
16 rooms, all with shower or bath and toilet

TELEPHONE
020-7935-2288

FAX
020-7935-8516

TUBE
Baker Street, Marble Arch

CREDIT CARDS
AE, MC, V

RATES
Single £65; double £93; suite £110; quad £130; full English breakfast included

Hart House is a sixteen-room bed-and-breakfast hotel superbly run by Andrew Bowden, who took it over from his parents about fifteen years ago. The building was part of an original terrace of Georgian mansions occupied by French nobility during the French Revolution. It is conveniently located for West End theaters, shopping, Hyde Park, Regent's Park, and the zoo.

Everything in the hotel is always very clean and in perfect order thanks to a committed redecorating schedule. In addition, most of the rooms have that hard-to-find commodity in London: *space*. Number 7 is a front-facing triple with a large bath and shower and two floor-to-ceiling windows. On the back of the hotel, No. 6, a spacious twin, has leaded windows you cannot see through, but amazingly enough, there is still plenty of light. I also like the bathroom, which has a stall shower, a lighted mirror over the sink, and two shelves for toiletries. Number 8 has windows overlooking a small balcony, and No. 11 is another sunny perch for two. All of the rooms are nicely fitted with mahogany furniture that includes an armoire, desk, comfortable chair, and chest of drawers. The lower-floor breakfast room has three skylights and a coal-burning fireplace, making it a cheerful spot for guests to enjoy the traditional English breakfast included in the price of a room. Large tables set with blue and white china encourage sharing and getting to know the other guests. Andrew Bowden's outgoing hospitality and reasonable rates make this a favorite, so get your reservation as soon as you know your London dates.

FACILITIES AND SERVICES: Central heat, direct-dial phones, hair dryer, no lift, office safe, TV, tea and coffee-makers, desk open for reservations 7:30 A.M.–10:30 P.M.

HAZLITT'S (27, $)
6 Frith Street, W1
23 rooms, all with shower or bath and toilet

There is no question about it: Hazlitt's is one of London's best small hotels. The combination of history, charm, and character, along with the hotel's unique surroundings and personal service, all in a super location, have made the hotel a standout from the moment it opened its doors in 1986. It is on the edge of Soho, within interesting and easy walking distance of more than thirty West End theaters, twenty cinemas, the Royal Opera House, and dozens of restaurants in every price category (see *Cheap Eats in London*). Named for the great English essayist and critic William Hazlitt, who boarded here, wrote his last essay here, and died here, the hotel occupies three Georgian townhouses built in 1718. All twenty-three rooms are named after the eighteenth- and early-nineteenth-century residents or visitors of the original houses. Many celebrities of our own day have stayed here, and it is especially popular among authors. Traditionally, guests who have had a recent work published leave a signed copy of their latest book in a special cabinet in the sitting room.

The entire hotel is a study in tasteful decorating, dominated by a sensational collection of more than two thousand original prints hung throughout the hotel, including in all of the guest bathrooms. The individually decorated bedrooms have high ceilings, comfortable beds—many of which are four-posters with snowy white Egyptian cotton duvet coverings. Most of the classic bathrooms have original Victorian claw-footed bathtubs and brass faucet hardware, lovingly polished by a full-time staff member solely employed for this purpose.

The ground-floor Baron Willoughby Suite is magnificent, with a massive four-poster bed, marble fireplace, leather-tufted chesterfield, and corner cabinet with a display of antique plates, teacups, and teapots. The Earl of St. Albans has a half-canopy bed, mirrored armoire, and a beautiful collection of bird prints hung in

TELEPHONE
020-7434-1771

FAX
020-7439-1524

EMAIL
hazlitts.co.uk

TUBE
Tottenham Court Road

CREDIT CARDS
AE, DC, MC, V

RATES
Single £140; double £185; suite £270; all rates subject to VAT of 17½ percent; Continental breakfast only, £8 extra per person, served in the room or in one of the sitting rooms

the bathroom. The Sir William Ross Room is perfect for a single. Although it doesn't have a view, it does have the advantage of more space and a marble washstand in the bathroom. A beautiful collection of framed prints of water animals highlights the Mary Baker Room, which also has a sweet corner fireplace and a beautifully carved headboard on its four-poster bed. For those requiring as much space as possible, consider the Jonathan Swift Room, with its 300-year-old bed frame; the Prussian President Room, with a walk-in closet and an extra sofa bed; or the William Duncombe Room, which has a fireplace discovered a few years ago during a renovation project, a marvelous, massive double bed, and a five-drawer dresser.

It is the nature of old buildings that nothing is perfect. The management asks guests to "Please be kind to the furniture, and if it is not being kind to you let us know and we will attend to it." Because the original character of the buildings has been kept, some floors may lean a little and there might be a ray or two of light under the doorway, and there is no elevator. However, the hotel has succeeded beautifully in maintaining the comfort of twentieth-century life, without sacrificing the historical spirit of its surroundings for its grateful and contented guests.

FACILITIES AND SERVICES: Central heat, direct-dial phones, hair dryer, laundry service, room safe, satellite TV, modems, no lift, 24-hour desk

NOTE: See page 157 for The Gore, another hotel under the same ownership.

IVANHOE SUITE HOTEL/PENSION (19)
1 St. Christopher's Place, W1
7 rooms, all with shower or bath and toilet

TELEPHONE
020-7935-1047
FAX
020-7724-0563
INTERNET
www.scoot.co.uk/
ivanhoe_suite_hotel
TUBE
Bond Street
CREDIT CARDS
AE, DC, MC, V

One of the best Cheap Sleeps in London is the seven-room Ivanhoe Suite Hotel/Pension. Located on a pedestrian walkway, this hotel consists of attractive singles and doubles, each with its own sitting area and tiled bathroom with stall showers. At street level on St. Christopher's Place, there is a hidden security system whereby guests view the front door below when someone rings their private doorbell. The white-glove test will never be necessary, as the rooms are nothing short of antiseptically clean and tidy. I like No. 4, done in soft peach with blue accents, with a view onto St.

Christopher's Place and the metal fountain, and the similar No. 6, a sunny double with a large closet, plenty of shelf space in a nice bathroom, and an interesting view of the square below. Another of my favorites is the bright No. 3, large enough for three people. For shoppers, this hotel almost qualifies as Mecca. Besides the interesting boutiques along St. Christopher's Place, you are only minutes from New and Old Bond streets and all the temptations of their elegant shops. Good restaurants and typical pubs are also only minutes away (see *Cheap Eats in London*).

FACILITIES AND SERVICES: Electric heat, fans in all rooms, direct-dial phones, hair dryer, laundry service, minibar, office safe, cable TV, radio, some room clocks, individual security for each room, trouser press, tea and coffeemakers, no lift, office open 7:30 A.M.–midnight

RATES
Single £66; double £80; triple £95; Continental breakfast included and served in the room

LANGHAM COURT HOTEL (9, $)
31–35 Langham Street, W1
56 rooms, all with shower or bath and toilet

The Langham Court, between Oxford Street and Regent's Park, is a full-service hotel where if you pay the rack rate, you will have paid too much. The Cheap Sleeping deal at this hotel is to get the corporate rate, and to absolutely forget eating breakfast here, either of which will save you more than enough to buy lunch for two in the hotel's brasserie or wine bar.

Originally built in 1899, the Langham Court provides comfortable, up-to-date accommodations in a friendly atmosphere. The elegant reception area, accented by blue and white Oriental plant holders and fresh flowers, has a welcoming bar with settees and armchairs where guests are provided with the local newspapers. Off to one side is a small outdoor terrace. Another advantage of this hotel, especially for businesspeople who want to entertain clients, is that they won't have to leave the comfort of the hotel to eat and drink well.

The bedrooms are color-coordinated and offer all the perks, including satellite television and computerized door locks. I found them to be appealing with the exception of the viewless, depressing few located on the ground floor, those one level below, and the back rooms, which suffer noise from the hotel fans.

FACILITIES AND SERVICES: Air-conditioning in some rooms, bar, central heat, conference room, direct-dial

TELEPHONE
020-7233-7888 (central reservations); 020-7436-6622 (hotel); 800-44-UTELL (toll-free from the U.S. and Canada)

FAX
020-7835-1888 (central reservations); 020-7436-2303 (hotel)

EMAIL
sales@grangehotels.co.uk

INTERNET
www.grangehotels.co.uk

TUBE
Oxford Circus

CREDIT CARDS
AE, DC, MC, V

RATES
Single from £140, corporate from £110; double from £160, corporate from £125; Continental breakfast £11 extra, English breakfast £15 extra

phones, hair dryer, laundry service, lift, porter, restaurant, 24-hour room service, office safe, tea and coffeemakers, trouser press, satellite TV, 24-hour desk

FORTE POSTHOUSE LEISURE BREAKS

TELEPHONE
0345-40-40-40; 0800-40-40-40 (toll-free within the U.K.); 800-225-5843 (toll-free from the U.S.)
FAX
01384-486159 (U.K.); 602-735-7296 (from the U.S.)
INTERNET
www.forte-hotels.com
CREDIT CARDS
AE, DC, MC, V

For one of the better hotel values in the capital, schedule your visit around one of the Forte Posthouse Leisure Breaks. These offer excellent package plans not only for London visitors but for those of you traveling elsewhere in the U.K. where there are Posthouse hotels. In London, the Cheap Sleeping deals can range from a simple room upgrade to five nights for the price of four; midweek, weekend, or holiday stays that include dinner, bed, and breakfast; and Theatre Breaks tickets to all the top West End shows, the opera and ballet, rock concerts, or the Chelsea Flower Show. Dinner vouchers, travel cards, and free (or greatly reduced) rates for children sharing their parents' room are usually part of the plans. In some cases you can use your dinner voucher at another participating hotel or restaurant, or have lunch or afternoon tea instead. There is a minimum two consecutive nights stay required, a full English breakfast is included, and other restrictions apply. For complete details and a price breakdown, contact the numbers to the left and ask for a brochure.

Forte hotels participating in the London Posthouse Leisure Breaks are the Posthouse Bloomsbury, WC1 (page 105); the Posthouse Kensington, W8 (page 80); the Posthouse Regent's Park, W1 (below); and the Regent Palace Hotel, W1 (page 55).

POSTHOUSE REGENT'S PARK (4)
Carburton Street, W1
323 rooms, all with shower or bath and toilet

TELEPHONE
020-7388-2300; 0800-40-40-40 (toll-free within the U.K.); 800-225-5843 (toll-free from the U.S.)
FAX
020-7383-7741
INTERNET
www.forte-hotels.com
TUBE
Euston, Marylebone, Paddington
CREDIT CARDS
AE, DC, MC, V
RATES
Singles from £80; doubles from £110; English breakfast included

This big Forte chain hotel offers a uniform and comfortable haven about five minutes from the West End. Fitness fanatics will be happy to run in Regent's Park, and the children in your group will love Madame Tussaud's and the Planetarium . . . all of which are nearby. The hotel participates in the Posthouse Leisure Breaks, which are described above.

FACILITIES AND SERVICES: Bar, central heat, direct-dial phones, hair dryer, lift, minibar, restaurant, room service, office safe, tea and coffeemakers, trouser press, satellite TV

REGENT PALACE HOTEL (43)
Piccadilly Circus, W1
920 rooms, 120 with shower or bath and toilet

Situated overlooking Eros and Piccadilly Circus, no hotel could be nearer the bright lights and bustle of London than the Regent Palace Hotel, which is part of the Forte Posthouse Hotels. It is one of the largest hotels in London and the perfect point from which to sample all that London has to offer. From here you will be steps away from theaters, nightclubs, restaurants, shops, tube and bus transportation, and several major museums. The 920 rooms, which are strung out along never-ending halls, are acceptably furnished in typical tailored-hotel style. Forty-four of them are geared to families. If you are arriving with children, they will receive a gift pack, and baby-sitting can be arranged. If sleep is part of your nightly plan, avoid the rooms on the eighth and ninth floors, which are often filled with school groups. Most of the rooms are without private facilities other than a sink with hot and cold water. In my opinion, it does not make Cheap Sleeping sense to pay one penny more to upgrade to a room with your own tight-fitting, airless "phone-booth" shower and toilet. The institutional hall facilities are large, and remind me of most you would find in a health club or college dorm. A maid opens the door to the shower or bath on request and cleans it immediately after each use. Save even more money and avoid eating breakfast here, especially the boxed editions that are made up "who knows when" and passed out every morning at a central distribution point on each floor. Almost every service you can imagine is in the hotel, including a Callahans Irish Pub, a themed restaurant that shows up in many other Posthouse Hotels. The hotel also partici-pates in the Forte Posthouse Leisure Breaks, which offer a host of significant Cheap Sleeping, money-saving plans that are loaded with benefits. Please see page 54 for further information.

FACILITIES AND SERVICES: Bars, central heat, direct-dial phones, hair dryers available, ironing rooms, laundry service, lift, office safe, some trouser presses, tea and coffeemakers, TV, 24-hour desk, baby-sitting, children gift packs

TELEPHONE
020-7734-7000; 0800-40-40-40 (toll-free within the U.K.); 800-225-5843 (toll-free from the U.S.)

FAX
020-7734-6435

INTERNET
www.forte-hotels.com

TUBE
Piccadilly Circus

CREDIT CARDS
AE, DC, MC, V

RATES
Single £55; double £80; English breakfast included

MISCELLANEOUS
Nonsmoking floors available

WIGMORE COURT HOTEL (11)
23 Gloucester Place, W1
18 rooms, 16 with shower or bath and toilet

TELEPHONE
020-7935-0928
FAX
020-7487-4254
EMAIL
info@wigmore-court-hotel.co.uk
INTERNET
www.wigmore-court-hotel.co.uk
TUBE
Baker Street, Marble Arch
CREDIT CARDS
MC, V
RATES
Single £50–60; double £70–95; triple £110; quad £120; five £130; six £140; 10 percent discount given if you mention *Cheap Sleeps in London* when reserving; English breakfast included

The Wigmore Court Hotel building was designed in the 1700s by John Elwes. Since that time many notables have resided here, including William Pitt. The address is less than a ten-minute walk to three tube stations, shopping on Oxford Street, and the tourist favorites of Madame Tussaud's, Hyde Park, Regent's Park, and enough restaurants listed in *Cheap Eats in London* to keep you well fed almost indefinitely. If you don't want to eat out, you can whip something up on the six-burner stove, bake a pie in the oven, or zap a quickie from a takeaway in the microwave in the hotel kitchen, which is equipped for the guests' use. And everyone will appreciate the convenient money- and time-saving coin-operated washers and dryers in the basement, along with the iron and ironing board. Finally, all Cheap Sleepers in London will receive a 10 percent discount if they mention this book when reserving.

What about the rooms? They are clean and come with an electric kettle, televisions, and fans and minibars in a few. My only problem with most of the rooms is the pattern overload thanks to the multicolored print and floral mixes and the varieties of wallpaper patterns. Separately, they would be fine, but all together it is a bit too much. However, I cannot fault the cleanliness, so if a smorgasbord of colors does not bother you, read on. In No. 2, the U-shaped, viewless room has twins and a sofa bed, space, and a nice bathroom with a tub and shower. Number 33 is a family room that can sleep four. The view from the two windows is pleasant; there is drawer, desk, and table space, and in the bathroom a tub for a nice bubblebath. In No. 31 you get a more put together room but have to go upstairs to the bathroom. The only room I found totally unacceptable (until redone) was No. 11, a two-room family affair with an old bathroom where the comment "It's a little bit tight for what's in there" holds very true. There is no lounge, but guests can meet in the pink-wallpapered breakfast room around its ornate metal tables.

FACILITIES AND SERVICES: Central heat, fans in some rooms, direct-dial phones, hair dryer and iron available, kitchen privileges, coin-operated laundry, some minibars, tea and coffeemakers, TV, no safe, no lift

W2

Paddington and Bayswater

Paddington is a good choice if you are on a budget or traveling by car. It is close to Hyde Park, where you can jog or walk off some of those full English breakfasts and your children can play and expend some of their pent-up energy. If you have a car, parking can be a nightmare, but not if you stay in one of the hotels on Sussex Gardens, where free parking is often part of the deal. Restaurants in the area are budget conscious and seldom gourmet. Many of the hotels that line both sides of the busy Sussex Gardens are geared for tourists spending one or two nights near the Paddington Train Station; in short, they're dull. However, the competition is stiff, making hotel prices here among the lowest in London. Transportation is superb. The area is served by four Underground lines: Metropolitan, Bakerloo, District, and Circle. In addition, all the Cheap Sleeps in W2 have the bonus of being within walking distance, or a short cab ride away, of Paddington Station, where the fast-rail link to Heathrow Airport runs every fifteen minutes between 5:30 A.M. and 11:30 P.M. and takes under thirty minutes either way. You can also check in for your onward flight at Paddington, which has twenty-seven desks for nine airlines with full luggage check-in facilities. This means you will save the hassle of getting to and queuing at Heathrow with luggage in tow.

Bayswater lies north of Kensington Gardens and is known as a residential area of contrasts. It is home to many Indians, Pakistanis, and Arabs, budget hotels, and shops of all types. Queensway, its main thoroughfare, has everything from the large Whiteleys of Bayswater indoor shopping mall, which houses stores, cafés, and cinemas as well as tacky shops and restaurants serving a multitude of ethnic and local foods. On Sunday, it is pleasant to walk along Bayswater Road, where artists and craftspeople display their works for sale (see Bayswater Road Art Exhibition, page 256).

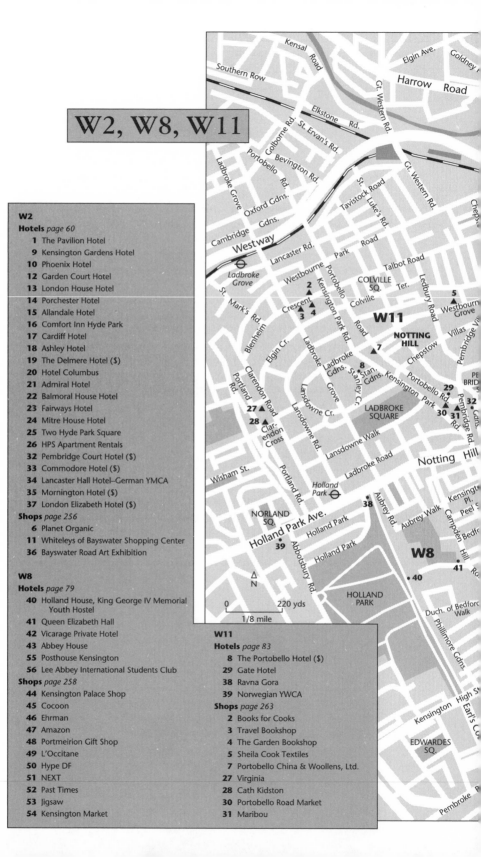

W2, W8, W11

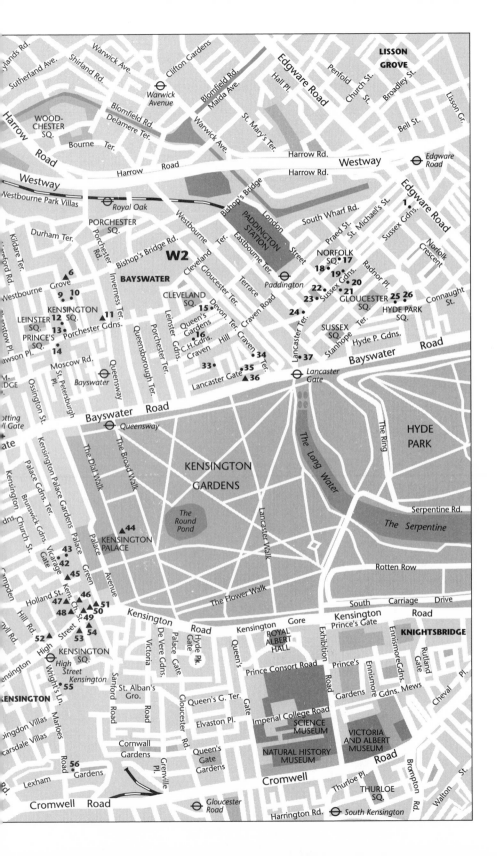

HOTELS in W2

OTHER OPTIONS

($) indicates a Big Splurge

ADMIRAL HOTEL (21)
143 Sussex Gardens, W2
20 rooms, all with shower or bath and toilet

Franco and Gloria Vales run a reliable Cheap Sleep for those voyagers insisting on a private bathroom but willing to overlook something less than perfectly matched rooms. Nonsmokers presently have the second floor to themselves, and if Franco has his way, the entire hotel will soon be entirely nonsmoking. Space is tight in some bathrooms, and the prefab arrangements might turn some off. However, the tidy rooms have drawer and closet space, a chair, and reading lights over the bed. Breakfast is served on English china in a sweet pink and white room that is as clean as the rest of the twenty-room hotel.

FACILITIES AND SERVICES: Central heat, direct-dial phones, double-glazed windows along the front, hair dryer and iron available, electric tea and coffeemakers, one free parking space that must be reserved, office safe, TV, no lift, some nonsmoking rooms, office open 8 A.M.–midnight

TELEPHONE
020-7723-7309/3975
FAX
020-7723-8731
EMAIL
frank@admiral143.demon.co.uk
INTERNET
www.admiral143.demon.co.uk
TUBE
Lancaster Gate, Paddington
CREDIT CARDS
MC, V
RATES
Single £45; double £70; extra person £30; English breakfast included

ALLANDALE HOTEL (15)
3 Devonshire Terrace, W2
25 rooms, 24 with shower or bath and toilet

Look for the orange-and-white-striped awning hanging over the entry to this budget basic on Devonshire Terrace, where owner Mr. Hussein has been offering Cheap Sleeps with no apologies for more than twenty years. There is no lift and no private phone or electric teapot in your room, but you do get satellite television reception in a clean room at a price that leaves something left over for you to enjoy London. Pink and rose dominate the color scheme, and the fabric of choice on the beds is my old fave . . . chenille. Some of the bathrooms are throwbacks to the days when bright blue tile was popular; few have hooks, but some have shower doors. Room No. 2, in the basement, is sold as a family room, but I think it is far too cramped for four people. Number 7, a triple, has a phone booth–style shower and slightly more space. Your breakfast will be served in a simple pink dining room with real plants flourishing along the windowsill.

FACILITIES AND SERVICES: Central heat, hall phone, hair dryer available, office safe, satellite TV, luggage storage (£2 per day), no lift

TELEPHONE
020-7723-8311/7807
FAX
020-7723-8311
TUBE
Lancaster Gate, Paddington
CREDIT CARDS
AE, DC, MC, V
RATES
Single £48; double £60; triple £75; quad £85; lower rates in off-season; English breakfast included

ASHLEY HOTEL (18)
15–17 Norfolk Square, W2
51 rooms, 39 with shower or bath and toilet

TELEPHONE
020-7723-3375
FAX
020-7723-0173
TUBE
Paddington
CREDIT CARDS
MC, V
RATES
Single £36–48; double £31–38 per person; triple £33 per person; family room £38 per person; add £1 per person if stay is for one night only. Special rates for children up to sixteen years sharing parents' room. English breakfast included
MISCELLANEOUS
Closed from December 24 to January 2

Many hotels around Norfolk Square are leased to managers and show very little pride of ownership, but not so at the Ashley, which has been proudly owned for over a quarter century by Welsh brothers John and David George. A sign on the front door of the hotel sums up their philosophy: "This is a highly respectable hotel, and management reserves its legal right to refuse admission to anyone of dubious or untidy appearance, or without visible luggage. The management also reserves the right to ask for positive ID." You get the message right away: This is a no-nonsense hotel that does not tolerate a hint of hanky-panky. The brothers cater to repeat visits from couples, families, and businesspeople. They even have guests who spent their honeymoon with them and return now with their children.

A genuine interest is taken in each guest. A family member is at the hotel during the day and one of them always presides over breakfast. Near the breakfast room is a bulletin board with helpful hints and tips on what to see and do in London, from street markets and river cruises to day trips in the country, unusual shopping advice, and what to do on a Sunday.

If you are a family group, you probably will have No. 23, a lower-ground-floor room with bunk beds that sleeps up to five. Despite its location, it is a cheerful room, with pink floral bedspreads and wallpaper. Security rails on the windows ensure safety. Best bets for singles or doubles are on higher floors. Number 9, one of the ten bathless singles, has a view onto Norfolk Square. Number 6 is a double in the back with not much of a view, but it is quiet, cute, and cozy.

FACILITIES AND SERVICES: Central heat, direct-dial phones, hair dryer available, office safe, TV, no lift, office open 8 A.M.–10:30 P.M.

BALMORAL HOUSE HOTEL (22)
156–157 Sussex Gardens, W2
34 rooms, 31 with shower or bath and toilet

Sussex Gardens is a noisy double boulevard not far from Hyde Park and Marble Arch in an area that once offered countless Cheap Sleeps geared to long-term stays for those down on their luck or on the dole. There have been definite improvements since then, however, and the area continues to be on the upswing. One of the better budget addresses, and one definitely in the top 1 percent for cleanliness, is the Balmoral House, run by the Vieites family. When you reserve, ask to be in the building at 156 Sussex Gardens, unless you like crossing a busy street to have your breakfast, which is served in a plant-filled room at the 156 address. The rooms at both addresses are generally well decorated, with no questionable color and pattern mixes. Those facing the street will have some noise. Above all, every room in both locations is spotlessly clean, thanks to the daily vigilance of Mrs. Vieites, who lets nothing escape her sharp eyes. When I commented on the cleanliness to one of her daughters, she dutifully replied, "Well, you have met my mother and you know she keeps us marching." The bottom line is a good budget Cheap Sleep with very few complaints.

FACILITIES AND SERVICES: Central heat, hall phone, hair dryer available, electric tea and coffeemakers, free parking for four cars, office safe, TV, no lift, desk open 7 A.M.– 11 P.M.

TELEPHONE
020-7723-7445/7402-1833
FAX
020-7402-0118
TUBE
Paddington
CREDIT CARDS
MC, V (5 percent surcharge)
RATES
Single £40–45; double £70–75; extra person £25; off-season rates in winter depending on availability; English breakfast included

CARDIFF HOTEL (17)
5–9 Norfolk Square, W2
60 rooms, 40 with shower or bath and toilet

All trains from Wales arrive at Paddington Station, so it is not surprising that many hotels in the neighborhood were owned by Welsh. These days most of them have been sold, but not the one run by the Davies family, which has been holding strong at the Cardiff for more than thirty years. Their sixty-room hotel is nothing fancy, but the small, clean rooms are adequately laid out for short-term living. Blond built-ins offer desk and closet space and a place to store luggage. Bathrooms are decidedly small, so I recommend cashing in a few Cheap Sleep vouchers and opting for a bathless abode. If your sight-seeing includes day trips outside of London to Stratford-upon-Avon, Windsor Castle, Oxford, or Bath, your train leaves from Paddington Station, a few minutes

TELEPHONE
020-7723-9068/3513/4500
FAX
020-7402-2342
INTERNET
www.cardiff-hotel.com
TUBE
Paddington
CREDIT CARDS
MC, V
RATES
Single £42–52; double £59–75; triple £87; quad £95; lower rates in January and February subject to availability; English breakfast included

walk from the hotel's front door. This also means that arrival or departure in London through Heathrow Airport will be a snap, what with the fast-rail link between Paddington and the airport.

FACILITIES AND SERVICES: Central heat (morning and evenings only), direct-dial phones, hair dryer available, electric tea and coffeemakers, office safe, some trouser presses, TV, no lift, desk open 7 A.M.–10 P.M.

COMFORT INN HYDE PARK (16)
18–19 Craven Hill Gardens, W2
60 rooms, 7 flats; all with shower or bath and toilet

TELEPHONE
020-7262-6644; 0800-44-44-44 (toll-free within the U.K.); 800-228-5150 (toll-free from the U.S.)

FAX
020-7262-0673

EMAIL
101445.425@compuserve.com

INTERNET
www.comfortinn.com

TUBE
Paddington, Bayswater

CREDIT CARDS
AE, DC, MC, V

RATES
Single £78; double £100; flats £130–180 per night; lower rates in hotel and flats subject to availability; Continental breakfast included with both

The Comfort Inn Hyde Park on Craven Hill Gardens is in a neighborhood of stately Georgian homes with manicured private gardens. The London Toy and Model Museum is across the street, and for other kinds of fun, there is an Internet café around the corner. The sixty rooms are frankly charm-free (i.e., shut your eyes and you are anywhere), but they do offer the advantage of being nonsmoking if you land on the fourth or fifth floors. These top-floor rooms are also recommended because they have more light and bigger bathrooms. Smokers can check into No. 101, a twin in the back with a limited view but with the plus of a sitting area with a desk and chair, and a real window in the bathroom. If you are staying for a few days and/or want plenty of space, reserve one of the hotel's flats, which range from roomy one-bedrooms to huge three-bedroom accommodations, all with maid service and Continental breakfast included. Also included are washing machines and kitchens with microwaves. There is no dishwasher or oven, which shouldn't be a problem unless you were planning on whipping up a turkey dinner with all the trimmings.

FACILITIES AND SERVICES: Bar, central heat, conference room, direct-dial phones, hair dryer, laundry service, lift, office safe (£1.50 per night), tea and coffeemakers, TV and radio, 24-hour desk, nonsmoking rooms on fourth and fifth floors. Apartments: all the above plus fitted kitchen with microwave and washing machine

COMMODORE HOTEL (33, $)
50 Lancaster Gate, W2
89 rooms, all with shower or bath and toilet

Big bear hugs go to the Commodore, a popular choice a stone's throw from Kensington Gardens. Scottish manager Malcom Hendry and his staff strive to make each guest feel welcome and important. This in part is also carried out by the hotel's mascots, a collection of bears. Their largest mascot, made in the U.K. at a cost of one thousand dollars and wearing a jaunty bow tie, stands a full six feet tall (look for him in the lobby). Be sure to smile when you have your picture taken with him. The little ones in your party will receive their own stuffed bear, wearing a red Commodore sash, to take home, and at Christmastime, they give out chocolate bears. I was touched to learn that the hotel donated one hundred stuffed bears to the children hospitalized as a result of the Oklahoma City bombing.

The hotel itself is a Victorian building dating from the 1860s. Many of the original features have been kept, including the hand-carved wooden fireplace in the lobby and the ceiling details. Five new townhouse rooms done with English furnishings add a note of luster to the remaining rooms on the fourth through the seventh floors, which have been redone. They are not lavish, but they are equipped with the basics, including private bathrooms, electric teakettles, and televisions in all and modems in some. Neutral colors and good housekeeping standards increase their appeal. The split-level family rooms are good buys.

FACILITIES AND SERVICES: Bar, business center with conference room, central heat, direct-dial phones, electric tea and coffeemakers, hair dryer, laundry service, lift, modems in some rooms, nonsmoking rooms on the fourth and fifth floors, office safe, TV, 24-hour desk

TELEPHONE
020-7402-5291; 800-44-UTELL (toll-free from the U.S.)
FAX
020-7262-1088
INTERNET
www.commodore-hotel.com
TUBE
Lancaster Gate
CREDIT CARDS
AE, DC, MC, V
RATES
Single £88–102; double £105–120; split-level and townhouse rooms £170; triple £160; family room £175; Continental breakfast included

THE DELMERE HOTEL (19, $)
130 Sussex Gardens, W2
38 rooms, all with shower or bath and toilet

The Delmere Hotel is a townhouse in Sussex Gardens, part of a legacy of early-nineteenth-century design by architect Samuel Pepys Cockerell, whose star pupil, Latrobe, built the Capitol in Washington, D.C. This area in London was built to provide luxurious homes for fashionable Victorian families. Lord Baden-Powell, founder of the Boy Scouts (see Baden-Powell House,

TELEPHONE
020-7706-3344; 800-55-CONSORT (toll-free from the U.S.)
FAX
020-7262-1863
EMAIL
delmerehotel@compuserve.com
INTERNET
www.delmerehotels.com

TUBE
Paddington
CREDIT CARDS
AE, DC, MC, V
RATES
Single £65–80; double £85–100; extra bed £15; Continental breakfast included, English breakfast £7 extra

page 154), was christened in St. James's Church. Sir Arthur Conan Doyle's family lived in Sussex Gardens, and at St. Mary's Hospital, Sir Alexander Fleming discovered penicillin.

As you enter, there is a comfortable sitting room and library stocked with daily papers and current magazines, and a black-and-white jazz bar where cocktails are served. Guests can also eat in the hotel restaurant, La Perla, which serves Italian and Continental cuisine, but frankly, it needs work. Consult *Cheap Eats in London* for better choices. The rooms range from spacious to extremely snug, but almost all are well thought out, with built-ins and compact baths offering good towels and bright lighting. Each color-coordinated room has a soft easy chair, luggage and desk space, and an electronic key card for extra security. Computer modems are standard. Only a few rooms fail to get my stamp of approval: No. 12, a dated, small double, and No. 103, a double with twin beds that's simply too small for comfort. Number 105 is a better twin, facing the front.

NOTE: The hotel has recently renovated the Hotel Columbus, also in Sussex Gardens. For further details, please see page 68.

FACILITIES AND SERVICES: Bar, central heat, computer modem ports, direct-dial phones, hair dryer, electric tea and coffeemakers, laundry service, lift, restaurant, room safe (£1 per day), satellite TV, radio, nonsmoking rooms, 24-hour desk

FAIRWAYS HOTEL (23)
186 Sussex Gardens, W2
10 rooms, 7 with shower or bath and toilet

TELEPHONE
020-7723-4871
FAX
020-7723-4871
EMAIL
fairwayshotel@compuserve.com
INTERNET
www.scoot.co.uk/
fairways_hotel
TUBE
Lancaster Gate, Paddington
CREDIT CARDS
MC, V

Steve and Jenny Adams run the homey Fairways Hotel, where you will find an abundance of ruffles and flourishes along with large portions of family hospitality. Nothing is modern, but this is part of the charm that keeps their regulars coming back. In an effort to keep up with the times, some rooms have had portable bathroom boxes added to them. Steve had a fit when he saw this comment, but I still maintain that the hall facilities are nice—so why not save a few pounds and avoid the bedrooms with the phone booth–size bathroom in the corner? That said, I must tell you about their top-selling room, No. 1, which is on the ground floor facing front. It is a pink room (even the ceiling), with lacy curtains, a brass four-poster bed, and a modular (box) bathroom.

Number 2, viewless and in blue, has great closets, a double bed, and a full bathroom. The photos in the breakfast room tell the story of this friendly family, and the growing collection of worldwide knickknacks and scores of Christmas cards suggest how fond their guests are of them. You, too, will soon feel right at home with all the others who gather here each morning to enjoy a hearty home-cooked breakfast while plotting their day in London. Motorists will appreciate the *free* parking spaces in front of the hotel, and walkers will be able to pace themselves nicely walking through Hyde Park or on to the West End. For the less athletically inclined, bus and tube transportation are within easy reach.

NOTE: If the Fairways Hotel is full, try the James Cartref House, owned by Jenny's brother Derek James and his wife, Sharon (see page 121).

FACILITIES AND SERVICES: Central heat (mornings and evenings), hall phones, hair dryer available, electric tea and coffeemakers, free parking, office safe (no charge), room safe (£1 per night), TV, no lift, desk open 7 A.M.–10 P.M.

RATES
Single £45–60; double £65–70; four-poster room £75 for two; triple £85; quad £95; lower rates in January and February; English breakfast included, plus cereals and fruit for vegetarians

GARDEN COURT HOTEL (12)
30–31 Kensington Gardens Square, W2
35 rooms, 16 with shower or bath and toilet

Edward Connolly's grandfather opened the Garden Court Hotel in 1954. Since taking it over a few years ago, Edward has made vast improvements from top to bottom, turning it into a stylish Cheap Sleeping choice that doesn't scream "budget!" Downstairs there are two sitting areas, one with a writing desk and a complimentary tray of tea, coffee, and biscuits, and the other slightly more formal, with a fireplace and a wall of assorted mirrors. Classical music adds a calming note. Summer guests are invited to sit in the back garden. Upstairs, the rooms vary from the very compact No. 27 to the larger No. 31, in yellow and white with whitewashed furniture that includes twin beds, a double dresser, a desk, and a folding chair. The bathroom is serviceable, with its stall shower, door hook, tiny basin, and glass-and-tile shelf for your toiletries. I also like No. 7, on the first floor, nicely done in yellow wallpaper with a teapot and china vase pattern in blue and white. There is a rattan cushioned chair, two bedside lights, and a view of a tree. A threesome will be given No. 26, which faces out and has mahogany furniture, a double and single bed, luggage

TELEPHONE
020-7229-2553

FAX
020-7727-2749

TUBE
Bayswater, Paddington, Queensway

CREDIT CARDS
MC, V

RATES
Single £35–50; double £55–76; triple £75–85; quad £80–95; English breakfast included (no beans, but yogurt and fresh fruit with your eggs and bacon)

and desk space, and a bathtub. Edward is on site daily with his Border terrier, Mutley, to welcome guests and attend to their needs. Plans are on the drawing boards for a lift, a computer center for guests, some nonsmoking rooms, and more bathrooms. You can trust it will all be done very tastefully.

NOTE: If you cancel your reservation within fourteen days of your arrival, you forfeit your deposit, though you can apply the deposit amount toward another stay within a year of your cancellation date.

FACILITIES AND SERVICES: Bar, central heat, direct-dial phones, hair dryer, office safe, TV, desk open 7 A.M.–midnight

HOTEL COLUMBUS (20)
141 Sussex Gardens, W2
15 rooms, 11 with shower or bath and toilet

TELEPHONE
020-7262-0974
FAX
020-7262-6785
EMAIL
hotelcolumbus@compuserve.com
INTERNET
www.delmerehotels.com
TUBE
Paddington
CREDIT CARDS
AE, DC, MC, V
RATES
Single £55; double £75; triple £85; quad £100; Continental buffet breakfast included

The Columbus is located on the south side of this leafy avenue. The building, which is approaching its two hundredth birthday, served mainly as a Cheap Sleeping crash pad for undiscerning backpackers and other rock-bottom budget seekers for most of its lifetime. No longer! Thanks to a complete refurbishment, it has been turned into a recommendable bed-and-breakfast, less than a five-minute walk from Paddington Underground and the Heathrow Airport link. As you walk in, note the French-inspired garden breakfast area with modern Miró-like framed prints on your right. There is no getting around the small bathrooms and the noise along the front, despite double glazing (which won't work if you open the windows), but the rooms are color coordinated and offer closet and drawer space, orthopedic beds, and electronic room locks for added safety. I would avoid any of the triples or quads, which are too squeezed for even a chair, and the dismal basement rooms that all share the same bathroom. But if it's a simple double you are after, this is a Cheap Sleep worth consideration. For something a bit more upmarket, try the sister hotel across the street, The Delmere Hotel (see page 65).

FACILITIES AND SERVICES: Central heat, direct-dial phones, hair dryer available, office safe, satellite TV, no lift, desk open 8 A.M.–11 P.M.

KENSINGTON GARDENS HOTEL (9)
9 Kensington Gardens Square, W2
17 rooms, 13 with shower or bath and toilet

All of the seventeen coordinated rooms have showers, and only four do not have a private loo. Please don't worry, the hall facilities are some of the best I have seen in London. The rooms are snug, with limited luggage space, but for those who travel light, they do have the extras that add up to a pleasant short-term stay. The best views are from the top-floor rooms, but you must be prepared to climb stairs to get there. A Continental breakfast is served in a rather formal basement breakfast room.

FACILITIES AND SERVICES: Central heat, direct-dial phones, hair dryer, electric tea and coffeemakers, minibar, office safe, satellite TV, no lift, 24-hour desk

TELEPHONE
020-7221-7790
FAX
020-7792-8612
EMAIL
info@kensingtongardenshotel.co.uk
INTERNET
www.kensingtongardenshotel.co.uk
TUBE
Bayswater, Queensway
CREDIT CARDS
AE, DC, MC, V
RATES
Single £50–55; double £75–80; triple £95–100; lower rates subject to time of year and availability; Continental breakfast included, English breakfast £6 extra

LANCASTER HALL HOTEL–GERMAN YMCA (34)
35 Craven Terrace, W2
In the hotel: 80 rooms, all with shower or bath and toilet

This is a top Cheap Sleep in London if there ever was one. The Lancaster Hall Hotel is owned by the German YMCA. The aim is to provide excellent accommodations for any traveler, and I assure you, they succeed in meeting their goal. The setup consists of the hotel itself and the student and group annex. Unless you are around twenty and traveling with a dozen pals, you probably want the hotel section, because the twenty-four-room refurbished annex is geared for groups and those under twenty-six, and none of the rooms have private baths (for complete information on the annex, see the description under YMCAs, page 231). German efficiency and sparseness in detail are reflected from the main hotel lobby, throughout the eighty rooms, and on into the annex. An army of uniformed maids pushing heavy-duty vacuum cleaners swoops through each day making sure everything is shipshape. The basic hotel rooms are coordinated with matching curtains and bedspreads on twin beds, laminated pine furniture, private safes, closets with both hanging and shelf space, and tiled bathrooms that are small but acceptable. For most pleasant results, request a high back room with a sunny view, perhaps Nos. 301 to 304, or 401 to 404. Breakfast is laid out buffet

TELEPHONE
020-7723-9276
FAX
020-7706-2870
TUBE
Lancaster Gate, Paddington
CREDIT CARDS
MC, V
RATES
Hotel: Single £60; double (all with twin beds) £78; Continental buffet breakfast included

style in a large, sedate dining room. Later on in the day a licensed bar opens in the lounge for guests. The hotel also caters for banquets, conferences, lectures, and seminars in function rooms that may be reserved by the day, or for any three part-day sessions.

FACILITIES AND SERVICES: Bar (6–11 P.M.), central heat, conference rooms, direct-dial phones, hair dryer available, lift, room safe, tea and coffeemakers, satellite TV

LONDON ELIZABETH HOTEL (37, $)
Lancaster Terrace, W2
48 rooms, all with shower or bath and toilet

There is still only one word to describe the London Elizabeth . . . *wonderful!* It has been in the Newman family since the 1950s and is now run by the dynamic husband and wife duo Peter and Karen Newman. Karen is an American, and met Peter while she was a guest in the hotel. Her attention to detail is evident. She not only decorated all the rooms, she did all the upholstering (with the exception of the sofas) and displays her growing collection of Czech crystal throughout. As soon as you cross the threshold, you enjoy a warm feeling of welcome extended by the Newmans and their helpful staff, many of whom are into three decades of service, and whose knowledge of London will go a long way toward making your stay here the best it can be.

The location, just inches from the Lancaster Gate tube stop and across the road from Kensington Gardens and Hyde Park, allows guests to be almost anywere in London within twenty to thirty minutes. Another bonus: The bus from Heathrow Airport stops at the hotel's front door. If you prefer the fast-rail link to Paddington, you are only a brief taxi ride from the station.

The reception area and living room display true British ambience, with a mixture of sofas and chairs clustered for good conversation. To one side is the rich red Theatre Bar and the Rose Garden Restaurant, which has a hand-painted mural along one wall and specializes in an international menu of country classic cuisine. On warm days, guests are invited to sit on the garden terrace, which is encircled with pots of herbs, green shrubs, and blooming flowers.

Many repeat guests have a favorite room and ask for it again and again. However, whatever style or size you have will be a quantum leap ahead of most of the competition, for the rooms display the best in furnishings,

TELEPHONE
020-7402-6641; 800-721-5566 (toll-free from the U.S.)
FAX
020-7224-8900
EMAIL
reservations@londonelizabethhotel.co.uk
INTERNET
www.londonelizabethhotel.co.uk
TUBE
Lancaster Gate
CREDIT CARDS
AE, DC, MC, V
RATES
Single £110; double £125; deluxe rooms and suites £180–250; child in parents' room: up to fourteen £10; over fourteen £25; buffet breakfast included

LONDON BREAKS RATES
THEATRE BREAK
£195 per person per night; includes two nights accommodation, ticket to a top West End show of your choice, champagne cocktail before three-course dinner in hotel restaurant, early morning tea and newspaper, and buffet breakfast; theater tickets cannot be exchanged or canceled if you change your booking.

fabrics, carpeting, and window treatments. Each has an excellent bathroom stocked with plenty of fluffy towels and nice toiletries. Closet space is adequate. The deluxe rooms and suites are all nonsmoking and air-conditioned, and have soft hangers in the closets and a welcome tray of fruit and a bottle of mineral water. If you reserve a suite, you will have fresh flowers, an ornamental fireplace, lighted magnifying mirrors in the bathrooms, televisions with VCRs, a deck of playing cards, and your own library bookshelf.

If you have just won the lottery, or are celebrating a very special occasion with an equally special person, treat yourself to the Hyde Park Suite, the Newmans' newest creation and a real tour de force when it comes to hotel accommodations. Three rooms were combined to make this magnificent suite, and great care was taken to restore it to its original 1850 form. The two marble fireplaces—massive mirrors over them, arched windows and shutters enclosing them—all date from the building's inception. The two-room suite is now graced with beautiful custom-built furnishings that include a set of matching bookshelves. If you are here for work, there is a large desk with the necessary computer modems to keep you in touch. For entertaining, there is a dining table that seats six, a wet bar, chess and checker sets, plus two satellite televisions and your own VCR. On sunny days, you can enjoy a drink on the terrace, which overlooks the Italian fountains in Hyde Park, or step onto the rear balcony. The sumptuous gray marble bathroom has the usual fine points, plus a twelve-inch showerhead, heated towel racks, a half dozen shelves, and a full-length beveled mirror. When you reluctantly have to leave, be sure to sign the guest book, where a Catholic monsignor from Dublin wrote, "A premature taste of paradise for a poor parson. God forgive me for enjoying it so much." I certainly hope he is forgiven, because I am sure he deserved every minute of enjoyment he had staying here, and you will too.

Another treat for expanded budgets is the Conservatory Room, with its fabulous stained-glass domed ceiling and panoramic, handmade leaded-glass windows designed to flood the room with both sun and moonlight. The bed sits on a raised platform; there is a small rooftop patio; and the view from the desk is of the fountains in the park. The bathroom is divine, the little fireplace warm and comforting, and, of course, the

WELCOME BREAK
£255 per person per night; children under fourteen sharing parents' room £90 per child per night; includes three nights accommodation, sight-seeing tour of London, champagne cocktail before dinner in the hotel restaurant, early morning tea and newspaper, and buffet breakfast; a fourth night that includes a Sunday night, £65 extra per person.

ROMANCE AND CELEBRATION BREAK
From £200–300 per person per night depending on accommodation; includes two nights in a deluxe or four-poster bedroom or a suite, bottle of champagne, bouquet of flowers, fresh fruit basket, and box of luxury chocolates in room upon arrival, gourmet candlelit dinner for two on the evening of your choice, buffet breakfast.

CHRISTMAS PROGRAMME
Single, three nights £345–375, five nights £475–520; all double rates are per person: double, three nights £325–475, five nights £450–675; extra child (under fourteen sharing parents' room) three nights £150, five nights £220; extra adult sharing bedroom, three nights £250, five nights £350. An optional charge of 5 percent gratuity will be added.

atmosphere speaks of true romance. The double, deluxe Victorian Room, with a crystal chandelier from Czechoslovakia, is bright and airy in soft yellow. The two wing chairs, a fireplace, and large mirrored dressing table make it very livable. Travelers who judge a room by square footage will be pleased with the lower-ground-floor garden Montagu Suite. The tiled bathroom has a set-in sink, gold fixtures, and plenty of space. The entry, with a closet, leads to a sitting area with a sofa and two high-back chairs covered in soft blue. The coal fireplace, bookshelf, and desk make it even more enjoyable. If you are in a standard room, you don't have to feel like Cinderella after the ball. These rooms have sitting areas, writing desks, and enough space to live comfortably. I like No. 116, with a few steps up to a bathroom that has loads of shelf space. Number 110, another standard twin room, is rather narrow, but it does have a little balcony facing front and a fan to cool you on hot afternoons.

To entice you further, the hotel offers a festive Christmas Programme plus three special Break Packages: the Theatre Break, the Welcome Break, and the Romance and Celebration Break. With your selection of either the Theatre Break, which features a two-night stay and the best available ticket to a top West End show of your choice, or the Welcome Break, which runs for three to four nights and includes a sight-seeing tour of London, you will be served a champagne cocktail in the bar each evening before a three-course dinner in the hotel restaurant. A pot of bracing tea is brought with your morning newspaper before you venture downstairs for the buffet breakfast. The Romance and Celebration Break means you will stay two nights in your choice of a deluxe bedroom (one with a four-poster bed) or one of the luxurious suites, have a bottle of champagne, a fresh fruit basket, and a box of chocolates in your room on arrival, and enjoy a gourmet candlelit dinner for two in the hotel restaurant on the night of your choice. These three Breaks are available any night of the week or on the weekend. I have saved the best for last. The Christmas Programme starts with a champagne reception hosted by the Newmans on Christmas Eve, followed by a four-course dinner, then a tour of the festive lights of London and Midnight Mass at St. Paul's Cathedral. Back at the hotel afterward, there is a late-night snack. On Christmas Day you start with early morning tea and the papers brought to your room, then an English breakfast. At noon, guests gather around the gaily decorated Christmas tree to receive their personal gifts from Karen and Peter. A traditional Christmas lunch is served, followed by a musical recital, high tea, and, if you can imagine, more food—another late-night snack. The next day, Boxing Day, you are treated to morning tea, an English breakfast, cocktails, and a midday dinner, then a Christmas pantomime and a grand buffet afterward. Guests staying another night receive tickets to any West End show they wish. The Christmas Programme is booked up to a year in advance by regulars, including a ladies bridge group who somehow find the time to play a few hands between all the eating and events.

NOTE: If you have any particular requirements, such as flowers or champagne in your room, tickets to any show, concert, or sporting events, baby-sitting, or anything else, let the staff know and they will provide it if at all possible.

FACILITIES AND SERVICES: Air-conditioning in deluxe rooms and suites, fans in the standard rooms, bar, concierge and porter, direct-dial phones with voicemail, hair dryer, laundry service, lift, modems in suites, parking (£9 for guests, £18 for nonguests), restaurant and 24-hour room service for light snacks, office safe, TV, VCR and stereo TVs in suites; nonsmoking deluxe rooms, suites, and selected standard rooms

MITRE HOUSE HOTEL (24)
178–184 Sussex Gardens, W2
70 rooms, all with shower or bath and toilet

It is always rewarding to return to a hotel and find that it's getting better. Andrew and Michael Chris grew up in the hotel, which their parents ran for thirty years. Today you can see their father's photo hanging by the lift. The two brothers are now in charge of the hotel, which includes three junior suites with Jacuzzis. These rooms, which are naturally the largest and most expensive, also have big closets, two television sets, and minibars. Several of the other rooms connect, an advantage for families with children who want some privacy. Those who need sunlight and moonbeams should avoid the viewless ground-floor rooms. If you arrive at Heathrow without a trolley full of luggage, the walk from Paddington Station is less than five minutes by foot. During your stay, the Lancaster Gate tube stop increases your mobility around London. Free parking for a

TELEPHONE
020-7723-8040

FAX
020-7402-0990

EMAIL
reservations@mitrehousehotel.com

INTERNET
www.mitrehousehotel

TUBE
Lancaster Gate, Paddington

CREDIT CARDS
AE, DC, MC, V

RATES
Single £65; double £75; junior suite £110; triple £85; quad £95; English breakfast included

few cars in front is another advantage, as is the youthful and outgoing desk staff, who try hard to please.

FACILITIES AND SERVICES: Bar, central heat, direct-dial phones, hair dryer, iron available, laundry service, lift, minibars and Jacuzzis in junior suites, free parking, office safe, tea and coffeemakers, satellite TV, trouser press in junior suites, nonsmoking rooms, 24-hour desk

MORNINGTON HOTEL (35, $)
12 Lancaster Gate, W2
66 rooms, all with shower or bath and toilet

TELEPHONE
020-7262-7361; 800-528-1234
(toll-free from the U.S.)

FAX
020-7706-1028

EMAIL
mornington.hotel@mornington
.co.uk

INTERNET
www.mornington.se

TUBE
Lancaster Gate

CREDIT CARDS
AE, DC, MC, V

RATES
Single £110; double £125–135;
split-level rooms £150;
Scandinavian breakfast included

Swedish-owned and -operated, the Mornington is an exceptional hotel, with a delightful staff dressed in bright red tartan in winter and lighter colors in summer. The pristine rooms have some of the best, and definitely the cleanest, bathrooms in London. All have wonderful mirrors, lots of space for your things, a drying rack for your hand washables, and a selection of shampoo, soap, and other items you might have forgotten to pack. The bedrooms display Swedish modern comforts with an easy chair, floor lamp, desk, portable fan in summer, and firm beds with fluffy duvet comforters. I could move right into most of their split-level accommodations, especially No. 84, which has floor-to-ceiling windows and an upstairs bedroom and a downstairs work/sitting room. Numbers 103, 107, and 108 are other split-levels with plenty of light. All rooms on the third floor are nonsmoking and many rooms throughout the hotel have polished hardwood floors, which are appreciated by allergy sufferers. The only rooms and split-levels to avoid are those facing "The Well," a blank-walled courtyard.

Downstairs by the reception desk is a book-lined lounge where you can order a snack from the bar or have afternoon tea. Breakfast is served Scandinavian style, which means a large buffet with fresh orange juice, fruit, hard-boiled eggs, cheese, meat, herring, plus assorted breads and cereals. It's enough to keep most Cheap Sleepers going strong until dinner. En route to the dining room, take a few minutes to look at the remarkable bird posters, which are a collection painted by Olof Rudbeck in 1693. Rudbeck, who studied at Oxford, portrayed the birds in their original size, and in great detail.

Also by the dining area is an office that allows guests who bring their own computer to hook up, send and receive email, or log on to the Internet.

FACILITIES AND SERVICES: Bar, central heat, direct-dial phones, fans on request, hair dryers, electric tea and coffeemakers, laundry lines in the bathrooms, laundry service, lift, office and room safes, nonsmoking rooms on third floor, TV with pay movies, guest computer service center, airport transfers by prior arrangement

THE PAVILION HOTEL (1)
34–36 Sussex Gardens, W2
31 rooms, all with shower or bath and toilet

TELEPHONE
020-7262-0905
FAX
020-7262-1324
INTERNET
www.eol.net.mt/pavilion
TUBE
Edgware Road
CREDIT CARDS
AE, DC, MC, V
RATES
Single £65–70; double £95–100; triple £110; Continental breakfast included and served in the rooms

Question: Is this a fantasy land or a hotel?

Answer: It's both . . . and what a place it is!

The Pavilion Hotel exceeds in providing jaw-dropping whimsical glamour for its high-gloss, high-wattage guests who populate the fashion, media, and music worlds. Brother and sister team Danny and Noshi Karne have combined their talents (she designs the rooms, he names them and works with her to produce them) to create a uniquely amazing boutique hotel that appeals to an artistically minded clientele. If you receive your mail at a Sun City or Leisure World address, need to have a daily Internet fix, or are coolly conservative and buttoned down in thought and deed, please . . . don't check in here. If, on the other hand, you love a kaleidoscope of colors, decor, and people, then check into one of London's hottest crash pads for high-style fashion bees.

All thirty-one rooms have a different theme to project a funky yet glamorous image. Honky Tonk Afro is an over-the-top tribute to kitsch gone wild. Heart-shaped mirrors hang over twin beds divided by beaded curtains. Pink feather boas ring the lime green room filled with fifties-style furnishings, including a cowhide-covered square stool, black chairs with furry pink cushions, fuzzy dice to hold back the black and white sparkling curtains, a guitar-shaped mirror, and twirling above it all, a mirrored disco ball. It is one of the hotel's most known and popular rooms, and is routinely used for television backdrops and tapings. One guest aptly summed it up by declaring, "Wow! This looks like Mick Jagger's dressing room!" I have never seen his dressing room, but it couldn't be any more bizarre.

Enter the Dragon is a mystical cocktail of Oriental treasures complete with blue and white Chinese teacup and teapot printed wallpaper, carved wooden window screens, a red and gold chest, and vibrant red and blue satin bedcovers. In Monochrome Marilyn, guests are enveloped by an Andy Warhol–inspired black and silver wallcovering of Monroe's face. The black velvet–draped bed is accented by a satin headboard studded with rhinestones. War and Peace, swathed from top to bottom in red fabric, puts you into a Napoleonic War–style tent, highlighted with a dozen or more military pictures and a great hat rack hung with Napoleonic hats. There isn't much closet space, but you get atmosphere in spades. History buffs may be interested to know that this building was once occupied by Napoleon's private surgeon. I don't need to tell you the theme of Highland Fling, lined in MacGregor tartan and showcasing a clan flag. The antlers and other hunting memorabilia will make you want to suit up and ride with the hounds. In the ground-level room Chapter and Verse, a love poem wraps itself around the walls, which are hung with Venetian prints. The low-to-the-floor beds are draped in black and gold, and there is a black furry bedside rug in which to wiggle your toes. A marble sideboard doubles as a desk and is lighted by an ornate crystal chandelier. This is the hotel's only nonsmoking room. Better Red Than Dead is a voluptuous symphony of vermilion, claret, and crimson, while Casablanca Nights is a deco-inspired Moorish fantasy. Other rooms have equally intriguing names: Funky Zebra, Diamonds Are Forever, and Green with Envy. In the planning stages are futuristic bathrooms and three more rooms: Indian Summer, Quiet Please (with a literary theme), and a minimalistic Lighter Shade of Pale. Downstairs is the Silver Salon, an Ali Baba's cave used for fashion shoots and more television filming. Upstairs, near a table that seems to serve as the reception desk, is a picture of the current "Phone Queen," a model who stayed at the hotel and managed to ring up the most outrageous phone bill in the shortest period of time. In addition to being honored with a framed photo, each "Phone Queen" receives a crown, a listing on the hotel website, and a certificate. The current record holder holds firm at £510.40 for a week, which equals about £3 per hour on a twenty-four-hour basis.

FACILITIES AND SERVICES: Central heat, direct-dial phones, hair dryer available, electric tea and coffee-makers, parking (£5 per day), room service for drinks, office safe, one nonsmoking room (Chapter and Verse), satellite TV, no lift

PEMBRIDGE COURT HOTEL (32, $)
34 Pembridge Gardens, W2
20 rooms, all with shower or bath and toilet

People always ask me to tell them about my favorite London hotel. I have several, and the Pembridge Court is one of them. I could occupy any of its rooms and be delightfully happy. Obviously another guest from Derbyshire felt even more strongly—he has just bought it. Don't worry, nothing will change. Nicola, the charming assistant manager, will be at the desk to greet you, ably assisted by Spencer and Churchill, the hotel's famous cat mascots, who are featured in all of the advertising and have been written up in the London *Sunday Times.*

It is hard to know just where to begin telling you about the hotel because everything about it is so well done and beautiful. It has won many certificates of distinction for its excellence in all categories, and after one visit, you will know why. It has, without question, the most colorful flower arrangements and outdoor blooming potted plant displays I have seen in London. I also love the antique lace collars, Victorian beaded bags, delicate ivory fans, tortoiseshell combs, frilly baby dresses, and other vintage pieces of clothing that have been framed and artistically incorporated throughout the hotel. Dogs and cats are as welcome as people, but management must be notified in advance and pet owners must be approved by Spencer and Churchill.

Every room is different and all are fully recommended. If someone told me I would like a stunning orange room facing a wall, I would have thought they were mad, but the ground-floor Chepstow Room is just this, with a nice bath and a framed flapper dress and wonderful pearl belt gracing the bedroom walls. The Churchill Room, named after one of the house cats, looks out toward Portobello Market. The color scheme is deep salmon with rose accents, the bed is king-size, and the bathroom has a shower and tub with gold fittings and a dressing table. Frames holding Edwardian ladies gloves, a child's bib, and a sweet camisole decorate the walls. If space is important, reserve the rich, ruby red Lancaster Room: its bathroom offers all the counter space you will need and enough towels to last almost forever. Accent pieces include a pageboy jacket and a black lace peignoir. For romance, the Belvedere Room, with a four-poster bed and sitting area by a sunny window, is a good choice. The hotel's intimate restaurant is open *only* for guests,

TELEPHONE
020-7229-9977

FAX
020-7727-4982; 800-709-9882 (toll-free from the U.S.)

EMAIL
reservations@pemct.co.uk

TUBE
Notting Hill Gate

CREDIT CARDS
AE, DC, MC, V

RATES
Single £120–155; double (small twin) £145; deluxe twin or double £185

and room service is always available for light snacks.

If your travels will take you to Cornwall, please consider their other hotel, the Cross House Hotel set in the Cornish harbor town of Padstow. It is a charming Georgian house, once owned by John Tredwen, the last of the local sailing ship builders. The hotel is open from April to October, and all eleven beautifully furnished rooms are nonsmoking. For more information, contact them at Church Street, Padstow, Cornwall PL28 8BG; tel: 01841-532391; fax: 01841-533633.

FACILITIES AND SERVICES: Air-conditioning in deluxe rooms, bar, central heat, direct-dial phones, hair dryer, laundry service, lift, free parking for two cars, restaurant for guests only, room service, office and room safe, trouser press, satellite TV, VCRs in deluxe rooms, 24-hour desk, two friendly cats for continued spoiling

PHOENIX HOTEL (10)
1–8 Kensington Gardens Square, W2
130 rooms, all with shower or bath and toilet

TELEPHONE
020-7229-2494; 800-528-1234
(toll-free from the U.S.)

FAX
020-7727-1419

EMAIL
phoenixhotel@dial.pipex.com

INTERNET
www.phoenixhotel.co.uk

TUBE
Bayswater

CREDIT CARDS
AE, DC, MC, V

RATES
Single £75; double £95

Most London hotels around Kensington Gardens Square began life as family homes of some note. The Phoenix is no exception. It is made up of eight townhouses built in 1854. The buildings now encompass 130 bedrooms that provide no surprises. Everything is here in uniform rooms done in mauve and green, each with a luggage rack, desk, cable television reception, and a framed print on the wall. Bathrooms are tiled and many have both a tub and stall shower. The split-level suites are recommended for those needing more space. If you ask to have the mezzanine in one of them made into a sitting room, you will have a pleasant place to sit and work, especially for a longer stay.

To relax outside your room, you can sit in a chair by one of the fireplaces either in the entry or in the small room off the bar and order a cup of tea, or something stronger. The bar also provides twenty-four-hour room service for beverages and light snacks. The hotel is affiliated with Best Western International, so booking from your own home on their 800 number won't cost you a penny, but breakfast will. If you book directly with the hotel, they will include it in your nightly rate.

FACILITIES AND SERVICES: Bar, central heat, direct-dial phones, hair dryer, iron available, lift, laundry service, room service for drinks and light snacks, individual safes at reception (50p per day), satellite TV, 24-hour desk

W8

Kensington

Kensington, especially in a summer afternoon, has seemed to me as delightful as any place can or ought to be. . . .
—*Nathaniel Hawthorne,* Our Old Home, *1863*

The Royal Borough of Kensington became an important section of London when William III commissioned Sir Christopher Wren to rebuild Kensington Palace. The palace, where Princess Diana lived, stands at one end of Kensington Gardens, which with Hyde Park forms the largest open space in London. Kensington High Street is one of London's premier shopping streets, lined with a wonderful variety of shops, several department store branches, and some of the wildest fashions this side of Mars. To the north is Kensington Church Street, famous for its magnificent antiques shops filled with museum-quality examples with very high price tags. But it costs nothing to window shop and dream. The area also boasts several excellent restaurants; please see *Cheap Eats in London* for details.

HOTELS in W8 (see map page 58)

Abbey House	**80**
Posthouse Kensington	**80**
Vicarage Private Hotel	**81**

OTHER OPTIONS

Student Dormitories

Queen Elizabeth Hall	**216**

Student-Only Accommodations

Lee Abbey International Students Club	**227**

Youth Hostels

Holland House, King George IV Memorial Youth Hostel	**235**

ABBEY HOUSE (43)
11 Vicarage Gate, W8
16 rooms, none with shower or bath and toilet

TELEPHONE
020-7727-2594

TUBE
High Street Kensington

CREDIT CARDS
None; cash only

RATES
Single £42; double £67; triple £80; quad £95; English breakfast included

The Abbey House, on a tranquil Victorian square close to Kensington Gardens, was built around 1860 for a wealthy businessman and has since been the home of a bishop and a member of Parliament. Now it is a small hotel and classic example of what twenty years of hard work can do to create a prime, budget B&B. The owners, Albert and Carol Nayach, offer Cheap Sleeps to those willing to give up the comfort and convenience of a private bathroom in the name of saving money. Their hospitality and genuine value is not lost on their regulars, who book rooms far in advance. If you want to stay here in high season, it will never be too early to make a reservation and to secure it with a deposit.

As you enter the front door of the hotel from the wide porch, you will see a beautiful interior staircase that winds up from the entry hall. The rooms are done in a flowery Laura Ashley style and are kept up to snuff with painting and redecorating when needed. Every room has a live plant, two pillows per person on an orthopedic bed with reading lights, and simple, nick-free furniture. Number 12, on the ground floor, is a ruffly double with good drawer and hanging space. Number 11 is also on the ground floor and has enough all-around space. The red-carpeted breakfast room has hunting pictures on the walls and white linen napkins and cloths on tables surrounded by red chairs. Free ice, tea, and coffeemaking facilities around the clock as well as a pay phone are available for guests.

FACILITIES AND SERVICES: Central heat, hall phones, TV, no safe, no lift

POSTHOUSE KENSINGTON (55)
Wright's Lane, W8
550 rooms, all with shower or bath and toilet

TELEPHONE
020-7937-8170; 0800-40-40-40 (toll-free within the U.K.); 800-225-5843 (toll-free from the U.S.)

FAX
020-7937-8289

INTERNET
www.forte-hotels.com

TUBE
High Street Kensington

The Posthouse Kensington belongs to the Forte Hotels and participates in its Posthouse Leisure Breaks scheme (for a further description of these money-saving hotel deals, see page 54). While this hotel is geared principally to tour groups, it has a good deal to offer individual guests who want a full-service hotel that includes a restaurant, spa, pool, Jacuzzi, beauty salon, and fully equipped fitness center. Unless further refurbishments have taken place, request a superior room on the fourth or seventh floors, and positively avoid anything on the first thanks to poor security on this level. Guests are given free membership in the hotel health club, which also has a small sport boutique in case you forgot your bathing suit or workout clothes. From this location, you will be close to shopping on Kensington High Street; the Victoria and Albert, Natural History, and Science museums; and one tube stop from the convention facilities at Olympia and Earl's Court.

FACILITIES AND SERVICES: Bar, central heat, direct-dial phones, hair dryers, free use of hotel health club with pool, Jacuzzi, steam room, spa, beauty salon, and equipped fitness gym, laundry service, lift, parking (£18 per 24 hours), restaurant and 24-hour room service, office safe, tea and coffeemaking facilities, satellite TV, pay movies, concierge, theater bookings, one nonsmoking floor

CREDIT CARDS
AE, DC, MC, V

RATES
Single £90; double £120–140; English breakfast included

VICARAGE PRIVATE HOTEL (42)
10 Vicarage Gate, W8
18 rooms, none with shower or bath and toilet

For the price and the value it represents, the Vicarage Private Hotel is a good Cheap Sleep buy in this part of London. The hotel is situated in a splendid turn-of-the-century mansion in a quiet section of the Royal Borough of Kensington. The impressive entry hall has a natural grillwork staircase leading up to the eighteen practical bedrooms, all of which have hot and cold running water but no private bathrooms. The large hall showers and WCs are above average and have attractive touches like framed prints or playbills on the walls. Number 12 is a spiffy single done in blue and yellow and boasting a view to the flats in the distance. Number 11, on the third floor, has high ceilings, two windows facing out, and bed space for three with room to spare. Number 6 is a front-facing double with forties-style furniture, and No. 19 is a top-floor nest for the sturdy solo traveler with a pretty oak armoire and beveled mirror. A stick-to-your-ribs English breakfast is served downstairs in a room set with assorted antique dining chairs around white linen–covered tables and old peasant prints on the walls. For those traveling alone, there is a special "singles" table.

TELEPHONE
020-7229-4030
FAX
020-7792-5989
EMAIL
reception@londonvicaragehotel .com
INTERNET
www.londonvicaragehotel.com
TUBE
High Street Kensington
CREDIT CARDS
MC, V
RATES
Single £48; double £75; triple £96; quad £105; English breakfast included (hot porridge available if ordered the night before)

Another way to get to know fellow guests is in the television lounge, with its leaded window and framed cameos. The hotel is close to Kensington High Street and its trendy shopping, as well as the complex housing the Royal Albert concert hall and the Victoria and Albert, Natural History, and Science museums. If plans to put in some private bathroom facilities and TV sets, and to re-cover the lounge furniture materialize, this already very nice selection will be even better.

FACILITIES AND SERVICES: Central heat, hall phones, hair dryer available, office safe, no lift

W11

Notting Hill and Portobello Road

Notting Hill is a mixture of radical ethnic types, hipsters, and Londoners on their way up, as well as those who scrape by on a $100,000 yearly trust, all of whom frequent the area's growing supply of trendy eating places, artistic boutiques, and offbeat shops. Its most interesting feature, from a visitor's point of view, is around Portobello Road, site of the famous outdoor flea and antiques market that is best seen on Saturday morning (5:30 A.M.–4 P.M.), when stalls and shops display a bewildering array of goods (see "Outdoor Markets," page 290). On the August bank holiday Monday and the Sunday before, the Notting Hill Carnival, Europe's biggest outdoor festival, is celebrated with nonstop music, dancing, and thousands of revelers.

HOTELS in W11 (see map page 58)

Gate Hotel	**84**
The Portobello Hotel ($)	**85**
Ravna Gora	**86**

OTHER OPTIONS
YMCAs
Norwegian YWCA	**232**

($) indicates a Big Splurge

GATE HOTEL (29)
6 Portobello Road, W11
6 rooms, 5 with shower or bath and toilet

TELEPHONE
020-7221-2403
FAX
020-7221-9128
EMAIL
gatehotel@aol.com
INTERNET
www.go-london.co.uk/hp/
gatehotel.html
TUBE
Notting Hill Gate
CREDIT CARDS
AE, DC, MC (must use to
guarantee room; 4 percent
service fee if used to pay final
bill)
RATES
Single £50–65; double £75–80;
triple £90; Continental
breakfast included

The Gate Hotel is a Cheap Sleep that many readers of *Cheap Sleeps in London* have come to appreciate. Others seem to forget where they are and have expectations that do not fit the category of this budget pick. Please consider the pluses and the minuses and depending on your stance, decide which one outweighs the other.

In spring and summer, the tiny outside facade is dotted with blooming flower boxes, which have won awards for manager Debbie Fletcher. The resident parrot, Sergeant Bilko, continues to welcome guests to the bright, compact single and double rooms, most of which offer a decent measure of comfort and practicality. Each has a built-in wardrobe, a full-length mirror, a small refrigerator, some desk space, tea and coffeemakers, and a TV and radio. There are no random styles; everything is coordinated in shades of blue and white. Original paintings depicting the early days of the Portobello Road market and its famous habitués add a touch of local character to each room. Private facilities in five rooms are a bonus, as is the fact that the sixth room's hall facilities are private to that room. A Continental breakfast will be served on white china in your room.

It sounds perfect, doesn't it? But a few cautionary words are in order. For those of you who do not like stairs, the ones here are quite steep and there are many to climb, especially if you have a room above the ground floor. Unless you have youth on your side, some of the extra beds are a backache waiting to happen. The regular beds are orthopedic, but not those that fold out to make a room into a triple. If you are a solo Cheap Sleeper, opt for something other than room 3, which is really too small for anyone traveling with more than a meager backpack. However, for most of us, Debbie's welcoming enthusiasm, as well as that of owner Brian Watkins, more than make up for the stairs and less-than-perfect beds, especially if you don't need a triple and can avoid No. 3.

FACILITIES AND SERVICES: Central heat, room fans, direct-dial phones, hair dryer, office safe, tea and coffeemaking facilities, TV, radio and clock, minibar, no lift, desk open 8:30 A.M.–10:30 P.M.

THE PORTOBELLO HOTEL (8, $)
22 Stanley Gardens, W11
22 rooms, all with shower or bath and toilet

Staying at the Portobello can be the next best thing to sampling life in the "Upstairs-Downstairs" era, but with twentieth-century plumbing. The owners of this sophisticated hotel did not miss a trick in adapting their hotel from several side-by-side Victorian townhouses. Their personal collection of art, armoires, rich antiques, and Oriental rugs are only a few of the nice touches that will carry you back to an era when graciousness and lovely surroundings mattered. If all of this plus rooms overlooking well-tended private gardens, four-poster beds, soft goose-down duvets, and an arty clientele used to impeccable service is your style, things don't get much better than the Portobello.

The entry and ground-floor sitting room are almost an English stage setting, with lush fabrics on overstuffed furniture and masses of fresh flowers and green plants. It looks like an American idealization of what a London drawing room should be. The twenty-two dramatically decorated rooms are inviting, with both whimsy and flamboyance working together to create unique atmospheres. Room No. 22 has a four-poster bed with side drapes. The sitting area overlooks the garden and is furnished with an inlaid antique desk and a fabulous bathroom with a green and white enamel shower and working Victorian "bathing machine"—a deep tub on legs surrounded by shower jets. From a horizontal position in your bubble bath, you can watch either television or the VCR. A favorite top-floor nest is No. 45, with dormer windows and a sofa and chair. The tub with gold feet is painted pink to go with the room, which also has a mirrored bed, an adorable makeup stand, and a small shower. For a slice of heaven, request No. 13, which is worth the trip to London just to sleep in the bed with angels and clouds painted on the canopy and side curtains. This room has a large bath with mirrors, brass, and all the extra amenities. For something unusual and fabulous, reserve No. 16, with a Chinese motif, a naughty round bed in the middle of the room, and another amazing Victorian bathtub with original copper and brass fittings, also in the main room. Another favorite is No. 6, with a gold-footed bathtub, a "tester" bed—a half four-poster draped in the back and covered with fluffy duvets—and French doors opening onto the garden.

TELEPHONE
020-7727-2777

FAX
020-7792-9641

TUBE
Notting Hill Gate

CREDIT CARDS
AE, DC, MC, V

RATES
Single £120; double £165–189; suite £235–285; Continental breakfast included

MISCELLANEOUS
Closed from around December 23 to January 3

Some of the top-floor rooms are referred to as "cabins" and that they are, minuscule havens with bathrooms to match. Some people wouldn't stay elsewhere. If this appeals to you, try No. 39, in bright red, which makes you feel you are enveloped in a big, warm hug.

Besides all the extras you would expect to find in an exceptional hotel, there is a bar and restaurant serving light meals; fax, copy, and courier services; theater bookings; and full-service health-club facilities within a four-minute walk. For guests who don't want to eat at the hotel, a 10 percent discount and preferential reservations are given at the hotel's Julie's, a popular upmarket wine bar and restaurant that's not too far away.

FACILITIES AND SERVICES: Air-conditioning in top-floor rooms, bar, direct-dial phones, hair dryer, laundry service, lift to third floor only, restaurant serving light meals, room service, office safe, satellite TV, VCRs, tea and coffeemakers, minibars, 24-hour desk, business services, theater bookings, health club privileges

RAVNA GORA (38)
29 Holland Park Avenue, W11
21 rooms, 5 with shower or bath and toilet

TELEPHONE
020-7727-7725
FAX
020-7221-4282
TUBE
Holland Park
CREDIT CARDS
MC, V
RATES
Single £30; double £50–60; triple £60–80; quad £80–88; English breakfast included

For a no-frills Cheap Sleep, the Ravna Gora is a smart address that budgeteers have been visiting for years. In its heyday, this palatial mansion, set back from busy and noisy Holland Park Avenue, must have been something. Standing in the rotunda and looking up at the sweeping staircase, I can just imagine the grand parties and balls that were staged here. Since 1956 it has been a B&B, and for the last twenty years or so it has been managed by the hardworking Jovanovic family and Mica, their gray and white cat. I have always wished that more than just the morning meal was served to guests, because the smells floating out from Mrs. Jovanovic's kitchen every time I have been to the hotel are tantalizing indeed.

The back-to-basics rooms, geared for students and the backpacking crowd, are generally snag- and tear-free and offer dependably clean chenille-covered beds for as many as six in a room. Even though the hotel is off the beaten tourist track, the Holland Park tube stop is down the street, and if you are driving, plenty of free parking is available in a locked lot right by the hotel.

FACILITIES AND SERVICES: Central heat, hair dryer available, public hall phones, free parking, office safe, TV, no lift, desk open 7 A.M.–midnight

WC 1

Bloomsbury

**London is incredibly beautiful. . . . I find Bloomsbury so
adorably lovely that I could look out of my window all day long.**
*—Virginia Woolf, letter to Katharine Arnold-
Forster, April 12, 1924*

Bloomsbury is one of London's most popular areas in which to stay,
and for good reason. Transportation is excellent and it is within walking
distance to West End theaters, Soho, shopping on Oxford and Regent
streets, and many good restaurants (see *Cheap Eats in London*). Consisting
of elegant and leafy squares and parks surrounded by lovely Georgian
townhouses, Bloomsbury is the home of the British Museum, which tops
the list of London's most popular tourist attractions, as well as the University of London and many well-known hospitals. In the early 1900s, the
area around Gordon Square was the base for the Bloomsbury Group, an
intellectual, liberal group whose members included Virginia Woolf,
Lytton Strachey, D. H. Lawrence, and John Maynard Keynes. Other
places of note in Bloomsbury include some lovely pubs, especially The
Lamb on Lamb's Conduit Street; Coram's Fields, a playground where no
adult is admitted unless accompanied by a child; the new British Library
next to St. Pancras Station; and the Gothic wonder formerly known as
Midland Grand Hotel but now referred to as St. Pancras Chambers. Next
door is King's Cross Station, where you begin your train journey if
heading north to Scotland. The area around the station is run-down and
should be avoided if alone, and always at night.

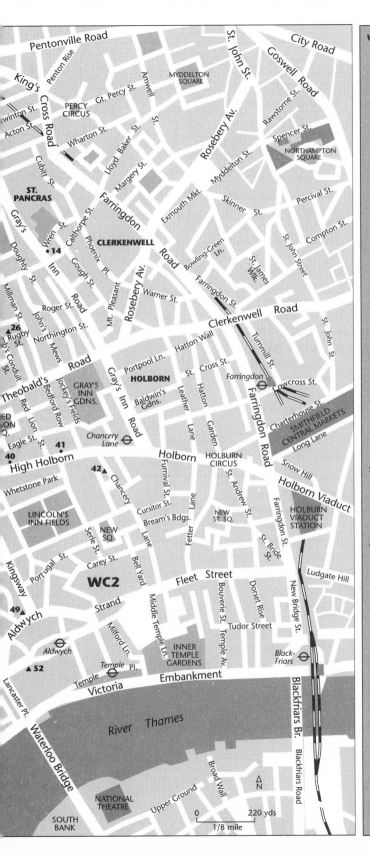

HOTELS in WC1

OTHER OPTIONS

Apartment Rentals

Student Dormitories

Student-Only Accommodations

($) indicates a Big Splurge

THE ACADEMY HOTEL (28, $)
17–21 Gower Street, WC1
48 rooms, all with shower or bath and toilet

The Academy ranks as one of the better hotels in Bloomsbury if you are looking for an upmarket choice that offers all the perks for either a personal or business-dictated stay in London. The management and staff pride themselves on providing the type of personal service one expects to find when paying a bit more. Whether it is securing a seat for a popular West End play in advance of your arrival, reconfirming ongoing reservations, or serving you breakfast in your room (at no extra charge), they are only too happy to be of service.

Located in the heart of London's publishing world and very close to the British Museum, the hotel was once a series of five Georgian houses built in the late 1700s. The original colonnades, the intricate plaster on the facade, and the delicate glass paneling are still in place today, despite several refurbishments, including the most recent one at a cost of £2.5 million. This ambitious project included enlarging the Alchemy restaurant and bar into a radically modern yet very stylish choice for visitors and locals to stop by for a drink, listen to live jazz, or enjoy a gourmet lunch, bar snacks, or a full-fledged dinner prepared by award-winning John O'Riordan. The food is exceptionally well presented and reflects the imagination and skill of this highly regarded chef. Public areas feature attractive trompe l'oeil murals leading to the restaurant and the masterful pastel bird prints by noted California artist Barbara A. Wood. The library, with a coal-burning fireplace, writing desk, and selection of good books, opens onto a garden. Now there is the addition of an enclosed glass conservatory garden where drinks and meals can be served year-round.

The rooms are individually decorated, with duvets on all the beds, well-lit work areas, excellent closet space, and up-to-date marble bathrooms with shelves, mirrors, and plenty of absorbent towels. All suites and deluxe rooms have air-conditioning. Number 54, a double suite with a large sitting area, has a lively coral color scheme, two telephones in the room, another in the executive bathroom, and double closets. Number 22 is a standard single with a separate entrance. I like the two windows, which let in lots of daylight, the floral theme of the room, and, of course, the closet space. In No. 2, you will

TELEPHONE
020-7631-4115; 800-678-3096 (toll-free from the U.S.)

FAX
020-7636-3442

EMAIL
academyh@aol.com

INTERNET
www.academy@aol.com

TUBE
Goodge Street, Russell Square, Tottenham Court Road

CREDIT CARDS
AE, DC, MC, V

RATES
Single £100–115; double £125–145; suite £185; extra bed £22; Continental breakfast £9 extra, English breakfast £11 extra, both served in your room at no extra charge

be in a standard double, with Barbara Wood prints on the wall and a small fireplace in a sitting area that has a settee.

NOTE: When booking your hotel reservation, ask for the American Friends Rate, which allows significant discounts, enabling many to upgrade and still be within a moderate budget.

FACILITIES AND SERVICES: Air-conditioning in deluxe rooms and suites, bar, central heat, conference rooms, direct-dial phones, hair dryer, laundry service, modems in all rooms, restaurant and room service, office safe, porter, satellite TV, tea and coffeemaker, theater bookings, no lift

THE AROSFA HOTEL (23)
83 Gower Street, WC1
16 rooms, 2 with shower or bath and toilet

TELEPHONE
020-7636-2115

FAX
020-7636-2115

TUBE
Euston Square, Goodge Street

CREDIT CARDS
MC, V

RATES
Single £35; double £48–62; triple £65–75; quad £88; English breakfast included

Hats off to Mr. and Mrs. Dorta for sheer determination and elbow grease. Together they have transformed this former crash pad for the homeless into one of the best Cheap Sleeps in London. When they bought the hotel a few years ago, it was such a wreck they had to close it completely in order to get rid of all the debris and overcome the neglect by the previous occupants. Murphy's Law was at work, and whatever could go wrong for the hardworking Dortas did, including the boiler breaking. All that is behind them now, and they and their sixteen-room completely nonsmoking hotel shine with pride.

The rooms don't aim to impress an interior decorator, but at prices this low they don't have to. They all provide matching laminated furniture, color-coordinated curtains and chenille bedspreads, a television, and some garden views, and a germ doesn't stand a chance in any of them. The hall facilities, which rate among the best in Bloomsbury, are newly tiled and always as clean as the rooms. Windows in the front rooms have double glazing, but for ensured quiet, I like something on the back side facing the hotel garden. Try No. 2, a double; No. 3, which is small but has a wide window view; or No. 4, a triple big enough, as one of my favorite British sayings goes, to "swing a cat." The only room I would not recommend is the basement dugout on the back, which I think is claustrophobic. Mr. and Mrs. Dorta disagree with me on this, promising that this is the quietest room in the hotel and the coolest in the summer. It is up to you to decide. In the morning, an English breakfast will be served in a pretty cream-colored dining room with rose-colored velvet chairs and a shelf loaded with touristy memorabilia brought by the growing roster of returning guests who appreciate the Dortas' hardworking, honest commitment to Cheap Sleeping in London.

FACILITIES AND SERVICES: Central heat, hair dryer available, tea and coffee in the lounge, TV, office safe, desk open 7:30 A.M.–10:30 P.M.

BLOOMS HOTEL (29, $)
7 Montague Street, WC1
27 rooms, all with shower or bath and toilet

The hotel building dates from the early 1700s, when it was occupied by Richard Penn, the Whig (liberal) member of Parliament from Liverpool. Today, service and attention to detail are the hallmarks of this very appealing selection, which has an attractive private walled garden backing up to the British Museum. While definitely in the Big Splurge category, it can be a more affordable sleep if you time your stay to take advantage of the weekend rates whenever they are available.

The richly appointed hotel is decorated with panache in an updated version of classic English style. The drawing room has the comfortable look of a grand house, with antiques positioned around a marble fireplace, and vases of fresh and dry flowers adding color accents. It is a delightful place to order a light snack and sip a cup of afternoon tea or an early evening sherry while catching up on the daily papers or current magazines provided for guests. The color-coordinated rooms have original paintings, a lounge chair, full mirrors, out-of-sight luggage space, and excellent bathrooms. Many of them are attractively themed. Number 4, the Lords, an executive double with a view onto the terrace, is named after the Lords cricket ground, and the autographed cricket bat of former Prime Minister John Major and his celebrity team is framed and hanging in the room. If you love going to the theater in London, be sure to request No. 104, the Theatre Royal, which takes its cue from London theaters. In the Dickens Room you will be surrounded with genuine articles on loan to the hotel from the Dickens Museum, including his shaving mirror, a monogrammed dinner plate, and a bust, as well as many photos of the author and a portrait of him hanging over the bed. In the Pickwick Room, a double, guests are

TELEPHONE
020-7323-1717
FAX
020-7636-6498
EMAIL
blooms@mermaid.co.uk
TUBE
Russell Square, Holborn
CREDIT CARDS
AE, DC, MC, V
RATES
Single £130–170; double £160–200; extra person £50; special weekend rates on request depending on availability; English breakfast and morning newspaper included

treated to a collection of wall-hanging tiles of Mr. Pickwick and Mrs. Bardell, and a framed check written by Dickens to his solicitor for £185 . . . quite a sum in those days. Number 307, facing the street, has no particular theme, but it is especially comfortable with its four-poster bed, working desk, and bathroom large enough to include a bidet. Numbers 1 and 2 have the advantage of being on the garden or can be combined to make a suite. The price of your room includes a cooked-to-order breakfast served in the formally set dining room, or on the garden terrace in summer. In addition to the usual breakfast fare, you can order hot porridge, haddock, kippers, or Lancashire black sausage. If you are hungry at other times and don't feel like going out, you can call 24-hour room service for a light meal. If you are eating out, the hotel works with several restaurants in granting preferential treatment to guests of the hotel.

FACILITIES AND SERVICES: Bar, ceiling fans, central heat, direct-dial phones, hair dryer, laundry service, lift, modems in all rooms, 24-hour room service, office safe, trouser press, satellite TV, radio, terry-cloth robes, 24-hour desk

BONNINGTON (27)
92 Southampton Row, WC1
215 rooms, all with shower or bath and toilet

TELEPHONE
020-7242-2828

FAX
020-7831-9170

EMAiL
sales@bonnington-hotels.co.uk

TUBE
Russell Square

CREDIT CARDS
AE, DC, MC, V

RATES
Single £120; double £155; triple £195; quad £245; Executive Single £145; Anniversary Room with spa and bottle of champagne £210. Getaway Weekends: single £90; double £130; triple £170; quad £190; Executive Single £115; Anniversary Room £190. All rates include an English breakfast, and children under fourteen are free when sharing parents' room. Ask for special rates, which are available at Christmas, Easter, and during the summer.

The Bonnington has an interesting history. When Scotsman John Frame built the hotel in 1911, he used the latest technology. The building was steel and concrete and had central heating, double-glazed windows, and lifts to every floor. He named it the Bonnington, a nostalgic reminder of the spectacular falls on his native River Clyde. With its two hundred bedrooms, large lounges, and noted dining room, it was hailed as something new and exciting in London because for a modest five shillings visitors were treated as valued guests and given a taste of luxury. The Bonnington, which is still owned by John Frame's family, is now a 215-room business hotel. But it's useful for Cheap Sleepers if they are able to take advantage of their Getaway Weekend bargain rates, which include bed, breakfast, and dinner. These rates are good for a stay of up to three nights on a Friday, Saturday, and Sunday. Also available are Easter, summer (mid-July to end of August), and Christmas special rates. The hotel is a good choice anytime for those who want a pivotal location within two miles of almost forty of London's top attractions, ranging from Bond Street and the High Courts of Justice to Madame Tussaud's and Trafalgar Square. Excellent tube and bus connections will take you further.

In general, the well-kept rooms are efficient and practical, but mundane when it comes to imagination. Some older bathrooms fall into the dated column, but most have both a tub and shower. Many of the doubles offer a small sitting area, a built-in wardrobe with shelf space, and a full-length mirror. Decorating caution was tossed to the winds in Nos. 259 and 359. Number 259, the Anniversary Room, "is designed for romance," with a draped bed and an ornate, gaudy bath complete with a mirrored double Jacuzzi and swan fittings. Slightly less over the top is No. 359, the Executive Single, done up in red velvet and shiny mahogany, also with a Jacuzzi, but no swans.

The dining room has a pitched glass ceiling and overlooks a real waterfall. For the children with you, there is a play area at the back of the hotel.

FACILITIES AND SERVICES: Bar, central heat, conference rooms, direct-dial phones, hair dryer, laundry service, lift, office safe, restaurant (three meals Mon–Fri, breakfast and dinner Sat–Sun), room service, satellite TV, rooms for disabled persons, trouser press, tea and coffeemaker, small children's playground, business center with free access to photocopying and a complimentary computer

CAMBRIA HOUSE (12)
37 Hunter Street, WC1
37 rooms, 3 with shower or bath and toilet

Both the Vandon House Hotel (see page 130) and the Cambria House are owned and operated by the Salvation Army. This means no smoking, no boozing, and no fooling with the rules. It's not that this is a prison with impossible standards, but rather that it's an extremely safe bet for those in the slow lane who want value for their money in a Bloomsbury location. The hotel has been redone once again, and the thirty-seven uniformly plain rooms continue to provide squeaky-clean accommodations. The only drawbacks to them seem to me to be dim lights and thin towels with no racks for hanging them. The new communal bathrooms are stellar, with tubs, showers, *and* heated towel racks. Bookings can be made for a maximum of twenty-eight days. Those of one

TELEPHONE
020-7837-1654

FAX
020-7837-1229

TUBE
Russell Square

CREDIT CARDS
MC, V

RATES
Single £29 per night, £193 per week; double £46 per night, £303 per week; triple £68 per night, £448 per week; children under three £6 per night, £40 per week; children three to fourteen £14 per night, £88 per week; English breakfast included

week or less must be paid in full upon arrival; guests with longer stays pay in advance on a weekly basis. Children between three and fourteen receive special rates if sharing with an adult. Breakfast is served and box lunches can be made up for a nominal charge.

FACILITIES AND SERVICES: Central heat, public phone, office safe, box lunches available, TV lounge, tea and coffeemaker, 24-hour desk, no lift, no smoking in hotel, no booze allowed

CRESCENT HOTEL (10)
49–50 Cartwright Gardens, WC1
27 rooms, 18 with shower or bath and toilet

TELEPHONE
020-7387-1515
FAX
020-7383-2054
TUBE
Euston, King's Cross, Russell Square
CREDIT CARDS
MC, V
RATES
Single £42–65; double £80; triple £90; quad £100; special rates on request if you stay longer than seven nights in low season; English breakfast included

The Crescent Hotel occupies a quiet position directly on Cartwright Gardens, a private square owned by the City Guild of Skinners and looked after by the University of London, whose residence halls are across the street. Keys to the garden and the four tennis courts are available to hotel guests (£1.50 per hour), and if you forgot your tennis racket and balls, they are available on loan from the hotel.

What sets this family-owned hotel apart from dozens like it? Aside from the clean, well-kept rooms, the lovely sitting room with a fireplace, and the impressive perfume-bottle collection in a glass display case in the dining room, which also has a cast-iron range found during a recent renovation project, the key to success here is the warmth and genuine hospitality of Mrs. Cockle and her mother, Mrs. Bessolo. Mrs. Cockle admits she was not formally trained in hotel management, but she did not need to be. She grew up in this hotel and inherited her mother's charm and graciousness. The word-of-mouth clientele, including many *Cheap Sleeps* readers, have been returning for more than forty years, and are welcomed each time as family. As Mrs. Cockle said, "The hotel is an extension of our home and we treat our guests accordingly."

The simple rooms are put together well, with the odd piece of vintage furniture to give them a hint of character. The largest family room is No. 5, on the ground floor, which has three twin beds and in the bathroom a curtained shower, pedestal sink, and a shelf for toiletries. For a more quiet stay, and in my opinion a more secure one, ask for No. 18, a sunny triple on the back, again with a stall shower. Three singles have a shower but no toilet. The other singles are completely bathless, but public facilities are above average and boast an enviable collection of plants the family has been nurturing for years.

FACILITIES AND SERVICES: Central heat, fans, direct-dial phones, hair dryer and iron available, office safe, TV, tea and coffeemaker, desk open 7:30 A.M.–10 P.M., no lift

EUSTON–TRAVEL INN CAPITAL (5)
1 Duke's Road, WC1
220 rooms, all with shower or bath and toilet

The London Travel Inns keep their pricing structure simple: one price for all rooms. Whether you are a single Cheap Sleeper or a family of four (with two adults and two children under sixteen) willing to share the same room, the price per room per night is a mere £60, breakfast extra. The plain, identical rooms have private bathrooms, hanging space, and a telephone that requires a phonecard (sold at the desk) to activate. Each location has a bar, restaurant, and "room service" dispatched from the vending machines in the halls. In addition to this location, there are two others in central London: County Hall–Travel Inn Capital, with some great views over the River Thames, and the newest location, Tower Bridge–Travel Inn Capital, near the Tower of London. Please see page 172 for information on these two. Other than the telephone and fax numbers and the tube stops, the information given at right applies to all three locations.

FACILITIES AND SERVICES: Bar, central heat, direct-dial phones (requires phonecard to activate), lift, restaurant, office safe, tea and coffeemakers, TV, one floor for non-smokers

TELEPHONE
0870-242-8000 (central reservations); 020-7554-3400 (Euston–Travel Inn Capital)

FAX
0870-241-9000 (central fax); 020-7554-3419 (Euston–Travel Inn Capital)

INTERNET
www.travelinn.co.uk (central website)

TUBE
Euston

CREDIT CARDS
AE, DC, MC, V

RATES
All rooms £60 per night; Continental breakfast £4, English breakfast £6

HARLINGFORD HOTEL (9)
61–63 Cartwright Gardens, WC1
43 rooms, all with shower or bath and toilet

The caring management of the Davies family at their B&B hotel on the Cartwright Gardens Crescent in Bloomsbury is reflected in the many repeat customers who value consistency, not only in the hotel and its upkeep but in its attention to the little details that make a difference in any hotel stay. For instance, at Easter you will find Easter candies on your pillow, and at Christmas, chocolates. The breakfast room is one of the nicest on the Crescent because it has three big windows overlooking the park in front. In addition to the usual cholesterol-laden English breakfast, they offer a buffet of

TELEPHONE
020-7387-1551

FAX
020-7387-4616

TUBE
King's Cross, Russell Square

CREDIT CARDS
AE, DC, MC, V

RATES
Single £70; double £86; triple £98; quad £110; buffet or English breakfast or both included

yogurt, fresh fruit, cheese, croissants, and more than twenty-four (I counted) cereal choices.

All the rooms are generally light and pleasing, with floral prints, tiled baths, and double-glazed windows. The best ones are on the second and third floors facing front or on the top floor with views over the gardens. These perches on the top require climbing stairs, because there is no lift in the hotel. The basement rooms have been renovated, but you can still hear the tube rumble from Nos. 4 and 8. Keys are available for the tennis courts in front of the hotel, and the nominal fee charged goes to the University of London to maintain them.

NOTE: The Mabledon Court Hotel and the Thanet Hotel (please see pages 104 and 109) are also owned by members of the Davies family.

FACILITIES AND SERVICES: Central heat, direct-dial phones, hair dryer available, office safe, TV, desk open 7 A.M.–midnight, no lift

HOTEL CALIFORNIA (1)
4–8 Belgrove Street, WC1
65 rooms, all with shower or bath and toilet

TELEPHONE
020-7837-7629

FAX
020-7278-5836

EMAIL
t.megaro@virgin.net

TUBE
King's Cross, St. Pancras

CREDIT CARDS
None

RATES
Single £40; double £55; triple £70; quad £80; buffet breakfast included

You have to admire the sheer determination and vision displayed by Tony Megaro, who grew up in the hotel business but has stepped out on his own and is developing two smart hotels in what was once a wilderness area for decent hotels. Simplicity and convenience prevail in the small but spunky rooms at his Hotel California, where the Cheap Sleeps are identically dressed with built-ins and complemented by matching duvet covers and curtains. All of them have tiled baths, and some even have tubs and heated towel racks. You can also bank on closet space, a color television, and in some, a private safe. A large buffet breakfast is served in a stunning modern room with fruit prints hanging on a backdrop of orange faux-finished walls.

Stay tuned for Tony's next project, a complete transformation of the hotel next door. Even though it will not offer Cheap Sleepers as friendly prices as the Hotel California, it will be well within many budgets.

FACILITIES AND SERVICES: Bar, central heat, hall phones (but direct-dial planned), hair dryer available, office safe, some room safes, TV, no lift

HOWARD WINCHESTER HOTEL (3)
9–10 Argyle Square, WC1
70 rooms, 60 with shower or bath and toilet

No lift, no lounge, and no telephones in your room tells you that things are kept to a bare Cheap Sleeping minimum at the Megaro family's seventy-room hotel not far from King's Cross. The spartan rooms are not for those who require space, or look for such "extras" as a table and chair. No, these are clone-designed rooms where you can hang your hat, take a fast shower, and sleep tight. All are clean and identically decked out with dark blue carpeting and blue and white fabrics. A full English breakfast is available each morning in two large modern rooms that are set with granite tables and have a mildly Italian feel to the faux-finished sienna-colored walls. Lina Megaro is an enthusiastic and friendly hostess, and along with her brother Tony (see Hotel California, page 98) welcomes many returning guests whose principal goal in London is to save money by Sleeping Cheap.

FACILITIES AND SERVICES: Central heat, hall phones, office safe, TV, no lift, 24-hour desk

TELEPHONE
020-7837-7930

FAX
020-7837-9146

TUBE
King's Cross, St. Pancras

CREDIT CARDS
None (but they expect to accept them soon)

RATES
Single £35; double £45; triple £60; one-night stands, add £5 per room; English breakfast included

IMPERIAL LONDON HOTELS LTD.

The Imperial London Hotels Ltd. is a group of six centrally located hotels with more than six thousand beds. For Cheap Sleepers in London, they are recommendable thanks to their long list of amenities and "Let's Go" Weekend package rates. The hotels deal mainly with budget tour groups, so personalized service is not high on the list of benefits for guests. As a result, expect big, bustling, impersonal, unimaginative hotels that move the herds in and out in processed precision. The hotels are within a five-minute walk of each other and less than a mile from the City of London, theaterland, Piccadilly Circus, main northern railway stations, and tube stops on the Central and Piccadilly lines going directly to Heathrow Airport.

Lower daily rates are available on request for groups. Their "Let's Go" Weekends are good from Friday through Sunday and include two nights in a room with private bath and television; daily English breakfast in all but the Royal National, where it is Continental; two three-course meals (lunch or dinner) in any of the hotel restaurants in the group; two days free parking in the underground garage; a welcome cocktail in the hotel bar

GENERAL INFORMATION FOR ALL IMPERIAL LONDON HOTELS

TELEPHONE
020-7278-7871 (central reservations)

FAX
020-7837-4653 (central fax)

EMAIL
101455.1271@compuserve.com

INTERNET
www.imperialhotels.co.uk

CREDIT CARDS
AE (2 percent service charge added), DC, MC, V

RATES
For daily rates, please see individual hotel listings; English breakfast included except at the Royal National, where it is Continental. "Let's Go" Weekend rates: £90 per person per night for a two-night stay; optional supplementary Sunday night (dinner, bed, and breakfast, including car parking) when booked together with the two-night weekend is

£50 per person. In addition to the above-quoted "Let's Go" Weekend base rate, some of the hotels have a per person per night supplement; please check below for details on each hotel.

on arrival; no single-room supplement; first child under fourteen occupying a cot or mini-bed in parents' room is free; other children in parents' room are half price. An optional third night that includes dinner, bed, and breakfast is available at all the hotels. It is important to note that no special offers or package rates are available through travel agents. They must be booked directly, either through central reservations or with the hotel itself. Includes the Bedford, Imperial, President, Royal National, and Tavistock.

NOTE: The sixth hotel in the group, the County, is not recommended.

FACILITIES AND SERVICES: Private baths, direct-dial phones, hair dryers available, televisions, radios, tea and coffeemakers, lifts, restaurants, conference facilities, and underground parking. Consult listings below for other services offered by each hotel.

BEDFORD HOTEL (33)
Southampton Row, WC1
184 rooms, all with shower or bath and toilet

TELEPHONE
020-7636-7822
TUBE
Russell Square
RATES
Single £70; double £90; third person (folding bed) add £18 to double rate, third person (cot) add £8 to double rate; "Let's Go" Weekend supplement £24 per person per night; English breakfast included in all rates

The Bedford, close to the British Museum, is the best of the group, with its uniformly boring rooms equipped with built-in furniture, luggage racks, good closet space (especially in the twin-bedded rooms), and pretty back views over the hotel garden and row houses beyond. Those with windows facing the busy street have double glazing to reduce the traffic noise. For an increase in sleep time and a breath of fresh air away from the traffic fumes on the clogged London road in front, book a room facing the back garden. In warm weather, tables are arranged on the patio, which has a reflecting pond and a fountain.

FACILITIES AND SERVICES: Bar, central heat, conference room, direct-dial phones, hair dryer available, lift, nonstocked minibars in some rooms, car park (£15 per 24 hours), office safe (50p per day), restaurant, coffee shop, room service, TV, radio, same-day laundry, trouser press, nonsmoking rooms, 24-hour desk

IMPERIAL HOTEL (24)
Russell Square, WC1
447 rooms, all with shower or bath and toilet

TELEPHONE
020-7837-3655
TUBE
Russell Square

The Imperial has everything from a car park to a casino next door. The rooms have been renovated, and those on the third and eighth floors have minibars. The best rooms for sleeping are on the eighth floor, with Russell Square views that overlook the entry and fountain area.

FACILITIES AND SERVICES: Bar, central heat, conference room, direct-dial phones, hair dryers available, lift, car park (£15 per 24 hours), satellite TV, radio, trouser press, tea and coffeemakers, office safe (50p per day), restaurant, room service, money exchange office (terrible rates), laundry service, tours, tickets, 24-hour desk

RATES
Single £72; double £94; third person (folding bed) add £18 to double rate, third person (cot) add £8 to double rate; "Let's Go" Weekend supplement £30 per person per night; English breakfast included in all rates

PRESIDENT (25)
Russell Square, WC1
523 rooms, all with shower or bath and toilet

The President has been revamped in budget style and now includes modems in all the rooms on the first floor and minibars in first-floor twins. It has all the goodies the others do in this group, but because volume is so big here, the prices are a bit less for standard nightly rates. An arcade joins this hotel with the Imperial.

FACILITIES AND SERVICES: Bar, central heat, direct-dial phones, hair dryer available, lift, minibars in first-floor twin rooms, modems in all rooms on first floor, restaurants, office safe (50p per day), TV and radio, trouser press and tea and coffeemakers in rooms from the second floor up, 24-hour desk

TELEPHONE
020-7837-8844
TUBE
Russell Square
RATES
Single £66; double £86; third person (folding bed) add £18 to double rate, third person (cot) add £8 to double rate; "Let's Go" Weekend supplement £24 per person per night; English breakfast included in all rates

ROYAL NATIONAL HOTEL (21)
Bedford Way, WC1
1,630 rooms, all with shower or bath and toilet

The Royal National sleeps two thousand persons in more than sixteen hundred rooms, making it the biggest hotel in London. The hideous lifeboat orange–colored curtains in this monstrous piece of architectural blight are gone, but the fleets of tour buses that disgorge budget revelers in from the sticks for a few days of booze and fun are not. The utilitarian rooms, joined by never-ending hikes down endless corridors, are clean and reasonably large, with only a few dings here and there, but the faded pink color scheme gives them a dull feeling. If you can take the hotel's "bus station at rush hour" atmosphere, you will find everything you need from an underground car park and a money changer (poor rates unless you are desperate) to a bar, gift shop, theater booking agency, and restaurants that serve predictable English fare.

TELEPHONE
020-7637-2488
TUBE
Russell Square
RATES
Single £67; double £82; third person (folding bed) add £18 to double rate, third person (cot) add £8 to double rate; "Let's Go" Weekend supplement £22 per person per night; Continental breakfast included in all rates

NOTE: The corridors are endless; be sure you learn the fire escape route from your room.

FACILITIES AND SERVICES: Bar, central heat, direct-dial phones, car park (£15 per 24 hours), lift, money changer, office safe (50p per day), restaurants, room service, TV, radio, laundry service, trouser press, three floors of non-smoking rooms, 24-hour desk

TAVISTOCK (17)
Tavistock Square, WC1
343 rooms, all with shower or bath and toilet

TELEPHONE
020-7636-8383
TUBE
Russell Square
RATES
Single £61; double £78; third person (folding bed) add £18 to double rate, third person (cot) add £8 to double rate; no supplement for "Let's Go" Weekend package deal; English breakfast included in all rates

The Tavistock is another of this chain's "tour group central" hotels, and with over three hundred rooms catering mainly to large Cheap Sleeping groups, one could hardly expect much of a personalized approach from the staff. They simply don't have the time or the training. Like all the others, the rooms are bigger than average, and every possible convenience is offered within the hotel, from a wine bar to laundry services. The best rooms here are those overlooking Tavistock Square.

FACILITIES AND SERVICES: Bar and wine bar, car park, central heat, direct-dial phones, hair dryer available, lift, restaurant, room service, TV, radio, office safe (50p per day), theater bookings

THE JENKINS HOTEL (6)
45 Cartwright Gardens, WC1
14 rooms, 7 with shower or bath and toilet

TELEPHONE
020-7387-2067
FAX
020-7383-3139
EMAIL
reservations@jenkinshotel.demon.co.uk
INTERNET
www.jenkinshotel.demon.co.uk
TUBE
Euston, King's Cross, Russell Square
CREDIT CARDS
MC, V
RATES
Single £52–68; double £68–78; triple £91; English breakfast included

Cheap Sleepers return to the fourteen-room Jenkins year after year, drawn by the tranquil location, the outgoing manner of owners Felicity Langley-Hunt and Sam Bellingham and their Labradors Georgie, Charlie, and the youngest, Tiggy, who take their duties as official greeters very seriously. Many guests have been known to actually complain if the dogs are not around, and have become coconspirators in playing havoc with their girth. To try to keep the dogs in fit form, Sam has been forced to place a sign in the dining room asking guests, "Please, do not feed the dogs."

The hotel has been listed in every edition of my book, which has pleased the majority of readers—I have received many favorable letters about this particular Cheap Sleep—and displeased a minority of readers, who have written to me with a laundry list of complaints (including, amazingly enough, the dogs). On my most recent London visit, I did what I always do when I recheck a current Cheap Sleep: I carefully inspected all fourteen rooms, the hall facilities, the reception/office area where the dogs hold court most of the time, the kitchen, and the dining room. Frankly speaking, I do not see the big beef with this hotel. Admittedly the rooms are nothing fancy, and in some cases they are small, but they are sweetly coordinated with a sprinkling of interesting pieces of furniture that give them a bit of personality. Room 10, on the top floor, is a sunny double and recommended, and so is No. 9, one of the largest, which has been redone in yellow and blue and has a corner modular shower and toilet. Number 11, a bathless twin on the top floor with a view, is without facilities and slated for renewal, so purists may want to avoid this one until it is redone. Number 1 is still below ground level (quite common in many B&B hotels), and the bathroom is just outside, but for some, the extra space and new decor may overshadow the semipublic bathroom situation. Room No. 7 faces the front and is a tiny double. When I commented on this to Sam, he said it was going to be turned into a single with its own bathroom. Good idea. Please make sure this has been done before you reserve it. The feeble water supply (which has drawn heavy criticism) has been corrected by shower pumps that ensure full-force hot showers anytime. The hotel is now entirely nonsmoking, a great feature for most Cheap Sleepers in London. I make no bones about the presence of the dogs, so if they pose a problem, look elsewhere. I recommend two other hotels right on Cartwright Gardens, neither of which have visable pets of any kind.

When you are at the hotel, be sure to admire the delicately hand-embroidered silk flowers framed with a poem that are hung throughout the hotel. In the 1920s, these flowers came in cigarette packages along with seeds, instructions on how to grow them, and a poem describing each flower variety. Mr. Bellingham found a large collection of these in a box belonging to his grandfather and had them framed for the hotel. They are a special touch that everyone seems to enjoy.

There is no downstairs reception or sitting room, so you will be received in the large kitchen with a big table in the center. Guests gather each morning in the green and white breakfast room with lacy white covers and fresh flowers on the tables. Keys to the gardens opposite the hotel are available for anyone who wants to play a set or two of tennis or just relax from sight-seeing and shopping for an hour or two.

FACILITIES AND SERVICES: Central heat, direct-dial phones, hair dryers, minibars, room safe, TV, tea and coffeemakers, the hotel is completely nonsmoking, no lift

MABLEDON COURT HOTEL (4)
10–11 Mabledon Place, WC1
31 rooms, all with shower or bath and toilet

TELEPHONE
020-7388-3866
FAX
020-7387-5686
TUBE
Euston, King's Cross
CREDIT CARDS
AE, MC, V
RATES
Single £68; double £78; ask about corporate rates for Friday, Saturday, and Sunday, or for stays of one week or more; English breakfast included

The Mabledon Court is an oasis in a desert of acceptable hotels. Just on the edge of Bloomsbury, close to Euston and King's Cross rail stations, it is owned by members of the Davies family, who also own the Harlingford Hotel (see page 97) and the Thanet (see page 109). When the Davies family bought this hotel, they tossed out the terrible furnishings and dismal color schemes. In their place they installed good beds in rooms that have pleasant, direct colors and blond built-in furniture that allows as much space as possible. Bathrooms have no tubs, only showers There are no twin-bedded rooms, and those on the front are noisy and lack security if you are on the ground floor and open the window. Better to request something on an upper floor along the back.

A basement lounge with broken-in chintz love seats leads to a breakfast room where the tables are covered in pink linen with white overlays.

FACILITIES AND SERVICES: Central heat, direct-dial phones, fans, hair dryers, office safe, TV, tea and coffeemakers, lift, desk open 7 A.M.–midnight

MORGAN HOTEL (36)
24 Bloomsbury Street, WC1
17 rooms, 4 flats; all with shower or bath and toilet

TELEPHONE
020-7636-3735
FAX
020-7636-3045
TUBE
Tottenham Court Road
CREDIT CARDS
MC, V with a 3 percent surcharge unless it is a direct debit charge card

For a stay of a few nights, a week, or a month or more, the Morgan Hotel and apartments receive my highest recommendation . . . and that of the many Cheap Sleepers who write to me saying this is their favorite London B&B address. In fact, once people find the Morgan Hotel, they *never* consider staying anyplace else in London. Reservations for this jewel in Bloomsbury are absolutely vital as far in advance as possible, and a year ahead is not *too* soon to begin making your plans.

The Morgan and the four adjacent apartments are owned by Joy Ward and her brothers, John and David.

For more than two decades they have worked very hard and spared no effort in creating a marvelous B&B where attention to every detail and their guests' comfort is their number one priority. They are so dedicated to their high level of excellence that they do all of the work in the hotel themselves, from greeting guests at the door to cleaning the rooms and preparing breakfast each morning.

David Ward, a carpenter and craftsperson par excellence, has done all the fine interior paneling and cabinetry. Everything is well planned, from the blooming flower boxes under the windows to the carefully maintained rooms, most of which are air-conditioned at no extra cost. Bathrooms are equally as nice, with a magnifying mirror and enough shelf and counter space. The dining room is comfortably fitted with booths and accented with fresh and dried flower arrangements. Adding to the warmth here is an impressive collection of English china, a display case of crystal and ceramics, along with toby jugs and early London photographs.

The four stunning apartments, which can sleep up to three, are decorated in the best of taste with polished furniture, beautiful fabrics, and framed English prints lining the walls. All include a television and VCR, an eat-in kitchen with a view, a large en suite bathroom with a separate shower and bathtub, a security system, daily maid service, and breakfast each morning at the hotel.

FACILITIES AND SERVICES: Air-conditioning in all but three hotel rooms and the four apartments, central heat, direct-dial phones, hair dryer, magnifying mirrors in bathrooms, room safe, satellite TV in hotel and apartments, no lift in hotel or for apartments

RATES
Hotel: Single £55; double £80; triple £120. Apartment: £100; extra person £40; English breakfast included for hotel and apartment guests. They prefer at least a five-night stay in the apartments, but will consider shorter stays depending on time of year and availability. Must cancel reservations more than 48 hours prior to arrival or forfeit deposit.

POSTHOUSE BLOOMSBURY (20)
Coram Street, WC1
284 rooms, all with shower or bath and toilet

It has everything except pizzazz (and a street number!). The modern rooms are distinguished only by their mediocrity. That goes double for the lackluster staff. However, it is a Forte Posthouse and does participate in their money-saving Leisure Breaks; otherwise I simply cannot whip up much enthusiasm about this unexciting choice.

FACILITIES AND SERVICES: Bar, central heat, conference facilities, direct-dial phones, hair dryer, lift, restaurant,

TELEPHONE
020-7837-1200; 0800-40-40-40 (toll-free within the U.K.); 800-225-5843 (toll-free from the U.S.)
FAX
020-7837-5374
INTERNET
www.forte-hotels.com
TUBE
Russell Square
CREDIT CARDS
AE, DC, MC, V

RATES
Singles from £85; doubles from £105–125; English breakfast included

room service, office safe, satellite TV, tea and coffee-makers, trouser press, 24-hour desk, three nonsmoking floors

THE PRINCESS HOTEL (2)
35–37 Argyle Square, WC1
21 rooms, 3 with shower or bath and toilet

TELEPHONE
020-7278-6895
FAX
020-7833-0984
TUBE
King's Cross, St. Pancras
CREDIT CARDS
MC, V
RATES
Single £30; double £40–52; triple £80; English breakfast included

I love surprises, especially when I can pass the good news on to readers. On my latest visit to the hotel, I was reminded by owner Coco Aronica of my first visit a few years ago, which was on a cold March day. I was in the neighborhood looking for a pub, and passed her perched on a ladder washing the windows in what I considered to be arctic conditions. We struck up a conversation, she invited me in, I liked what I saw, and the rest, as they say, is history: the discovery of this clean Cheap Sleep in London run by Coco, her brother Jessie, and their families, who manage the hotel and live on-site, which lends a homey, family air many Cheap Sleepers like.

Argyle Square is in the northern tip of Bloomsbury and quickly accessible to the St. Pancras railroad station. It is far (thirty minutes) from the usual tourist trails in London, and to get to them you will have to depend on tube, bus, taxi, and shank's mare. However, if you are a certified Cheap Sleeper in London, the Princess Hotel definitely lives up to its name. It is as well scrubbed inside as it is out, with rooms a big step up from the dark Dickensian decor that is the rule in most of the area's budget lodgings. The rooms are snug and lean, with colors that blend well to allow for pleasant dreams, not wild nightmares. Hall bathrooms are the norm (none of the singles have private facilities). The public areas are done in easy-care materials that are a cinch to keep washed and don't show wear and tear. The tiled dining room is set with three communal tables where guests can stoke up for the day on bacon, eggs, beans, and all the trimmings.

FACILITIES AND SERVICES: Central heat, hall phones, hair dryer and iron available, TV, tea and coffeemakers, 24-hour desk, no lift

RUSKIN HOTEL (31)
23–24 Montague Street, WC1
33 rooms, 6 with shower or bath and toilet

An enviable location (around the corner from the British Museum) and clean rooms are offered by the Spanish family that runs the Ruskin Hotel. The bedrooms do not all quite mix and match, and in some the lighting is very dim, but nothing is badly worn and the front windows are double-glazed to help muffle the constant street noise. The rooms on the back are quieter because they overlook a lovely private park. There is a lift to every floor and all major credit cards are accepted, two rarities in most small, family-operated B&Bs in London. The prices depend on the amount of private plumbing in your room. For Cheap Sleepers, there is absolutely no need to pay extra to get a cramped private bathroom when the ones in the hall are not only bigger and better but save you significant money. The owners, Mr. and Mrs. Sedeno, have green thumbs, which is especially evident in the cheerful mirrored dining room where they display many of their plants. When you are in the television lounge, you will not be able to miss the beautiful oil painting done right on the plaster above the mantle. It is by James Ward, who painted animals for the Duke of Bedford, and depicts the area around Camden Town in the early 1800s.

FACILITIES AND SERVICES: Central heating, public phone in hall, hair dryers, lift, office safe, tea and coffeemakers, front desk open 7:30 A.M.–midnight

TELEPHONE
020-7636-7388

FAX
020-7323-1662

TUBE
Holborn, Russell Square, Tottenham Court Road

CREDIT CARDS
AE, DC, MC, V

RATES
Single £45; double £65–80; triple £75–85; English breakfast included

ST. MARGARET'S HOTEL (30)
26 Bedford Place, WC1
64 rooms, 10 with shower or bath and toilet

During their many years at the St. Margaret's, Rosanna and Betino Marazzi have served a quiet circle of regulars, the sort of people who would not return if they were not fully satisfied. My next-door neighbor and his family have been coming here for more than thirty years and have no plans of staying in any other London hotel. The keynote of the hotel is friendly, personal service by a dedicated staff that has worked here for years. As Mrs. Marazzi told me, "My staff changes only when someone retires!"

The eclectically furnished, slightly old-fashioned rooms are fresh and bright and impeccably maintained. The views along the back overlook the Duke of Bedford's

TELEPHONE
020-7636-4277/580-2352

FAX
020-7323-3066

TUBE
Holborn, Russell Square

CREDIT CARDS
MC, V

RATES
Single (none with private baths) £47; double £58–76 (No. 53 is £85); £2.50 supplement for one-night stays; £6 cancellation fee; English breakfast included

gardens and are truly magnificent in the spring and early summer when the trees and flowers are in full bloom. Even the tiniest single has a generosity of space and is clean. Almost all the rooms still have their original fireplaces, which in the early days maids had to stoke several times a day to keep the guests warm. With the addition of central heat, stoking the fires is no longer one of the maids' responsibilities, and the fireplaces serve as decorative reminders of a long-lost era in hotel living. For a family, or anyone actually, No. 53 is a great room with a glassed-in conservatory along the gardens, the original marble fireplace dating from 1803, and a nicely tiled bathroom. I can't imagine that anyone could be disappointed by it. There are other rooms that are very nice, and most of them have their own baths and face the gardens, which are available for guests to use and enjoy. Try for No. 40, a family room for four; No. 28, a double or triple with windows onto the garden and a tiled stall shower in the bathroom; No. 33, also with a new stall shower and pink carpet; or No. 23, a favorite because it is so light and has excellent closet and luggage space. Numbers 24 and 41 are quiet L-shaped bathless singles, with enough room to fully unpack and stay for a week or more.

I think the dining room is one of the nicest in Bloomsbury because it is bright and airy with fresh flowers and green plants. I like to sit in the back section, overlooking the gardens below. As you walk from the lounge to the dining room, please be sure to take a minute to look at the original hand-painted glass featuring birds, flowers, and plants you might see in the neighborhood. Also displayed here are a series of interesting photographs taken by the Marazzis's son of important events in and around Bedford Place.

FACILITIES AND SERVICES: Central heat, direct-dial phones, satellite TV, hair dryer available and in all rooms with private baths, office safe, tea and coffee served anytime, no lift

THANET HOTEL (32)
8 Bedford Place, WC1
16 rooms, all with shower or bath and toilet

Believe me, the Thanet Hotel is an exceptionally good value and very nice for the price. Hotels around Russell Square are a dime a dozen and range from luxury stays to utter dumps with rooms qualifying as dark horror stories. The key is to find one that is not only clean and fairly priced but comes without the usual dime-store style of decorating that pits clashing colors against patched carpets, shrunken bedspreads, and furnishings that can charitably be called "curbside." If you like Bloomsbury and want to be close to the British Museum, Covent Garden, and the theaters, the Thanet should be a top contender for your stay because now it is even better than before. The hotel is owned and managed by third-generation hoteliers Richard and Lynwen Orchard. Thanks to their continued efforts, the hotel has improved by leaps and bounds since my last visit.

The hotel stands out with a bright-blue awning over the door and the colored-tile entry leading up two steps from the street. As you enter, look up to admire the original glass dome in the ceiling that sheds light on a winding staircase. A ground-floor dining room with seven linen-covered tables looks over window boxes to the street. There is no formal lounge, but the rooms are nice enough to encourage you to spend more than just minimum time sleeping in them. Every one of them has plain walls above wooden wainscoting, is decorated with floral bedspreads and dusty rose carpets, and has an en suite bathroom. All but two have ornamental fireplaces. The suite on the garden level is the only one with a bathtub; the other rooms have stall showers. Number 5 is a smart twin or triple with a balcony view of the garden. The beauty of the room is the magnificent eight-by-ten-foot gold mirror hanging over the tile and metal fireplace. Numbers 9 and 10 also look out onto green space and have slightly larger corner bathrooms.

NOTE: Two other Bloomsbury hotels are run by family members: the Harlingford Hotel and the Mabledon Court Hotel, see pages 97 and 104.

FACILITIES AND SERVICES: Central heat, direct-dial phones, fans, hair dryers, office safe, TV and radio, tea and coffeemakers, no lift

TELEPHONE
020-7636-2869/580-3377
FAX
020-7323-6676
TUBE
Holborn, Russell Square
CREDIT CARDS
AE, MC, V
RATES
Single £64; double £82; triple £98; quad £110; English breakfast included

WC2

Charing Cross, Covent Garden, Leicester Square, and The Strand

Why are Trafalgar Square fountains like Government Clerks? Because they play from 10 till 4.
—Punch, *July 17, 1858*

All distances in London are measured from Charing Cross, the official center of London, just south of Trafalgar Square.

Covent Garden, London's first planned square, was laid out in 1630 by architect Inigo Jones on behalf of the Duke of Bedford, who owned the land. Before that, it was the Covent Garden for Westminster Abbey, thus the name. In Victorian times, Covent Garden was London's fruit and vegetable market, the place that the legendary Professor Henry Higgins met Eliza Doolittle. In the mid-sixties, the market was converted into a complex of shops, cafés, restaurants, and wine bars that draw crowds every day and night of the week. Because of the density of theaters in the area (including Drury Lane), many of these restaurants offer well-priced pre- and post-theater menus. There always seems to be something going on around Covent Garden—street entertainers perform in the plaza, and the narrow streets fanning out from the market are lined with interesting boutiques and dozens of coffeehouses that can easily take up an afternoon of browsing and sipping.

Leicester Square, sandwiched between Piccadilly Circus and Charing Cross Road, is perpetually crowded with people milling about, waiting to attend one of the first-run cinemas, or queuing at the Half-Price Ticket Booth (see "Saving Money at London's Theaters and Concerts," page 242). Chinatown is close and so are the stage theaters along Shaftesbury Avenue.

The Strand is a rich assortment of former noblemen's homes occupying the area between The Strand and the River Thames. For the tourist, it is the principal route between the West End and the City.

($) indicates a Big Splurge

THE FIELDING HOTEL (48)
4 Broad Court, WC2
24 rooms, all with shower or bath and toilet

TELEPHONE
020-7836-8305

FAX
020-7497-0064

TUBE
Covent Garden

CREDIT CARDS
AE, DC, MC, V

RATES
Single £75–85; double £95–120; Continental breakfast £3, English breakfast £4.50; must cancel within 48 hours of arrival or forfeit deposit

MISCELLANEOUS
Closed between Christmas and New Year's

For those London visitors who want to be only a heartbeat away from theaters, Soho, Piccadilly Circus, and West End restaurants and shopping, the Fielding is a popular destination. The hotel is named after the novelist Henry Fielding, who lived in Broad Court with his brother; both were magistrates at the Bow Street Magistrates' Court next door. The building seems to have been here since time began. Some Cheap Sleeping readers love the hotel, calling it "quaint" and/or "historical." Others find it dreadfully cramped, with depressing views and lacking in flashy amenities. Frankly, I am somewhere in between, believing that the location, pleasant management, and several of the redone rooms with new bathrooms save the day.

The hotel is on a paved pedestrian walkway next to the Bow Street Magistrates' Court, site of the world's first police station, and almost opposite the Royal Opera House in Covent Garden. Diamond-paned windows and flower-filled window boxes frame the entrance. The downstairs breakfast room desperately needs a face-lift, but hardly anyone notices thanks to Paco, who runs the show here and whips up a mighty fine Spanish omelette. If you choose not to take breakfast here, which is extra anyway, countless cafés and coffeehouses are within a five-minute walk.

Most of the rooms are far from spacious, and thanks to their city center location, more than a few have gloomy vistas, but in general they do have a cozy cottage air. The new bathrooms in many, especially the singles, add further appeal. Numbers 10, 20, and 30 are corner locations on Broad Court. Their small sleeping areas are bolstered by well-lighted sitting areas and new bathrooms. Number 5 is another room to keep in mind. The new bath has a regulation glass-enclosed shower and heated towel rack, and the room itself features a dressing area and newer pine furnishings. Hiking enthusiasts who climb to the top floor will be rewarded with No. 35, which has a rather interesting view to a block of apartments that once were government council flats (i.e., subsidized). Number 3, a standard twin, has a grim view and needs redoing from start to finish. Until that has happened, this room is a definite no-no.

FACILITIES AND SERVICES: Bar, central heat, direct-dial phones, hair dryer available, office safe, TV, no lift, no children under twelve allowed

THE PASTORIA (54, $)
3 St. Martin's Street, WC2
58 rooms, all with shower or bath and toilet

Tucked away in a traffic-free side street off Leicester Square is the Pastoria. For those with flexible budgets and more demanding needs who want a key location in the center of the West End, this lovely hotel has a great deal to offer, especially if you take advantage of the Weekend, Corporate, or Super Saver rates, which in some cases can cut the rack rate almost in half. Look at it this way: what you save on time, taxi, and tube costs at this location you can apply to upgrading your stay. Piccadilly Circus, Regent Street, Covent Garden, Parliament Square, and Buckingham Palace are all within walking distance; and with Leicester and Trafalgar Squares on the hotel's doorstep, many of London's top theaters and cinemas are only minutes away.

The hotel, which originally began as a gentlemen's private club and restaurant, was converted into a hotel in 1931. The rooms have an intimate Edwardian theme, with a hint of the Orient provided by the rich red and green fabrics that enhance the walls and upholstery. The only drawback to the hotel are the singles facing the back, with creepy views of a fire escape. The newest rooms, with marble baths, are on the sixth floor, which is also one of the hotel's three nonsmoking floors. Number 608, a double, has a peekaboo look at Big Ben and Nelson's Column. Number 603, which can be made up as either a king or twin, is as well presented as all the

TELEPHONE
020-7930-8641; 800-333-3333 (toll-free from the U.S.—Radisson)

FAX
020-7925-0551

TUBE
Leicester Square

CREDIT CARDS
AE, DC, MC, V

RATES
Single £170; double £200 (always ask about Corporate, Super Saver, and Weekend rates, which are much less); English breakfast included

other rooms and has even more closet and drawer space, plus a bathroom window, but the view from both the room and the bathroom is nothing.

The hotel's dining room faces Leicester Square, but the food is only okay if you just want a quick bite. Consult *Cheap Eats in London* for better choices that are all within easy walking distance.

FACILITIES AND SERVICES: Air-conditioning is planned, bar, central heat, direct-dial phones, hair dryer, laundry service, lift, porter, restaurant, room service, room safe, satellite TV, pay movies, radio, clock, tea and coffee-makers, 24-hour desk, three nonsmoking floors

SEVEN DIALS HOTEL (44)
7 Monmouth Street, WC2
10 rooms, 7 with shower or bath and toilet

TELEPHONE
020-7681-0791/240-0823

FAX
020-7681-0792

TUBE
Covent Garden, Leicester Square

CREDIT CARDS
AE, EC, MC, V

RATES
Single £55–75; double £65–90; triple £105; Continental or English breakfast included; 48-hour cancellation policy enforced

As my Scottish auntie used to say, "You never know what's 'round the corner, dear, until you look." I am glad I kept looking "'round the corner" in this high-priced neck of the London woods, determined to find another acceptable Cheap Sleep. The ten rooms at the Seven Dials Hotel don't offer all the amenities of the big-spender neighbor down the block, which has tabs in the high triple digits, but they do offer clean, cut-rate Cheap Sleeps for those coming to London to concentrate on the theater. The building is old and narrow and there are stairs to climb, but the small rooms are just fine if you are looking for a safe crash pad between curtain calls. In your room, where everything matches, you can brew a cup of tea, call your friends anywhere in the world, or watch the BBC news reports on the telly. Your choice of an English or Continental breakfast is included, and so is the friendly charm of Hanna, the sweet Polish girl who oversees the running of the hotel.

FACILITIES AND SERVICES: Central heat, direct-dial phones, hair dryer and iron available, office safe, tea and coffeemakers, TV, no lift

SW1

Belgravia, Knightsbridge, Pimlico, Victoria, Westminster, and Whitehall

Belgravia is owned by the Duke of Westminster, perhaps the richest man in England. It is no wonder, then, that Belgravia has the most expensive real estate in London, especially around Eaton Square, where two or three million pounds for a fixer-upper is considered a bargain. Ebury Street, one of London's better B&B streets, is on the edge of Eaton Square. Mozart lived at 180 Ebury Street and composed his first symphony here. Noël Coward lived for twenty-five years with his mother at 111 Ebury Street in what is now the Noël Coward Hotel (see page 125). There are some good restaurants and charming small pubs in this area (see *Cheap Eats in London*).

Knightsbridge is another top-drawer address where residents can shop at Harrods and the even more expensive and exclusive Harvey Nichols, gaze longingly at the designer boutiques on Sloane Street, and browse through the tempting shops along Beauchamp Place.

Other than the Tate Gallery, a strip of antiques shops along Pimlico Road, Princess Margaret's son Lord David Linley's design shop, and a cluster of shops around Warwick Way, Pimlico does not have tourist sites drawing crowds of visitors. Belgrave Road features an expanse of terraced town homes, many of which house a variety of Cheap Sleeping B&Bs, most of which are definitely not included in this book.

Victoria hasn't much to recommend it, other than the massive Victoria Station, through which every visitor to London probably passes at least once. If you are leaving London via coach (on the bus), you will leave from the Victoria Coach Station, about a five-minute walk from the Victoria rail and tube station. Restaurants in this area are geared mainly toward the hungry onetime tourist, so you know they are basically terrible.

Westminster and Whitehall are devoted to running the country. In Westminster you will set your watch according to Big Ben; visit the Houses of Parliament and Westminster Abbey, the burial site of many historical figures; and tour the Cabinet War Rooms used by Winston Churchill and his generals during World War II.

Two of the most famous addresses in the world are here: No. 10 Downing Street, home of the British prime minister, and Buckingham Palace. You can't even get close to No. 10 Downing Street, but you can to Buckingham Palace when you witness the famous Changing of the Guard, or in August, when the queen is away and the doors are opened to the paying public.

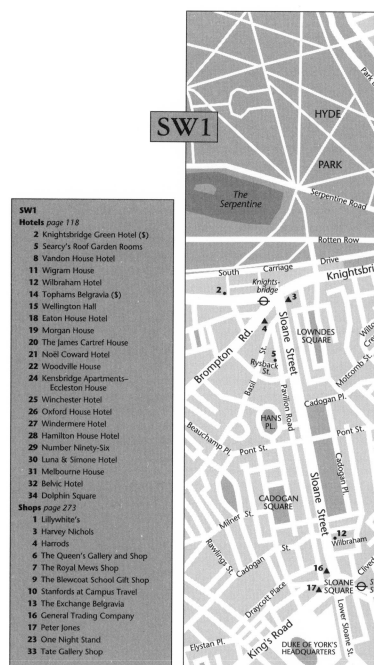

SW1

HYDE PARK

MAYFAIR

The Serpentine

Park St.
South Audley St.
Mount Street
Farm St.
Park Lane
Park Lane
Curzon Street
Brick
Piccadilly
Serpentine Road
Rotten Row
Hyde Park Corner
HYDE PARK CORNER
Duke of Well. Place
Knightsbridge
Grosvenor Place
South Carriage Drive
Knights-bridge
Brompton Rd.
Sloane Street
LOWNDES SQUARE
Wilton Crescent
Halkin St.
Chapel St.
Basil St.
Rysback St.
Motcomb St.
BELGRAVE SQUARE
Upper Belgrave St.
HANS PL.
Pavilion Road
Cadogan Pl.
Belgrave Place
Beauchamp Pl.
Pont St.
Pont St.
Cadogan Pl.
Lowndes Pl.
Eaton
King's Rd.
Lyall St.
CADOGAN SQUARE
Sloane Street
Milner St.
St.
EATON SQUARE
BELGRAVE
Eccleston
Elizabeth St.
Ebury Mews
Rawlings St. Cadogan
12 Wilbraham
King's Rd
Eaton Gate S. Eaton Place
Eaton Terrace
Chester Row
Draycott Place
16
17 SLOANE SQUARE
SLOANE SQUARE Sloane Square
Cliveden Pl.
18 EBURY PL.
19 20
21
23 22
Pimlico Rd.
Ebury
Ebury Br.
St.
Lower Sloane St.
Elystan Pl.
King's Road
DUKE OF YORK'S HEADQUARTERS
Smith Ter.
St. Leonard's Ter.
Royal Hospital Road
Chelsea Bridge Road
Ranelagh Gro.
Ebury Bridge Road
Ormond
RANELAGH GARDENS
Christchurch St. Gate
Chelsea Gate

0   220 yds
1/8 mile

N

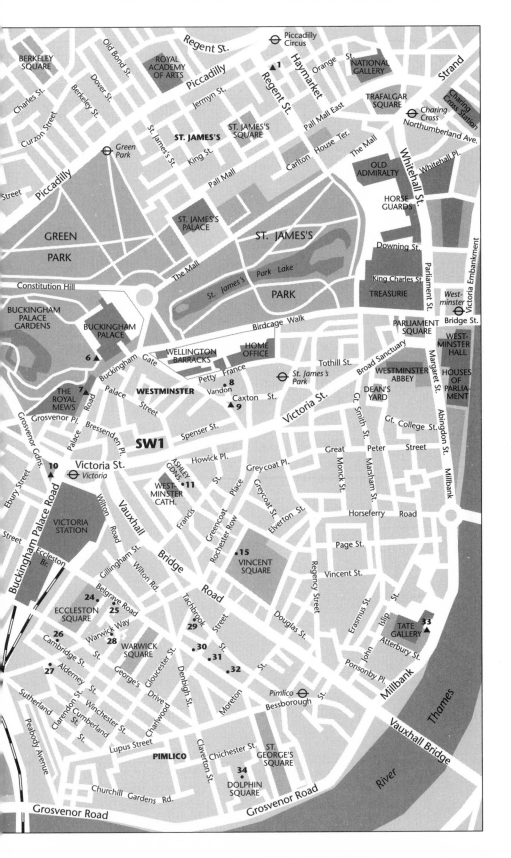

HOTELS in SW1

OTHER OPTIONS

Apartment Rentals

Bed and Breakfast in a Private Home

Student Dormitories

($) indicates a Big Splurge

BELVIC HOTEL (32)
105 Belgrave Road, SW1
14 rooms, 8 with shower, none with toilet

The Belvic Hotel's business card contains the promise "terms moderate." That should be corrected to "terms positively philanthropic"! Not only are they low to start, but they get even lower the longer you stay.

Mr. and Mrs. Coleman have the cheapest Cheap Sleep going on Belgrave Road, an area filled with dirt-bag hotels where charm, cleanliness, and comfort are not the mottoes of most of the absentee owners. When I asked Mrs. Coleman how long she had owned the Belvic, she said, "Too long." Then she told me the building itself is more than 250 years old, and that she had the house blessed 36 years ago, so there was my answer.

At the Belvic, space in spades will be yours in rooms large enough to entertain twenty of your closest friends. You won't have to apologize for a shabby clutter of exhausted reject furniture holding snoozing cats, or floral wallpaper competing for color dominance with garish drapes and multipatterned carpets. No, you will be pleased with a clean room in quiet but hardly coordinated colors, your own TV, and a decent bed. Each room has a sink and some have a shower booth as well, but toilets are communal. In the morning, Mrs. Coleman will cook you a sturdy English breakfast, using eggs from free-range chickens, and serve it to you in her breakfast room with freshly pressed brown and white tablecloths.

FACILITIES AND SERVICES: Central heat, no private phones, office safe, TV, no lift, desk open 7:30 A.M.– 11 P.M.

TELEPHONE
020-7821-0813
TUBE
Pimlico
CREDIT CARDS
None; cash only
RATES
Single £30; double £45; triple £60; lower rates for longer stays; English breakfast included

EATON HOUSE HOTEL (18)
125 Ebury Street, SW1
10 rooms, 5 with shower or bath and toilet

If you stay in an Ebury Street B&B, chances are you will encounter noise in front-facing rooms and some uninspiring views in the quieter rooms along the back. Some visitors overlook these drawbacks in favor of a genuinely friendly owner of a small and tidy B&B who treats her guests like family. A stay at Eaton House means just that. Owner Josephine Belgrano and her daughters Anabel and Maria have been treating their devoted guests like long-lost relatives for thirty years. All of the rooms are painted white and kept clean. Each

TELEPHONE
020-7730-8781
FAX
020-7730-6535
TUBE
Victoria, Sloane Square
CREDIT CARDS
AE, MC, V
RATES
Single £40–50; double £55–65; triple £70–85; lower winter rates; English breakfast included

has its own tea and coffeemaker and color television, in case you want to brew a cup of tea and catch up on your British telly programming. Private facilities have been added to five rooms, but if you are trying to cut costs, you can safely book a room without a private bathroom—the hall toilet and tiled communal bath facilities (on alternate floors) are some of the best of any B&B on the entire street. Breakfast is served piping hot each morning in a room with green and white cushioned chairs and shared tables, where guests swap shopping discoveries and restaurant tips. Both Anabel and Maria are former London tour guides and are happy to help plan your days in London.

FACILITIES AND SERVICES: Central heat, hall phone, hair dryer and iron available, office safe, tea and coffeemakers, TV, office safe, no lift, desk open 7:30 A.M.–11 P.M.

HAMILTON HOUSE HOTEL (28)
60 Warwick Way, SW1
40 rooms, all with shower or bath and toilet

TELEPHONE
020-7821-7113

FAX
020-7630-0806

EMAIL
hamiltonhhotel.demon.co.uk

TUBE
Victoria

CREDIT CARDS
MC, V

RATES
Single £75; double £85; triple £110; ask for lower off-season rates; English breakfast included

The 150-year-old Victorian building has its limitations, but for the Cheap Sleeper who doesn't demand anything more than a functional room with space-saving built-in furniture and private facilities, the Hamilton House should do. Most of the rooms have no views to speak of, and those on the front are noisy and lacking in any security. To avoid this, request something on the back side of the third floor, which has the advantage of being quiet. When reserving, I also recommend asking for a room with a tiled bath, not one with an airless portable metal unit placed in a corner of the room. The hotel is clean . . . and that counts. So does the big cooked breakfast to get you going each morning and the plans afoot to install a lift and redecorate some rooms.

FACILITIES AND SERVICES: Central heat, direct-dial phones, hair dryer, office safe, satellite TV, tea and coffeemakers, no lift, 24-hour desk, ten nonsmoking rooms

THE JAMES CARTREF HOUSE (20)
108/129 Ebury Street, SW1
James House: 9 rooms, 3 with shower or bath and toilet
Cartref House: 11 rooms, 8 with shower or bath and toilet

It would be hard to imagine a better London B&B than the two-in-one James Cartref House on Ebury Street run by Derek and Sharon James, energetic hosts who are adept at making everyone feel right at home. After a stay with the James family in either of their two B&Bs, you will undoubtedly join the many Cheap Sleepers who have come before you, returning each time you are in London.

Ranking high on my list of top budget bets in London, these two small hotels reflect the couple's dedication to the needs of their guests, who receive the kind of attention seldom seen in this busy, impersonal world. They have now taken the bold step (one that's appreciated by many) and declared their B&Bs to be completely nonsmoking. Hurray!

Both Sharon and Derek take tremendous pride in keeping everything in tip-top condition by repainting, refinishing, and redecorating whenever necessary. The addition of a glass conservatory breakfast room at the James House has been such a success that one is planned for the Cartref House across the street. At the Cartref House, each floor has its own color scheme, with the differently decorated rooms designed to give guests a sense of cozy comfort. In the nine-room James House, each room is individually done in a different color scheme. The sense of coziness in them all is achieved by Sharon's use of simple and sweet fabrics that are coordinated with the carpeting, color of the walls, and the window treatments. Cheap Sleeping families will appreciate the low rates, large rooms (some with bunk beds), and proximity to the Victoria train, bus, and tube station. If you arrive via British Air at Gatwick, the train whisks you from the airport directly to Victoria for a fraction of the taxi fare and in half the time a bus ride takes.

NOTE: If the James Cartref House is fully booked, try the Fairways Hotel, run by Derek's sister, Jenny, and her husband, Steve Adams (see page 66).

FACILITIES AND SERVICES: Central heat, hall phone, hair dryer available, no lift or safe, tea and coffeemakers, TV, no smoking allowed, desk open 7 A.M.–10 P.M.

TELEPHONE
020-7730-7338 (James House);
020-7730-6176 (Cartref House)

FAX
020-7730-7338

EMAIL
jandchouse@c.s.com

TUBE
Victoria, Sloane Square

CREDIT CARDS
AE, MC, V

RATES
Single £50–60; double £70–80; triple £85–95; family room £115–135; English breakfast included. These rates apply to both houses.

KNIGHTSBRIDGE GREEN HOTEL (2, $)
159 Knightsbridge, SW1
28 rooms, all with shower or bath and toilet

TELEPHONE
020-7584-6274
FAX
020-7225-1635
EMAIL
theKGHotel@aol.com
TUBE
Knightsbridge
CREDIT CARDS
AE, DC, MC, V
RATES
Single £100–105; double
£135–145; suite £160–175;
lower off-season rates subject to
availability; express breakfast
£4, Continental breakfast £6,
English breakfast £10

"I can't wait to come back!" wrote one contented guest. Another described the Knightsbridge Green as "intimate, elegant, and warm." I am equally enthusiastic about this special hotel, especially after inspecting it again for the fourth edition of *Cheap Sleeps in London*. New for guests this time around is a modem in each room, a smart ground-floor lounge with a sleek L-shaped sofa accented by royal blue chairs, and a no-smoking policy enforced throughout the entire hotel.

The area known as Knightsbridge epitomizes classic fashionable London, and this wonderful hotel fits the image perfectly. It is situated adjacent to Hyde Park, and is within easy bag-carrying distance of Harrods, Harvey Nichols, and the designer boutiques lining Sloane Street and Beauchamp Place.

From the outside, it resembles many other London townhouse hotels. However, the minute you walk into the sea green entryway and step up to the marble reception desk, you know that this hotel is several notches above the rest. Director Tim Marler opened the hotel in 1967, and began a tradition of quality and service he and his friendly staff uphold to this day. The rooms, most of which are spacious suites, are exquisitely planned in decorator colors, have enough storage space for you to stay almost forever, and offer marble baths with power showers and plenty of daylight. Number 32, done in burgundy, has tartan drapes framing five curved windows and a romantic sleigh bed. The long wall of closets separating the sitting room and bedroom will house a season's worth of clothes.

If I am alone, I ask for No. 42, a warm, sunny room with Jane Churchill's "fat animals" print draperies at the three windows and a super bathroom where I can spread out, or No. 46, on the back, with a turquoise faux finish on the desk and dressing table. If there are two of you, ask for No. 43, a two-room suite with adobe-colored walls and a peek at Hyde Park, or No. 24, with a bay window and sofa in the sitting room and a large bedroom facing the back to ensure calm and quiet.

In the smartly attired Club Room you can read the daily papers while sipping a hot or cold drink. Breakfast, which you order the night before, is specially prepared for you and served in the comfort and privacy of your room.

FACILITIES AND SERVICES: Air-conditioning, central heat, direct-dial phones, hair dryers, laundry service, lift, modems, room safe, no-smoking allowed, satellite TV, tea and coffeemakers, trouser press, desk open 7:30 A.M.–10:30 P.M.

LUNA & SIMONE HOTEL (30)
47–49 Belgrave Road, SW1
36 rooms, 27 with shower or bath and toilet

Belgrave Road is a good location if Victoria Station plays heavily in your London plans. However, the street is loaded with grubby little B&Bs catering to determined but budget-tied travelers of all nationalities, and it's all too easy to get stuck in a dump. To avoid that, head for one of the best selections on the street: the Luna & Simone Hotel, owned for thirty years by twin brothers Peter and Bernard Desira. The modern reception area has a curved desk backed by four clocks showing the time in New York, London, Tokyo, and Sydney. Keeping pace with the modern theme are two downstairs breakfast rooms with wraparound banquette seating, recessed lighting, and a no-smoking policy. The noise in rooms on the street will drive insomniacs mad, and those on the back have uninspiring views. But—and this is important—this very well maintained family-run hotel provides friendly accommodations consisting of a clean bed in a nonsmoking room (if requested), double-locked doors, your own TV, and a substantial English breakfast to all monetarily constrained Cheap Sleepers.

FACILITIES AND SERVICES: Central heat, direct-dial phones, hair dryers, office safe, some nonsmoking rooms, TV, no lift, desk open 7 A.M.–11 P.M.

TELEPHONE
020-7834-5897
FAX
020-7828-2474
TUBE
Pimlico, Victoria
CREDIT CARDS
MC, V
RATES
Single £30–45; double £44–70; triple £70–85; lower rates in off-season; English breakfast included

MELBOURNE HOUSE (31)
79 Belgrave Road, SW1
16 rooms, 14 with shower or bath and toilet

When you look up and down Belgrave Road, all you see are signs for the numerous B&Bs that line both sides. These rooms range from cheap and cheerful to down-and-out dirty and depressing. Melbourne House falls into the cheap and cheerful category, thanks to the enthusiastic owners, John and Manuela Desira, whose cousins operate the Luna & Simone down the street (see

TELEPHONE
020-7828-3516
FAX
020-7828-7120
TUBE
Pimlico, Victoria
CREDIT CARDS
MC, V

RATES
Single £35–55; double £75;
triple £95; family room £110;
English or Continental
breakfast included

above). All sixteen exceptionally clean and whitewashed rooms are the same, with hot-pink chenille spreads, burgundy carpets, and brownish curtains. Laminated knotty-pine furniture and tiled baths with stall showers behind glass doors make housekeeping easy, as does the fact that the rooms are small and have limited or nonexistent seating space. The worst example of this is No. 5, nothing more than a small sleeping cubicle with no space for even a table. The double-glazed windows in front drown out the incessant traffic noise that starts at 0-dark-hundred and goes until the wee hours; and wardrobes are there for a few hanging clothes. No smoking is allowed in any of the bedrooms. You are invited to watch cable TV or plug in a video in the lounge.

NOTE: At press time, plans were being made to have two nonsmoking luxury flats nearby with prices starting in the neighborhood of £75 per night—which is a bargain rate, especially if you're traveling with a family. Be sure to inquire if this interests you.

FACILITIES AND SERVICES: Central heat, direct-dial phones, free luggage storage, office safe, TV, tea and coffeemakers, no lift, no smoking, desk open 7:30 A.M.–midnight

MORGAN HOUSE (19)
120 Ebury Street, SW1
11 rooms, 3 with shower or bath and toilet

TELEPHONE
020-7730-2384
FAX
020-7730-8442
TUBE
Victoria, Sloane Square
CREDIT CARDS
MC, V
RATES
Single £45; double £70–85;
triple £90–95; quad £105;
English breakfast included

Rachel Joplin and Ian Berry are the friendly owners of two B&Bs on Ebury Street: this one and the Woodville, a little farther along the road (see page 133). For a small operation, the entryway at Morgan House is indeed grand, with a crystal chandelier hanging over white wainscoted walls with gold floral wallpaper on top. The miniature breakfast room is brightly outfitted in yellow and blue with a pine buffet. Rooms are more than you would expect for the price, offering an imaginative blend of mirrors, a black marble fireplace or two, and a smattering of antiques and metal bed frames added for spice. Bits and pieces of contemporary furniture, à la Pier One or Cost Plus, round out the picture. If you like noise, Rooms 3 and 7 are full of it, but it's better to request other rooms—perhaps No. 2, a basic double with some space; Room B, on the back, with a little fireplace, twin beds, and shared facilities; or No. 9, the family room with a new white-tiled bathroom. Avoid at all costs Room A, on the street, with zip in the security department.

While singles don't have private facilities, you can rent a double (with bathroom) as a single for £70.

FACILITIES AND SERVICES: Electric heat, no private phones, hair dryer available and in some rooms, office safe, TV, tea and coffeemakers, no lift, desk open 7:30 A.M.– 10 P.M.

NOËL COWARD HOTEL (21)
111 Ebury Street, SW1
14 rooms, 6 with shower, none with toilet

From 1917 until 1930, actor and playwright Sir Noël Coward occupied the first two floors of this house, which belonged to his mother, who ran it as a boardinghouse. She lived in the bungalow that is still in back of the hotel with a garden beyond it, the servants lived in what is now the basement dining room, and Noël Coward had his room on the first floor (now No. 3 Piccadilly). After he moved out to much grander quarters, his mother sold the property, and since then a series of proprietors have run it as a B&B of varying quality. Now, thanks to owner Mark dos Santos, the fourteen rooms, all named after tube stops in central London, are recommendable for Cheap Sleepers. Fancy and large they are not . . . serviceable and clean they are. Victoria, facing front, has two double beds, a shower, washbasin, television, and minibar. In Covent Gardens and Piccadilly you will find a marble fireplace and original bookshelf but no chairs. For stair climbers, Wimbledon, almost to the top, has twin beds but no sitting space. Because some of the hall bathrooms are unheated in winter, it would be wise to request a room with its own shower, even if they are what I call "phone booths" in the corner of the room. For theatergoers, the hotel can book tickets, and offers theater promotions that give two tickets for the price of one for popular West End shows selected monthly by the hotel.

FACILITIES AND SERVICES: Individual room heating, laundry service, some minibars, office safe, secretarial service and mobile phones on request, advance arrangements can be made for guests to be met at Heathrow Airport, tea and coffeemakers, TV, theater promotions and bookings, no lift

TELEPHONE
020-7730-2094

FAX
020-7730-8697

EMAIL
a.hill@ic.ac.uk

TUBE
Victoria, Sloane Square

CREDIT CARDS
AE, DC, MC, V

RATES
Single £45–55; double £65–75; triple £95

OXFORD HOUSE HOTEL (26)
92–94 Cambridge Street, SW1
17 rooms, none with shower or bath and toilet

TELEPHONE
020-7834-6467/9681

FAX
020-7834-0225

TUBE
Victoria

CREDIT CARDS
MC, V to guarantee reservation
(5 percent surcharge if bill is
paid by credit card)

RATES
Single £36–38; double £46–50;
triple £60–65; quad £80–85;
English breakfast included

If you want a clean, family sort of place to stay, this could be your spot. All rooms have American-style wallpaper reasonably color coordinated with the curtains. The chenille spreads blend in most of the time and so do the carpets. The owners, Mr. and Mrs. Kader, live at the hotel with their two grown sons, pet rabbits, a whistling bird (who does "Jingle Bells"), and two cats—a fat one called Mr. China, who had his tail amputated, and Keyser, with a tail, who thinks he is a part-time bunny. Before going to his office in the morning, Mr. Kader prepares breakfast in the open kitchen just off their downstairs dining room. During the day, Mrs. Kader is at the desk, managing the hotel and making sure guests' needs are met. Over the years I have watched their boys grow from little chaps in short pants to one now an engineering graduate from Imperial College and married and another ready to enter university and study law. I like the family atmosphere here, and especially the Kaders' commitment to their hotel and to each person who stays with them. If you like this sort of homespun lodging, send your one-night deposit soon. While you must guarantee your first night with a credit card when booking, avoid using your credit card to pay your bill at the hotel, as there will be a 5-percent surcharge.

FACILITIES AND SERVICES: Central heat, hall phones, hair dryer available, TV in lounge, no safe, no lift, desk open 7 A.M.–10 P.M.

SEARCY'S ROOF GARDEN ROOMS (5)
30 Pavilion Road, SW1
11 rooms, 2 flats; all with shower or bath and toilet

TELEPHONE
020-7584-4921

FAX
020-7823-8694

TUBE
Knightsbridge

CREDIT CARDS
AE, DC, MC, V

RATES
Single £90–110; double £130;
suite £160 for two, £135 for
one; apartment £200 per night;
extra bed £15 per night;
Continental breakfast included
in hotel rate only

As the saying goes, you can't tell a book by its cover. Truer words were never spoken when it comes to this sleeping beauty only a heartbeat and credit card toss from Harrods, the designer boutiques along Sloane Street, and all of exclusive Knightsbridge. You arrive in front of an unassuming white building with a green door. You must press the buzzer by the door to be let in, then ride a red freight elevator to the third floor, where you will step into the comfortable world of Searcy's Roof Garden Rooms, a surprisingly peaceful London oasis owned and operated by Searcy's, one of London's finest catering firms. Each room is elegantly and individually designed, the service is impeccable, and the price considerably less than most hotels in the area. All rooms are nonsmoking and beautifully furnished, with pretty fabrics and a collection of antiques you wish you could sneak home with you. Some rooms have canopy beds; others have sitting alcoves. A few of the rooms with baths are just that—a bathtub is right in the room, not in a separate bathroom. You are just going to have to trust me on this: Everything fits right in and you *will* like it. A special room is No. 15, with a forest mural wrapping from the bedroom into the bathroom. Number 7 is a comfortable double with lots of space, especially in the bathroom, with a stretch tub and mirrored wall. Pink and very feminine are the words to describe room No. 14, with a mural, tiled bath, and stall shower. Room 9, with a purple spring flower motif, is pictured on the brochure, and No. 5, with a sofa bed, comfortable wing chairs in a small lounge, end-to-end twins, and the bathtub in the room, is the only suite. A Continental breakfast, which includes yogurt, cereals, boiled egg, toast, and croissants, is included, and it will be served in the comfort of your own room. There is a sunny roof garden for guests, and the large kitchen is open to those who want to fix a cup of tea or store snacks in the refrigerator.

If your stay is longer or you need more room, *one* of their two flats is worth consideration. The first is on Brompton Road, and so desperately in need of a total renovation that it is out of the question until totally revamped and soundproofed. However, the second flat, on Beaufort Gardens, is completely recommended, provided you can be happy in a basement (lower ground floor) setting. It offers a sitting room, two bedrooms, a little terrace, a washer and dryer, and a small but fully fitted kitchen. You will never feel gypped by excessive add-on charges when dialing your friends and business colleagues, because the telephone is a pay phone that accepts credit cards and telephone cards.

FACILITIES AND SERVICES: Electric heat, ceiling fans, pay phones, laundry service, hair dryer, lift (but not to fourth floor), room service for breakfast only, office safe, TV, tea and coffeemaking privileges, some trouser presses, 24-hour desk, no smoking allowed in the hotel or flats

TOPHAMS BELGRAVIA (14, $)
28 Ebury Street, SW1
39 rooms, 37 with shower or bath and toilet

TELEPHONE
020-7730-8147
FAX
020-7823-5966
EMAIL
Tophams_Belgravia@
compuserve.com
INTERNET
www.tophams.com
TUBE
Victoria
CREDIT CARDS
AE, DC, MC, V
RATES
Single £120; double £130–160;
triple £170; cancellations must
be made at least 48 hours prior
to date of intended arrival or
there will be a one-night room
charge; off-season package rates
on request; English breakfast
included

How do I love Tophams Belgravia? I can't begin to count the ways. Behind the long success of this lovely hotel, wrapped in understated elegance and discreet British good taste, are three generations of the Topham family. Currently run by Marianne Topham and her husband, Nicholas Kingsford, the hotel has earned a worldwide reputation for caring for guests, who return year after year. Marianne Topham's artistic background is impressive. Her great-great-grandfather, noted artist F. W. Topham, was a contemporary and friend of Charles Dickens and also illustrated some of his work. Marianne studied art at the Byam School of Art and, having worked with many prominent interior designers and architects, including Nina Campbell, David Hicks, and Christopher Smallwood, has developed into one of England's best-known visual artists. In addition to her beautiful decoration of the entire hotel, guests are also treated to displays of her lovely oils and watercolors, which are available for purchase.

The individually created bedrooms in the five adjoining buildings have the friendly feel of a country home, with flowery Colefax and Fowler fabrics, little sitting alcoves where guests can take tea or read a newspaper, loads of family antiques, and a dedicated staff that has been with the hotel for decades. While the rates dictate that your stay will be a Big Splurge, there is usually a package of some sort on offer during the off-season. For example, there might be a Theater Break in January and February that requires reserving any of the double rooms for three nights. Guests will receive a complimentary dinner for two in their restaurant and a performance of their choice (subject to availability) for a West End theater production followed by a glass of champagne.

The comfort of each guest is always the primary consideration. Bedrooms are furnished in the genteel style of an old-fashioned home, with attention to the details that transform an impersonal hotel room into a pleasing temporary residence: a pretty plate hanging on the wall, a framed lithograph, a Limoges vase filled with spring flowers. With thirty-nine outstanding rooms, it is almost impossible to select a favorite (though two of the rooms have hall bathrooms, they are completely private to those rooms). However, some stand out, such as No. 9, with a tiny room sink and a canopy bed; it was the favorite of Sir Michael Redgrave when he stayed at the hotel in his early theater days. It is a quiet room, with soft chairs and French floral prints on the bed pillows, canopy, and drapes. New and slightly more expensive are the seven mews rooms on the lower ground floor. They are a sterling example of how to use otherwise wasted space and transform it into rooms filled with charm and appeal. Mews 5 is tucked into the old cellars and decorated in pink and white stripes. There is no real view, but no one seems to mind. In Mews 4 you will sleep in a four-poster bed, and in Mews 2, a popular triple, there is a separate room with a twin bed—ideal for a small family with one child or to use as a sitting room. Another popular family room is No. 39, with a separate sleeping loft under a sloping roof that is a favorite with children. If you are a man traveling alone, request No. 17, which was especially decorated for an American guest who visits London frequently. The theme of the room is cricket, carried out by hanging cricket bats, trophies, and a series of black-and-white photos of the man's school days. An interesting room for some might be No. 15, a small double, or perfect single, with a direct view of Margaret Thatcher's London townhouse.

Lunch and dinner are served Monday through Saturday in a streetside restaurant, or downstairs in the Tophams Bar daily. The menu runs from simple sandwiches to three-course meals, all well prepared and served with care. Guests of the hotel become automatic members of Tophams Club, a private club in the hotel where members gather for drinks and substantial snacks in congenial surroundings.

Another *very* special feature of this extraordinary hotel is Jennifer Dorn. Ms. Dorn is a noted travel authority on Great Britain, and she runs her own consulting business in New York. As a complimentary favor of the hotel to its American guests, the services of Ms. Dorn are included. When your reservation is confirmed, she will telephone you and, if you wish, help you to organize your trip to London or anywhere else you might be traveling in the U.K. Even if you don't stay at Tophams Belgravia, please consider using her services. When you think of what you could save in time, energy, and money on costly mistakes, it is worth the investment toward a better trip. You can contact her by writing, calling, or faxing her at: Oh, To Be in England, 2 Charlton Street, New York, NY 10014; tel: 212-255-8739; fax: 212-252-0157; email: rldorn1@aol.com.

FACILITIES AND SERVICES: Membership in Tophams Club during stay, central heat, direct-dial phones, hair dryer, laundry service, lift, restaurant and room service, office safe, satellite TV, tea and coffeemakers

VANDON HOUSE HOTEL (8)
1 Vandon Street, SW1
35 rooms, 17 with shower or bath and toilet

TELEPHONE
020-7799-6780
FAX
020-7799-1464
TUBE
St. James's Park
CREDIT CARDS
AE, DC, MC, V
RATES
Single £38–48; double £60–75; triple £110; quad £140 (see deposit requirements); English breakfast included
MISCELLANEOUS
The hotel is closed from December 24 to January 2. Deposits: When a reservation is accepted by the hotel, a deposit of £10 per person per week or part thereof is required. If the reservation is canceled, the deposit is forfeited. There is a maximum stay of 28 nights.

Any Cheap Sleeper knows that there is a shortage of rooms in London for under £80 per night that are not geared for those with youth on their side and a pack on their back. One line of thinking at the London Tourist Board is that new hotels should be targeted toward the needs of rich visitors, and let the chips (or beds) fall where they may for the less wealthy. Obviously, the board has overestimated the wide-ranging appeal of a £375-a-night hotel room . . . breakfast extra.

Hello, Vandon House!

For thirty years this hotel served as the Salvation Army's headquarters and as a charity for down-and-outers needing a free bed and meal. After a few face-lifts and a recent radical renovation, the hotel is now an unpretentious budget hotel for those seeking honest value in a key London location. Because it is under the auspices of the Salvation Army, some strict rules are enforced, which make it unappealing to those determined to vacation in London's fast track. For starters, there is no smoking and no liquor allowed on the premises. The reception desk is staffed by a congenial crew that still keeps an eagle eye out for anything unbecoming to the hotel and its valued clientele. The hotel is far from lavish, naturally, but it is neat as a pin, with meticulously cared for rooms that will bring back memories of college dorms with their utilitarian furnishings. Space is one of their virtues, especially in the bathrooms, which in some cases are bigger than a few hotel rooms I could mention, and unfortunately have had to endure.

FACILITIES AND SERVICES: Central heat, conference facilities, direct-dial phones, hair dryer and iron available, laundry service, lift, office safe, restaurant, TV, tea and coffeemakers, trouser press in some rooms, 24-hour desk, photocopying and fax facilities, no smoking and no liquor allowed

WILBRAHAM HOTEL (12)
1 Wilbraham Place, SW1
52 rooms, all with shower or bath and toilet

Those who remember visiting their grandmother in a big Victorian home with lots of small, meandering rooms will be able to picture this bastion of traditional British decorum, where almost nothing has changed since the days when the sun never set on the British Empire. With a staff straight out of central casting, this well-known hotel offers a top location off Sloane Square. It would be nice if some of the rooms were combined to create more space, but management foresees no more radical changes than *maybe* redecorating a few rooms each year. They haven't even embraced the concept of accepting credit cards or including the 17½ percent VAT into either their room or breakfast rates. Email, Internet, computer modems . . . my goodness gracious, no! How quaint it all is—hardly the stuff twenty-first-century hotel operations are all about. And this seems to be the cachet that endears it to its loyal fans, who have been coming here since childhood and are now back with their grandchildren . . . and all having a great time.

The mostly frumpy rooms are filled with antiques of varying degrees of quality and other furnishings with that "rescue-me" look. This isn't to say the hotel is over the hill, but in my opinion, it is certainly right on the edge. If you need a large room, reserve one of the four suites or a deluxe twin. The double-bedded rooms are quite small, especially if you have large pieces of luggage. Numbers 1 or 26 are better choices for a long stay. Number 1 is a ground-floor deluxe twin with lovely wood paneling, a fireplace, a sofa and two easy chairs, leaded windows, and a big bathroom with heated towel racks. Number 26 has a bay window, somewhat coordinated fabrics, and a small sitting area with a desk. The bathroom has a tub and a handheld shower. I would nix No. 2, which wins my ugliest-bathroom-tile award with its beyond hideous daisy flower design.

Breakfast, which is extra, is brought to your room, but lunch and dinner are served in a paneled dining room on the main floor. The food is not gourmet but tried-and-true English fare guaranteed to stick to your ribs.

FACILITIES AND SERVICES: Bar (closed Sundays and holidays), portable electric heaters, direct-dial phones, hair dryer, two lifts, office safe, restaurant (Mon–Sat lunch and dinner, sandwiches on Sun), room service, TV

TELEPHONE
020-7730-8296

FAX
020-7730-6815

TUBE
Sloane Square

CREDIT CARDS
None; cash only

RATES
Single £75–85; double £95–110; deluxe twin from £125; extra bed £20; crib £8; Continental breakfast £5 extra, English breakfast £7 extra. *Note:* All prices, including breakfast, are exclusive of VAT of 17½ percent, which will be added to your bill.

WINCHESTER HOTEL (25)
17 Belgrave Road, SW1
18 rooms, 4 flats; all with shower or bath and toilet

TELEPHONE
020-7828-2972
FAX
020-7828-5191
TUBE
Victoria
CREDIT CARDS
None; cash only
RATES
No singles, 1–2 people £75;
triple £105; family room £120.
Flats (no children under 12 in
any flats, 4–5-night minimum
stay): 1 bedroom £95 per night,
2 bedroom for 4 people £190
per night (all flats have daily
maid service and linen change);
English breakfast included for
both hotel and flat guests
MISCELLANEOUS
Closed on Christmas Day

If you are a Cheap Sleeper looking for a bed for the night with bacon, eggs, and beans on your breakfast plate in the morning, you are in the right place on Belgrave Road, a long bottom-budget hotel strip leading from Victoria Station into Pimlico. Of course there are exceptions, and the Winchester Hotel is one of them. For those of you who prefer something more, Jimmy McGoldrick's hotel is a class act, offering all the benefits of a small hostelry that prides itself on the high standards of comfort and service expected by today's travelers. It is not cute and cozy, nor is it filled with English antiques and picture-postcard-perfect floral displays. However, it is well thought out, with acceptable color and fabric coordination and good maintenance. All rooms have an armchair, enough closet space, reading lights, and tiled private bathrooms with high-pressure showers, a real bonus for those tired of holding a limp nozzle with two weak squirts of water erratically spraying. If noise disturbs your sleeping patterns, avoid front-facing rooms. For guests looking for the space and independence of a private apartment, four fully equipped units display the same attention to detail as the hotel rooms. An added treat for both hotel and flat residents is the English breakfast, cooked personally for you by Jimmy in his stainless-steel kitchen.

FACILITIES AND SERVICES: Central heat, no private phones, TV, no lift, no safe, office open 6 A.M.–midnight

WINDERMERE HOTEL (27)
142–144 Warwick Way, SW1
23 rooms, 20 with shower or bath and toilet

TELEPHONE
020-7834-5163/5480
FAX
020-7630-8831
EMAIL
100773.1171@compuserve.com
TUBE
Victoria
CREDIT CARDS
AE, MC, V

Nick and Sylvia Hambi are a hardworking, friendly couple who take very good care of their guests. Just glance through their visitor's book at reception to see the comments from the contented travelers from around the world who stay here time and again.

Yes, the building is old, but it has an interesting history dating back to medieval England, when Warwick Way was called "The Abbot's Lane" because it was the road that connected Westminster Abbey with the abbot's residence, known as Abbott's Grange. The hotel stands at the point where the gate to the Abbott's Grange existed. The Victorian building now housing the hotel was constructed in 1857, and was known as the "Pimlico Rooms," the earliest B&B in the area.

During the past ten years that I have been including the Windermere Hotel in *Cheap Sleeps in London,* I have watched the hotel grow and improve by leaps and bounds. Nick is a go-getter who must lie awake nights devising ways to improve his twenty-three-room hotel, and he succeeds on every level. All the individually arranged and decorated rooms offer travelers up-to-the-minute benefits. In addition to color coordination, recessed lighting, satellite television, and a private safe, he has installed two modem sockets so you can check your email or go on the Internet. I like No. 25, done in sunny oranges, and No. 11, a floral-themed room with a king-size bed that can be split into twins if requested. Some rooms on the front are noisy. Double glazing on the windows helps, but if you are a light snoozer, get a room in the back. Bathrooms come with heated towel racks in most, hair dryers, and very good showerheads. I also like the fact that there is a restaurant, The Pimlico Room, that is open for dinner not only to hotel guests but to the neighborhood regulars. Each night there is a set-priced meal in addition to à la carte suggestions. This convenience pays dividends if you are trying to make an early curtain call, cannot face going out again after a hard day traipsing through London, or if you have tired and hungry children on your hands.

FACILITIES AND SERVICES: Bar and restaurant, central heat, direct-dial phones, hair dryer, two modems per room, public car park next door with special rates, room service, room safe, satellite TV, tea and coffeemakers, some trouser presses, no lift

RATES
Single £65–85; double £75–110; triple £120; quad £130; English breakfast included

MISCELLANEOUS
There is a 72-hour cancellation policy

WOODVILLE HOUSE (22)
107 Ebury Street, SW1
12 rooms, none with shower or bath and toilet

Ian Berry and Rachel Joplin own the Woodville House, which reminds me of comfy Olde England thanks to its creatively compacted rooms highlighted by almost and real antiques. Beyond the narrow Georgian entry are two breakfast rooms, accented by floor-to-ceiling gold-toned silk draperies and a view onto a garden wall. The house cat, Beasty, who has a definite preference for men, reigns supreme here and on the hotel patio.

TELEPHONE
020-7730-1048

FAX
020-7730-2574

TUBE
Victoria, Sloane Square

CREDIT CARDS
MC, V

RATES
Single £42; double £62; family rooms for 3–5 people from £80; English breakfast included

Room A, designed for families, is on the ground level. If you like warm and fuzzy, this is your room. Bunk beds help create more space, and the collection of teddy bears occupying a corner spot adds a welcoming touch. Family Room C is also home to related teddys and has access to the patio. I like No. 6, a twin with mini-coronets over the bed, a detailed ceiling, two miniature wing chairs, and wooden window shutters. The focal piece in this room is a Parisian Victorian morning clock. Another handsome clock, a copy of a Louis XIV timepiece, sits in No. 4, which also had a white and gold metal bed with a lace drape over it. The hotel is under the same ownership as the Morgan House, also on Ebury Street (see page 124).

FACILITIES AND SERVICES: Electric heat, hall phones, hair dryer available, TV, guest refrigerator and electric kettle, no lift, no safe, desk open 7 A.M.–11 P.M.

SW3

Chelsea

In the nineteenth century, Chelsea gained fame as London's Bohemia, where writers and artists lived, including Thomas Carlyle, George Eliot, Henry James, James Whistler, and Oscar Wilde. It is unlikely the area will ever again be an impoverished artists' colony because now it is one of the most desirable London neighborhoods, and one of the most costly. Chelsea is also where garden and flower enthusiasts from around the globe congregate in May for the dazzling Chelsea Flower Show. King's Road, starting at Sloane Square and lined with boutiques and restaurants, runs the length of Chelsea. When you are walking along, keep your eye out for the distinguished elderly gentlemen wearing smart dark blue and red uniforms and black hats. These are the well-loved Chelsea pensioners who live here and serve as the area's goodwill ambassadors. King's Road is one of London's most popular upmarket shopping destinations for everyone from preteens to thirty- or forty-somethings. Sloane Square is where you will rub cashmere-clad elbows with these Sloane Rangers, London's equivalent of yuppies and DINKS (Double Income, No Kids couples). You will find them out in full force on Saturdays around Peter Jones Department Store and browsing through Justin de Blanks' General Trading Company. As you wander down King's Road, take a few detours on some of the side streets, where you will see brightly painted mews houses with manicured postage-stamp gardens.

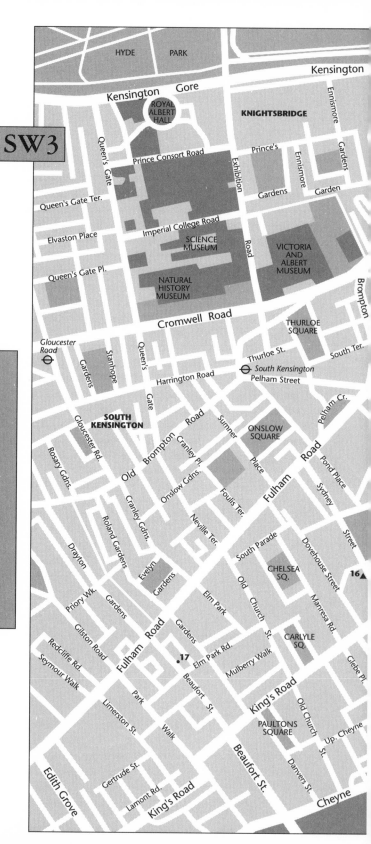

SW3

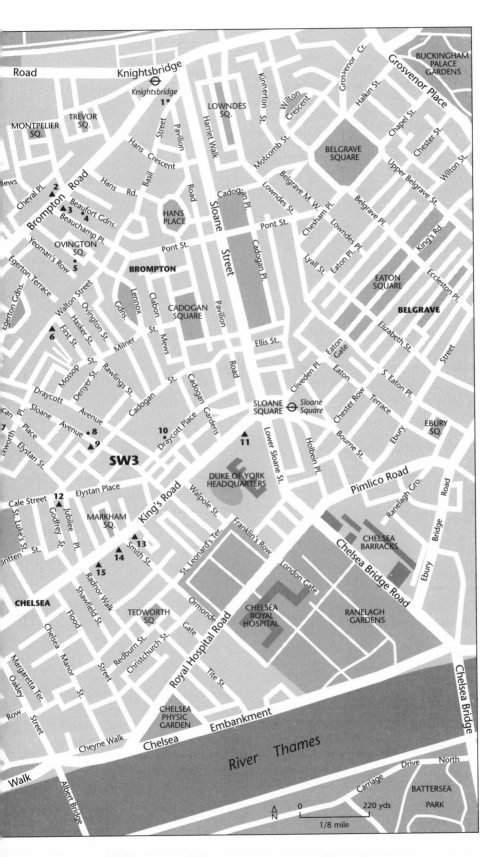

Road   Knightsbridge

Knightsbridge

1•

MONTPELIER SQ.

TREVOR SQ.

LOWNDES SQ.

Kinnerton St.

Wilton Crescent

Grosvenor Ct.

Grosvenor Place

BUCKINGHAM PALACE GARDENS

Halkin St.

Chapel St.

Chester St.

Upper Belgrave St.

Wilton St.

BELGRAVE SQUARE

Belgrave M. W.

Belgrave Pl.

Cheval Pl.   **2**▲

Mews

Brompton Road

Hans Rd.

Hans Crescent

Basil   Street

Pavilion   Road

Harriet Walk

Motcomb St.

Cadogan Pl.

Lowndes St.

Pont St.

Chesham Pl.

Lowndes Pl.

Eaton Pl.

King's Rd.

Eccleston Pl.

▲**3**   Beaufort Gdns.
▲   **4**

Beauchamp Pl.

OVINGTON SQ.

• **5**

HANS PLACE

Sloane   Street

Cadogan Pl.

Lyall St.

Eaton Pl.

EATON SQUARE

BELGRAVE

BROMPTON

Yeoman's Row

Egerton Terrace

Egerton Gdns.

Walton Street

Lennox Gdns.

Clabon St.

Milner St.

CADOGAN SQUARE

Pavilion Road

Ellis St.

Elizabeth St.

Street

Hasker St.

First St.   ▲**6**

Ovington St.

Cadogan Gardens

Eaton Pl.
Eaton Gate

Eaton Terrace

S. Eaton Pl.

Mossop St.

Denyer St.

Rawlings St.

Cadogan St.

St. Mews

Cadogan

Cliveden Pl.

Chester Row

EBURY SQ.

Draycott

Sloane

Avenue

ican Pl.

Place

Elystan St.

Avenue

• **8**
▲ **9**

10•
Draycott Place

SLOANE SQUARE   *Sloane Square*

Lower Sloane St.

Holbein Pl.

Eaton Square

Bourne St.

Ebury

Ebury

7

SW3

▲ **11**

DUKE OF YORK HEADQUARTERS

Pimlico Road

Ranelagh Gro.

Bridge

Road

Cale Street   ▲**12**

St. Luke's St.

ritten St.

Godfrey St.

Jubilee Pl.

Elystan Place

MARKHAM SQ.

▲ **13**

Smith St.

▲ **14**

▲ **15**

Radnor Walk

Shawfield St.

King's Road

Walpole St.

Franklin's Row

St. Leonard's Ter.

CHELSEA BARRACKS

Chelsea Bridge Road

Ebury

CHELSEA

Flood

Chelsea

Manor

Street

Redburn St.

Christchurch St.

TEDWORTH SQ.

Ormonde

Gate

London Gate

CHELSEA ROYAL HOSPITAL

RANELAGH GARDENS

Margaretta Ter.

Oakley

Row

Street

Cheyne Walk

CHELSEA PHYSIC GARDEN

Royal Hospital Road

Tite St.

Embankment

Chelsea

Chelsea Bridge

Walk

Albert Bridge

River   Thames

Drive   North

Carriage

BATTERSEA PARK

△ N   0   220 yds

1/8 mile

HOTELS in SW3

OTHER OPTIONS

($) indicates a Big Splurge

THE BASIL STREET HOTEL (1, $)
Basil Street, SW3
93 rooms, all with shower or bath and toilet

TELEPHONE
020-7581-3311

FAX
020-7581-3693

EMAIL
TheBasil@aol.com

INTERNET
www.absite.com/basil

TUBE
Knightsbridge

CREDIT CARDS
AE, DC, MC, V

RATES
Single £130; double £190; family room £260 (two bedrooms and one bath for two adults and up to three children); extra bed £20; Continental breakfast £8 extra, English breakfast £14 extra. Rack rates do not include 17½ percent VAT.

The Basil Street Hotel began when Mr. Charles Winslow-Taylor bought the hotel in 1910. During the twenties, extensive construction enabled Mr. Winslow-Taylor to realize his dream of creating a home away from home in the heart of Knightsbridge, one of London's most exclusive areas, and it remains family-owned, one among a handful of large London hotels that do not belong to a larger group or consortium. With two grand-daughters now at the helm, the Basil Street celebrates more than ninety years of providing a "hotel for people who don't like hotels." As one guest said, "I knew I would like the hotel when I arrived and discovered that my room, No. 278 I think, was on the third floor, and that No. 305 was on the second. You've got to love a hotel with that kind of disdain for conformity."

Throughout its long history, the hotel has adapted to more demanding standards of its faithful guests, but one essential quality remains unchanged: the style and personal service we remember from a more generous and gracious age. The staff's devotion to duty is remarkable. The three senior managers have more than one hundred years of service between them. Nine of the staff have served over twenty years, and twenty-seven more than ten years. The real service awards, however, go to the two Polish porters who arrived in 1949 and retired at ages eighty and eighty-four in 1993.

The hotel has the hospitable air of a spacious country home where you would like to live forever. Rooms and corridors are fitted with admirable examples of the family's lovely English furniture and collectibles, including pieces of Sheraton and Hepplewhite, and the largest collection of mezzotints in Great Britain. In the entrance hall is a magnificent lantern that once hung in the Duke of Norfolk's home in St. James's Square. If you look, you will see his crown, which is the hotel's logo. Each bedroom differs in size, shape, and decoration, but all meet every standard of quality, taste, and comfort any guest could ever want.

In 1971, a unique club for women was established in the stunning Art Deco lounge. The Parrot Club took its name from Basil, the resident parrot, who greeted guests for many years. During his hotel residency, the waiters taught him disreputable language, and he had to be retired, so he was sent away to luxurious exile, where he enjoyed himself until a ripe old age. Mothers, daughters, and granddaughters continue to gather at this ladies-only retreat, which is not only a welcome refuge from busy London but a base for businesswomen seeking a quiet place to meet clients, send and receive messages, entertain guests for morning coffee, lunch, or afternoon tea, or use the office facilities. Men are allowed, but only in the company of a woman. Women hotel guests are invited to use the Parrot Club freely during their stay, which is appreciated by those who are traveling alone and need office support or conduct business meetings. That is not all the club offers. You can order morning coffee, a light lunch or a glass of champagne, call for a taxi, book theater tickets, take a shower, press your ball gown, change your child's nappy, prepare its bottle and arrange for a baby-sitter, or borrow an umbrella. If you are staying long enough you may be able to attend one of their interesting lectures, or perhaps squeeze in a quick day trip to Paris that includes shopping and guided tours of some of the smaller museums.

For many of the guests who call this their London home, the hotel developed the Basilite Scheme, which entitles frequent visitors (those who've had four stays within the past three years) to significant discounts and privileges; call or email for complete details. There are also special rates for minimum two-night weekend stays, for stays of five nights or more, and discounts offered through August, on bank holidays, Christmas, and during the January sales. That last discount time period alone could tip the scales for some dedicated shoppers, because Harrods is just a one-minute walk away.

If this isn't enough, there is a comfortable lounge where afternoon tea is served, a bar, and a beautifully appointed dining room where members of the Royal College of Music play four nights a week, starting at 7 P.M.

Reservations are not held beyond 4 P.M. unless guaranteed. If rooms are canceled after 12 P.M. on the day prior to arrival, one night's accommodation will be charged unless the room is re-let. Whenever you cancel, be sure to get a cancellation number because claims for refunds are considered only when a cancellation number is quoted.

FACILITIES AND SERVICES: Air-conditioning on request at no additional cost, bar, central heat, direct-dial phones, hair dryer, electric kettle on request, ironing room, laundry service, lift, two parking spaces (must be booked—£22 per 24 hours), Parrot Club, restaurant and room service, office safe, satellite TV, radio, clock, theater bookings, 24-hour desk, porter, meeting rooms, one floor exclusively reserved for nonsmoking guests

BLAIR HOUSE HOTEL (10)
34 Draycott Place, SW3
11 rooms, all with shower or bath and toilet

TELEPHONE
020-7581-2323/7255-0771

FAX
020-7823-7752

TUBE
Sloane Square

CREDIT CARDS
AE, DC, MC, V

RATES
Single £90; double £110–120; extra bed £20; lower rates in the off-season; Continental breakfast included

On a quiet Chelsea side street, you will find the Blair House Hotel. The small rooms are old hat and styleless, but clean and reasonable for the area, especially when you consider that the boutique hotel down the street charges *six* times as much, and that's with VAT at 17½ percent and breakfast extra. The hotel changed hands in 1994, and the new Malaysian/Chinese owners installed cubicle bathrooms and a lift, and freshened the painting. There are four rooms similar to No. 101, a twin on the back with a quiet and pleasing view, but only one like No. 111, a larger, better furnished back room with a view of trees and and an ivy-covered wall. Its high ceiling gives the feeling of space, but I would not stay in it until the mold is removed from the bathroom. For shoppers, the location is sheer heaven. Peter Jones Department Store and the trendy King's Road are only a few minutes' walk from the hotel. For further shopping safaris, direct bus service to Knightsbridge, with Harrods, Harvey Nichols, and all the name designer showcases, is only a few stops away. Culture buffs will be able to take a bus or the tube at Sloane Square to almost any site or museum on their list of must-dos. For night-time enjoyment, there are plenty of good restaurants and typical pubs to keep you going for at least a week (see *Cheap Eats in London*).

FACILITIES AND SERVICES: Central heat, direct-dial phones, hair dryer, lift, satellite TV, tea and coffee-makers, trouser press in double rooms, office safe, 24-hour desk

KNIGHTSBRIDGE HOTEL (4, $)
10 Beaufort Gardens, SW3
40 rooms, 10 flats; all with shower or bath and toilet

Occupying a prime position on tree-lined Beaufort Gardens, only a mere whisper away from Harrods, the fully equipped Knightsbridge Hotel meets the needs and expectations of travelers in the Big Splurge category. If I listed every service and facility offered, I would not have space to tell you about the lovely accom-modations. Even though there is a full-time mainte-nance person on duty, ten private apartments with enviable kitchens, and a very outgoing staff—what good is it all if your room is unpleasant and you feel as though you are living in a cell? This will never happen here. The professionally orchestrated rooms are large enough for a long stay and complemented by traditional fabrics, marble and tiled bathrooms with Jacuzzis in some, and walk-on balconies in others. Two executive rooms (Nos. 311 and 312) on the back of the hotel have small sitting rooms with pitched ceilings and gray-tiled baths with gold fixtures. The deluxe apartments not only have wash-ers and dryers, but dishwashers and microwaves, plus all the other equipment you'll need to prepare everything from a cup of tea to your Christmas goose. Number 421 is a good example, with two televisions, a large bedroom, and a modern kitchen with a microwave oven and a four-burner stove. To make the hotel more appealing, there is a 10 percent discount for weekly stays and special rates during the low season.

FACILITIES AND SERVICES: Air-conditioning on request (£10 supplement), central heat, conference facilities and

TELEPHONE
020-7589-9271
FAX
020-7823-9692
EMAIL
reception@knightsbridgehotel
.co.uk
INTERNET
www.knightsbridgehotel.co.uk
TUBE
Knightsbridge
CREDIT CARDS
AE, DC, MC, V
RATES
Single £100–120; double £150–195; triple £195; flat £165–300; English breakfast included; 10 percent discount for weekly stays, special rates upon request in low season

secretarial services, direct-dial phones, fax machine and private line in room or suite on request, hair dryer, laundry service, ironing facility, lift to all hotel rooms and most of the flats, office safe, satellite TV with in-house movies, minibars in some rooms, Jacuzzis in some rooms, theater booking, fully fitted kitchens in all flats

SW5

Earl's Court

Earl's Court is usually a reliable, if seedy barometer of the changes in social and political pressure in the world beyond. When anything happens on some outcrop of the globe with an unpronounceable name, it will show up a few months later on Earl's Court Road. The street swarms with the world's latest arrivals.

—Jonathan Raban, Arabia Through the Looking Glass, *1979*

Earl's Court is often called "Kangaroo Court" because it serves as unofficial headquarters for London's sizable Australian student community. It is also known for its two large exhibition centers: Earl's Court and Olympia. The area has a mixed bag of hotels, ranging from charming antiques-filled restored townhouses to chains and some of the worst fleabags London has to offer. Many accommodations are geared toward people with low budgets and an abundance of youth on their side. To go with these Cheap Sleeps are a multitude of budget restaurants, with only a handful serving anything approaching quality food. From a tourist's point of view, the area offers very little. The major reason I see to recommend it is if you are involved in an event at one of the exhibition centers and need a Cheap Sleep, or can spring for something listed in the following section that has been carefully evaluated and inspected, and does not represent the underside of Earl's Court. Transportation is good from the Earl's Court tube; you have a direct link to Heathrow Airport and about a thirty-minute ride to the action in central London.

SW5, SW7, SW10

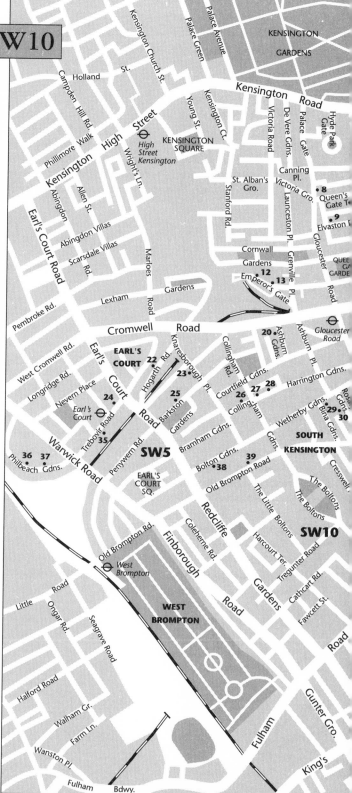

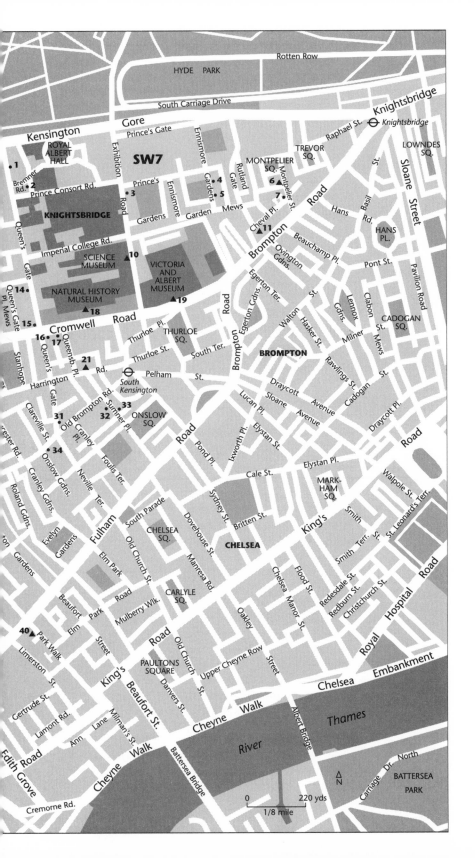

HYDE PARK

Rotten Row

South Carriage Drive

Knightsbridge

Knightsbridge ⊖

Gore

Kensington

Prince's Gate

ROYAL
ALBERT
HALL

SW7

Ennismore Gardens

Exhibition Road

MONTPELIER
SQ.

Raphael St.

TREVOR
SQ.

LOWNDES
SQ.

•1

Bremner
Rd. •2

Prince Consort Rd.

Prince's

•4

Rutland Gate

6▲

Montpelier St.

Sloane Street

St.

KNIGHTSBRIDGE

•3

Ennismore

•5

7•

Hans

Basil

Road

HANS
PL.

Gardens

Garden

Mews

Cheval Pl.

▲11

Beauchamp Pl.

Rd.

Pont St.

Pavilion Road

Imperial College Rd.

Brompton

Ovington
Gdns.

SCIENCE
MUSEUM

▲10

Egerton Ter.

Walton

Hasker St.

Lennox Gdns.

Claton

CADOGAN
SQ.

Queen's Gate

14•

NATURAL HISTORY
MUSEUM

VICTORIA
AND
ALBERT
MUSEUM

▲19

Egerton Gdns.

St.

Milner

St.

Mews

Pl. Mews

▲18

Road

Rawlings St.

Cadogan

15•

Cromwell   Road

Thurloe
Pl.

THURLOE
SQ.

South Ter.

Brompton

BROMPTON

St.

16•

17•

Queensb.

Thurloe St.

South Ter.

Draycott

Sloane

Avenue

Cadogan

Draycott Pl.

Harrington

21
▲

Rd.

Pelham

Lucan Pl.

Avenue

Road

Stanhope

Gate

⊖

South
Kensington

St.

Ixworth Pl.

Elystan St.

Elystan Pl.

Walpole St.

Clareville St.

31•

Old Brompton Rd.

Summer Pl.

33•

ONSLOW
SQ.

Road

Pond Pl.

Cale St.

MARK-
HAM
SQ.

St. Leonard's Terr.

Cranley

32•

King's

Smith

•34

Onslow Gdns.

Neville Ter.

Foulis Ter.

Sydney St.

Britten St.

Smith Terr.

St.

Roland Gdns.

Cranley Gdns.

Evelyn

Gardens

Fulham

South Parade

CHELSEA
SQ.

Dovehouse St.

CHELSEA

Flood St.

Redesdale St.

Redburn St.

Christchurch St.

Royal

Hospital

Road

Elm Park

Old Church St.

Manresa Rd.

Chelsea Manor St.

40▲

Park Walk

Elm

Beaufort

Park

Mulberry Wlk.

Road

CARLYLE
SQ.

Oakley

Street

Limerston

St.

Street

Old Church St.

PAULTONS
SQUARE

Upper Cheyne Row

Chelsea   Embankment

King's

Beaufort St.

Danvers St.

Gertrude St.

Lamont Rd.

Ann

Lane

Milman's St.

Cheyne

Walk

Albert Bridge

Thames

BATTERSEA
PARK

Edith Grove

Cheyne

Walk

Battersea Bridge

River

N

Carriage Dr.

North

Cremorne Rd.

0   220 yds

1/8 mile

HOTELS in SW5

OTHER OPTIONS

($) indicates a Big Splurge

AMSTERDAM HOTEL (24)
7 Trebovir Road, SW5
20 rooms, 8 flats; all with shower or bath and toilet

TELEPHONE
020-7370-2814/5084

FAX
020-7244-7608

INTERNET
www.cityscan.co.uk

TUBE
Earl's Court

CREDIT CARDS
MC, V

RATES
Single £70–85; double £80–95; triple £105–110; family £115–125. Apartments (studio to two bedrooms) £95–160

The appealing plant-lined entry has a corner seating area and a collection of Thomas McKnight prints of world-famous vacation destinations. It may not seem like much, but in this corner of London it is notable: the Amsterdam has a lift to all floors in the hotel (and to the third floor for the apartments), individually controlled room heat, a twenty-four-hour porter, plus guest fax and copying facilities. All the twenty cheerful and bright rooms have slightly differing colors and functional bathrooms. In addition to the hotel rooms, there are eight apartments ranging in size from a studio to two bedrooms. On first glance they are very nice, with coordinated fabrics and enough space to move around and live in. On second look I realized the following flat basics were missing: a work area, dining table and chairs, and drawer space. Obviously the owner of this hotel has never spent a night in one of these apartments.

FACILITIES AND SERVICES: Central heat, direct-dial phones, hair dryer available, tea and coffeemakers, equipped kitchens in the apartments, lift to all floors in hotel (to the third floor for apartments), office safe, TV, 24-hour desk, guest fax and copy services

BARKSTON GARDENS HOTEL (25)
33–34 Barkston Gardens, SW5
83 rooms, all with shower or bath and toilet

The Barkston Gardens Hotel, on a quiet square just far enough away from the trashy tourist part of Earl's Court to make it recommendable, greets its guests with bright, ample rooms and baths. It is a big, rambling hotel, exhibiting bold primary colors accented by modern prints and wallpaper with the sponged or marbleized look. The parrot seems to be the hotel mascot because you see a picture of a napping bird on every room door. The furniture is blond Swedish modern, rooms have luggage space, a place to sit other than the bed, views over the gardens in front, and enough closet space. Significant money was saved by doing the reception area as simply as possible. Seating here consists of a porch swing. The whimsically constructed lounge is colorfully decorated with elephants, parrots, fish, and a peacock staring at you from around the walls in the room.

FACILITIES AND SERVICES: Bar, central heat, direct-dial phones, hair dryer, laundry service, lift, restaurant, room service, office safe, satellite TV, radio, clock, tea and coffeemakers, no smoking in the second-floor rooms, 24-hour desk

TELEPHONE
020-7373-7851
FAX
020-7370-6570
TUBE
Earl's Court
CREDIT CARDS
AE, DC, MC, V
RATES
Single £85–95; double £100–120; Continental breakfast £7 extra, English breakfast £9 extra; children six and under sharing parents' room are free, and so are baby cots. Always ask for seasonal rates.

BEAVER HOTEL (36)
57–59 Philbeach Gardens, SW5
38 rooms, 22 with shower or bath and toilet

In this far corner of London, the well-kept Beaver Hotel delivers more for your battered Cheap Sleeping pound than most. Bonus points are earned for their car park, which charges a £5 twenty-four-hour fee; a 10 percent discount for longer stays; and complimentary tea and coffee available whenever you want. The simple rooms are clean and vary from small without bath to reasonably spacious with all facilities. They are priced accordingly, starting at £35 for a snug single. The only drawbacks I found were the lack of bedside reading lights and the old-fashioned individual square toilet paper. The wood-paneled Austrian-style breakfast room has cushioned chairs and banquettes. For socializing, you can play pool in the next room, or join the sports fans who gather around the satellite television in the lounge. The tube stop is only a five-minute walk away, and the management is accommodating, two more reasons this is a good pick if Earl's Court is your Cheap Sleeping stomping ground.

TELEPHONE
020-7373-4553
FAX
020-7373-4555
TUBE
Earl's Court (take the Warwick Road exit)
CREDIT CARDS
AE, DC, MC, V
RATES
Single £35–50; double £50–75; triple £85; lower rates for weekly stays; English breakfast included

FACILITIES AND SERVICES: Central heat, direct-dial phones, hair dryers in rooms with private bathrooms, laundry service, parking (£5 per day), TV in some rooms, radio, office safe, lift, office open 7:30 A.M.–midnight, nonsmoking rooms on the ground floor

THE CRANLEY (29, $)
10–12 Bina Gardens, SW5
36 rooms, all with shower or bath and toilet

TELEPHONE
020-7373-0123; 800-553-2582
(toll-free from the U.S.)
FAX
020-7373-9497
EMAIL
thecranley@compuserve.uk
INTERNET
www.thecranley.co.uk
TUBE
Gloucester Road
CREDIT CARDS
AE, DC, MC, V
RATES
Single £120–140; double £150–160; executive twin £170–180; suite £180–200; penthouse or flat £240–260; Continental breakfast £11 extra, English breakfast £15 extra; special rates in January and February

If you appreciate the finer things in life, a stay at the Cranley is guaranteed to be memorable. It is one of the best small hotels in London and serves as a textbook example of how to run a small hotel with great style and elegance. In 1990, former owner Bonnie De Loof, from Ann Arbor, Michigan, restored three townhouses in South Kensington. In the process, she kept intact the high ceilings with handsome moldings, the floor-to-ceiling windows, and several Victorian fireplaces. The stunning interior follows the English country recipe of chintz, traditional antiques, swagged draperies, beautiful flower arrangements, and a lovely garden in back. Mrs. De Loof also incorporated all the touches Americans love to find in a small hotel, matching modern facilities with those of a large luxury hotel. The individually decorated rooms include kitchenettes hidden behind paneled doors, complete with a microwave and enough equipment to do light cooking. The mattresses are American made. The bathrooms are wonderful, with warm terry-cloth robes, assorted English toiletries, and deep bathtubs. All of the rooms, of course, are lovely, but a few stand out. Number 105, a deluxe double, has an Oriental motif and its own fireplace. The fourth-floor one-bedroom suite has a balcony and a view of St. Paul's Cathedral, as does No. 204, a smaller double on the back. The two ground-floor suites have private terraces and Jacuzzis. I could check into flat No. 107 and stay comfortably for weeks. I like the large sitting room, with its marble fireplace and two sofas, the working table space, the loft bedroom, and the oversize kitchen with a full refrigerator, separate freezer, stove, and microwave. Service is of the old school and taken seriously by the hospitable staff, which does its utmost to provide attentive personal service for each guest.

IMPORTANT NOTE: A few years ago Mrs. De Loof sold The Cranley and began another related business called Small & Elegant Hotels International, a hotel- and apartment-booking service that represents boutique-style hotels and elegant serviced flats with character and personality in London, Paris, and New York. There are several good reasons to book through this well-run agency: (1) generally they can get you a better rate; (2) rooms are allotted to them, so if the hotel tells you they are fully booked, chances are good that they may be able to get you in; and (3) you are dealing with an experienced hotelier who knows what pleases Americans.

Other *Cheap Sleeps in London* listings represented by Small & Elegant Hotels International are: Harrington Hall hotel (see page 159), One Thirty serviced flats (see page 188), and Roland House serviced flats (see page 191). For further informantion on Small & Elegant Hotels, please see page 199.

FACILITIES AND SERVICES: Air-conditioning and ceiling fans, central heat, direct-dial phones, hair dryer, laundry service, lift to third floor, parking by arrangement, office safe, satellite TV, trouser press, free use of gym at Harrington Hall (see page 159), kitchenettes with microwaves in all rooms, some with large kitchens

HOGARTH HOTEL (22, $)
Hogarth Road, SW5
85 rooms, all with shower or bath and toilet

If you want a full-service hotel for a reasonable tab near both Earl's Court and Olympia Exhibition Centers, this is your best bet. The Hogarth has been owned and operated by the Marston family since they built it in 1971. They pride themselves on the level of service offered to all guests, and have received many awards for the warm welcome extended. They are especially proud of the Automobile Association's Courtesy Care Award for outstanding customer care. They are the only hotel in England to have won it twice, which is impressive considering it is only awarded to two London hotels each year. The list of amenities in this modern-style hotel is long and appealing for both tourists and businesspeople. Everyone always appreciates the tasteful and pleasant rooms, especially those on the fifth floor with balconies. All have a private room safe, modem points, and a bathroom drying rack for quick laundries. There is also a convenient car park, 24-hour room service, and a nicely appointed dining room with menu choices ranging from a burger and chips to vegetarian and daily fixed-price features. There are nonsmoking rooms and a floor with

TELEPHONE
020-7370-6831; 800-528-1234 (toll-free from the U.S. and Canada)

FAX
020-7373-6179

INTERNET
www.marstonhotels.co.uk

TUBE
Earl's Court, Gloucester Road

CREDIT CARDS
MC, V

RATES
Single £95; double £110; triple £125; executive room £140; English breakfast buffet £10 extra; special rates on weekends, for long stays, bank holidays, Christmas, and New Year's

extra security measures geared to women traveling alone. Business travelers enjoy the eight air-conditioned executive rooms, which have two telephones, a larger television set, minibar, and just enough extra space to make a difference. Weekend breaks and holiday rates are further enticements at this Best Western–affiliated hotel.

FACILITIES AND SERVICES: Bar, central heat, direct-dial phones, hair dryer, iron and ironing board available, laundry service, lift, minibars in executive rooms, private car park (£10 per day, £15 for 24 hours), restaurant and 24-hour room service, room safe, nonsmoking rooms on second floor, and rooms designed with extra security for women traveling alone, satellite TV, tea and coffeemakers, trouser presses, conference facilities, 24-hour desk

MAYFLOWER HOTEL (35)
26–28 Trebovir Road, SW5
48 rooms, 25 flats; all with shower or bath and toilet

TELEPHONE
020-7370-0991
FAX
020-7370-0994
EMAIL
mayfhotel@aol.com
INTERNET
members.aol.com/
MAYFLHOTEL/private/
MAY.HTM
TUBE
Earl's Court
CREDIT CARDS
AE, MC, V
RATES
Single £55; double £70; triple £80; quad £90. *Flats:* studio from £90–110; one bedroom £99–155, two bedrooms £135–185; Continental breakfast included with both hotel and flats. There is a 48-hour cancellation policy.

Earl's Court is known for many things, and one of them is its proliferation of Cheap Sleeps. You have to be careful here not to get caught in one of the grunge palaces, where the world of London on the cheap takes on an undesirable new meaning. To avoid such potential trauma, check into the Mayflower, a functional, clean budget refuge a block or two from the tube station.

One look at the price and you know it is not an annex of Claridges. The forty-eight frill-free rooms have private baths and benefits of good housekeeping. The bathrooms are all different, in color at least. I assume these colors are a result of whatever bright tile was on special offer when renovation time rolled around. Room No. 40 is a habitable double with dormer windows, a multicolored duvet, and checked curtains. The bath is citrus yellow and gray. Number 6, on the ground floor with a depressing view, has its bath decorated in glowing mint green. Singles will be given No. 43 on the back, in pink and white with a shower in the bathroom. Breakfast is served in two basement rooms, one with upholstered bench seats and the other vaguely Art Deco in tone, with round tables draped in red paper.

The hotel also owns the Court Apartments, older standard flats cheerfully done with wooden floors, simple furnishings, and limited closet and drawer space. Each has its own equipped kitchen and safe but no lifts. The more luxurious flats have a lift, light wood furnishings, larger kitchens, nice bathrooms, and more closet space but, unfortunately, limited drawer space and no bedside lights.

NOTE: The Rushmore Hotel across the street is owned and managed by the same group. This hotel used to be recommended in *Cheap Sleeps in London,* but until it has been refurbished, unfortunately I can no longer include it.

FACILITIES AND SERVICES: Central heat, direct-dial phones, hair dryer, lift, office safe, tea and coffeemaking facilities, satellite TV, 24-hour desk. *Court Apartments:* central heat, direct-dial metered phone lines, lift to luxury flats, fitted kitchen (some luxury flats with dishwashers, washers, and dryers), daily maid and linen service, private safe, satellite TV, video player on request

SWISS HOUSE HOTEL (39)
171 Old Brompton Road, SW5
16 rooms, 15 with shower or bath and toilet

When you arrive at the Swiss House, you know immediately that someone is taking care to put the best foot forward. It is a small B&B, only sixteen rooms, but one look at its ivy-covered facade and flower boxes and you will feel as though you have come home. One of the nicest rooms is No. 212, a top-floor triple with a fireplace and a garden view. Other quiet garden rooms to remember are Nos. 2, 5, 8, 12, and 17. Room 201, a street-side triple with a pretty white fireplace outlined in fruit-patterned tiles, is decorated in soft lavender with a light rose floral print fabric on the spreads and curtains. If it is space you are after, consider lower-ground-floor No. 217, the only room with a tub. It has a walk-in closet and either a king or twin beds. If you are in one of these street-side rooms, better bring earplugs, because traffic along Old Brompton Road never seems to stop. A large self-service Continental breakfast is offered in the basement breakfast room, with a cheerful blue and white color scheme carried out on the china and curtains, complemented by dried floral arrangements and mirrors along one wall. Light snacks, an almost unheard of extra in a modest B&B of this type, include soup, sandwiches, tea, and coffee provided from noon until 9 P.M.

TELEPHONE
020-7373-2769 (reservations);
020-7373-9383 (guests)

FAX
020-7373-4983

EMAIL
recep@swiss-hh.demon.co.uk

INTERNET
www.webscape.co.uk/
swiss_house/index.html-ssi

TUBE
Gloucester Road

CREDIT CARDS
MC, V (5-percent discount for cash payment)

RATES
Single £45–65; double £80–90;
triple £100; quad £115;
Continental breakfast included,
full English breakfast £5 extra

FACILITIES AND SERVICES: Central heat, fans in rooms, direct-dial phones, hair dryer available, office safe, light snacks noon–9 P.M., tea and coffeemaking facilities, satellite TV, iron and ironing board available, no lift, some nonsmoking rooms, office open 8 A.M.–11 P.M.

YORK HOUSE HOTEL (37)
27–29 Philbeach Gardens, SW5
27 rooms, 2 with shower or bath and toilet

TELEPHONE
020-7373-7519/79
FAX
020-7370-4641
TUBE
Earl's Court (take the Warwick Road exit)
CREDIT CARDS
AE, DC, MC, V
RATES
Single £34–36; double £53–55; triple £62–66; quad £72–76; five £80; English breakfast included; special weekly rates for longer stays in the low season quoted on request

Winnie, the friendly manager, has been welcoming guests to this thrifty Cheap Sleep in London since 1981. The hotel is low-tech yet sensible, sturdy, and to the point when it comes to this pocket of London. The rooms are clean and sunny, with high ceilings and no musty odors, nicks, dents, or tears. Rates are indeed bordering on charitable compared to some of the almost obscene prices charged by a few others in the neighborhood. Your final bill will be even less if you stay a week or more and can take advantage of the discount given for long stays in the off-season.

There is the usual television lounge paying homage to overstuffed low seating and a few determined plants. Breakfast is served in two whitewashed rooms with red and white tablecloths brightening the morning meal. On warm days, chairs and table are set out in the garden. The good news is that the twenty-seven rooms can house around forty-five people. The bad news is they often do, so make your reservations as early as possible and be *positive* about your dates because the deposit is nonrefundable, period.

FACILITIES AND SERVICES: Central heat, direct-dial phones, TV lounge, office safe, no lift, office open 7 A.M.–11 P.M.

SW7

South Kensington

South Kensington (referred to as "South Ken") is a treasure trove for culture seekers. The Royal Albert Hall is here, as well as the vast complex that includes the Victoria and Albert, Natural History, Geological, and Science museums. Stately Victorian homes, Georgian mansions, and charming mews houses with picture-perfect gardens characterize this very desirable residential area. In springtime, clusters of pink and white blooms on the ornamental cherry trees turn it into a fairyland that draws many photographers. For most of the hotels listed, there is easy tube access from Heathrow Airport.

($) indicates a Big Splurge

BADEN-POWELL HOUSE (15)
Queen's Gate at Cromwell Road, SW7
180 beds, all rooms with shower or bath and toilet

TELEPHONE
020-7584-7031

FAX
020-7590-6902

EMAIL
bph.hostel@scout.org.uk

INTERNET
www.scoutbase.org.uk

TUBE
Gloucester Road

CREDIT CARDS
AE, MC, V

RATES
Scout Rate: single £40; double (with twin beds) £32 per person; 3- to 4-bedded room £26 per person, extra bed £9; dorm room for those under 16 £14, over 16 £19; Continental breakfast included. Non-Scout Rate: single £60; double (with twin beds) £40 per person; 3- to 4-bedded room £23 per person, extra bed £12; dorm room for those under 16 £20, over 16 £26; Continental breakfast included. Please note group and individual booking and cancellation policies.

MISCELLANEOUS
The hotel is closed two days before Christmas until after New Year's. The restaurants, especially in winter, are not always open in the evening, so call ahead to check.

Every time I go back to the Baden-Powell House I cannot believe how much more value is offered. For serious budgeteers with a Scout in the family, you can't afford not to take advantage of this outstanding Cheap Sleep in London.

Opened in 1961 by Queen Elizabeth, the Baden-Powell House fulfills the dream of the founder of the Boy Scouts, Lord Baden-Powell, that there be a permanent place where the Boy Scouts and Girl Guides of the world might meet or stay when they come to London. I think it is interesting to note that the Scouts purchased the site in 1956 for the net cost of £39,000 and in 1997 spent £2 million to totally refurbish the facility. Talk about rising costs! The wonderful part is that the facilities of this remarkable hotel are open not only to members of the Scouts and Guides, but to their families, whether or not the member is present. Even if your child or grandchild is a first-year Cub Scout or Brownie, you are eligible to take advantage of this Cheap Sleeping deal.

The hotel is situated in the heart of London's museum district. The Natural History Museum is across the street; the Science Museum and the Victoria and Albert are minutes away. Also within easy reach are the Royal Albert Hall and Kensington Palace. Other famous places such as the Tower of London, Westminster Abbey, and the West End are an easy tube or bus ride away. The simple rooms vary from singles to bunk-bedded dorms and are all nonsmoking. In addition to private bathrooms and air-conditioning, you will have an electric kettle for making your own tea and coffee, a color television, and daily maid service. If you forgot your hair dryer, you can borrow one from the front desk. Other attractive bonus points at this Cheap Sleep in London include conference rooms, fax machine, and photocopying (fee charged), a coin-operated laundry and dryer, ironing facilities, two restaurants, a few first-come parking spaces (the only non-bargain offered), a young staff happy to help with your sight-seeing plans, and a notice board to keep everyone up to the minute on theater and concert performances.

Breakfast is included in the nominal rate, and for very little more, two- and three-course lunches and dinners are served daily in the cafeteria and, more formally, in the Kingfisher Restaurant. If you are going on a day trip, or leaving London via train, consider having the kitchen pack a box lunch to avoid subjecting yourself to the poor quality of food offered on all the British rail lines.

BOOKING POLICIES: *British Groups:* A nonrefundable deposit of £5 per person required as confirmation. The balance of no less than 50 percent of the full payment is required eight weeks prior to arrival. *Groups other than British:* A nonrefundable deposit of £5.50 per person per night and 50 percent of full payment required eight weeks prior to arrival. *All Groups:* Evening meals must be booked a minimum of two weeks in advance. *Families and Individuals:* A nonrefundable deposit of £7 per person required for each booking. *Cancellation for all groups and individuals:* If a booking is canceled in whole or in part more than thirty days prior to arrival, there will be a 50 percent cancellation fee. If a booking is canceled less than thirty days before arrival, the Baden-Powell House reserves the right to charge a 100 percent cancellation fee.

FACILITIES AND SERVICES: Air-conditioning (no added charge), central heat, conference facilities, direct-dial phones, garage (£3 per hour, £15 for 12 hours, £30 for 24 hours), hair dryer available, tea and coffeemaking facilities, coin-operated washer and dryer, iron and ironing board, cafeteria-style restaurant open for three meals a day to residents and nonresidents, Kingfisher Restaurant for more formally served meals, office safe, no smoking allowed in any part of the building, no liquor allowed except in the Kingfisher Restaurant, TV, 24-hour desk, luggage room. In the cafeteria: three-course lunch for £6.50, two- to three-course dinner from £5–6; packed picnic (must be ordered in advance) £2–4; Kingfisher Restaurant (by reservation only) set meal including wine £9.

FIVE SUMNER PLACE (32, $)
5 Sumner Place, SW7
13 rooms, all with shower or bath and toilet

TELEPHONE
020-7584-7586
FAX
020-7823-9962
EMAIL
no.5@dial.pipex.com
TUBE
South Kensington
CREDIT CARDS
AE, MC, V
RATES
Single £90; double £145; triple £165; large breakfast buffet included; lower rates in January and February

Many small, select London hotels have turned genteel coziness into an art form. Five Sumner Place is no exception. The hotel's loyal and discerning clientele give it top marks for its lovely tone and decor, pleasing service, and appealing residential location along a beautiful row of white Victorian townhouses built in 1848. When you arrive, you will recognize the understated, luxurious air of a well-run country home. Comfortable furniture in traditional English style are in the guest rooms that, due to the nature of the building, vary in size and shape. If you want to face the front, No. 3, decorated in soft gray with mahogany furniture and a white-tiled bath with a shower, is a popular selection. So is No. 6, in deep rose and burgundy. This room has recently been renovated, and has a small balcony and a good shower in a well-lit bathroom. I like No. 4, overlooking the garden on the first floor, with a comfortable wing chair and writing desk. If living subterraneanly does not bother you, check into No. 2 in the basement. The soft yellow room itself is certainly quiet and the new bathroom with a tub and shower adds to its appeal.

A stunning glass breakfast room with hanging plants overlooks a pretty side garden. What a wonderful place to begin your London day, enjoying a buffet breakfast while glancing through a stack of complimentary daily newspapers. The hotel is ideally placed for visiting the sights of London by bus, tube, or taxi. The South Kensington tube, with a direct link to Heathrow Airport, is less than five minutes away on foot, and major museums and a score of restaurants and shops in all price ranges are within an easy stroll (see *Cheap Eats in London*).

FACILITIES AND SERVICES: Central heat, direct-dial phones, hair dryer, laundry service, lift, minibar, office safe, TV, trouser press, 24-hour desk, complimentary afternoon tea, nonsmoking rooms on request

THE GORE (1, $)
189 Queen's Gate, SW7
54 rooms, all with shower or bath and toilet

"Pure joy . . . about as far as you can get from an American corporate hotel," writes the *Wall Street Journal*. *Elle* states, "Six storeys of Old English charm, made cosy with open fires and 5,500 paintings and prints that cover the walls." "The only plastic you will find is the telephone and TV," says the *Financial Times*. Everything said about this charming hotel is absolutely true. It is a very special one-of-a-kind hotel filled with character and personality where the owners strive to provide for their guests what they themselves want in a hotel: mellow surroundings; an intelligent, friendly staff; good food and wine; and affordable prices.

The two impressive townhouses have quite a history. They were first developed into a hotel in the late 1800s when a William Kirby converted them into "discreet hotel suites" and advertised to visitors as "an hotel in all but name." It was listed as "an establishment of superior standard, in the most favourite and fashionable part of the Metropolis," boasting menservants in livery, hot and cold running water, carriages for the use of clients, and a hydraulic lift worked by underground pressure supplied by the London Hydraulic Company. In 1904, Kirby fell on hard times and sublet No. 189 to the Turkish Embassy. Four years later, Misses Fanny and Ada Cook took over, and the Gore has been a privately owned hotel ever since, still filled with "the kind of Victorian clutter the sisters would have been proud of." It is also well known for its magnificent collection of more than five thousand vintage English prints and paintings hung throughout the hotel and in each room. As you enter, beautiful old paintings of Queen Victoria line the back of the reception area and the walkway leading to an emerald green sitting room filled with large, comfortable sofas and chairs. A roaring winter fire adds a cheerful touch. For a stylish and delicious meal, you can walk into Bistrot 190 (see *Cheap Eats in London*); for a more formal experience, the downstairs dining room serves traditional food in elegant and expensive surroundings.

There are regular single and double rooms with all the nice furnishings and appointments one expects to find in a small hotel of this caliber. However, the *real* fun at the Gore begins when you reserve one of their special

TELEPHONE
020-7584-6601; 800-637-7200 (toll-free from the U.S.)

FAX
020-7589-8127

EMAIL
reservations@gorehotel.co.uk

TUBE
Gloucester Road

CREDIT CARDS
AE, DC, MC, V

RATES
Single £115–155; double £160–230; Tudor Room £250; all rates exclusive of 17½-percent VAT; Continental breakfast £8 extra

suites. Probably the best known and most popular is No. 101, the Tudor Room, where a dark-wood-paneled entrance leads to a massive Gothic room with Oriental rugs scattered on its wooden plank floors. Further touches include a huge carved wood-burning fireplace, leaded stained-glass windows, and a carved beamed ceiling with gargoyles. To one side, a ladder, or a secret door, takes you to the "minstrel's gallery," which is a perfect sleeping loft for children. Downstairs, Mom and Dad can share the four-poster canopy bed. The bathroom keeps pace with a Victorian bathtub and throne-seat lavatory. For another unusual experience in hotel living, check into Venus, No. 211, and sleep in a gilded bed that once belonged to Judy Garland and was used in the 1963 musical *I Could Go on Singing,* in which she and Dirk Bogarde costarred. A four-by-six-foot copy of Titian's *Lady of Modena* looms over the room, and in the marbled bathroom, a hand-painted Zeus driving a chariot rides over the bathtub.

The Miss Ada and Miss Fanny rooms (Nos. 208 and 308) are named after the spinster sisters who ran the Gore as a rooming house. In No. 308 you will sleep in Miss Fanny's four-poster bed, which is so high it has a set of steps that actually was her Georgian commode. In both rooms the bathrooms have improved. They have mahogany paneling with wonderful throne-seat toilets and cast-iron baths with showerheads the size of large dinner plates. Another suite of note is No. 314, the Dame Nellie, named after Dame Nellie Melba, an Australian opera singer renowned during Queen Victoria's time; Dame Nellie's picture hangs to the right of the fireplace in the hotel lounge (King Edward III is on the left). The bedroom itself, popular with honeymooners, is an opulant mixture of mirrors, nineteenth-century French cupboards, and Victorian chaise lounges. The hotel admits that "the bathroom is an experience in itself," with its two bronze statues. Rates are higher at the Gore, but for its many followers, it is well worth the extra for its unique atmosphere and cordial service.

FACILITIES AND SERVICES: Bar, central heat, direct-dial phones, hair dryer, laundry service, lift, minibar, office and room safe, restaurant, room service, TV, nonsmoking rooms

HARRINGTON HALL (28, $)
5–25 Harrington Gardens, SW7
200 rooms, all with shower or bath and toilet

Harrington Hall sets a benchmark for every possible comfort and convenience and, more important, at lower prices if you go on a weekend or in the off-season. The elegant marbled lobby and reception areas are the curtain-raisers for what awaits beyond. The bar, finished in exotic Burr Vavona, and the beautiful marble fireplace combine warmth and comfort with traditional furniture in complementary colors. The rooms and suites offer stylish accommodations and pour on the extras for the appreciative occupants. In addition to air-conditioning and rooms exclusively reserved for nonsmokers, you will find cable television, a minibar, and a telephone answering machine. Bathrooms are stocked with a variety of toiletries and absorbent towels, and offer good light and plenty of mirrors. The business center, for the exclusive use of guests, has secretarial services, including photocopying, and fax services. Conference and banquet facilities for several hundred are beautifully arranged. In addition to all this, guests can work out in the hotel gym, listen to quiet piano music while sipping a drink before dinner, or order something from room service and watch a video. The concierge will secure tickets for any West End production, and uniformed porters will see to it that you never lift anything heavier than your purse.

FACILITIES AND SERVICES: Air-conditioning, bar, central heat, direct-dial phones and answering machines in each room, hair dryer, minibar, same-day laundry and dry cleaning, lift, office safe, restaurant, 24-hour room service, business and conference facilities, satellite TV, VCR, in-house movies, radio, tea and coffeemakers, trouser press, fitness center with sauna and workout room, 24-hour desk, nonsmoking rooms

TELEPHONE
020-7396-9696; can also be booked through Small & Elegant Hotels International (see page 199) and 800-44-UTELL (Utell International)

FAX
020-7396-9090; 402-398-5484 (from the U.S.)

EMAIL
101752.2030@compuserve.com

INTERNET
www.harringtonhall.co.uk

TUBE
Gloucester Road

CREDIT CARDS
AE, DC, MC, V

RATES
Single or double £170; triple £175; suite £190; lower corporate and weekend rates subject to availability; Continental breakfast £10 extra, English breakfast £14 extra

JARVIS EMBASSY HOUSE HOTEL (14, $)
31–33 Queen's Gate, SW7
80 rooms, 1 flat; all with shower or bath and toilet

First, some historical trivia about this hotel: from the end of the eighteenth century until the early 1960s, the four buildings that make up the hotel housed a women's hospital where Elizabeth Taylor is reported to have had her first face-lift. Now, in room No. 5, there is supposedly a ghost who was one of the hospital nurses.

TELEPHONE
020-7584-7222; 800-344-1212 (Golden Tulip: toll-free from the U.S.; Mon–Sat 7:30 A.M.–8 P.M., Sat 9 A.M.–3 P.M. central time); 800-44-UTELL (Utell International)

FAX
020-7589-3910

INTERNET
www.jarvis.co.uk
TUBE
Gloucester Road
CREDIT CARDS
AE, DC, MC, V
RATES
Single £100–110; double
£110–150; triple £120–170;
apartment rate depends on
length and time of stay;
corporate, summer, and
weekend rates on request;
children 16 or under staying in
parents' room free; Continental
breakfast £8 extra, English
breakfast £11 extra

A few years ago, a well-conceived refurbishing turned this downcast hotel into a recommendable location close to Hyde Park and Kensington Gardens, the Royal Albert Hall, and three of London's most famous museums, including the Victoria and Albert. During the remodeling, every effort was made to preserve the tone of this nineteenth-century building. You can still see the stuccoed facade, the elaborate ceilings, the York stone staircase, and the mirrored doors of the original private residence. The spacious rooms have luggage racks, good bathrooms, neutral decor, and two telephone lines so you can plug in and check your email or log on to the Internet. The addition of several suites and executive rooms offer guests more living space and bigger bathrooms. Suite No. 1010 has triple windows and a terrace, two television sets, a walk-in closet, double sinks, and a separate stall shower in the bathroom. If you are a light sleeper, avoid anything facing Queen's Gate, where the traffic noise lasts twenty-four hours a day. When booking, check first with the Golden Tulip or Utell toll-free numbers and then with the hotel for the best price. As with most hotels of this type, you can often strike a better deal by contacting the hotel directly. If you do, ask for the best rate: weekend, leisure, corporate, special holiday, and so on.

NOTE: The hotel has a two-bedroom, two-bath apartment with kitchen and sitting room. Rates depend on length of stay.

FACILITIES AND SERVICES: Air-conditioning in apartment, central heat, direct-dial phones with separate line for email hookup, hair dryer, iron and ironing board in executive rooms and suites, laundry and cleaning service, lift, TV, tea and coffeemakers, trouser press, 24-hour desk, nonsmoking rooms

NUMBER SIXTEEN (33, $)
16 Sumner Place, SW7
36 rooms, 32 with shower or bath and toilet

TELEPHONE
020-7589-5232; 800-592-5387
(toll-free from the U.S.)
FAX
020-7584-8615
EMAIL
reservations@
numbersixteeenhotel.co.uk
TUBE
South Kensington
CREDIT CARDS
AE, DC, MC, V

On a cold day, when I am sitting in a comfortable chair sipping a cup of tea in front of the fire in the sitting room at Number Sixteen, it is hard for me to remember I am in a London hotel and not in a friend's living room. This is the effect the hotel has on its guests; everyone feels right at home and is eager to return to a place that has that well-worn (yet far from seedy) look of a pretty English country home.

Four Victorian townhouses have been linked together to create this hotel. As each house was added, the gardens were expanded in back, and the result is one of the loveliest expanses of flowers and greenery in South Kensington, especially in the spring when the tulips are a riot of color. The addition of a glass conservatory overlooking the garden makes its enjoyment a year-round pleasure. Throughout the day, tea and coffee are available in your room, the drawing room, or the conservatory. In the evening, you can pour yourself a drink from the honor bar in the library.

The bedrooms are a well-broken-in mixture of antiques and traditional furniture that represent a certain English taste and old charm. Four special ground-floor rooms have their own terraces overlooking the gardens and many others have balconies. All rooms include remote-controlled television sets, stocked minibars, private safes, and bathrooms with terry-cloth robes and baskets of English soaps and creams. In the morning, the Continental breakfast includes cold cereal, rolls, an egg, and juice and is brought to your room. Guests can also pay special rates to use the facilities of a nearby fitness center that includes a swimming pool and beauty services.

If you are planning to be in London several times in one year, consider becoming a member of Club Sixteen, a package that offers members these benefits: priority booking, preferential room rates with £15 supplement for sharing partner and room upgrade when possible, free newspapers and bottled water, telephone and fax charges at 10p a unit, and access to Aquilla Health Club. Personal membership is £120; corporate membership is £500.

FACILITIES AND SERVICES: Bar, central heat, fans, direct-dial phones, hair dryer, laundry service, lift, room safe, minibar in rooms, TV, radio, 24-hour desk, use of a nearby gym with pool, sauna, and beauty treatments at nominal fee

RATES
Single £95–125; double £170–200; junior suite £215; weekend rates in October, November, and January; Continental breakfast included

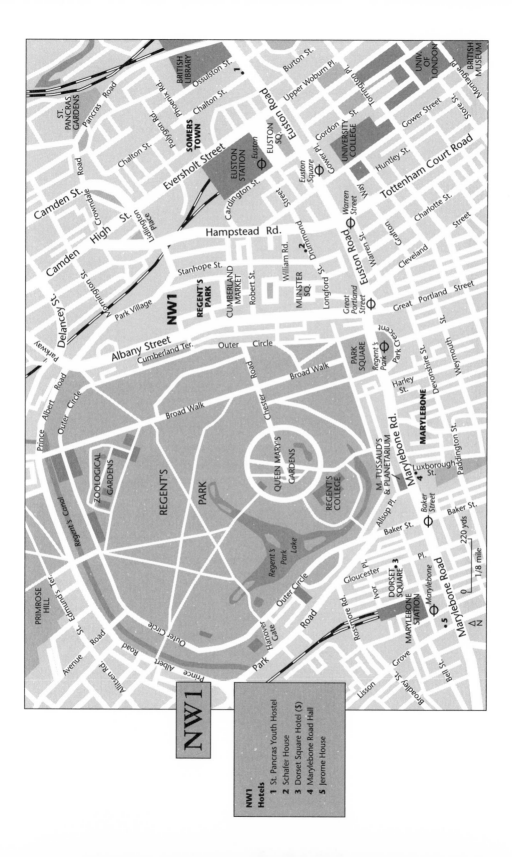

NW1

Regent's Park

Originally the private hunting ground for Henry VIII, this 400-acre park is famous for its zoo, concerts, summer open-air theater, puppet shows, and live bandstand. There is a boat pond, acres of gardens and lawns, and the Regent's Canal, where you can take a leisurely boat ride on a lazy Sunday afternoon and contemplate moving to London for good.

HOTELS in NW1
Dorset Square Hotel ($)	163

OTHER OPTIONS
Apartment Rentals

Jerome House	181

Student Dormitories

Schafer House	221
Marylebone Road Hall	223

Youth Hostels

St. Pancras Youth Hostel	236

($) indicates a Big Splurge

DORSET SQUARE HOTEL (3, $)
39–40 Dorset Square, NW1
38 rooms, all with shower or bath and toilet

For whatever reason you can think of—a birthday, an anniversary, or just to celebrate being in London with someone special—the Dorset Square Hotel receives my highest recommendation and praise. I must warn you, however, that once you stay here, all other hotels will pale by comparison.

The hotel overlooks two acres of gardens that were the site of Thomas Lord's (the famous English cricket player) first cricket ground. Everything about this beautiful hotel is in magnificent taste, from the exclusive, individually designed bedrooms to the Potting Shed, a rustic garden restaurant. Like all rooms in the hotel, the sitting room is furnished with lovely pieces that owners Kit and Tim Kemp would select for their own home. An honor bar laid out with wines, spirits, and champagne sits along one wall. Staffordshire bowls of potpourri,

TELEPHONE
020-7723-7874; 800-553-6674 (toll-free from the U.S.)

FAX
020-7724-3328

EMAIL
dorset@firmdale.com

INTERNET
www.firmdale.com

TUBE
Baker Street, Marylebone

CREDIT CARDS
AE, MC, V

RATES
Single £105; double £130–195; four-poster double £225; rates do not include 17½-percent VAT; ask for seasonal rates; Continental breakfast £12 extra, English breakfast £15 extra

artistic faux finishes, lovely fabrics on overstuffed sofas and chairs, silk draperies, and beautiful floral arrangements and potted plants complete the serene room.

No detail has been overlooked in any of the thirty-eight bedrooms and suites, all of which are a pure joy to occupy. Everything you can imagine has been done in each one to create a luxurious yet livable atmosphere, where antiques, bold color pairings, laces, lush green plants, and flowers are mixed with lavish abandon. The polished bathrooms have scales; baskets of Molton Brown soaps, creams, and shampoos; terry-cloth robes; huge towels; big mirrors; telephones; and even a tissue box covered in a fabric that coordinates with those used in the adjoining bedroom. For that very special person in your life, reserve room No. 202. The sitting room, with its fireplace and view of the square and private gardens, divine four-poster bed with side curtains, marble bath, and double-mirrored armoire, is guaranteed to capture anyone's heart. Just below it on the first floor is No. 102, a deluxe double with two comfortable chairs and two big windows on the square. Even the standard rooms, though somewhat smaller, are exceptional, and of course have all the amenities.

Just to show how seriously the hotel upholds its extremely high standards of service and maintenance, there is someone permanently on the staff just to care for its collection of decorative antique laces; another makes sure the floral displays never wilt and that the potted plants don't fade. In addition, a full complement of maids, porters, and valets is always on hand to see to a guest's every need. This is, of course, a Big Splurge, but one you will never regret.

NOTE: The hotel has one side that is not serviced by a lift and some of the stairs here are steep and narrow. If stair climbing is not part of your daily workout routine, be sure to request accommodations on the side with the lift.

FACILITIES AND SERVICES: Air-conditioning in most rooms, honor bar, restaurant and 24-hour room service, central heat, direct-dial voicemail phones in rooms and bathrooms, hair dryer, laundry and cleaning services, office safe and room safes, lift to most rooms, 24-hour room service, minibar, satellite TV, radio, clock, modems in all rooms, secretarial and office services

EC1

Farringdon and Clerkenwell

While not the West End nor near any tourist excitement, the area of London known as Farringdon and Clerkenwell is becoming more popular thanks to its handful of trendy eating places and more affordable real estate prices. It is close to the Barbican Centre, where the Royal Shakespeare Company and the London Symphony Orchestra perform, and where the Museum of London and the Barbican Art Gallery are located. St. Giles Church and the City of London School for Girls are in the central courtyard of the center. Early birds can raise a pint or two with the market workers in a pub around the famous Smithfield Market, a meat and poultry wholesale market since the twelfth century. One of the tube stops, Farringdon Station, is the original terminus of the Metropolitan Line, the world's first underground. The walk to The City is not far.

OTHER OPTIONS in EC1

Apartment Rentals

Orion–Barbican   **189**

Student Dormitories

Rosebery Avenue Hall   **219**

YMCAs

London City YMCA   **231**

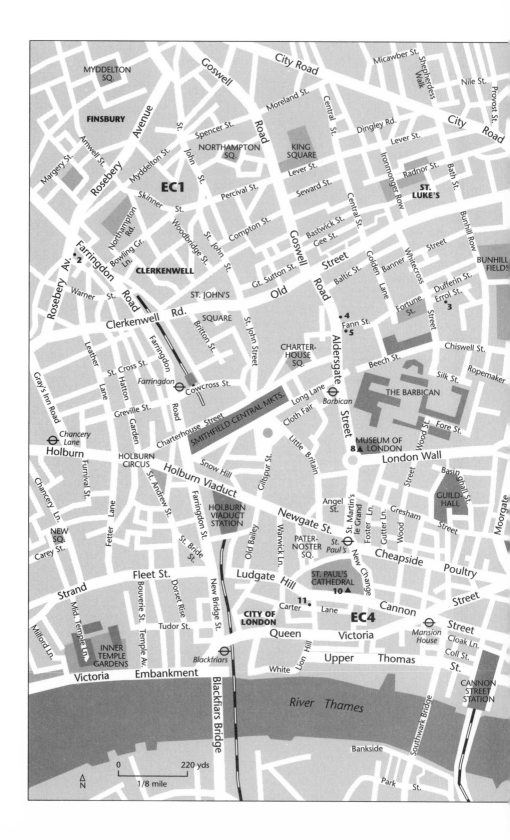

MYDDELTON SQ.

City Road

Micawber St.
Shepherdess Walk

Nile St.

Provost St.

Goswell

FINSBURY

Moreland St.

Dingley Rd.

Avenue

Spencer St.

Central St.

City

Road

NORTHAMPTON SQ.

KING SQUARE

Lever St.

Ironmonger Row

Radnor St.

Bath St.

Road

Amwell St.

Margery St.

St. John St.

Rosebery

Myddelton St.

EC1

Percival St.

Seward St.

Central St.

ST. LUKE'S

Bunhill Row

Skinner

Northampton Rd.

St.

Woodbridge St.

Compton St.

Bastwick St.

Gee St.

Golden Lane

Banner

Whitecross

Street

BUNHILL FIELDS

Bowling Gr. Ln.

St. John St.

Goswell

Baltic St.

Dufferin St.

Errol St.

CLERKENWELL

Gt. Sutton St.

Old

Street

3

Rosebery Av.

2

Warner St.

Clerkenwell Rd.

ST. JOHN'S

SQUARE

Britton St.

St. John Street

4

Fann St.

5

Fortune St.

Chiswell St.

Ropemaker

Farringdon Road

Leather Lane

St. Cross St.

Hatton Garden

Farringdon Road

CHARTER-HOUSE SQ.

Aldersgate

Beech St.

THE BARBICAN

Silk St.

Fore St.

Chancery Lane

Greville St.

Cowcross St.

Charterhouse Street

SMITHFIELD CENTRAL MKTS.

Cloth Fair

Long Lane

Barbican

Street

St. Paul's

Gray's Inn Road

Holburn

HOLBURN CIRCUS

Snow Hill

Little Britain

MUSEUM OF LONDON

8

London Wall

Basinghall St.

Furnival St.

Chancery Ln.

St. Andrew St.

Holburn Viaduct

Giltspur St.

Angel St.

St. Martin's le Grand

Foster Ln.

Gutter Ln.

Wood

Gresham

GUILD HALL

Street

Moorgate

NEW SQ.

Fetter Lane

Farringdon St.

HOLBURN VIADUCT STATION

Newgate St.

PATER-NOSTER SQ.

St. Paul's

Cheapside

Poultry

Carey St.

St. Bride St.

Old Bailey

Warwick Ln.

New Change

Fleet St.

Bouverie St.

Dorset Rise

New Bridge St.

Ludgate Hill

ST. PAUL'S CATHEDRAL

10

Cannon

Street

Strand

Mid. Temple Ln.

Temple Av.

Tudor St.

CITY OF LONDON

11

Carter

Lane

EC4

Mansion House

Cloak Ln.

Milford Ln.

INNER TEMPLE GARDENS

Blackfriars

Queen

Victoria

Lion Hill

Upper

Thomas

Coll St.

St.

CANNON STREET STATION

Victoria

Embankment

White

River Thames

Blackfriars Bridge

Bankside

Southwark Bridge

0   220 yds

1/8 mile

N

Park St.

EC1, EC2, EC3, EC4, E1

EC2

The Barbican

The Barbican Centre serves as one of London's arts centers and is home to the London Symphony Orchestra. In addition to attending concerts, you can visit the art gallery, cinema, or theater. Other than this center, the area offers little of interest to most visitors.

OTHER OPTIONS in EC2 (see map page 166)
YMCAs
Barbican YMCA   **229**

EC4

The City

The one-and-a-quarter-square-mile area known as The City was, in fact, the original city of London and is loaded with history and beautiful churches. It was devastated in 1666 by the Great Fire, and again during the Blitz in World War II. Today it is the heart of London's business and financial world, and fills each working day with a quarter of a million people who lend it an air of importance and excitement. On the weekends it is a ghost town . . . even some of the pubs and most of the restaurants are closed. You definitely want to time your visit here on a weekday, and I recommend going on one of the walking tours that concentrate on the importance of this interesting part of London.

OTHER OPTIONS in EC4 (see map page 166)
Youth Hostels
City of London Youth Hostel   **234**

SE1

South Bank and Waterloo

Development along the South Bank of the River Thames has brought this once run-down and neglected area of London into prominence. It takes in Shakespeare's Globe Theatre and museum, Southwark Cathedral, the wharves housing several well-known restaurants in Sir Terence Conran's vast empire, and the new Tate Gallery of Modern Art, which will be housed in a former power station. The sprawling area also includes the Royal Festival Hall and South Bank Centre on one side of the Waterloo Bridge and the Royal National Theatre on the other. A riverside walkway links the Royal Festival Hall to Waterloo Station; the magnificent view of The City from the Waterloo Bridge has inspired many artists.

HOTELS in SE1

OTHER OPTIONS

Student Dormitories

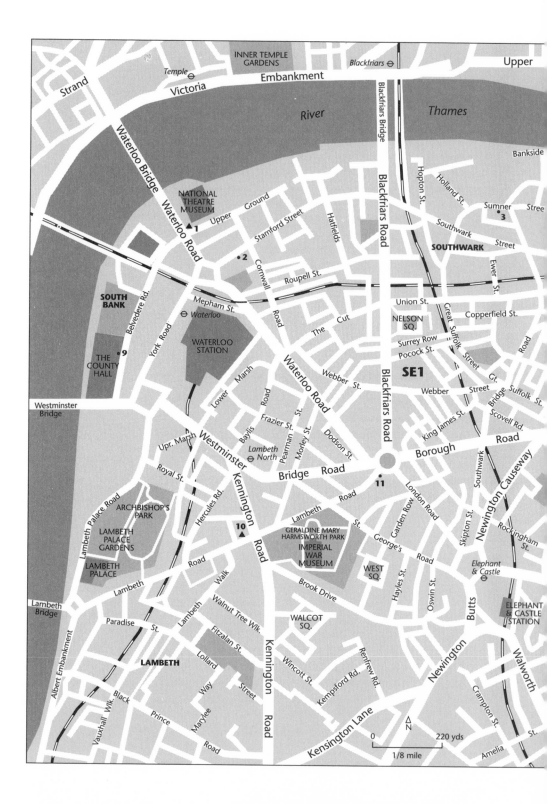

Strand

Victoria

INNER TEMPLE GARDENS

Temple ⊖

Embankment

Blackfriars ⊖

Upper

River

Thames

Bankside

Blackfriars Bridge

Waterloo Bridge

NATIONAL THEATRE MUSEUM

Upper Ground

Stamford Street

Hatfields

Hopton St.

Holland St.

Sumner Stree

3

▲1

Southwark

Waterloo Road

2

Cornwall

Roupell St.

Road

Union St.

Southwark Street

SOUTHWARK

SOUTH BANK

Mepham St.

⊖ Waterloo

The Cut

NELSON SQ.

Copperfield St.

Great Suffolk Street

Ewer St.

Belvedere Rd.

York Road

WATERLOO STATION

Surrey Row

Pocock St.

Road

THE COUNTY HALL

9

Lower

Marsh

Road

Webber St.

SE1

Gt.

Suffolk St.

Scovell Rd.

Waterloo Road

Webber Street

Bridge

Westminster Bridge

Baylis

Frazier St.

St.

Pearman St.

Morley St.

Dodson St.

King James St.

Borough Road

Upr. Marsh

Westminster

Lambeth North ⊖

Bridge Road

11

London Road

Garden Row

Southwark

Newington Causeway

Royal St.

Kennington

Skipton St.

Rockingham St.

ARCHBISHOP'S PARK

Hercules Rd.

10 ▲

Lambeth Road

St. George's

Butts

Lambeth Palace Road

LAMBETH PALACE GARDENS

GERALDINE MARY HARMSWORTH PARK

IMPERIAL WAR MUSEUM

Road

Elephant & Castle ⊖

ELEPHANT & CASTLE STATION

LAMBETH PALACE

Road

WEST SQ.

Hayles St.

Oswin St.

Lambeth Bridge

Lambeth

Walk

Brook Drive

WALCOT SQ.

Albert Embankment

Paradise St.

Lambeth

Walnut Tree Wlk.

Fitzalan St.

Wincott St.

Kempsford Rd.

Renfrew Rd.

Newington

Walworth

LAMBETH

Lollard Street

Kennington Road

Crampton St.

Vauxhall Wlk.

Black

Prince

Manlee

Way

Road

Kensington Lane

N

0   220 yds

1/8 mile

Amelia St.

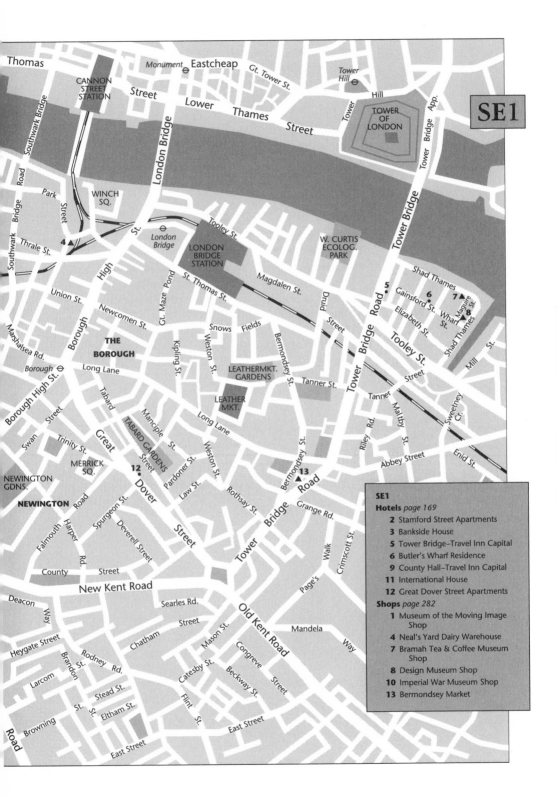

Thomas Monument Eastcheap Gt. Tower St.

Tower Hill

Hill

CANNON STREET STATION

Street

Lower Thames Street

Tower Hill

TOWER OF LONDON

Tower Bridge App.

SE1

Southwark Bridge

London Bridge

Tower Bridge

Park Street

WINCH SQ.

Road

Bridge

Southwark

Thrale St.

4 ▲

St.

London Bridge

Tooley St.

LONDON BRIDGE STATION

Magdalen St.

W. CURTIS ECOLOG. PARK

Shad Thames

5 • Gainsford St. Wharf 6 St. 7 ▲ 8 ▲

Tower Bridge Road

Elizabeth St.

Shad Thames

Mill St.

High

Union St.

Newcomen St.

Gt. Maze Pond

St. Thomas St.

Snows Fields

Bermondsey St.

Tooley St.

Tanner St.

Street

Tanner

Sweeney Ct.

Borough

THE BOROUGH

Long Lane

Kipling St.

Weston St.

LEATHERMKT. GARDENS

LEATHER MKT.

Druid Street

Riley Rd.

St.

Maltby

Abbey Street

Enid St.

Marshalsea Rd.

Borough High St.

Borough ⊖

Tabard

Street

Long Lane

MANCIPLE St.

Street

TABARD GARDENS

Weston St.

Rothsay St.

Bermondsey St.

Road

Grange Rd.

Swan

Trinity St.

Great

MERRICK SQ.

12 •

Dover

Pardoner St.

Law St.

13 ▲

NEWINGTON GDNS.

NEWINGTON

Falmouth Rd.

Harper Rd.

Spurgeon St.

Deverell Street

Street

Tower Bridge Road

Page's Walk

Crimscott St.

County Street

New Kent Road

Searles Rd.

Street

Mandela Way

Deacon Way

Heygate Street

Larcom

Brandon St.

Rodney Rd.

Stead St.

Eltham St.

Chatham

Mason St.

Catesby St.

Beckway St.

Congreve Street

Flint St.

Old Kent Road

Browning St.

East Street

East Street

Road

COUNTY HALL–TRAVEL INN CAPITAL (9)
Belvedere Road, SE1
313 rooms, all with shower or bath and toilet

For central reservations information, rates, and a description of this hotel chain, please see page 97.

TELEPHONE: 020-7902-1600
FAX: 020-7902-1619
TUBE: Waterloo

TOWER BRIDGE–TRAVEL INN CAPITAL (5)
Tower Bridge Road, SE1
185 rooms, all with shower or bath and toilet

For central reservations information, rates, and a description of this hotel chain, please see page 97.

TELEPHONE: 020-7940-3700
FAX: 020-7940-3719
TUBE: London Bridge

Other Options

London hotels are among the most expensive in the world, and the busiest. What does a Cheap Sleeper do when everything is booked and the budget purse strings cannot be stretched one pound further? The answer is: seek other options.

Besides traditional hotel rooms, visitors to London have a wide variety of other options that make Cheap Sleeping sense; they include everything from staying in an apartment to pitching a tent under the stars. With many of these alternative Cheap Sleeps, you will be asked to pay in cash and be required to make a hefty deposit in advance of arrival. Many private B&Bs and flat rentals demand that the balance of your stay be paid on arrival. Refund policies can be merciless, and are *never* in your favor. Many keep their policies simple and to the point: no refunds, period. To avoid costly headaches and financial anguish if you have to cancel or cut your trip short, *please* invest in trip-cancellation insurance whenever possible. These policies are available through various state automobile associations, your travel agent, and, in some cases, from the flat rental agency you are dealing with in London. I cannot overemphasize the importance of carrying this insurance. I hope you never need it, but if you do, it could save you thousands of dollars in forfeited money.

Apartment Rentals

There is no place like home, so on your next trip to London, why not consider renting a flat? A stay in a flat gives you more space than a hotel, and for less money. Almost as important, it allows you to get to know a neighborhood of London that you will soon think of as your own. If you are staying longer than a few days, a flat makes sense because discounts can often be negotiated based on the time of year and length of stay. If you are traveling with children, the kitchen convenience can be a big money-saver, even if you only fix breakfast and a few snacks a day.

When researching the London flat scene, I can promise you I ran across some real bomb sites that were not only ugly, run-down, and depressing but dirty and operated by unfriendly people who would never darken the door of your flat if you faced any sort of maintenance problem. Others, sadly, have not followed routine maintenance or done any upgrading and thus have been dropped from this edition. Just as with all of the hotels and shops listed in *Cheap Sleeps in London,* I have personally inspected all of the apartments I recommend to you.

Even though I mention it as the number one tip for apartment rentals, it is so important it bears repeating here: If you plan on renting a flat, be sure you clearly understand the payment, cancellation, and refund policies. It is beyond the scope of this book to detail the various policies you will encounter, but they are usually draconian and hit hardest when the chips are down and you must change your plans. If you accept only one piece of advice from me on apartment rentals, this is it: *Buy cancellation insurance.* This small investment will pay off handsomely if you have to change plans about dates, cancel altogether, or must suddenly cut your stay short.

CHEAP SLEEPING TIPS ON RENTING A LONDON APARTMENT

1. Most important: Know the cancellation policy and buy cancellation insurance.

2. Be very specific when stating your needs: size of flat and number of occupants; stall shower versus handheld shower nozzle in a tub; kitchen equipment (i.e., microwave, fully outfitted for major cooking sprees, or are you just going to peel an orange and drink instant coffee?). Don't forget to consider the beds. Do you want a double or twin beds, or will a pullout sofa or Murphy bed do? Ask that color photographs of the flat you are considering be sent to you.

3. Is there a phone? How much are the calls? Is there an answering machine in your flat or a switchboard to take calls when you are out? What about a fax in your apartment or access to one in the office? And don't forget about a modem if you plan on accessing the Internet and picking up your email.

4. Who pays for utilities, other than the telephone, which you are always charged for? Be careful on this one . . . especially if you are going to run the heat or air-conditioning full blast.

5. How far is the flat from *your* center of interest in London? Where is the nearest market, laundry and dry cleaner, tube and bus stops, pub, restaurant? Ask for a map with the location of the flat, nearest tube stop, and grocery shopping pinpointed.

6. Is maid service included, and if not, is it available and how much does it cost?

7. Who is responsible for laundering the sheets and towels? If you are, you will probably want a washer and dryer in the unit, or at least in the building.

8. Is the apartment suitable for children? Is a park or playground nearby?

9. Is there a lift to your flat? While that fifth-floor penthouse has a million-dollar view, do you really want to lug suitcases up and down, as well as bags of groceries and shopping finds? Think about this one carefully . . . stairs get old *fast*.

10. If dealing with an apartment rental agency, find out about other services the company may offer, such as airport transfers, sightseeing in London, help with ongoing travel in the U.K., and air travel arrangements. The list can be long, cost effective, and very helpful.

HOTELS IN LONDON WITH APARTMENTS AND/OR KITCHENETTES

Amsterdam Hotel, Earl's Court, SW5	**146**
Comfort Inn Hyde Park, Hyde Park, W2	**64**
The Cranley, South Kensington, SW5	**148**
Jarvis Embassy House Hotel, South Kensington, SW7	**159**
Knightsbridge Hotel, Knightsbridge, SW3	**141**
Mayflower Hotel, Earl's Court, SW5	**150**
Morgan Hotel, Bloomsbury, WC1	**104**
Searcy's Roof Garden Rooms, Knightsbridge, SW1	**126**
Winchester Hotel, Victoria/Pimlico, SW1	**132**

APARTMENTS IN UNIVERSITY DORMITORIES

BUAC–British Universities Accommodation Consortium Ltd.	**212**
King's College London–King's Campus Vacation Bureau	**215**
London School of Economics Halls and Residences	**218**

SERVICED APARTMENTS

ASHBURN GARDEN APARTMENTS (20)
3–4 Ashburn Gardens, South Kensington, SW7
25 flats, all with shower or bath and toilet

TELEPHONE
020-7370-2663
FAX
020-7370-6743
TUBE
Gloucester Road
CREDIT CARDS
None; cash in British sterling only

For an economical Cheap Sleep, Ashburn Garden is a basic budget bet, provided that the bathrooms and kitchens have been completely redone and the folding beds removed from the hallways. Otherwise, pass this one by until renovations are complete.

I continue to list the flats for several reasons: price, location, and the resident housekeepers, Susan and James Covey, whose Scottish warmth and cheerful hospitality have endeared them to scores of regulars. James serves as porter and handyman and is full of great tips about what to see and do in London. Susan supervises the housekeeping staff and looks after the guests with the same care and dedicated enthusiasm she gives to her own family. The flats are functional, but woefully short on the latest styles. Hopefully the owner, Andrew Aresti, will remedy this by updating them as planned. I also hope he will start taking credit cards. The best flats are those on the higher floors, because the bedrooms in these are on the quiet side of the building and get more light. There is a launderette close by, and a huge Sainsbury's and a Waitrose, two of London's best supermarkets, are only a block away. Public transportation is a snap and less than five minutes away by foot.

FACILITIES AND SERVICES: Central heat, direct-dial phones with private number, lift, equipped kitchens, satellite TV, office safe, iron and ironing board, maid service Monday through Friday

RATES
One bedroom for 1–2 persons £85 daily, £465 weekly; two bedrooms for 4 £120 daily, £810 weekly; lower rates November–March; additional beds/cots £20 daily, £90 weekly

ASTONS APARTMENTS (30)
39 Rosary Gardens, South Kensington, SW7
49 flats, all with shower or bath and toilet

Astons Apartments have a new owner and a new look. Gone are the dated bathless budget studios, now replaced by streamlined units with equipped kitchens and private bathrooms. The three stately Victorian homes that make up Astons are tucked away in South Kensington on a quiet side street off Old Brompton Road. This puts you close to almost any place in London, either on foot, via the Gloucester Road tube station, or on a red double-decker bus. If you decide to eat in, good supermarkets are not far, or if you are stepping out to dine, the scores of wonderful restaurants will make it hard to decide which to select, but *Cheap Eats in London* will come to your rescue.

The coordinated accommodations are divided into standard and designer studios. The standard studios are small, basic, and somewhat cramped for long stays involving more than one person with any degree of luggage. They do have equipped kitchens with microwaves and hot plates, satellite television, and private telephones (with answering machines on request). The designer choices have a touch more space and luxuriousness, and include a marble shower, iron and trouser press, and private room safe in addition to all of the above amenities. Those on the front have balconies and those on the

TELEPHONE
020-7590-6000; 800-525-2810 (toll-free from the U.S.)

FAX
020-7590-6060

EMAIL
sales@astons-apartments.com

INTERNET
www.astons-apartments.com

TUBE
Gloucester Road

CREDIT CARDS
MC, V

RATES
Standard single from £55 per day; double from £75–80 per day; triple from £110 per day; quad from £140 per day; 15 designer studios for 1–2 £115 per day. Lower rates for longer stays. All rates exclusive of 17½-percent VAT. Strict 48-hour cancellation or change of plans policy absolutely enforced.

back overlook a green space. When booking, please be aware that management strictly adheres to an ironclad forty-eight-hour cancellation policy, which will not be waived for any reason whatsoever. In addition, if you cut your stay short without giving forty-eight hours notice, you will pay for the entire stay. They also quote their rates without the hefty $17\frac{1}{2}$ percent VAT.

FACILITIES AND SERVICES: Central heat, direct-dial phones, answering machines on request, hair dryer on request, equipped kitchens, office safe (standard studios), room safe (designer studios), satellite TV, no lift

CITADINES–SOUTH KENSINGTON (8)
35A Gloucester Road, South Kensington, SW7
92 flats, all with shower or bath and toilet

TELEPHONE
020-7543-7878
FAX
020-7584-9166
INTERNET
www.citadines.com (central reservations)
TUBE
Gloucester Road
CREDIT CARDS
AE, MC, V
RATES
Studio 1–2 persons £110; one bedroom for 1–4 persons £150; lower rates for longer stays and during the off-season

The ninety-two apartments at the Citadines in South Kensington offer foolproof, predictable lodgings. You have your choice of a studio or a two-level apartment decked out in cookie-cutter style, meaning if you've seen one, you've seen them all. Kitchens are fitted, bathrooms stocked with towels, and the service gracious. In the basement you can work out in the fitness studio while doing a load of laundry in the launderette. There is no dining room, but special rates can be arranged for guests to have breakfast at the restaurant next door. From the doorstep, you are within walking distance of the Victoria and Albert, Natural History, and Science museums; concerts at the Royal Albert Hall; and grocery shopping at the mammouth 24-hour Sainsbury's on Cromwell Road.

FACILITIES AND SERVICES: Central heat, direct-dial phones, fitness studio, hair dryer, iron, baby cots and nappy-changing facilities on request, coin-operated laundry, lift, satellite TV, 24-hour desk

COLLINGHAM SERVICED APARTMENTS (26)
26–27 Collingham Gardens, Earl's Court, SW5
25 flats, all with shower or bath and toilet

TELEPHONE
020-7244-8677
FAX
020-7244-7331
EMAIL
Collingham@infiniti.demon.co.uk
TUBE
Earl's Court, Gloucester Road
CREDIT CARDS
AE, DC, MC, V

The fashionable and understated apartments in these two converted Victorian townhouses feel like private residences. The location is convenient for early morning jogs in Kensington Gardens, and you are also close to the Royal Albert Hall and the complex with the Victoria and Albert, Natural History, and Science museums. For day-to-day household shopping there is Sainsbury's, an enormous supermarket, plus the usual neighborhood spots where you can pick up the daily paper or buy water. Each apartment has a sitting and dining area, a very well equipped kitchen that includes a four-burner stove, refrigerator/freezer, and microwave, plus all the nice pots, pans, and crockery you will need to do a full range of cooking. The modern tiled bathrooms have blue trim and enough light and space to make them serviceable. Closet space is good. Number 120, a huge three-bedroom, two-bath unit tastefully done in blues, faces Collingham Gardens. It has a dining table that seats six, and a large kitchen with a pass-through to the living and dining room. Number 122 is a one-bedroom choice on the back facing other apartments. I like its large sitting room, great kitchen with loads of counter space, and the roof terrace—especially on a sunny day.

FACILITIES AND SERVICES: Central heat, direct-dial phones, hair dryer, iron and ironing board available, fully fitted kitchens, laundry service, lift, office safe, maid service six days a week, satellite TV, 24-hour desk. On request they can arrange airport pickup, office services, theater and tour bookings, and video rental.

RATES
Studio (sleeps two) £90; one bedroom (sleeps two) £135; two bedrooms (sleeps four) £180–200; three bedrooms (sleeps six) £245; penthouse (sleeps four to six) £215–260; free baby cots; lower rates from October 1 to March 31

DOLPHIN SQUARE (34)
Dolphin Square, Pimlico, SW1
151 flats, all with shower or bath and toilet

Dolphin Square, a seven-and-a-half-acre riverside block of flats and gardens near the Tate Gallery, has been called home in the past by an illustrious group of residents, including Christine Keeler, the prostitute at the center of the Profumo scandal; Sir Oswald Mosley, the World War II leader of British Fascists; John Vassal, the Admiralty spy; and, more recently, Princess Anne and her husband, Commander Timothy Laurence, both of whom spent a few months in a flat here.

If you enjoy the services offered by a deluxe hotel, plus the advantages of sports facilities, shops, and a place to park your car, it would be hard to imagine a better address than Dolphin Square. The flats range from studios to three-bedroom accommodations with fireplaces, above-average kitchens, large baths, and loads of actual storage and living space. All are highly recommendable. Aside from just staying in nice surroundings, guests are extended free membership in the Health Club, with a sixty-foot heated indoor swimming pool, sauna, and steam room. A staff is on hand to provide massages and beauty treatments at reasonable rates. Energetic visitors

TELEPHONE
020-7834-3800; 800-44-UTELL (toll-free from the U.S.)
FAX
020-7798-8735
EMAIL
reservations@dolphinsquarehotel.co.uk
INTERNET
www.hotelbook (Utell)
TUBE
Pimlico
CREDIT CARDS
AE, DC, MC, V
RATES
Studio: single use £130–165; double use £150–175; classic suites: 1 bedroom £185–195; 2 bedrooms, sleeps 3 £230; 2 bedrooms, sleeps 4 £240; 2 bedrooms, 2 baths, sleeps 4 £270; 3 bedrooms, 3 baths, sleeps 6 £320; monthly rates depending upon availability and time of year; Continental breakfast £8, full English breakfast £15

can book a tennis court or join a squash game on one of eight courts. Others can attend yoga or aerobics classes. Two restaurants and room service take care of those not in the mood to cook. For those who are, shopping in the arcade is a cinch with a greengrocer, supermarket, deli, wine shop, travel and theater booking agent, car hire, chemist, newsstand, dry cleaner, and hairdresser all right there.

All flats have fully equipped kitchens and seven-day-a-week maid service, but the prices do *not* include breakfast.

FACILITIES AND SERVICES: "The works," including but not limited to: bar, business and conference center, central heat and ceiling fans, direct-dial phones, answering machine in all flats, hair dryer, iron and ironing board, fully fitted kitchens, microwaves in smaller flats or on request in larger flats, laundry and dry cleaning shop on premises, lift, office safe, parking (£15 per 24 hours), restaurants and room service, satellite TV, sports club, swimming pool, squash and tennis courts, full-service beauty salon, fax and modem facilities, Internet access, mobile phone rental, travel agency, shops, theater booking, car hire, porters, 24-hour desk

EIGHT KNARESBOROUGH PLACE (23)
8 Knaresborough Place, Earl's Court, SW5
12 flats, all with shower or bath and toilet

TELEPHONE
020-7244-8409/7373-0323

FAX
020-7373-6455

TUBE
Earl's Court, Gloucester Road

CREDIT CARDS
AE, DC, MC, V

RATES
£100–165 per night for up to four people; minimum stay of two days, breakfast not included; lower rates on request for stays of more than three weeks

Eight Knaresborough Place and Five Emperor's Gate (below) are owned and managed by Robert and Polly Arnold, his sister Susan Noah, and their father, Walter Arnold. Robert is in charge of the business end, while the others handle the interior decorating and day-to-day running of these two blocks of serviced flats. Judging from the repeat guests, especially Americans, this is a winning team. I prefer the block of twelve flats at Knaresborough Place because they are better located, have good security, and offer the added convenience of a laundry room. The interiors are up-to-the-minute and comfortably coordinated, and several flats have their own private patio gardens or balconies with chairs and tables for sunny days. For shopping needs, you will have to go no farther than Cromwell Road, to two of the best supermarkets in London that have everything you could ever need and then some.

There is always someone at the desk from 7 A.M. to 11 P.M. at Knaresborough Place, whereas at Emperor's Gate there is no office or on-site manager at any time.

FACILITIES AND SERVICES: Central heat, direct-line private phones in each flat, hair dryer, fitted kitchens, iron and ironing board, drying rack, coin-operated laundry, TV, linen and maid service six days a week, no lift, no safe, complimentary daily newspapers

FIVE EMPEROR'S GATE (12)
5 Emperor's Gate, South Kensington, SW7
6 flats, all with shower or bath and toilet

The six flats at Five Emperor's Gate—which is run by the same people who run Eight Knaresborough Place (above)—have their devotees, especially those with the newer bathrooms and kitchens hidden behind folding louvered doors. If you are willing to climb some steep stairs, ask for Flat F, with a sofa bed and a bird's-eye view from the arched windows. It's a bit of a tight squeeze in the twin bedroom, but it does have appeal. So does the Flat First Level West, with a large mirrored closet, small balcony, and a separate sitting area. If stairs are not part of your program, reserve Flat A, a basement location with a separate entrance and a bricked-floor entry. There isn't much sunshine here, but that doesn't seem to bother those who appreciate the cozy electric fireplace, rather modern furniture, and one of the better kitchens in the building.

Emperor's Gate has no office or on-site manager; phone the office at Eight Knaresborough Place for information and reservations.

FACILITIES AND SERVICES: Central heat, direct-line private phones in each flat, hair dryer, fitted kitchens, iron and ironing board, drying rack, TV, linen and maid service six days a week, no lift, no safe, complimentary daily newspapers

TELEPHONE
020-7244-8409/7373-0323

FAX
020-7373-6455

TUBE
Gloucester Road

CREDIT CARDS
AE, DC, MC, V

RATES
£100–165 per night for up to four people; minimum stay of two days, breakfast not included; lower rates on request for stays of more than three weeks

JEROME HOUSE (5)
14 Lisson Grove, Marylebone, NW1
24 flats, all with shower or bath and toilet

Finding and renting a flat in a strange city and country can cause aggravation . . . and I'm talking aggravation with a capital A. You can save yourself the hassle and book into Jerome House, part of the Westminster Apartment Services. This agency can meet almost all budgets and lifestyles in very well managed,

TELEPHONE
020-7706-1871 (Jerome House); 020-7221-1400 (Westminster)

FAX
020-7723-3277 (Jerome House); 020-7229-3917 (Westminster)

EMAIL
westminsterapartments@
viennagroup.co.uk
INTERNET
www.vienna-group.co.uk
TUBE
Marylebone
CREDIT CARDS
AE, DC, MC, V
RATES
Weekly: studio £620; one
bedroom £910; two bedrooms
£1,140

nicely maintained flats in central London. My focus is on Jerome House, which I found outstanding on every level with the possible exception of the area, which is rather remote for tourists. That said, there is a tube a few minutes away; buses run up and down Marylebone Road; and there is some great antique hunting not far away on Church Street (see "Indoor Antiques Markets" in the "Cheap Chic" section of this book, page 288).

Space, space, and more space—this is what you get at Jerome House. The fifth-floor apartments have skyline views, others overlook the Old Marylebone Grammar School, and most have good sunlight. Even the studios have plenty of room to settle in and call it home. Beds range from king-size to sofa style. Closets are, in a word, fabulous. Bathrooms are marble. Big modern kitchens provide you with all you need to cook and eat in grand style. After, put the dishes in the dishwasher, the towels in the washing machine, and stretch out on the couch and watch CNN or a video in a nicely decorated sitting room.

FACILITIES AND SERVICES: Central heat and fans, direct-dial phones with answering machines (on request), hair dryer, kitchens with microwaves and dishwashers, laundry service, washers and dryers, lift, parking (£10 per day), room safe, satellite TV with video and video rentals in lobby, maid service Mon–Fri, linen changed twice weekly, 24-hour desk, welcome grocery pack if staying three nights or more

KENSBRIDGE APARTMENTS
Main office: 38 Emperor's Gate, South Kensington, SW7

TELEPHONE
020-7589-2923 (central
reservations)
FAX
020-7373-6183 (central
reservations)
TUBE
Gloucester Road
CREDIT CARDS
None; British sterling only

There is not a chance you will become bored with perfection in one of Walter Harris's unsophisticated Cheap Sleeping flats. If you need some place for a long-term London stay and can keep expectations to a rock-bottom level while living in a no-frills, no-charm spot with fifties veneer, dated colors, and user-friendly furniture, you will no doubt be just fine staying here and certainly pleased with the money you will save. If you are willing to share a bathroom with another flat, the Cheap Sleep gets even cheaper. Some of the singles are mighty small, closets are minuscule, and the kitchen (of sorts) does not always have a sink—you might have to use the one in the bathroom. Most of the flats have twin beds, but doubles can be requested. Remember, the money you save will make for wonderful evenings out. The locations are close to bus and tube transport, and household shopping needs can easily be met in nearby supermarkets and neighborhood shops. Despite the time-warp feel of these flats, they are *very* popular with determined budgeteers, so if you fall in that category, get your reservation in early . . . and read the fine print about refunds, cancellations, and so on. There is a one-week minimum stay.

Apartments in the group include Eccleston House, Elvaston Lodge, and Kensgate House, all briefly described below. For reservations contact the main office.

FACILITIES AND SERVICES: All flats have heat, hall phones, equipped kitchens, Mon–Fri maid service, linen changed weekly, TV, no safes, office hours Mon–Fri 9:30 A.M.–5:30 P.M., Sat 9 A.M.–2 P.M., closed Sunday and holidays

RATES
Singles start at £155 per week (shared facilities), no singles with bath, shower, and toilet; doubles start at £285 per week (shared facilities), £310–340 with facilities; triple or quad with private facilities £310–455; extra bed £25 per week; rates do not include 17½ percent VAT; a deposit of £100, paid in British sterling, is required to secure the reservation.

ECCLESTON HOUSE (24)
64–66 Eccleston Square, Victoria, SW1

Despite the historic location on lovely Eccleston Square, only three doors from one of Winston Churchill's former homes, the Eccleston House flats are recommended only for the hardest-core Cheap Sleeping enthusiasts on this planet. The flats are clean and the location good, but you know you are on a lean budget when you are Sleeping Cheaply here.

TELEPHONE
020-7839-0985
TUBE
Victoria

ELVASTON LODGE (9)
12 Elvaston Place, South Kensington, SW7

This block of flats in South Kensington features studios and two-room apartments and is the best of this group. That is not saying much, however, because just like all the others, it is very, very budget-basic with no decorating thought given to any of the flats. Forget bringing any electronic equipment more sophisticated than a transistor radio with earphones; the electricity won't take anything more. Email hookup? You must be joking. The only telephone is the one by the entryway in the downstairs hall. Top flat picks are No. 8, with a loft bedroom, and No. 9, a front studio for two with a porch.

TELEPHONE
020-7589-9412 (office); 020-7584-0873 (guests)
TUBE
Gloucester Road

KENSGATE HOUSE (13)
38 Emperor's Gate, South Kensington, SW7
17 flats, 13 with shower or bath and toilet

TELEPHONE
020-7370-1040 (office); 020-7370-6624 (guests)

TUBE
Gloucester Road

The decorating theme here follows the same "any chair will do" mentality as the others in the Kensbridge group. The four single flats do not have private facilities and in No. 10, the tiniest, the same sink doubles as your bathroom and/or kitchen washing facility. If you land in No. 1, a small basement double with facilities, you will get a double bed, two chairs, and a fold-down table mounted on one wall. A better choice is No. 9, with a separate kitchen, two chairs, and a proper table. Number 2, on the ground floor facing the street, is the largest and lightest choice. There is a double bed on the main level, but on the mezzanine above, anyone over four feet tall would not be able to stand erect.

KNIGHTSBRIDGE SERVICE FLATS (4)
45 Ennismore Gardens, Knightsbridge, SW7
12 flats, all with shower or bath and toilet

TELEPHONE
020-7584-4123

FAX
020-7584-9058

EMAIL
info@ksflats.demon.co.uk

INTERNET
www.ksflats.demon.co.uk

TUBE
Knightsbridge

CREDIT CARDS
MC, V

RATES
Single from £70 per night; double from £80 per night; lower off-season rates. They prefer a week's stay, but shorter stays can be accommodated if there is room. Reservations are guaranteed on receipt of one week's rent in advance, and all rents thereafter are payable weekly in advance. If you leave before your reservation is over, you will be charged for the full period unless the flat can be relet.

Because these flats are functional, clean, well located, and so reasonably priced, I consider them an excellent Cheap Sleep choice.

For the ultimate in London shopping, you can take a shortcut and sneak through "the hole-in-the-wall" and be at Harrods' door in minutes. However, if you are expecting to entertain dignitaries or want high-roller surroundings, these flats are not for you, despite the celebrity-studded neighborhood of stately mansions. Ava Gardner lived across the street for twenty years in a flat that rumor has it was paid for by Frank Sinatra, and Charles Gray, who played in early James Bond films, lives next door.

These twelve units are furnished in a mix from the forties and fifties. Some have been redecorated in bland beige, others are still in off-greens and pungent oranges. Most have beds in the sitting room and too many chairs. On the plus side, the bathrooms are good and the kitchens, even though they are old-style, have microwaves and everything else you will need for boiling water or preparing a feast. The top-floor flats are the best because they have better views, and remember, there *is* a lift. The basement garden flat, with an eat-in kitchen, opens onto a patio and has a sunroom with a sofa and two chairs.

FACILITIES AND SERVICES: Wall heaters, direct-dial phones with private number, lift, no safe, satellite TV, iron and ironing board, maid service Mon–Fri, office open 8 A.M.–8 P.M.

LONDON SUITES (5)
12 Ovington Square, Knightsbridge, SW3
8 flats, all with shower or bath and toilet

Location, location, location. This is what you will get in a London Suites flat. If you want to be within strolling distance to London's best shopping in Knightsbridge, close to scores of excellent restaurants catering to all budgets (see *Cheap Eats in London*), and near good transportation that has you anywhere in the West End in under thirty minutes . . . this is your neighborhood.

At the sedate London Suites you will have the use of a private garden, twice-weekly maid service, a fitted kitchen with microwave, a lift, TV with VCR on request, stereo CDs, your own washing machine or the use of one in the basement, plus attractive surroundings where you can move in, spread out, and actually live in London and pretend you are a native. Another good point: management is friendly and on-site. Accommodations range from studios to one-bedroom flats, two of which are nonsmoking.

While I am usually less than enthusiastic about subterranean-level accommodations, I do like the newly redone No. 12B, with its separate entrance and very nice kitchen. Number 491, a quiet studio on the back, has some of the owner's traditional furniture and a walk-in closet. Number 402 is also quiet and very nice, with a stained-glass domed skylight, but the view is not wonderful.

FACILITIES AND SERVICES: Central heat, private telephone line, answering machine at no extra charge, private door-entry buzzer, hair dryer, laundry facilities in units or in building, iron and ironing board, fitted kitchens with microwaves, lift, TV (VCR on request), stereo CD players, maid and linen service twice weekly, office hours Mon–Fri 8:30 A.M.–5 P.M. (but someone is always on call for guests)

TELEPHONE
020-7581-5466

FAX
020-7584-2912

EMAIL
info@londonsuites.com

INTERNET
www.londonsuites.com

TUBE
Knightsbridge

CREDIT CARDS
AE, MC, V

RATES
All rates are per week and there is a minimum three-night stay: studio £550–650; one bedroom £700–850

NELL GWYNN HOUSE: NGH APARTMENTS LIMITED AND THE ACCOMMODATION OFFICE (8)
Sloane Avenue, Chelsea, SW3
NGH Apartments Limited: 130 flats, all with shower or bath and toilet
The Accommodation Office: 200 flats, all with shower or bath and toilet

NGH Apartments Limited

TELEPHONE
020-7589-1105

FAX
020-7589-9433

EMAIL
101562.1120@compuserve.com

INTERNET
www.demon.co.uk/hotel-net/ ngh.html

TUBE
Sloane Square, South Kensington

CREDIT CARDS
AE, MC, V

RATES
All rates are per week and include VAT. There is a one-week minimum stay. Studios for 1–2 persons £310–370; studio for 2–4 persons £375–550; one bedroom for 2–4 £525–900; two bedrooms for 3–5 persons £800–900; extra-large two-bedroom for 4–6 persons £1,200–1,350; a refundable deposit of £250–500 is required in advance to reserve against cancellation, for the use of the telephone, and for any potential damages. The balance of the deposit is refunded in about four weeks, after the monthly phone bill has been received and paid. Four week's cancellation notice is required. Payment for the first week is due upon arrival. Discounts for longer stays.

The massive apartment block is so well known in London that it doesn't even need a street number—all you need to know is Nell Gwynn House, Sloane Avenue.

Over the years I have inspected many, many London flats, but when I am in London for any length of time I stay at Nell Gwynn. For its price and location, between Old Brompton Road and King's Road, it is a stellar choice. In short, I cannot imagine wanting or needing more than Nell Gwynn and its location have to offer.

The apartments stand in the heart of Chelsea, one of the most exclusive residential districts in London. The spacious choices range from studios to one- and two-bedroom apartments, individually furnished to provide comfort and convenience. All the accommodations have abundant closets with plenty of shelves, hanging space, and out-of-sight luggage storage. There is an equipped kitchen, some with microwaves; a color television, some with cable; an iron and ironing board; a large bathroom with good light and a huge tub; central heat; direct-dial phones; and answering machines available for a small weekly charge. Washers, dryers, and dishwashers are available in many of the newer flats. Maid service is included Monday through Friday; towels are changed twice a week, bed linens weekly; and mail is delivered to your flat. If you need to do some photocopying or send a fax, you can do so during office hours. The staff of both agencies, from the hardworking upstairs maids to the office personnel and friendly porters (a few of whom have been here since time began), go out of their way to make guests feel welcome and to make your stay pleasant.

If you can't find what you need in the neighborhood, chances are you don't really need it. Across the street is a row of shops, including a dry cleaner, convenience grocery, liquor and wine shop, pharmacy, and upscale dress agency (see Levy and Friend, page 277). For long-term housekeeping and cooking needs, King's Road, with two supermarkets, is just a five-minute walk away; Harrods is fifteen. Walton Street, a wonderful street full of tempting boutiques and several restaurants listed in

Cheap Eats in London, is a block away. Elystan Place and Chelsea Green, an aristocratic square, is another block in the other direction. Here you can have tea and crumpets, indulge in magnificent French pastries, have your hair done, do your laundry, buy an expensive antique or custom-designed gown or a toy for a special little one, stop by the hardware store, have your clothes cleaned, and get your shoes shined. You can also buy fresh fish, meat, cheese, flowers, and the finest produce in London. If you are not in the mood to cook, there are a dozen or more excellent *Cheap Eats in London* restaurants, wine bars, and pubs within a two- to ten-minute walk. Taxis on Sloane Avenue take only three or four minutes to flag down, even during rush hour. Otherwise you can easily walk to two tube stops or buses that go directly to the West End and most points beyond. As you can see, when I say this location has it all I am *not* stretching the truth.

Two rental agency offices operate from here, one representing individual owners (the Accommodation Office) and the other a corporation managing its own flats (NGH Apartments Limited). Those at the Accommodation Office have a twenty-two-night minimum stay and are either studios or one-bedroom units. At NGH Apartments Limited, the minimum stay is one week and the flats range in size from studios for up to three to large two-bedroom units that can sleep six. I would declare it a photo finish in the race for which agency has the better flats, but if you are going to be here at least twenty-two days, I would say that the apartments represented by the Accommodation Office win by a nose thanks to their more up-to-date decoration and overall amenities.

FACILITIES AND SERVICES: Central heat, direct-dial phones (own private number), answering machines on request, iron and ironing board, washers, dryers, and dishwashers in many units, laundry service, lifts, parking, individual safes in office, TV (most with satellite), 24-hour porter, concierge, car hire, ticket bookings, fax and secretarial services during business hours, which are Mon–Fri 9 A.M.–6 P.M., Sat 10 A.M.–4 P.M.

The Accommodation Office
TELEPHONE
020-7584-8317
FAX
020-7823-7133
TUBE
Sloane Square, South Kensington
CREDIT CARDS
AE, MC, V
RATES
All rates include VAT. Studio £310–450 per week; one bedroom £550–750 per week. There is a minimum 22-day stay. This may be extended by the day or week thereafter, and is payable accordingly. Twenty-two days' rent is payable in advance and a minimum of one week's rent is required as a refundable deposit against telephone charges and damages.

NUMBER ONE (27)
1 Harrington Gardens, South Kensington, SW7
25 flats, all with shower or bath and toilet

TELEPHONE
020-7370-4044
FAX
020-7370-6741
TUBE
Gloucester Road
CREDIT CARDS
MC, V
RATES
Studio apartment: 1–2 persons £90; one bedroom: 1–2 persons £110; two bedrooms: 1–3 persons £145; two double bedrooms: 1–4 persons £160; special rates for long stays and groups

Number One is well named.

I love getting tips about good deals in London, or any place else I cover, and Number One certainly is one of the better ones I received in London.

Interiors of the twenty-five flats pay tribute to the days when big sectional sofas and one-inch mosaic-tiled bathrooms were in vogue. So what? Everything is clean, and the best part is that you will have *room . . .* room to hang your clothes in the mirrored wardrobes; room to lay out a few toiletries in the bathrooms, most of which have both tub and shower; room to get into the kitchen and cook a real meal and serve it in a dining area with a nice table and chairs. Even the satellite-connected television screens are bigger than normal. Add-on perks include office services, theater and tour bookings, car or VCR rental, and airport transfers. Shops and the tube in this sought-after London neighborhood are close by, as is the museum complex that includes the Victoria and Albert. Quiet rooms are on the back, but sunshine can be limited. Views and the light are better on the front, but the trade-off is some noise.

FACILITIES AND SERVICES: Central heat, direct-dial phones, hair dryer, iron and ironing board, laundry and dry cleaning service, lift, parking can be arranged, office safe, satellite TV, maid service every day, 24-hour reception. Also available on request: airport transfer, baby beds, car and VCR rental, office services (fax, photocopying, secretarial services), theater and tour bookings

ONE THIRTY (16)
130 Queen's Gate, South Kensington, SW7
53 flats, all with shower or bath and toilet

TELEPHONE
020-7581-2322; reservations can be made through Small & Elegant Hotels International (see page 199) or toll-free at 800-44-UTELL
FAX
020-7823-8488
TUBE
Gloucester Road, South Kensington
CREDIT CARDS
AE, DC, MC, V

One Thirty is defined by its hotel-like decor with dark woods, striped bedspreads, and coordinated wall coverings and carpeting. The location puts you between the Gloucester Road and South Kensington underground stations, both of which are on the Circle, District, and Piccadilly lines, with direct access (about thirty minutes) to Heathrow Airport. The flats range in size from tightly fitted studios to penthouse suites with all the bells and whistles one would expect for the price. The units have everything you will need for a London sojourn, short or long: fitted modern kitchens, good wardrobe space, double-glazed windows to buffer the traffic noise (this is London, and there is inescapable noise), private safes, lifts to all floors, and secretarial services. For maximum pleasure, ask for something on a high floor, preferably with a balcony and not facing a wall.

FACILITIES AND SERVICES: Air-conditioning in the penthouse, central heat and ceiling fans, direct-dial phones, hair dryer, laundry and dry cleaning service, lift, room safe, TV and radio, VCR available (£30 per week), trouser press, 24-hour desk, six-day maid service, secretarial services with fax and photocopiers

RATES
Studio £122; one bedroom £170; two bedrooms £210–228; three bedrooms £275; penthouse £260; corporate and lower rates for longer stays

ORION

Leave it to French ingenuity to design a good-value apartment hotel that doesn't remind you that you're on a *budget* at every turn, or make you feel *nouveau pauvre* while staying there. The exteriors are institutionally correct, and so are the studios and the large one- or two-bedroom flats, which have all the basics, plus a few extras. Besides pots, pans, nice crockery, and glassware in the kitchen, you will have a microwave and a dishwasher. The bathrooms are worth the price alone, with their sink space *and* shelves, plus a tub and shower. Another positive for many are the rooms reserved for nonsmokers. The studios interconnect and are all about the same size . . . twenty-five square meters. That, for the metrically challenged, is about three hundred square feet. The apartment hotels include the Barbican; Holborn/Covent Garden, and Trafalgar. The facilities and services may vary slightly at each location, but you can count on the perks listed after each individual hotel.

ORION–BARBICAN (4)
7–21 Goswell Road, Barbican, EC1
129 flats, all with shower or bath and toilet

The area around the Barbican is not tourist central, but there is tube and bus transportation, a huge modern Safeway grocery store, and the use of the Barbican Y Fitness Center or swimming at a nearby pool for lower fees. You are reasonably close to the historical City of London, Saint Paul's Cathedral, and the London Museum. If you want to take a peek at suburban London living, Islington, which has some interesting restaurants and shops, is close by. The Barbican also accepts pets (oh . . . how French!).

TELEPHONE
020-7566-8000; 800-755-8266 (toll-free from the U.S. for studio bookings only; must call the hotel directly for larger accommodations)
FAX
020-7566-8130
EMAIL
orionuk@aol.com
INTERNET
www.scoot.co.uk-orion
TUBE
Barbican

CREDIT CARDS
AE, DC, MC, V
RATES
Daily rates start at £100 for a studio and £145 for a flat; the longer the stay, the lower the rate (weekly, monthly); Continental breakfast £7 extra, English breakfast £9 extra

FACILITIES AND SERVICES: Central heat, a conference room, direct-dial phones, double-glazed windows, hair dryer, coin-operated laundry, ironing facilities, dishwasher, microwave, lift, office services for nominal fees, parking spaces (£15 per day), satellite TV, office or private room safe, rooms for the disabled, baby cots, nonsmoking rooms, 24-hour desk, maid and linen service once a week, towels changed twice a week

ORION–HOLBORN/COVENT GARDEN (40)
94–99 High Holborn, Covent Garden, WC1
192 flats, all with shower or bath and toilet

TELEPHONE
020-7395-8800
FAX
020-7395-8799
EMAIL
orionuk@aol.com
TUBE
Holborn
CREDIT CARDS
AE, DC, MC, V
RATES
Studio £110; flat £158, lower rates for longer stays; Continental breakfast £7 extra, English breakfast £9 extra

For pleasure visitors to London, this is a super address. From here you can walk to the British Museum and Covent Garden, one of the most vibrant and fashionable parts of London, brimming with restaurants, nightlife, and theaters, including the magnificent, newly redone Royal Opera House. Also within striking distance are the banks of the Thames, Piccadilly Circus, Oxford Street, and Dickens' House. In all, there are 152 studios for one to two people and 40 one-bedroom flats for one to four people.

FACILITIES AND SERVICES: Central heat, a conference room, direct-dial phones, double-glazed windows, hair dryer, coin-operated laundry, ironing facilities, dishwasher, microwave, lift, office services for nominal fees, parking spaces (£15 per day), satellite TV, office or private room safe, rooms for the disabled, baby cots, nonsmoking rooms, 24-hour desk, maid and linen service once a week, towels changed twice a week

ORION–TRAFALGAR (56)
18–21 Northumberland Avenue, Trafalgar Square, WC2
187 flats, all with shower or bath and toilet

TELEPHONE
020-7766-3700
FAX
020-7766-3766
EMAIL
orionuk@aol.com
TUBE
Charing Cross, Embankment
CREDIT CARDS
AE, DC, MC, V
RATES
Studio for 1–2 people £118; flat for 1–4 people £170; flat for 1–6 people £210, discounts for longer stays; Continental breakfast £7 extra, English breakfast £9 extra

The Orion–Trafalgar is close to the National Gallery, Trafalgar Square, and across the Hungerford Bridge from Waterloo Station and the artistic area of the South Bank, with the National Theatre, Royal Festival Hall, and Queen Elizabeth Hall. A bonus for guests is the use of the Royal Commonwealth Society's dining room, which has been dramatically redone in a stunning, colorful modern theme.

FACILITIES AND SERVICES: Central heat, a conference room, direct-dial phones, double-glazed windows, hair dryer, coin-operated laundry, ironing facilities, dishwasher, microwave, lift, office services for nominal fees, parking spaces (£15 per day), satellite TV, office or private room safe, rooms for the disabled, baby cots, nonsmoking rooms, 24-hour desk, maid and linen service once a week, towels changed twice a week

ROLAND HOUSE (34)
121 Old Brompton Road, South Kensington, SW7
89 flats, all with shower or bath and toilet

From the outside, Roland House has all the zip and pizzazz of a pair of sturdy English oxfords. That does not mean that it is not likable or recommendable. It is well priced, clean, pleasantly staffed, and *inside,* where you will be living, it is attractive and functional. Even better, you can arrive for one night, or move in lock, stock, and barrel for one year. After a month, there is a 10-percent reduction, and beyond that, the price is negotiable. Your apartment will come with six-day-a-week maid service, linen changes, cable television, lift, fitted kitchens with microwaves, ample closet space, bathrooms that are not new but well maintained, and decor that is simply done, with whitewashed oak furniture. Don't expect answering machines, laundry facilities (but you can send it out), or dishwashers. Best values are the one-bedroom apartments with a sitting room. The smallest studios are elfin in size, with no sofa and only a single bed, small table, and one upholstered chair. However, if you are traveling alone and not planning on cooking up a storm, they will do. I would also beware of ground-floor and first-floor rooms facing a dull brick wall. It is a good walk to the supermarket, especially if you have to lug back a lot, but tube and bus service from the South Kensington Station is excellent and only a five- or ten-minute walk away.

FACILITIES AND SERVICES: Central heat and some ceiling fans, direct-dial phones, equipped kitchens, lift, office safe, satellite TV, 24-hour desk, maid service Mon–Sat, laundry and dry cleaning service, secretarial (fax, photocopying) services

TELEPHONE
020-7370-6221; reservations can be made directly or through Small & Elegant Hotels International (see page 199) or 800-44-UTELL (toll-free from the U.S.)

FAX
020-7370-4293

EMAIL
rolandhouse@compuserve.com

TUBE
Gloucester Road, South Kensington

CREDIT CARDS
AE, DC, MC, V

RATES
Studios: 1–3 persons (twin beds) £95–110; one bedroom £120–145; two bedrooms £160. No minimum stays; corporate, group, and long-term rates upon request

SNOW WHITE PROPERTIES (5)
55 Ennismore Gardens, Knightsbridge, SW7
12 flats, all with shower or bath and toilet

TELEPHONE
020-7584-3307

FAX
020-7581-4686

EMAIL
snow.white@virgin.net

INTERNET
www.accomodata.co.uk/
070396.htm

TUBE
Knightsbridge

CREDIT CARDS
None; cash only

RATES
Studios £680–750 per week;
one bedroom £780–960 per
week; extra person £15 daily,
£80 weekly; lower off-season
rates and for long stays

Maxine White, along with the help of her sister and Custard the cat, offers twelve nicely appointed flats on Ennismore Gardens. They are well situated for shopping trips to Knightsbridge, performances at the Royal Albert Hall, the museum complex that includes the Victoria and Albert, and leisurely strolls or bracing morning jogs through Hyde Park. I can recommend all of the flats, which are charmingly done in the English school of decorating that leaves no ruffle or frill undone or over-looked. Everything is coordinated, right down to the colors of the shower curtains and the bows on the bowls of scented potpourri. In addition, the closet space is good, the bathrooms are nice, and the kitchens are especially well equipped, some with Maxine's own antique china. Number 2, a basement twin or double in pink florals, opens onto a small plant-filled terrace. Contrary to most lower-level accommodations in London, this one is cheerful and light. Flat No. 8 is a multilevel choice with a terrace, and No. 7, in blue and yellow, has two windows overlooking the gardens. I also like the top-floor flat, with the living area smartly done in gray and white, with yellow, cerise, and plum accent cushions. The twin bedroom has antique beds covered in gray quilted spreads. The large kitchen should inspire trips to Harrods' fabulous food halls, and the brick terrace with its table and chairs is the perfect place for a summer breakfast or late afternoon drink before going out to the theater. Maxine and her sister are charming hostesses, and their devoted regulars adore them . . . so if this is your kind of place, please book as far ahead as possible.

FACILITIES AND SERVICES: Air-conditioning (portable) in some, central heat, direct telephone line for each flat, iron and ironing board, fitted kitchens with stoves and microwaves, lift to all but the top-floor flat, office safe, satellite TV, radio, maid service five days a week, security phone at entrance with bell to each flat, fax facilities in the office, office open Mon–Fri 9:30 A.M.–5:30 P.M.

TWO HYDE PARK SQUARE (25)
2 Hyde Park Square, Hyde Park, W2
76 flats, all with shower or bath and toilet

With over seventy studios and one-bedroom flats, Two Hyde Park Square is not only positioned with perfection, it offers value for money for those who insist on high standards of comfort in a secure and private environment. This part of London boasts some of the most expensive real estate turf in the city, and these units keep pace except, surprisingly enough, in price. A variety of nearby shops and restaurants make wining and dining a pleasure either in your own flat or out. Business guests will find secretarial and office backup services, and motorists will have a secure car park for a nominal fee. All guests will be well located to strike out for all of London's major attractions.

Almost all of the units have been rejuvenated, with coordination well carried out. In my opinion, the older-style flats are very nice, and besides, they cost less and have more closet space. For studio dwellers, superior studio No. 4 provides a large work desk and twin beds in an area beside the sitting room. The bathroom has a tub and the kitchen a two-burner cooking stove and a micro-wave. Number 72 is another good studio, with a view, an attractive bedroom, and a nice bath. For something larger, No. 73 offers a separate lounge and dining area, a swivel television for either the bedroom or the lounge, good storage, and a nice bath. The kitchen is small but well equipped. If you plan on roasting your Christmas goose here, you will want No. 74, a top-floor corner unit that has a large, bright kitchen with a four-burner stove, oven, and microwave. The view of the trees in the small park below makes you pinch yourself to remember this is London. The bedroom has plenty of space and there are two televisions, one in the lounge and one to watch in bed.

FACILITIES AND SERVICES: Central heat, direct-dial phones, hair dryer available, laundry service, lift, parking (£10 per night), office safe, satellite TV , washers, dryers, and dishwashers in some, maid service Mon–Fri, linen changed twice weekly, fully fitted kitchens, concierge, business services, access to private gardens, 24-hour desk

TELEPHONE
020-7262-8271

FAX
020-7262-7628

TUBE
Lancaster Gate, Marble Arch, Paddington

CREDIT CARDS
AE, DC, MC, V

RATES
Studios: standard £85 for two, superior £100; standard one-bedroom flats £105 for 2; superior one-bedroom flat £110 for 2; senior apartment, one large twin-bed flat £125; extra bed in senior apartment £10. All rates include VAT; lower rates for long-term stays

Apartment Rental Agencies

CHEZ VOUS

TELEPHONE
415-331-2535

FAX
415-331-5296

EMAIL
bonjour@chezvous.com

INTERNET
www.chezvous.com

CREDIT CARDS
None; cash only

RATES
$900–4,050 per week, depending on size and amenities

1001 Bridgeway, Suite 245
Sausalito, CA 94965

Chez Vous, as its name implies, began with apartment rentals in Paris (see their listing in *Cheap Sleeps in Paris* as well), and as with all success stories, they grew by leaps and bounds because they filled a niche and provided good services at affordable prices. Now they can provide you with a home away from home in London. By consulting their website and/or flipping through their fifty-page catalog of London flats, you are bound to find something of interest. The catalog also clearly explains all the ins and outs of their payment and cancellation policies. The locations are desirably upmarket: Chelsea, Kensington, Mayfair, Knightsbridge, and Belgravia, and range from lower-ground-floor one-bedrooms to a four-bedroom family home with a garden. There is a minimum one-week rental period, scheduled to begin any day of the week. All reservations are made through their office in Northern California.

FACILITIES AND SERVICES: Vary with each apartment

HOBART SLATER (7)

TELEPHONE
020-7590-1200

FAX
020-7590-1210

EMAIL
shortlets@hobartslater.co.uk

INTERNET
www.hobartslater.co.uk

TUBE
Knightsbridge

CREDIT CARDS
None

6–8 Montpelier Street, SW7

Jeremy Lambourne is your contact man at the Hobart Slater agency if you are in the market for an exceptional short let in London. While you may not be reserving the home known as the "Telephone Exchange" on Portobello Road, an award-winner for architecture and design, set behind private gates, with two fifty-foot reception rooms, four bedrooms and baths, a gym, sauna, and underground parking for two limousines . . . all for a mere £7,000 per week, you might be interested in the cozy redone one-bedroom flat on the lower ground floor of an old Victorian home five minutes from High Street Kensington and Kensington Gardens that rents for around £350 per week. If you are a modernist, request the sleekly spectacular, hard-edge modern flat near Harrods, with its sensational collection of film posters and space-age kitchen. Having spent considerable time in the States, Mr. Lambourne understands the wishes and needs of most Americans. While his apartments are not among the Cheapest Sleeps in London, they are some of the better ones in the Big Splurge category.

FACILITIES AND SERVICES: Depends on apartment, but all are well done

HPS APARTMENT RENTALS (26)
2 Hyde Park Square, W2

Where there is a need, there is always a way to fill it. Martyn Lawson recognized the need in London for serviced apartments of a high standard, offering excellent value for money and located in prime London areas. The result is HPS Apartment Rentals, which offers some of the most spacious, well-decorated apartments for the money that can be found in London. All are central . . . nothing is located in a tourist fringe that requires long commutes to get to anything more marginally interesting than the local pub. If you are going to Rome, Paris, Madrid, Barcelona, or New York, HPS Apartment Rentals also has apartments in those cities. The following three apartments represent a good cross section of what HPS has available in London. For further information and to reserve, contact HPS directly. Apartments include Allen House, Lancaster Gate, and Mayfair Pied et Terre, which are described below.

ALLEN HOUSE
Allen Street, Kensington, W8
35 flats, all with shower or bath and toilet

These flats, in the Royal Borough of Kensington and Chelsea, just a block or so off High Street Kensington, provide you with all the conveniences of shopping, restaurants, and transportation around Kensington, while still maintaining a quiet neighborhood feel. All of the very spacious flats are named after famous London areas or streets. One of my favorites is No. 29, Savile, on the front, with two beautifully arched windows letting in loads of light. I also like the large No. 38, Winchester, and No. 25, Portobello. All have great closets. However, be sure your unit has been recently redone. That is not to say the older units are in shambles, but since the bright

RATES
One-bedroom flats from £350 per week, most flats represented are in the £400–800 per week range

TELEPHONE
020-7262-8271

FAX
020-7262-7626

EMAIL
reservation@apartments-hps -london-paris.co.uk

INTERNET
www.apartments-hps -london.co.uk

CREDIT CARDS
AE, DC, MC, V

RATES
See individual apartment rentals

TUBE
High Street Kensington

RATES
All prices are per night and include VAT: one bedroom £135; two bedrooms/two bathrooms £180; three bedrooms/two bathrooms £200; lower rates subject to season and availability

coordinated colors, new bathrooms, and modern kitchens in the redone units are the same price as the older units, why not? An extra summer bonus is the large enclosed garden. Allen House flats can be booked through HPS Apartment Rentals, page 195.

FACILITIES AND SERVICES: Central heat, direct-dial phones with security entry, fax machines on request, lifts, five-day maid service, porter, office safe, satellite TV, some washers, dryers, and dishwashers

LANCASTER GATE
49 Lancaster Gate, W2
6 flats, all with shower or bath and toilet

TUBE
Lancaster Gate, Queensway
RATES
All rates are per day and include VAT: two bedrooms/two bathrooms £165–175; three bedrooms/two bathrooms £190–200; lower rates depending on season and availability

The six beautifully furnished two- and three-bedroom flats at Lancaster Gate are only a few minutes from Hyde Park, in a quiet London square between Queensway and Marble Arch. The units are well equipped, meticulously maintained, and totally coordinated. All come with washers, dryers, dishwashers, and two television sets. Kitchens have a proper stove, microwave, and quality cooking utensils, crockery, and silver. As everyone knows, I am a great fan of closet and drawer space, but one of the oversize bedrooms here exceeds my wildest dreams, with six chests that hold twenty-seven drawers! Ah . . . heaven, and all in one room! The ground-floor bedrooms have no view, so if this is a problem, I would suggest a flat on a higher floor. Lancaster Gate flats can be booked through HPS Apartment Rentals, page 195.

FACILITIES AND SERVICES: Central heat, direct-dial phones with security entry, fax on request, lift, maid service, satellite TV, video, washer, dryer, dishwasher, six-day maid service

MAYFAIR PIED ET TERRE
20 flats, all with shower or bath and toilet

TUBE
Depends on apartment location
RATES
All rates are per day and include VAT: one bedroom £125–145; two bedrooms/two bathrooms £150–265, lower rates subject to season and availability

These apartments are so popular that people never want to leave . . . in fact, they want to buy them. Considering the platinum locations, scattered around the heart of Mayfair and on the edge of Grosvenor Square and Park Lane, I would hate to think what the prices would be if they actually were for sale. As with all HPS Apartments, these are comfortably livable and nicely decorated with all the conveniences to make your stay easy and pleasant. These apartments are in various Mayfair locations. Mayfair

Pied et Terre flats can be booked through HPS Apartment Rentals, page 195.

FACILITIES AND SERVICES: Central heat, direct-dial phones with security entry, fax on request, lift, five-day maid service, car park (rates on request), satellite TV, video available, washer, dryer

THE INDEPENDENT TRAVELLER
Thorverton, Exeter EX5 5NT, England

The Independent Traveller was established in 1980 for those who enjoy traveling on their own. Headed by Mary and Simon Ette, this business lists central and suburban London apartments, country cottages, small inns, hotels, and B&Bs from Cornwall to Inverness. They are used to working with people from around the globe, and regularly get inquiries from faraway places such as Papua New Guinea and Kathmandu. The prize for their most isolated request is still shared between missionaries in Nepal, who sent a letter that required a week's donkey journey just to get it to the post office to be sent to London, and another from archaeologists on a remote island in the Pacific with one mail boat per month. How did they book? By sending exact requirements and a deposit and instructions to "get on with it." So, as you can see, wherever you may be in the world, Mary and Simon are only a letter, telephone call, fax, or email away.

When requesting information about London properties, I recommend looking for something central. While their suburban London addresses are cheaper and give you more living space, weigh carefully what you save in money and gain in space against what you will spend in time commuting back and forth to London, if that is going to be the focal point of your trip. If it isn't, then living on the fringes should be fine.

While the accommodations are inspected regularly and there is an excellent group of owners, many of whom have been with Mary for years, you must remember that you are staying in a private flat. Maybe the sofa needs recovering, the paint redone, or the bathroom modernized. It is *not* a hotel . . . please don't expect one. More than half the clientele is repeat business, which is a very strong recommendation. There is a three-night minimum stay; low-season rates are offered from November through March; and cancellation insurance is always available. While you can't always take advantage of the

TELEPHONE
01392-860807

FAX
01392-860552

EMAIL
independenttraveller@
compuserve.com

CREDIT CARDS
MC, V

RATES
Weekly rates depend on property, what type of maid service is included, and the location; lower rates for longer stays; £280–950 (weekly maid service); £450–1,500 (Mon–Fri maid service)

lower seasonal rates, you should definitely take out cancellation insurance.

FACILITIES AND SERVICES: Vary with each property

IN THE ENGLISH MANNER
515 South Figueroa, Suite 1000
Los Angeles, CA 90071-3327

TELEPHONE
213-629-1811; 800-422-0799
(toll-free from the U.S. and
Canada)

FAX
213-689-8784

EMAIL
itemus@aol.com

INTERNET
www.english-manner.co.uk

CREDIT CARDS
AE, DC, MC, V

RATES
Weekly rates from $600 for a
studio or one bedroom; there is a
minimum one-week stay. They
strongly advise cancellation
insurance, and can provide you
with the details.

"Sketch us your idea of the dream vacation house and location and we will do our best to deliver." This is the motto of In the English Manner, which takes the guesswork and anguish out of spending a week or more in a flat in the heart of London, or in your own home almost anywhere in Great Britain. All properties are privately owned by well-to-do, and in some instances illustrious, British families, and reflect the owner's individual living style and taste. All are beautifully equipped and maintained to high standards. In London their properties are some of the best I encountered. You have a choice of delightful flats or homes located in the best neighborhoods. You can live in a classical house in the heart of Belgravia, a contemporary apartment on the second floor of a building near Harrods, a bright flat overlooking the banks of the River Thames, or a three-story mews house in popular Chelsea. When traveling beyond London, arrangements can be made to stay in some of England's finest country house hotels, situated on elegant estates. If staying in one place a week or longer, consider one of their magnificent period and historic cottages or castles. Traveling "in the English manner" allows you the luxury of arranging for a chauffeured car for airport transfers, food to be purchased for you and placed in your kitchen, a cook to prepare it, and private guide services in London and the countryside. They also can provide airline tickets, theater bookings, and help with whatever plans you have to make your vacation or business trip the best it can be.

FACILITIES AND SERVICES: Vary with each property, but almost all needs and desires can be met

SMALL & ELEGANT HOTELS INTERNATIONAL
9425 Whispering Sands
West Olive, MI 49460

American Bonnie DeLoof knows what she is doing when it comes to hotel and apartment accommodations in London. She is the former owner of The Cranley, which in my opinion represents the quintessence of British taste and style . . . and at a cost most of us can afford. While I write about The Cranley and her services as a hotel booking agent on page 148, her services concerning apartment rentals bear repeating here because she is able to book a wide range of apartments in all price categories anywhere in London. If you want to be thirty seconds from the main door of Harrods, call Bonnie. If it's a flat near Kensington Palace you're after, she has it. For a Big Splurge, ask her about the company she represents called Manors & Co. I could move into any one of their flats and happily call it home indefinitely. With Bonnie handling the details, you can sit back, relax, and pleasantly anticipate a memorable stay in London.

TELEPHONE
616-844-6000

FAX
616-844-6402

EMAIL
res@smallandeleganthotels.com

INTERNET
www.smallandeleganthotels.com

FACILITIES AND SERVICES: Vary with each property

VILLAS INTERNATIONAL
950 Northgate Drive, Suite 206
San Rafael, CA 94903

Villas International offers one of the widest selections of overseas rental properties for the independent traveler. With more than twenty-five thousand villas, cottages, châteaux, flats, and castles, surely they will have one that fits your needs and budget. Write, call, fax, or email them and describe your needs, where you want to be in London, and your price range. If you need a rental car, that can also be arranged, but I don't recommend a car in London unless it is used to get you out of town. When calling, speak with David Kendall, who maintains office hours Monday to Friday 9 A.M.–6 P.M. (Pacific standard time).

TELEPHONE
415-499-9490; 800-221-2260 (toll-free from the U.S.)

FAX
415-499-9491

EMAIL
villas@best.com

INTERNET
villasintl.com

CREDIT CARDS
None; cash or check only

RATES
Vary with each location, but start around $750 per week for a small studio

FACILITIES AND SERVICES: Vary with each property

Bed and Breakfast in a Private Home

It is an unfortunate fact of travel life: London hotel rates are some of the highest in the world, and show no signs of spiraling anywhere but up. In addition to the high rates, most London hotel service you will encounter today is impersonal, dictated by computers, fax machines, voice mail, and guests being numbers, not names. As a result, many travelers on holiday are becoming nostalgic for the personal touch accompanied by a genuinely friendly smile and warm hospitality. For a quality alternative to staying in a hotel, one of the best ways to save considerable money *and* add a personal approach to your next trip to London is to consider staying in a private home. London is full of small establishments advertising themselves as B&Bs. These are usually mum-and-pop hotel operations with homespun decor in fewer than twenty rooms with hall facilities, or private rooms consisting of airless modular units no bigger than a phone booth stuffed into an already too small space. There's not a lift, so there will be daily stair-climbing workouts up to your room and down to the basement dining room for breakfast. These have their place and many are listed in *Cheap Sleeps in London.* However, if you want to gain a greater insight into life in London, go for the *real* thing: a bed-and-breakfast stay in a private London home. Facilities and prices vary widely, depending on each residence and what it has to offer you. Think about it carefully before you reserve, because you are, in effect, a guest in someone's home and thus do not have hotel services as part of the package. Nor do you have kitchen privileges or the right to stretch out on the living room sofa and read the Sunday papers. To avoid disappointment, *be sure* to lay out all your needs and expectations in advance. Specify such things as whether a nonsmoking household is a must and whether you are allergic to dogs, cats, children, or noise; if you can't negotiate stairs, say so. And if you need a private bathroom or have specific dietary requirements for breakfast, make all this clear up front. You may also want to know whether liquor is allowed in your room, if entertaining in the host's living room is permitted, and if you have access to a telephone and fax.

NOTE: Each bed-and-breakfast agency has cancellation, no-show, and refund policies. Read and understand the fine print before reserving, *please.*

AT HOME IN LONDON
70 Black Lion Lane, W6

With more than seventy homes in greater London, Maggie Dobson's At Home in London will surely have just the B&B to suit you. Those that are the least expensive on her roster are in Location Two, *not* in central London, and require some lengthy commutes on the tube or bus to get to the center of things. These areas include Chiswick, Hammersmith, Kew, Putney, and so on. Location One B&Bs are more centrally located in areas such as Knightsbridge, Kensington, Mayfair, and Chelsea. Wherever you stay, your hosts, who include lawyers, teachers, architects, designers, and writers, will provide you with a comfortable bedroom and bathroom, plus breakfast in the morning. You will have your own key so you can come and go as you like, and stay only one night if that is all your schedule allows. Remember, these B&Bs are in someone's private home, so expect some homey touches: dogs, cats, children, comfy but well-loved furniture, personal collections, and probably some stairs. On the other hand, be sure to state your bottom-line requirements when reserving. If you want nonsmoking without pets and/or children in the household, say so, and Maggie will do her best to please you and match you with a compatible host family.

Maggie can also arrange for you and at least nine others to have high tea in a private London home. Prices for the tea party are provided on request. If you plan to travel elsewhere in the U.K., At Home in London can provide similar accommodations for you.

FACILITIES AND SERVICES: Vary with each home

TELEPHONE
020-8748-1943

FAX
020-8748-2701

EMAIL
AtHomeinLondon@
compuserve.com

INTERNET
www.athomeinlondon.co.uk

CREDIT CARDS
None

RATES
Rates are per night for the room and include breakfast. Location One: single £38–56; double £58–85; Location Two: single £28–36; double £50–56

THE BULLDOG CLUB
14 Dewhurst Road, W14

There is no question about it: The Bulldog Club is fabulous and offers the finest imaginable alternative to an expensive hotel stay, and at a fraction of the cost. Before I tell you just a few of the wonderful things about this bed-and-breakfast service, there is some interesting background information.

TELEPHONE
020-7371-3202; 800-727-3004
(toll-free from U.S.)

FAX
020-7371-2015

EMAIL
jackson@bulldogclub
.u-net.com

INTERNET
www.bulldogclub.com

CREDIT CARDS
AE, MC, V (paid to The Club, not your host; *only* open to members of the Bulldog Club; three-year membership is £25 per adult and includes a yearly newsletter)

RATES
London locations (all rates are per room, per night): single £85 (when available); double £105. *Country locations:* single £60; double £80; available at country homes only three-course dinner, £20–25 per person. There is a 10 percent single-night supplement. All rates include English breakfast.

With her last child off to boarding school and nothing to do while she and her husband rattled around in their large London home, founder Amanda St. George began to take in paying guests who were friends of friends. This was such an unqualified success that she convinced pals in Kensington, Chelsea, and other parts of central London to do the same. Thus was born The Bulldog Club, named for her bulldog, Emily. A few years ago Amanda moved to South Africa, and The Club is now owned and beautifully run by charming and energetic Maggie Jackson. It is in its eleventh year and flourishing more than ever with stunning properties in London and the countryside.

By paying a £25 three-year membership fee per adult you become a member of The Club and stay in some of London's most beautifully appointed homes, filled with museum-quality antiques, paintings, books, tapestries, and objets d'art at rates considerably less than those of a more moderate hotel. All of the five-star quality properties are magnificent, down to the last detail, offering guests personal and exclusive attention from the moment of arrival until departure. Many lone women travelers and businesspeople now think of their favorite Bulldog home as their own and would never consider the impersonal Hilton or Sheraton hotels again. Each lovely room in a Bulldog Club home is equipped with a color television, tea and coffeemaking facilities, telephone, and in some cases a fax. Fresh flowers and fruit are always in each room, and a bottle of Perrier or English Malvern water is by the bedside. The luxurious private bathrooms are complete with hair dryer, a basket of the best English bath soaps and oils, a terry robe, and beautiful towels. Each day guests are given a menu from which to decide what to have for breakfast the next morning. They might choose from juices and fruit, yogurt, cereals, eggs any style with bacon, sausages, mushrooms, and tomatoes, followed by toast and rolls, jams, and coffee or a pot of tea. If staying more than a few days, the host makes sure the menu changes. Breakfast is served in the guest's private dining area, and a complimentary newspaper is beside the tea or coffee cup. For relaxing during the day, the guest has the use of a sitting room. All homes maintain a nonsmoking policy.

There's more! Bulldog also offers country stays at more than twenty privately owned estates throughout the English, Welsh, and Scottish countrysides, as well as in Edinburgh, Oxford, and Salisbury. These historic private castles, mansions, and manor homes are set in exquisite gardens and parklands and cost even *less* than the Bulldog homes in London. Dinner, with three courses, can be booked in advance at £20–25 per person. All of these beautiful locations are selected and monitored by Maggie, and they must meet the same exacting standards required of the London properties. It is important to note two further important points: Every London Bulldog home, and most in the country, are exclusive to The Club, and because they are such special private residences, no general list is offered. Guests are told what is available when they give specific dates.

It is all very British, terribly upper crust, and "really a must for every civilized person visiting London or the countryside," as one delighted guest put it. I think he is 100 percent correct. The Bulldog Club stands alone at the top of its class and, as always, receives my highest recommendation and endorsement.

FACILITIES AND SERVICES: All locations include central heat, telephone (sometimes private), and fax in some, private sitting and dining rooms, TV, mineral water, hair dryer, terry robe, map and description of the location of the home. Homes are in South Kensington, Holland Park, Earl's Court, Parsons Green, Limehouse (the Docklands), Marble Arch, and Knightsbridge. *Country locations:* Many have tennis courts, swimming pools, and can provide dinner if booked in advance. There are country locations in or near Bath, Edinburgh, Oxford, Salisbury, Stonehenge, Stratford, York, Cotswold, Gloucestershire, Hampshire, Leicestershire, New Forest, Northumberland, Suffolk, Wiltshire, Scotland, and Wales. Of course, they do change, so if you have a particular area in mind, please be sure to ask. All Bulldog homes are nonsmoking.

THE LONDON BED & BREAKFAST AGENCY
71 Fellows Road, NW3

Dynamic Julia Stebbing runs her B&B agency with boundless energy coupled with a dose of British good sense. She provides rooms in private homes in and around London in four categories. Prices are quoted per person, include breakfast, and depend on the category location and whether or not you will share a bathroom. There are no one-night reservations accepted, a two-night

TELEPHONE
020-7586-2768
FAX
020-7586-6567
EMAIL
stay@londonbb.com
INTERNET
www.londonbb.com

minimum is required, and a £5 booking fee is added for all reservations.

For most Cheap Sleepers, homes in Category A will be the most appealing, even though they are the more expensive. This category includes central London and the immediate suburbs. If you stay in a Category B or C home, the quality will be the same and the price lower, but the distance to Piccadilly Circus is another matter. Even some in the A category are what I would consider in the tourist boondocks, so be careful. Check them out on a map first and find out the tube and/or bus connections, remembering that the cost of the accommodations in this category will be the same, so why waste valuable vacation time commuting back and forth to whatever action and bright lights you want to see in London.

RATES

Rates are per person per night, and include breakfast plus a £5 booking fee. There is a two-consecutive-night minimum stay and these can only be reserved seven days in advance. Stays of three nights or longer should be booked as far in advance as possible. Category A (Greater London): from £32 per person per night; Category B+ to B (edges of London and beyond): from £23–27 per person per night; Category C (far out): £20 per person per night.

All of her accommodations offer guest rooms in nice homes with friendly hosts, none of whom have what she termed "heaving bosoms," which she translated as "having problems that would affect a guest in any way." That is reassuring. Each home and host is, of course, different, but whether you stay in a large home toward outer London, a flat in Victoria, or a lovely rowhouse with a prize-winning garden overlooking the River Thames, you will be warmly received by your host family. Many of the homes are nonsmoking, so be sure to state if that is a priority for you.

FACILITIES AND SERVICES: Vary with each home, but expect stairs

NUMBER NINETY-SIX (29)
96 Tachbrook Street, Pimlico, SW1
2 rooms, each with shower or bath and toilet

TELEPHONE
020-7932-0969

FAX
020-7821-5454

EMAIL
helendouglas@btInternet.com

INTERNET
www.instaweb.co.uk/helendouglas

TUBE
Pimlico (take the Rampayne Street exit)

CREDIT CARDS
None; cash only

RATES
Single £85; double £95; Continental breakfast included, English breakfast £8 extra

An enthusiastic reader wrote to me about Helen Douglas's marvelous bed-and-breakfast home in Pimlico, and thank goodness she did, because unless you have insider knowledge, you would never know about this wonderful place, which, quite frankly, rates as one of my favorite new entries for the fourth edition of *Cheap Sleeps in London*. In my opinion, Number Ninety-Six is the perfect choice for discriminating Cheap Sleepers who value personal service in a quiet, elegant home surrounded by lovely heirloom antiques and chintzes. There is only one problem: once settled in, you will never want to leave!

Several years ago, Helen Douglas opened her large, beautifully furnished home to London visitors. Along with the help of her housekeeper, Jennie, who began as her children's nanny three decades ago and is now adored by all the guests, eveything is done to make you feel welcome and comfortably at home. There are only two graciously appointed bedrooms, each with a sitting area. There is one downstairs, with a large sitting room and breakfast area, and another upstairs, with a four-poster bed and a fabulous gold mirror. If you are staying in this room, your breakfast will be served in the main living room on the ground floor. The Continental breakfast includes freshly squeezed orange juice, homemade jam and marmalade to spread on your croissants, brioche, and toast, and hot tea and coffee. A full English breakfast is available for a supplemental charge. During the day, sandwiches and tea and coffee may be ordered. They also provide fax services, theater bookings, and will do your laundry and ironing (no laundry is allowed to be done by guests in the rooms, and there is a nominal charge for this service).

At Number Ninety-Six you will be within easy reach of most of London's musts, including Buckingham Palace, the Houses of Parliament, Westminster Abbey, the Thames, West End theaters, shopping in Knightsbridge, and the Tate and National galleries. Several longtime Cheap Eats are close by and you are also within five or ten minutes of Victoria Train and Coach Stations, which have easy links to Heathrow and Gatwick airports.

FACILITIES AND SERVICES: Central heat, direct-dial phones, laundry service, TV and radio, sandwiches, tea and coffee to order, daily newspaper, faxing, no lift

MISCELLANEOUS
Closed a few days around Christmas

UPTOWN RESERVATIONS
41 Paradise Walk, SW3

Uptown Reservations offers exclusive B&B accommodations *only* in the posh inner districts of London: Knightsbridge, Sloane Square, Chelsea, Mayfair, St. James's, and Kensington. The homes are carefully selected by Monica Barrington and Keith Stables, who personally monitor each to ensure that it is keeping pace with their standards. All will have private baths, and the price includes breakfast. From minimalistic modern to mews houses filled with enviable antiques and heirlooms, Uptown has it all. Many of the homes look as though Martha Stewart or Laura Ashley lived in them, or that *House Beautiful* should be called in to do a feature story. Efforts are made to match guests with hosts, who

TELEPHONE
020-7351-3445
FAX
020-7351-9383
EMAIL
inquiries@uptownres.co.uk
INTERNET
www.uptownres.co.uk
CREDIT CARDS
AE, MC, V

Single £65; double £85; family room £100; £5 supplement for a single-night stay; Continental breakfast included. There is a deposit of 28 percent of the total booking that is non-refundable but may be applied to a later booking if canceled at least seven days ahead. Deposits can be made by credit card, but the balance is to be paid in British sterling cash to the host upon arrival.

come from a variety of interesting backgrounds and professions. Be sure to state your needs when booking, and remember, you are a guest in a private home, so, even though you will be staying in lovely surroundings, you must not expect hotel services.

FACILITIES AND SERVICES: Depends on home. Nonsmoking homes are available. They offer car hire for general uses as well as airport transfer, individually guided sightseeing or shopping tours; details of all these services are given on request.

Camping

You are not going to get a Cheaper Sleep in London than sleeping under the stars in your own tent or camper in a campground on the edges of London. You may not be a happy camper, however, when you realize these sites are far removed from the center of the city, thus forcing you to make commutes of one or two hours *each* way, using a combination of foot, train, bus, and tube to get to your final London destination. If you have your own transportation, consider the heavy traffic, confusing one-way London streets, and steep parking fees before you drive yourself.

ABBEY WOOD CO-OP CAMPING & CARAVANING SITE
Federation Road, Abbey Wood, near Greenwich, SE2

FACILITIES AND SERVICES: Electrical hookups, public phones for outgoing calls *only*, no incoming calls, laundry room with iron, children's play area, free showers, toilets. Open all year.

TELEPHONE: 020-8311-7708

FAX: 020-8311-1465

TRAIN STOP: Abbey Wood Station, then a 10-minute walk

CREDIT CARDS: MC, V

RATES: Pitch fee for motor homes, tents, or caravan £8.50, plus £4 per person per night for adults over 17, £1.20 per person per night for children under 17; pitch fee for tents with cars £5 per night; with motorcycles, bicycles, or hikers £4 per night; electrical hookup £1.50 per night

MISCELLANEOUS: Advance reservations are necessary for Easter, spring holidays, July, and Aug. If you are in a motor home or have a car trailer, you can always reserve ahead. Send a £5 deposit and self-addressed envelope (with International Postal Coupon) for confirmation. No advance reservations made for tents, bicycles, or hikers. If you belong to a trailer or caravan club, bring your card for a discount.

CRYSTAL PALACE, CARAVAN CLUB SITE
Crystal Palace Parade, Crystal Palace, SE19

FACILITIES AND SERVICES: Coin-operated laundry, free showers and toilets, small convenience store selling milk, juice, and eggs. Advance booking for motor vans and trailers: send £5 to secure a spot (this will be deducted from total charge when you arrive). Tent space given out on first-come, first-served basis. Open all year.

TELEPHONE: 020-8778-7155

FAX: 020-8676-0980

TRAIN STOP: From Victoria Station to Crystal Palace stop on British Rail, followed by a twenty-minute walk to the campground, uphill all the way. Buses are a five- to ten-minute walk to the campground.

CREDIT CARDS: MC, V

RATES: Caravan pitch fee £9 plus £4 per person per day, £1.20 child under 5 per day; electrical hookup £1.45; tent pitch fee £2–4 depending on mode of transport (i.e., foot, motorbike, or car), plus the per person fees quoted above; electrical hookup £1.45; maximum stay twenty-one nights. Lower rates in off-season.

HACKNEY CAMPING
Millfields Road, Hackney Marshes, E5

FACILITIES AND SERVICES: Free showers and toilets, snack bar, shop, baggage storage, laundry facilities; open June–August, office open 24 hours

TELEPHONE: 020-8985-7655

FAX: 020-8749-9074

EMAIL: tentcity@btInternet.com

BUS STOP: Take bus No. 38 from Victoria or Piccadilly Circus to Clapton Pond and walk down Millfields Road; or take bus No. 242 from Liverpool Station to Mandeville Street and cross bridge to Hackney Marshes.

CREDIT CARDS: None; cash only

RATES: No pitch fee for caravans or tents; £5 per person per day; children under 12 half price

LEE VALLEY PARK
Picketts Lock Centre, Picketts Lock Lane, Picketts Lock, N9

This one is loaded with extras . . . when was the last time you played eighteen holes of golf at your campsite?

FACILITIES AND SERVICES: Free showers and toilet, coin-operated laundry, swimming pool (£1 per person per swim), 18-hole golf course (greens fee £8), golf pro and golf shop, two gyms, sauna, convenience store, public phone for outgoing calls only, no incoming calls, twelve-screen cinema next door and restaurant. No tents provided. Open year-round, office open 8 A.M.–10 P.M. daily.

TELEPHONE: 020-8345-6666

FAX: 020-8884-4975

TRAIN STOP: From Liverpool Station in London, take British Rail to Edmonton Green, then bus W8 to Picketts Lock. Bus stops in front of the cinema and it is another 200 yards to the campsite. Campground is six miles from center of London and trip to campground takes thirty minutes each way.

CREDIT CARDS: MC, V

RATES: No pitch fee; adults 15 years and up £5.50 per person per day; children under 16 £2.50 per child per day; electrical hookups £2.50 per night

TENT CITY
Old Oak Common, East Acton, W3

There is tent living *only* at this campsite, in field tents set up for men, women, or mixed. Or, bring your own tent and pitch it for the same price. Very popular. Open June–September.

FACILITIES AND SERVICES: Free showers and toilets, snack bar, baggage storage, laundry and cooking facilities

TELEPHONE: 020-8743-5708

FAX: 020-8749-9074

TUBE: East Acton, bus No. 12 or 52A, six miles from London

CREDIT CARDS: None; cash only

RATES: No pitch fee; £6 per person per day, £3.50 per child per day in dormitory-style tents or in your own

Student Dormitories

Some of the Cheapest Sleeps in London are in university and college dormitories after the students have left. The good news is that these are available to a Cheap Sleeper no matter what age. The bad news is that these accommodations are available only during holiday periods and in summer when classes are not in session. Most of these utilitarian sites are well located and many offer inexpensive cafeteria-style meals, but few have private bathrooms or any style. Some have dorm rooms that can sleep four to six persons who may or may not be traveling together. Lockers are provided, but theft is common. To protect your belongings, put valuables in the office safe and lock up your baggage, using the best lock you can afford. Since most of the bathing facilities are communal, it is a good idea to bring along shower shoes and soap. Linens and towels are usually provided. Each operation has its own payment and cancellation policy. A dim view is taken of cancellations, and penalties are usually at least 10 percent of the entire stay, and in some cases as high as 50 percent. No-shows rarely get one pence refunded. Cancellation insurance is strongly recommended.

ALLEN HALL UNIVERSITY DORMITORY (17)
28 Beaufort Street, Chelsea, SW3
About 40 rooms, none with shower or bath and toilet

TELEPHONE
020-7349-5615
FAX
020-7349-5601
TUBE
Sloane Square, then bus No. 19, 22, or 319, or No. 211 or 11 from Victoria
CREDIT CARDS
None; all payment in advance in British sterling
RATES
Single £27; double £47; English breakfast included. A nonrefundable £10 deposit is required when booking, but is deducted from the final bill.

Allen Hall is a seminary where men train for the priesthood ten months of the year. During mid-July and all of August it is open to groups, families, or individuals looking for a Cheap Sleep in London. The building was built on the site of the home of Sir Thomas More and his family, which makes it historically interesting. The location in Chelsea is close to King's Road and all the boutiques and restaurants it has to offer. The majority of rooms are singles, but there are a few twin-bedded rooms and those suitable for families. All are reminiscent of military comfort and decorating levels. The communal bathrooms are recent. There is a television lounge with tea and coffee provided. Breakfast is the only meal provided, but those really watching their pounds can prepare light snacks in the kitchenettes located on each floor. The staff includes some of the students of the college, which creates a friendly, easy atmosphere. There is a nonrefundable deposit of £10, and payment must be made in full upon arrival in *British sterling only.*

FACILITIES AND SERVICES: Central heat, public phone downstairs, kitchen privileges, tea and coffee always available, no lift

LINSTEAD HALL–IMPERIAL COLLEGE OF SCIENCE, TECHNOLOGY, AND MEDICINE VACATION ACCOMMODATIONS (3)
47 Prince's Gardens, Exhibition Road, South Kensington, SW7
724 rooms; during holiday periods, none with shower or bath and toilet

TELEPHONE
020-7594-9507/8
FAX
020-7594-9505
EMAIL
reservations@ic.ac.uk
TUBE
South Kensington (take the Thurloe Street exit)
CREDIT CARDS
MC, V
RATES
Single £32; double £50; Continental breakfast included

Trying to find the reception office in a maze of institutional brick buildings can be discouraging. If you are coming on the tube, you want the South Kensington stop, Thurloe Street exit. The entrance to the building is off Watts Way, not, as the address suggests, Prince's Gardens. To keep your frustration level to a minimum when you arrive, be sure to ask that a map of the facility be sent to you when you make your reservations. During school holiday periods, student rooms are available. None are en suite, and the bathrooms are shared with a maximum of three other people. A limited number of twin and single rooms are available year-round (170 singles, 24 twins), and these doubles are en suite. Children under ten years are not allowed, and the building is not suitable for the disabled. The rooms, of the usual student variety, are cleaned regularly, and linens and towels are provided. In addition to a dining room and a small grocery store, there is a bookshop, sports center, and bank. The hall is located in a nice residential area on the boundary of Kensington and Chelsea, not far from museums and the Royal Albert Hall, which is open at Easter and July through the end of September.

FACILITIES AND SERVICES: Central heat, public phones, lifts to some floors, laundry facilities, pizzeria on campus, grocery store, bookshop, bank, sports center, TV in lounge, office safe, some kitchen facilities, 24-hour reception

LONDON HOUSE FOR OVERSEAS VISITORS (13)
Mecklenburgh Square, Bloomsbury, WC1
350 rooms, 6 with shower or bath and toilet

This residence is open year-round to postgraduate students and visiting academics. Short stays are considered to be from one night to three months; most of the residents are here for an academic term.

FACILITIES AND SERVICES: Direct-dial phones, tea and coffeemakers and TV in some suites

TELEPHONE
020-7837-8888
FAX
020-7837-9321
TUBE
Russell Square
CREDIT CARDS
MC, V
RATES
Short term: single £28; double £60–70; breakfast not included. Prices for longer stays are available upon request.

MORE HOUSE (17)
53 Cromwell Road, South Kensington, SW7
60 rooms, none with shower or bath and toilet

If you are interested in a popular Cheap Sleep open only in summer, where gentle nuns treat their guests with the utmost kindness, get your reservation in ASAP, because the word is out on this one.

More House is named for Sir Thomas More, a famous saint of the English Reformation who was lord chancellor under King Henry VIII and lived in Chelsea. The house is run by the Sisters of St. Augustine, and during the school term is used as a dorm for students attending London University Colleges. In July and August, More House offers bed-and-breakfast accommodations at prices reminiscent of bygone days. Those planning to stay a week or more will have a 10 percent discount. Groups receive favorable rates, and children under six stay free if they share their parents' room. Each sparse room has hot and cold running water and dormitory

TELEPHONE
020-7584-2040
FAX
020-7581-5748
TUBE
South Kensington, Gloucester Road
CREDIT CARDS
None; British sterling only

RATES
Single £26 per night; double
£42 per night; triple £54 per
night; dormitory room £16 per
night. *Rates for students on
summer courses of four weeks or
more:* single £120 per week;
double £92 per person per
week. *Rates for nonstudents
staying more than four weeks:*
£145 per person per week. All
rates include an English
breakfast. There is a 10 percent
discount for each night after the
seventh night. A nonrefundable
£10 deposit is required on
booking, but is deductible from
the bill. This deposit may be
paid by international money
order or banker's draft.

decor. Baths, showers, and toilets are on each floor and so are tea and coffeemakers, a microwave, refrigerator, and telephone to receive incoming calls. A full English breakfast, with juice, bacon, sausage, eggs, beans or tomatoes, cereal, rolls, toast, tea, and coffee is served in the cafeteria. The South Kensington location is prime: right across from the Natural History Museum.

RESERVATIONS: To inquire about rooms here, write to The Warden, More House, 53 Cromwell Road, London, SW7 2EH. To reserve, a nonrefundable £10 deposit is required, which is deductible from the total bill. All payment must be in British sterling.

FACILITIES AND SERVICES: Central heat, public phones, microwave, refrigerator, tea and coffeemakers on each floor, TV in lounge, lift, coin-operated laundry, office safe

QUEEN ALEXANDRA'S HOUSE (2)
Bremner Road, Kensington Gore, South Kensington, SW7
110 rooms, none with shower or bath and toilet

TELEPHONE
020-7589-3635
FAX
020-7589-3177
TUBE
Gloucester Road, South
Kensington
CREDIT CARDS
None; cash only
RATES
£125 per week if stay is longer
than two weeks, otherwise £25
per day; Continental breakfast
included; dinner £4–6 extra

From July to mid-August (and other times if rooms are available), women of all ages can check into Queen Alexandra's House. It is definitely not sumptuous, but it is a safe, well-located selection next to the Royal Albert Hall. One advantage is that all of the rooms are singles, so you won't have to bunk with strangers. It is popular, and advance reservations are strongly recommended because drop-ins can rarely be housed. A dining room open for dinner, microwaves on each floor, plus coin-operated laundries and ironing facilities are further money-savers for many.

FACILITIES AND SERVICES: Central heat, dining room for breakfast and dinner, public phone, iron, coin-operated laundry, microwave on each floor, office safe, TV lounge, lift

BUAC–BRITISH UNIVERSITIES ACCOMMODATION CONSORTIUM LTD.
Box 1707, University Park, Nottingham, NG7 2RD

TELEPHONE
0115-950-4571
FAX
0115-942-2505
EMAIL
buac@nottingham.ac.uk
INTERNET
www.buac.co.uk

BUAC is the umbrella name for more than sixty universities in Great Britain where accommodations are available during the summer months and, in many cases, during Easter and Christmas holidays. There are eleven locations in London, three of which are central. Prices are very Cheap Sleeper friendly, with housing options ranging from a single room to a flat with a kitchen. Some of the universities offer special summer classes you can take, but that is not a requirement to stay. Many offer a range of sport and recreation facilities at little or no extra cost. Please contact BUAC directly and ask that a brochure and price list be sent to you.

INTERCOLLEGIATE HALLS

Intercollegiate Halls, which are connected to the University of London but independently operated, are dotted throughout London and open to Cheap Sleepers during the summer months. Each hall handles its own bookings. Basic information about some of the more desirable locations follows. As of press time, none of the halls had email or websites, but the university does.

EMAIL: ulao@lon.ac.uk
INTERNET: www.lon.ac.uk/accom.

Canterbury Hall, WC1	**213**
College Hall, WC1	**213**
Commonwealth Hall, WC1	**214**
Connaught Hall, WC1	**214**
International Hall, WC1	**214**
Nutford House, W1	**215**

CANTERBURY HALL (7)
12–18 Cartwright Gardens, Bloomsbury, WC1
250 rooms, none with shower or bath and toilet

Most bathrooms are shared by only two or three rooms. Canterbury Hall is open mid-June through July.

FACILITIES AND SERVICES: Central heat, direct-dial phones, TV lounge, squash and tennis courts, coin-operated laundry, lift

TELEPHONE: 020-7387-5526
FAX: 020-7383-7729
TUBE: Russell Square
CREDIT CARDS: None; cash only
RATES: For groups or individuals: £24 for bed and breakfast; £28 with dinner included

COLLEGE HALL (22)
Malet Street, Bloomsbury, WC1
250 beds, no private facilities

College Hall is open June, July, and September, but is closed in August.

FACILITIES AND SERVICES: Kitchen on each floor, coin-operated laundry, lift, restaurant, TV lounge

TELEPHONE: 020-7580-9131

FAX: 020-7636-6591

TUBE: Goodge Street, Russell Square

CREDIT CARDS: None; cash only

RATES: Single £25; double £35; Continental breakfast and dinner included

COMMONWEALTH HALL (8)
1–11 Cartwright Gardens, Bloomsbury, WC1
400 rooms, none with shower or bath and toilet

Commonwealth Hall is open mid-June through mid-August.

FACILITIES AND SERVICES: Two kitchens per floor, coin-operated laundry, library, lift, music room, safe, squash and tennis courts, TV lounge

TELEPHONE: 020-7387-0311

FAX: 020-7383-4375

TUBE: Russell Square

CREDIT CARDS: None; cash only

RATES: Groups or individuals £24 for dinner, bed, and breakfast; reservations must be made in advance

CONNAUGHT HALL (18)
41 Tavistock Square, Bloomsbury, WC1
200 rooms, none with shower or bath and toilet

Connaught Hall is open at Easter and from June through August.

FACILITIES AND SERVICES: Coin-operated laundry, garden, lift, TV lounge

TELEPHONE: 020-7387-6181

FAX: 020-7383-4109

TUBE: Euston, Russell Square

CREDIT CARDS: None; cash only

RATES: Prices are per person: bed and breakfast £21; dinner, bed, and breakfast £26

INTERNATIONAL HALL (19)
Brunswick Square, Bloomsbury, WC1
531 rooms, 20 with shower or bath and toilet

International Hall is open for Easter and from mid-June to mid-September; you must be over sixteen years old.

FACILITIES AND SERVICES: Direct-dial phones, kitchen, coin-operated laundry, lift, squash courts, TV lounge

TELEPHONE: 020-7685-4500
FAX: 020-7278-9720
TUBE: Russell Square
CREDIT CARDS: MC, V
RATES: Prices are per person: £26 for dinner, bed, and breakfast; £22 for bed and breakfast

NUTFORD HOUSE (10)
Brown Street at Nutford Place, Marylebone, W1
200 rooms, none with shower or bath and toilet

Nutford House is open for Easter and from mid-June to mid-September.

FACILITIES AND SERVICES: Kitchen on each floor, coin-operated laundry, leisure center with pool and gym (supplemental charge), TV lounge, no lift, no smoking allowed
TELEPHONE: 020-7468-5800
FAX: 020-7258-1781
TUBE: Marble Arch
CREDIT CARDS: None; cash only
RATES: Rates are per person: bed and breakfast £24; dinner, bed, and breakfast £30

KING'S COLLEGE LONDON–KING'S CAMPUS VACATION BUREAU
127 Stamford Street, London SE1 9NQ

While technically under the heading of BUAC accommodations, which are described on page 212, King's Campus Vacation Bureau is an entity in itself, and reservations for their residence halls should be made through their central London office. King's Campus Vacation Bureau has various college halls of residence offering dormitory and flat accommodations in and around London that provide an impressive number of beds and range of facilities for both groups and individuals. You can select an en suite apartment or a student single or double room. The residences offer breakfast, but the apartments do not. Conference facilities are available. Only those within central London that take both individuals and groups are described below. For a complete listing of all their London area residence halls, and those specifically for large groups, please contact the main office. The residences are open from early June to mid-September, and at Wellington Hall only, usually during the Christmas and Easter vacations as well. All bookings must be made through the King's Campus Vacation

TELEPHONE
020-7928-3777
FAX
020-7928-5777
EMAIL
vac.bureau@kcl.ac.uk
CREDIT CARDS
MC, V
RATES
Rooms: single £17–26; double £36–40; Continental or English breakfast included depending on location. *Apartments:* singles only £32–35, no breakfast included; discounts for stays of seven or more nights, groups, and students with university status.

Bureau office. When booking, bear in mind that discounts are available to individuals for stays over seven nights, groups, and university students holding current student status. Half- or full-board rates are available for groups of thirty or more.

GREAT DOVER STREET APARTMENTS (12)
165 Great Dover Street, London Bridge, SE1
769 rooms, all with shower or bath and toilet

TELEPHONE
020-7407-0068/9

FAX
020-7378-7973

TUBE
Borough

The apartments are close to the South Bank of the River Thames and within walking distance of Shakespeare's Globe Theatre and the new Tate Gallery of Modern Art, which opened in 2000. The 769 single flats (twins could be arranged) are in a modern residence built around a landscaped quadrangle. Each has a private bathroom and small refrigerator.

FACILITIES AND SERVICES: Central heat, each flat has a communal area with TV and, on request, direct-dial phones, four rooms and parking for disabled, coin-operated laundry. Minimum one-week stay.

QUEEN ELIZABETH HALL (41)
Campden Hill Road (on the Kensington Campus), Kensington, W8
242 beds, no private facilities

TELEPHONE
020-7333-4255 (office hours);
020-7333-4245 (24 hours)

FAX
020-7333-4401

TUBE
High Street Kensington,
Notting Hill Gate

The smart shopping along Kensington High Street, Kensington Gardens, and Holland Park make Queen Elizabeth Hall one of the more desirable choices. There are 242 beds in single and twin rooms, all with only a washbasin. Showers and toilets are on the hall. Meals for groups can be arranged; otherwise only breakfast is served.

FACILITIES AND SERVICES: Central heat, direct-dial phones only by arrangement, otherwise, you will use the hall phones, lift to some floors, coin-operated laundry, ironing facilities, maid and linen service, TV in lounge, squash and tennis courts (BYO rackets and balls), pool table, 24-hour desk

STAMFORD STREET APARTMENTS (2)
127 Stamford Street, Waterloo, SE1
560 rooms, none with shower or bath and toilet

The apartments are located by the South Bank arts complex on the River Thames. This complex houses the Royal National Theatre, National Film Theatre, Festival and Queen Elizabeth halls, Purcell Room, Hayward Gallery, and the Museum of the Moving Image. Covent Garden is just across the Waterloo Bridge and the Eurostar Terminal, and Waterloo Station, with trains direct to Paris and Brussels, is also close. The building was the first warehouse owned by W. H. Smith, the famous stationers and bookstore, and their crest can still be seen at roof level on the facade—the only part of the original building that's still there. The residence has 560 single bedrooms arranged in self-contained units of four to nine rooms, each with its own bathroom and small refrigerator.

FACILITIES AND SERVICES: Each unit has a communal area with a television and, by arrangement, each room may have its own direct-dial phone. There are rooms equipped for disabled guests and limited parking for them, but otherwise there is no parking on campus. Breakfast is not provided and there is no lift.

TELEPHONE
020-7873-2969 (office hours);
020-7873-2962 (all other times)
FAX
020-7873-2964
TUBE
Waterloo

WELLINGTON HALL (15)
71 Vincent Square, Victoria, SW1
125 beds, no private facilities

Wellington Hall is in the quiet, green Vincent Square, only a few minutes from Parliament Square. The building was designed by A. C. Martin, an Edwardian architect, and was used by the College Theology Faculty until 1983, when it became a student residence hall. This is the most central of the King's College residences, within walking distance of Victoria Station, Westminster Abbey, Big Ben, the Houses of Parliament, and the Tate Gallery. There are 125 beds in single and twin-bedded rooms, all with hot and cold water and the other facilities down the hall. There are two lounges with views of the gardens and the square. Lunch and dinner can be arranged for groups only, but an English breakfast is served. This is the only residence that is also open during the Christmas and Easter breaks.

FACILITIES AND SERVICES: Bar, central heat, conference room, laundry and ironing facilities, library, public phone, TV lounge, 24-hour desk

TELEPHONE
020-7834-4740
FAX
020-8233-7709
TUBE
Victoria, St. James's Park

LONDON SCHOOL OF ECONOMICS HALLS AND RESIDENCES

The LSE halls and residences offer thousands of comfortable Cheap Sleeps during Easter and summer vacation periods. All are within easy access to public transportation and are in the areas most tourists have on their lists. Reservations are made directly with the residences and all accept credit cards.

BANKSIDE HOUSE (3)
24 Sumner Street, South Bank, SE1
800 beds; most rooms have shower or bath and toilet

TELEPHONE
020-7633-9877
FAX
020-7574-6730
TUBE
London Bridge, Blackfriars
CREDIT CARDS
MC, V
RATES
Single £30–42; double £58; triple £75; quad: £88; breakfast included

LSE's largest residence is on the South Bank of the Thames, near the Globe Theatre and opposite the site of the new Tate Gallery of Modern Art. From here, Covent Garden, the West End, Tower of London, Tower Bridge, and St. Paul's Cathedral are all within a fifteen-minute walk.

FACILITIES AND SERVICES: Bar, games room, coin-operated laundry, TV lounge

BUTLER'S WHARF RESIDENCE (6)
11 Gainsford Street, Hays Wharf, SE1
250 rooms and flats; no rooms have private facilities; all flats have private facilities

TELEPHONE
020-7403-8533/7407-7164
FAX
020-7403-0847
TUBE
Tower Hill, London Bridge
CREDIT CARDS
MC, V
RATES
Single £22; double £38; Flats £18 per person per night: no breakfast

Butler's Wharf is a London School of Economics complex offering rooms and flats close to the Tower Bridge. It is opposite the St. Katharine Docks and close to the Design Museum, Hays Wharf, and across the river from the Tower of London, the Barbican, Covent Garden, and the West End. All rooms are centrally heated and linens are provided. The flats sleep up to seven in private bedrooms that share a communal living room, kitchen, and bathroom. Open from the end of July through the end of September.

FACILITIES AND SERVICES: Central heat, lift, linens, coin-operated laundry. *Flats only:* kitchen, tub and shower, two toilets, TV lounge

HIGH HOLBORN RESIDENCE (41)
178 High Holborn, Covent Garden, WC1
496 beds; 20 flats have shower or bath and toilet

You can't get more central than the school's newest residence, occupying prime territory in the West End opposite the Shaftesbury Theatre at the top of Drury Lane. Within five minutes on foot you can be in Covent Garden, Leicester Square, Oxford Street, Trafalgar Square and the National Gallery, or in Bloomsbury. Four or five people can stay in single or small twin rooms in a flat that has a shared kitchen, dining area, and bathroom.

FACILITIES AND SERVICES: Kitchen, coin-operated laundry

TELEPHONE
020-7379-5589

FAX
020-7379-5640

EMAIL
LSEhighholborn@compuserve.com

TUBE
Holborn, Chancery Lane

CREDIT CARDS
MC, V

RATES
Single £25–35; double £45–65; children under 12 £7, up to 12 £10; Continental breakfast included

PASSFIELD HALL (16)
1 Endsleigh Place, Bloomsbury, WC1
144 rooms, none with shower or bath and toilet

The Georgian building is divided into three blocks around a garden. It is a good location if you intend to visit the British Museum, British Library, Madame Tussaud's, and Covent Garden. Passfield Hall is open for Easter and from July to September.

FACILITIES AND SERVICES: Rooms have phones for in-coming calls, coin-operated laundry, kitchen, no lift

TELEPHONE
020-7387-3584

FAX
020-7387-0419

TUBE
Euston

CREDIT CARDS
MC, V

RATES
Single £22–28; double £45–50; triple £58–64; English breakfast included

ROSEBERY AVENUE HALL (2)
90 Rosebery Avenue, Clerkenwell/Angel, EC1
193 rooms; 18 twin rooms have shower or bath and toilet

From some of the rooms at Rosebery Avenue Hall you have a view of the famed Sadler's Wells Theatre; from others a peek at St. Paul's Cathedral. As in all dormitory rooms, you can expect only the basics: hot and cold water, a bed, desk, chair, and closet. Toilets and showers are shared on each floor. The tube stop here is Angel, which may seem like the edge of nowhere, but actually it isn't. The area is called Clerkenwell, and it was here that Oliver Twist was taught to pick pockets by the Artful Dodger. You are close to the Barbican Centre, St. Paul's Cathedral, and the City of London. From an entertainment side, you are in exploring distance from the Camden Passage Antiques Market, fringe theater, and a traditional London street market in Chapel Street. Open Easter and mid-June to late September.

TELEPHONE
020-7278-3251

FAX
020-7278-2068

TUBE
Farringdon

CREDIT CARDS
MC, V

RATES
Single £28; double £38–60; triple £65; Continental breakfast included

FACILITIES AND SERVICES: Bar, central heat, limited disabled access, TV lounge, coin-operated laundry, cafeteria, kitchen on each floor, lift, office open 7:30 A.M.–11 P.M.

UNIVERSITY COLLEGE LONDON

University College London has residence halls open to the public during term vacation periods and in the summer. Because of their locations in greater Bloomsbury, these dorms make excellent choices for independent budget seekers and groups of twenty or more who do not want to live in seedy hotels in order to keep Sleeping Cheap. The rooms have weekly maid service, and linens and towels are provided. Bathrooms, showers, and toilets are communal. For availability, bookings, and specific information, contact the site manager of the individual colleges directly.

Astor College, W1	**220**
Campbell House East, WC1	**220**
Langton Close, WC1	**221**
Ramsay Hall, W1	**221**
Schafer House, NW1	**221**

ASTOR COLLEGE (7)
99 Charlotte Street, Bloomsbury, W1
250 rooms, none with shower or bath and toilet

TELEPHONE
020-7580-7262

FAX
020-7636-6385

TUBE
Goodge Street, Warren Street, Tottenham Court Road

CREDIT CARDS
None; cash only

RATES
All rates are per person: less than 7 nights £22; more than 7 nights £20; no breakfast, but there is a cafeteria

Astor College is a brick pile of rooms about a five-minute walk from Oxford Street that is open from the first part of June until mid-September for groups and individuals.

FACILITIES AND SERVICES: Bar, central heat, private-line telephones in all rooms (require phonecards, available at the desk to call out), gym and squash court, coin-operated laundry, minibars, kitchens on each floor, TV lounge. Breakfast available only for groups by arrangement.

CAMPBELL HOUSE EAST (15)
5–10 Taviton Street, Bloomsbury, WC1
246 beds, no private facilities

TELEPHONE
020-7391-1479

FAX
020-7388-0060

TUBE
Euston Square

CREDIT CARDS
None; cash only

Converted from eleven early Victorian townhouses, the residence houses more than two hundred people in single or twin rooms that share kitchens and bathrooms. Bed linens are provided; towels are not. The hall is open from mid-June to the last part of September.

FACILITIES AND SERVICES: Central heat, public phone, communal kitchens, TV and music room, coin-operated laundry, garden

RATES
Single, less than 7 nights £18, more than 7 nights £16; double, less than 7 nights £34 per room, more than 7 nights £32 per room; no breakfast

LANGTON CLOSE (14)
Wren Street at Gray's Inn Road, Clerkenwell, WC1
268 rooms, none with shower or bath and toilet

Langton Close can sleep 268 in single rooms in flat clusters that share shower, toilet, and kitchen. All linens are provided. Access to central London and the City of London is convenient by foot or public transportation. Both groups and independent travelers are welcome from June to September.

FACILITIES AND SERVICES: Central heat, computer room, personal direct-dial phone line that requires a phonecard, kitchen privileges, coin-operated laundry, parking can be arranged, TV lounge. Groups only; no booking less than seven nights.

TELEPHONE
020-7833-8175
FAX
020-7833-8206
TUBE
Russell Square, King's Cross
CREDIT CARDS
None; cash only
RATES
£22 per person; no breakfast

RAMSAY HALL (6)
20 Maple Street, Bloomsbury, W1
480 rooms, none with shower or bath and toilet

Ramsay Hall provides mainly single rooms to individuals or groups of students or professors during the Easter holidays and from June to September. The basic rooms have hot and cold running water, and the rates include a cooked breakfast and all linens. Dinner, with two meat dishes and one vegetarian selection, is served, but costs extra. From here the walk to Regent's Park and the British Museum is easy, and the public transportation is good.

FACILITIES AND SERVICES: Bar, central heat, private phone lines that require phonecards to activate, coin-operated laundry, lift, car park, free bicycle storage, satellite TV and VCR in lounge, dining room for breakfast and dinner, 24-hour desk

TELEPHONE
020-7387-4537
FAX
020-7383-0843
TUBE
Great Portland Street, Warren Street, Goodge Street
CREDIT CARDS
None; cash only
RATES
Under 7 nights £22, breakfast included, £27 with breakfast and dinner; over 7 nights £20 with breakfast, £25 with breakfast and dinner. Individual dinner tickets are £8.

SCHAFER HOUSE (2)
168–182 Drummond Street, Euston, NW1
363 rooms, none with shower or bath and toilet

It is all more of the same: 363 single rooms all with sinks, arranged in clusters of up to five rooms around a kitchen/dining room and shower available to groups

TELEPHONE
020-7387-1286
FAX
020-7383-3920
TUBE
Warren Street, Euston Square

CREDIT CARDS
None; cash only
RATES
£16 per person

only for at least seven nights. The toilet is in the hall. All rooms have double-glazed windows and all linens are provided. You can cook here, arrange to eat breakfast and dinner at Ramsay Hall (see above), or just go there for a drink at the bar, which will probably seem like a very good idea after a few nights in these barracklike quarters.

FACILITIES AND SERVICES: Central heat, computer room, communal kitchens, hall phones, coin-operated laundry, TV

UNIVERSITY OF WESTMINSTER

Careful-shopping Cheap Sleepers sit up straight and pay attention! There is absolutely no need to reduce your stay to a grubby flophouse-style hotel when you can check into a room in one of these residence halls and get a clean, safe bed in a room with a maid and linen service, not to mention fringe benefits and a convenient location. The catch is that you have to time your visit around Easter and Christmas breaks, or from the first part of July to mid-September. Groups have first dibs, but with so many rooms scattered over London, individuals do stand a good chance, especially if they can book ahead. All reservations for both groups and individuals should be made through the central booking office, not through the individual halls.

Central Reservation Information
TELEPHONE: 020-7911-5807/5000 (booking office)
FAX: 020-7911-5141
EMAIL: comserve@westminster.ac.uk
INTERNET: www.wmin.ac.uk
CREDIT CARDS: MC, V
RATES: Prices are per person in single or twin-bedded rooms and depend on age and length of stay. Under 26 years: less than 7 nights £22, weekly £135; over 26 years: less than 7 nights £27, weekly £168; rates do not include breakfast. Group rates are quoted on request. The dates of opening for the individual halls may vary slightly, but all are open from the first part of July until mid-September. Some are open during the Easter and Christmas school holidays as well.

Alexander Fleming Halls, N1	**223**
International House, SE1	**223**
Marylebone Road Hall, NW1	**223**
Wigram House, SW1	**223**

ALEXANDER FLEMING HALLS
3 Hoxton Market, The City, N1

Situated on the edge of the historic City of London, Hoxton is close to the traditional East End markets and Brick Lane, famous for its Eastern cuisine. The accommodations consist of single bedrooms arranged in self-contained units of four to eight, each with private bathrooms, kitchen and dining area, and television. There is a coin-operated laundry on site.

TELEPHONE
020-7739-5730

FAX
020-7729-7918

TUBE
Old Street

INTERNATIONAL HOUSE (11)
1–5 Lambeth Road, South Bank, SE1

International House is a short walk from the Houses of Parliament, the River Thames, Waterloo Station, and the Eurostar Terminal. It is a modern nine-story building with singles and doubles for ninety. The rooms on high floors have great views of London. Each floor has a communal kitchen and bathrooms. There is a TV lounge and a coin-operated laundry.

TELEPHONE & FAX
020-7582-9688

TUBE
Lambeth North, Waterloo

MARYLEBONE ROAD HALL (4)
35 Marylebone Road, Marylebone, NW1

Of the twenty-one floors at Marylebone Road Hall, rooms on the top three are the best because they have washbasins, large wardrobes with good shelf space, and extra icing on the cake: sweeping views of greater London. The floors are coed, but not the rooms or the bathrooms. On every floor there is a bathroom for every six rooms, a kitchen for every twelve. There is also a common room with a satellite TV, bookstore, and coin-operated laundry. If you don't want to fix something in the hall kitchen, you can dine out at any number of Cheap Eating spots in the vicinity, or stop by the student canteen and snack bar. The locale is great, across from Madame Tussaud's and the Planetarium.

TELEPHONE
020-7911-5000, ext. 3139 or 5071

FAX
020-7911-5141

TUBE
Baker Street

WIGRAM HOUSE (11)
84/99 Ashley Gardens, Thirleby Road, Westminster, SW1

Located on a residential street off the paved piazza of the Westminster Catholic Cathedral, Wigram House is at the heart of London tourist sights. Westminster Abbey, the Palace of Westminster, Big Ben, and the Thames are less than ten minutes away by foot. The residence is a seven-story Victorian mansion block that

TELEPHONE
020-7828-5019

FAX
020-7828-3497

TUBE
Victoria

can accommodate up to two hundred guests, most in modernly furnished singles.

There are kitchens, bathrooms, and telephones on each floor, a common room with a TV, and laundry facilities.

Student-Only Accommodations

There are many places in London to stay that are only or mainly for students. Basically, from what I can see, they are the pits—run-down hotel dumps with absolutely no regard for cleanliness or safety, let alone eye appeal. Some are so bad I wouldn't even let my dog walk in, not to mention a young person . . . no matter how cash-strapped. There are some exceptions, and those listed here are recommended and safe.

THE GENERATOR (11)
MacNaghten House, Compton Place (off 37 Tavistock Place), WC1
810 beds, no private facilities

TELEPHONE
020-7388-7666

FAX
020-7388-7644

EMAIL
generator@lhdr.demon.co.uk

INTERNET
www.lhdr.demon.co.uk

TUBE
Russell Square

CREDIT CARDS
MC, V

RATES
Single £40; double £28 per person; 3–6 beds £24 per person; 7–8 beds £22.50 per person; one-night Saturday bookings in winter subject to a £2 supplement on all rate categories; lower rates in the off-season; Continental breakfast included

Mars to Earth, come in please.

The Generator is something else. If you know and like the architecture of the Georges Pompidou Centre in Paris, with its exposed piping, swirling neon tube lights, and open-grid ceilings, you will love the Generator. Designed along futuristic lines, with hard-edge graphics and decoration, it is a popular pit stop for Cheap Sleepers young enough in body, mind, and spirit to appreciate this far-out London sleeping factory designed to provide clean beds and a chance to meet other like-minded voyagers. You will bunk in dorm rooms designed to sleep up to eight, and shower down the hall in cubicles divided by corrugated tin. Food and drink are consumed in the Fuel Stop (cafeteria), the Turbine (dining room), and in the Generator Bar. Talking Heads is an additional facility where groups can meet. Breakfast is an all-you-can-eat affair and included in the room rate. Lunch and dinner are available only to groups with advance notice, but anyone can drink at the bar. Management states that the Generator is really beyond description and that you have to experience it to get the true flavor. Go and try it for yourself, but be sure to book early, because there is going to be a long queue ahead of you.

FACILITIES AND SERVICES: Bar, central heat, hall phones, lift, luggage storage, restaurant for groups, office safe (50p per opening), all rooms nonsmoking, TV lounge

INTERNATIONAL STUDENTS HOUSE (1)
229 Great Portland Street, Marylebone/Regent's Park, W1
200 rooms, 4 with shower or bath and toilet

For my money, the International Students House is one of the best of its kind in London. Most important for Cheap Sleepers, it is open throughout the year to *anyone* who is staying temporarily (under three months) and to students on a long-term basis. For sheer number of services offered in London, it is unequaled. Even if you are not staying here, but are a full-time student, you can pay a monthly or yearly membership fee and participate in their wide range of planned activities. Even better, if you hold an International Student ID card, you will get a discount (see page 23 for more about this super money-saver), and if you are an au pair or student nurse, you will pay half price. Members are eligible to buy discounted theater and concert tickets; take aerobics, ballroom dancing, or karate lessons; work out in the fitness center or play snooker, tennis, bridge, or chess. Anyone staying here is automatically a member and, in addition to the above, can eat the bargain meals served in the cafeteria; watch full-length films, surf the net in the cyber café, check the bulletin board for jobs, rides, or lonely hearts; change money; borrow a hair dryer or iron; or join the Travel Club and participate in London walking and sight-seeing tours, day trips into the country, and weekend excursions. If you think you might become a member, bring three passport-size photos and proof of full-time-student status.

FACILITIES AND SERVICES: Bar, cafeteria, central heat, cyber café, hair dryer and iron available, laundry room, lift in one building, hall phones, office safe, TV/VCR lounge, vast array of services and activities, fitness center, conference facilities. Reception desk open Mon–Fri 7:45 A.M.–10:30 P.M., Sat–Sun 8:30 A.M.–10:30 P.M.

TELEPHONE
020-7631-8300
FAX
020-7631-8310
EMAIL
accom@ish.org.uk
INTERNET
www.ish.org.uk
TUBE
Great Portland Street
CREDIT CARDS
MC, V

RATES: There is a complicated array of rates depending on length of stay and level of amenities. There are seasonal and group discounts, as well as breaks for longer stays, but only up to three months for nonstudents. If you hold an International Student ID card, there will be a 5-percent discount, except on the weekly rates.

Short stays:

Includes room with hot and cold running water, private telephone, and £2 breakfast voucher:

Single	£32
Twin	£22 per person, sharing
3–4 beds	£20 per person, sharing
Multibeds	£12 (bed only, no breakfast)

Includes room with private bathroom, private telephone, and £2 breakfast voucher:

Single	£32
Twin	£26 per person, sharing

Special weekly rates (from September to May):

Includes a £2 breakfast voucher—except for multi-bedded rooms—hot and cold running water, and club membership:

Single	£180
Twin	£135 per person

Long stays (three-month minimum):

	first 4 weeks	thereafter
Single	£100	£85
Twin	£80	£70
Triple	£65	£55
Dorm	£48	£43

The long-term rates are per person per week and do not include breakfast. There is a nonrefundable booking fee, an annual membership fee, and a security deposit. Long-term residents are issued meal cards, which give discounts in the cafeteria. If there is no prior arrangement, and the duration of your stay is *less* than three months, weekly rates apply. Permanent/long-stay residents should apply well in advance to the reservations office.

LEE ABBEY INTERNATIONAL STUDENTS CLUB (56)
57–67 Lexham Gardens, Kensington, W8
100 rooms, 20 with shower or bath and toilet

If you want to stay a cut above the usual student digs, check into this Christian-run students' club, founded in 1964 by the Lee Abbey Council, headed by the Right Reverend Lord Coogan, former archbishop of Canterbury. Here you will find clean and pleasing single or shared rooms offered to people of all faiths and nationalities. It is staffed by a group of young men and women who live on site and work together as a Christian community. Breakfast and dinner are served and vegetarians catered for; social programs are arranged during the academic year; there is a chapel, large garden, study area, photocopying service, and coin-operated laundry. Short-term stays are open to anyone over eighteen, but for three months or more, you must be a valid, card-carrying student.

FACILITIES AND SERVICES: Central heat, public phones, coin-operated laundry, dining room, lift, office safe, TV and VCR in lounge, pool and Ping-Pong tables, backyard barbecue

TELEPHONE
020-7373-7242

FAX
020-7244-8702

EMAIL
studentsclub@leeabbeylondon.freeserve.co.uk

INTERNET
www.leeabbeylondon.freeserve.co.uk

TUBE
Earl's Court, Gloucester Road

CREDIT CARDS
MC, V

RATES
Short-term (under three months) daily: single £30–35; twin or triple £22–28 per person depending on plumbing; weekly single £196–230; twin or triple £140–180 per person depending on plumbing; one-night deposit for short-term stays; 10 percent discount for 4 weeks or more, rates for longer stays on request; prices include breakfast and dinner Mon–Fri, lunch Sat–Sun. Guests pay £4.50 for dinner.

MISCELLANEOUS
No smoking allowed except in the smoking room and the garden

LONDON HOUSE HOTEL (13)
81 Kensington Gardens Square, Bayswater, W2
76 rooms; some with showers, none with toilets

This hotel and the Porchester described below are part of the Vienna London House Hotel group of bare-bones Cheap Sleeping budget hotels in London, and the only two of the lot worth considering. Geared mainly for student and college groups, they do accept individual Cheap Sleepers when they have room. At the London House, the seventy-six rooms are uniform in their basic approach to stripped-down living, with open closets, metal beds, and no chairs. Half the rooms have shower boxes and none have toilets, which leaves seven or eight people to share the one in the hall. If you are willing to take your chances on a room, show up at the last minute and hope for one of their dramatic discounts, which are *only* granted to walk-ins.

TELEPHONE
020-7221-1400 (central reservations)

FAX
020-7229-3917 (central reservations)

EMAIL
hotels@vienna-group.co.uk

TUBE
Bayswater, Queensway

CREDIT CARDS
AE, MC, V

RATES
Single £42; double £55; triple £70; quad £85; dorm room £20 per person; discounts (can be considerable for walk-ins) subject to season and availability; Continental breakfast included

FACILITIES AND SERVICES: Central heat, hall phone, hair dryer available for a £20 deposit and 50p per day, office safe (£1 per day), TV in lounge, no lift, 24-hour desk

PORCHESTER HOTEL (14)
33 Prince's Square, Bayswater, W2
58 rooms, 20 with shower or bath and toilet

TELEPHONE
020-7221-1400 (central reservations)
FAX
020-7229-3917 (central reservations)
EMAIL
hotels@vienna-group.co.uk
TUBE
Bayswater, Queensway
CREDIT CARDS
AE, MC, V
RATES
Single £40; double £54–65; triple £68–78; dorm £19–22 per person; deeply discounted weekly rates subject to availability; Continental breakfast included

If the London House Hotel described above is your kind of London pad, then so is the Porchester, part of the same budget group of hotels geared to student groups, backpackers, and other pound-pinching Cheap Sleepers. At the Porchester you do have the option of a single room without a bath or sleeping four to six in a dorm room that does have a private bathroom. Closets are open and no lockers are provided, but maid service along with linens are. Weekly rates are breathtakingly low, but can only be booked on the spot, subject to availability. The hotel refused to let me tell you how low these rates are, but I found a guest who knew and I can tell you that a single in a hotel around the corner costs more per night than a bed here for a week does. Both the Porchester and the London House are good starting places for the young at heart, mind, and body to become quickly plugged in to the scene of what to see and do in London on the cheap.

FACILITIES AND SERVICES: Bar, central heat, lift, restaurant for breakfast and dinner, office safe (£2 per stay), TV in some rooms and in the lounge, 24-hour desk

TOWNSEND HOUSE (31)
126 Queen's Gate, South Kensington, SW7
15 rooms, none with shower or bath and toilet

TELEPHONE
020-7225-3777/7589-9628
FAX
020-7245-1458
EMAIL
platform@gfs.u-net.com
TUBE
Gloucester Road, South Kensington
CREDIT CARDS
None; cash only
RATES
£20 per person per night; Continental breakfast included

The Townsend House, for women only, is run by the Girl's Friendly Society, an Anglican Church charity since 1895. The Christian accommodation facility is a clean, safe, well-located choice for women traveling alone on a Cheap Sleeping budget. There are two types of accommodations: a long-term hostel open to women between eighteen and thirty years of age (here there is a minimum stay of one month) and a B&B arrangement with no requirements for age or minimum length of stay, but a maximum stay of fourteen nights. This part of the facility closes between Christmas and the New Year. There are no single rooms, and they are basic, but with washbasins and weekly linen changes. The hostel floors each have a laundry and kitchen, but the B&B guests must do their laundry in the basement. Rooms are all nonsmoking; no men are allowed above the ground floor ever, and they must leave the building after 11 P.M.

FACILITIES AND SERVICES: Central heat, small chapel, public telephone, laundry and ironing facilities, kitchen on each hostel floor, lift, office safe, TV and video in lounge

YMCAs

For reliable, clean, safe accommodations at great prices, any Cheap Sleeper in London *must* consider staying at one of the YMCAs described below. For the price you will always get bed and breakfast, and if you stay a week or more, usually dinner as well. Even if you have to pay for your own dinner in a Y restaurant, you definitely will not be able to find a better Cheap Eat. At the Barbican Y and the London City Y, you get the added benefit of gym privileges. For a list of all the London YMCAs, call 020-8520-5599.

BARBICAN YMCA (5)
2 Fann Street, Barbican, EC2
196 rooms, none with shower or bath and toilet

Attention Cheap Sleeping fitness fanatics!

If you can handle very, very basic accommodations on the edge of things in London, and want to keep fit by pounding the flesh even on holiday, read on.

Some 196 single and double rooms on sixteen floors make this one of the biggest Ys in London. Metal beds, cafeteria food (which includes dishes for vegetarians), shared bathrooms, and low-watt (sometimes bare) lights in scruffy rooms . . . is this high-class incarceration? No! This is a Cheap Sleep with a big bonus: *free* membership in the Y Fitness Center and reduced fees to attend the various classes. The rooms may be a bit over-the-hill, but the Fitness Center is state-of-the-art, with enough equipment and loud, upbeat music to keep you pumping, stepping, and cycling until you drop. If you take advantage of all the classes, you won't have much time to

TELEPHONE
020-7628-0697

FAX
020-7638-2420

EMAIL/INTERNET
Admin@barbican.ymca.org.uk

TUBE
Barbican

CREDIT CARDS
MC, V

RATES
Daily rates are per person and include only bed and breakfast. Weekly rates are per person and include bed, breakfast, and dinner. Single: daily £24, weekly £140; double: daily £22; weekly £122; English breakfast included

see or do much else in London, but you will come home with a bronzed, buffed, and toned bod. Those who like to "fatburn" and sculpt in one workout should start with the Step and Sculpt class. Move on to Aerobics, the Abs Blaster, Body Sculpting, Circuit Training, or Yoga; whirl through a dancing class; try some belly dancing ("guaranteed to reduce beer guts while improving your sense of rhythm and sex life"); or, if you're over fifty, join a class of floor exercises or the Cardio-Combo class, which concentrates on "legs, bums, and tums." Worn out? Wrap up your workout with a session on a tanning bed and a steam bath.

FACILITIES AND SERVICES: Central heat, public hall phones, hair dryer available, lift, office safe, restaurant (cafeteria), TV lounge, 24-hour desk, free use of fitness center and reduced rates for classes. Bed linens and maid service provided, BYO towels and soap

INDIAN STUDENT YMCA (5)
41 Fitzroy Street, Soho, W1
110 rooms, 15 with shower or bath and toilet

The motto of the Indian Student YMCA is "We serve members, friends and well wishers and thank you for your patronage." On every visit I have made here, they have lived up to their words.

When I first asked to see these accommodations, I was ready to be unimpressed. However, when I saw how clean and well maintained the rooms were compared to many other Cheap Sleeping digs in London, I knew I had to include this as a very special Cheap Sleep in London. While still operating as a hostel for seventy-five full-time Indian students, it is also open to anyone of any age from any place on a short-term basis. The sunny rooms have light-colored wooden built-in furniture, three-drawer desks with shelves above, a chair, and acceptable beds. There is daily maid service for all short-stay visitors. The budget price includes breakfast and dinner "Indian style" and there is *no* reduction if you don't eat here. If you like Indian food, this is a deal you will never beat. Even if you skip dinner altogether, it is a Cheap Sleep you will have to go a long way to equal. (See *Cheap Eats in London* for more information about the cafeteria-style restaurant.) If you are a music lover, you are in luck: twice a week, the Westminster Philharmonic Orchestra practices next door, and Y guests can listen to the music from the balcony for absolutely nothing.

TELEPHONE
020-7387-0411
FAX
020-7383-7651
EMAIL
indianymca@aol.com
TUBE
Warren Street, Great Portland Street
CREDIT CARDS
None
RATES
Single £35; double £50–55; family suite £75; extra bed £12; children under 5 are free, children 6–12 have special rates on request; English breakfast and Indian dinner included
MISCELLANEOUS
Must pay a membership fee of £1 if not a YMCA member, and everyone pays a 50p reservation fee

FACILITIES AND SERVICES: Central heat, direct-dial phones, iron available, lift, cafeteria for breakfast, lunch, and dinner, TV in lounge and in a few rooms, minibars in a few rooms, study room, library, coin-operated laundry, badminton, billiards, Ping-Pong, 24-hour desk

LANCASTER HALL HOTEL–GERMAN YMCA (34)
35 Craven Terrace, Paddington, W2
In the annex: 22 rooms, none with shower or bath and toilet

The Lancaster Hall Hotel is owned by the German YMCA and consists of two parts: the hotel proper and the student and group annex. Because it will serve Cheap Sleepers in London more as a hotel than as a Y, I have also listed it under the hotel section for W2 on page 69. The redone annex is geared for groups and students under twenty-six years old, and none of the twenty-two rooms have private baths. However, you certainly can leave the Lysol spray in your suitcase when going to the communal bathrooms, which reflect German zeal for cleanliness.

FACILITIES AND SERVICES: Hotel and annex: bar after 6 P.M., central heat, conference rooms, hall phone, hair dryer available, lift, office safe, 24-hour desk

TELEPHONE
020-7723-9276
FAX
020-7706-2870
TUBE
Lancaster Gate, Paddington
CREDIT CARDS
MC, V
RATES
Single £21; double £36; triple £42; quad £52; Continental breakfast included
MISCELLANEOUS
Group rates available on request for parties of 20 or more.

LONDON CITY YMCA (3)
8 Errol Street, Barbican, EC1
111 rooms, 4 with shower or bath and toilet

Only single or double rooms are available at this Y, which is about a block from the Barbican Y, and a mile ahead in terms of room standards. During the year it is full of students, so getting space can be a problem. In the summer, you stand a better chance. Only four rooms have en suite bathrooms, but there is a bathroom for every two rooms, so it really isn't too bad to share. Each room has its own TV and a locked closet. Bed linens are provided, but towels are not. Guests can use the Barbican Y Fitness Center (see page 229 for details).

NOTE: A £10 key deposit is taken upon arrival and returned on day of departure. Bookings are accepted by telephone, letter, or fax. A nonrefundable first-night payment will be required.

FACILITIES AND SERVICES: Central heat, hall phones, coin-operated laundry, lift, restaurant for breakfast and dinner, TV in room, office safe, ironing facilities, access to Fitness Center at the Barbican Y

TELEPHONE
020-7628-8832
FAX
020-7628-4080
TUBE
Barbican, Moorgate
CREDIT CARDS
MC, V
RATES
Nightly: single £26, double £41 for bed and breakfast; weekly (must include four consecutive Saturday nights): single £182 for first 4 weeks, £162 for fifth week; double £287 for first 4 weeks, £257 for fifth week for bed and breakfast nightly, dinner Mon-Sat and lunch Sat and Sun. Long-term rates (3 months or more) on request.

NORWEGIAN YWCA (39)
52 Holland Park, Holland Park, W11
20 rooms; 18 with shower only, 2 with shower and toilet

TELEPHONE
020-7727-9346/9897
FAX
020-7727-9897
EMAIL
get47@dial.pipex.com
TUBE
Holland Park
CREDIT CARDS
MC, V
RATES
Single (some tiny) £27; double £25 per person; triple £21 per person; breakfast and packed lunch always included, dinner included September–June. Lower rates for stays of 4 weeks or more.

Oh, how I wish I was younger or Norwegian! Then I could stay at this wonderful YWCA, which is open *only* to women who are under thirty or carry a Norwegian passport. Men must be Norwegian citizens under thirty, or married and in the company of a woman who is. If you can get past the entrance requirements, let me assure you this is a fabulous Cheap Sleep in London.

Living in a Y can be an institutional and spartan experience. Not here, though—not by a long shot. I will start with the food. When I arrived I could smell bread baking, and was told by Iris, a warm, welcoming staff member, that they do all their own baking, especially the bread because "English bread is full of air and not nutritional." Already I was hooked. Even more so when I found that the rates from September until the end of June include breakfast, dinner, a packed lunch, and tea and coffee every evening, and on Wednesday and Sunday nights, homemade cakes are served. In July and August, when the students are gone, only breakfast and packed lunches are available, but there is a microwave, refrigerator, and electric kettle that anyone can use. The rooms are exceptional . . . simple in their Norwegian pale knotty-pine furniture with duvet covers on the beds, nightlights, and a wardrobe. All have a shower; two also have a toilet. You will be happy in No. 23, a huge room with a view over the Holland Park mews and the street beyond, where Richard Branson (Virgin Airlines owner and balloon enthusiast) has a home. If there are two of you, No. 17 is a good choice because it has its own shower and toilet. Whenever you arrive you will receive a welcome note on your bed with a biblical saying, or a poem and a piece of wrapped candy. Of course, smoking, boozing, and using drugs are absolutely prohibited. The lounge is a dignified yet homey room pleasantly outfitted with comfortable furnishings and a rogues' gallery of the Norwegian founders and benefactors of this YWCA, which was originally a club for Norwegian nannies and maids. The dining room is equally pretty, set with pine furnishings and colorful tablecloths. In back there is a large garden with a barbecue. A few years ago a group of music students raised enough money to build a sound-proof music room where guests can listen to music, study, or use the computer.

FACILITIES AND SERVICES: Central heat, phones for incoming calls only, dining room for breakfast, dinner, packed lunches, evening tea and coffee from September–June, breakfast and packed lunches only from July–August, kitchen privileges, office safe, satellite TV in lounge, soundproof music room, no lift, no laundry allowed (launderette close by), no smoking (except in the garden), no liquor, office open daily 7 A.M.–11 P.M.

NOTE: You must be a member of YWCA to stay here. The membership subscription is 1 night–1 week £2; 1 week–6 months £6; 6 months–1 year £12.

Youth Hostels

The London youth hostels listed below are associated with the nonprofit International Youth Hostel Association and are the *only* hostels to consider. Other crash pads may call themselves hostels, but they are some of the worst excuses for accommodations I have ever seen . . . anywhere. Please avoid any place calling itself a private hostel and *only* go to those associated with the YHA (Youth Hostel Association).

Despite their name, youth hostels are open to all ages, but those under fourteen years of age should be accompanied by an adult. Most hostels offer a variety of accommodation options—you can find single, double, family, and dormitory rooms in most major locations. To stay at a hostel, you must be a member of your National Youth Hostel Association (YHA), or pay a nominal extra fee for up to six nights, after which you become a member. Members can stay at any of the five thousand hostels in over seventy countries, from the United States to New Zealand, from South Africa to Ireland. In London there are seven hostels, five of which are central and two of which are in the boonies. In addition, members are eligible for a "suitcase of travel bargains" ranging from discounts on transportation, museums, theaters, restaurants, shops, special travel packages, and language courses. Hostels also provide a variety of programs and activities: walking tours, pub crawls, and movies, which adds up to much more than just a Cheap Sleep.

The YHA value is significant for anyone looking for a Cheap Eat and/or a Cheap Sleep in London. Sleeping accommodations range from modern bunk-bedded rooms for singles to fifteen-bed dorms with bathrooms on every floor. The hostels provide TV lounges, kitchens

U.S. Booking Information

Hosteling International/American Youth Hostels (HI-AYH), 733 15th Street, Suite 840, NW, Washington, D.C. 20005

EMAIL
hiayhserv@hiayh.org.com

INTERNET
www.hiayh.org; www.iyhf.org

London Booking Information

General Office, 14 Southampton Street, Covent Garden, London WC2; Reservations Office, 38 Bolton Gardens, London SW5

HOURS
Mon–Fri 9:30 A.M.–5:30 P.M.

TELEPHONE
020-7373-3400

FAX
020-7373-3455

EMAIL
lonres@yha.org.uk

INTERNET
www.yha-england-wales.org.uk.

(except at the City of London Youth Hostel), cafeteria-style lunches and/or dinners in most, a coin-operated laundry, and convenient extras that include money changing at bank rates, personal storage lockers (bring your own locks), onward bookings, discount tickets to major attractions, and theater reservations. Sheets are provided, but towels and soap are not, so you can either BYO or pay a nominal charge for one. Few have lifts; all have a nonsmoking policy in the bedrooms.

If the hostel way of traveling appeals to you, plan as far ahead as possible because hostel locations in popular destinations (especially London) fill up quickly, and you don't want to be left out in the cold. Reservations can be made six months in advance, using the on-line computerized booking network (IBN) with payment by either MasterCard or Visa. The IBN Reservations Line is 202-783-6161. The cost is $5 per hostel booking. Allow at least five days to receive your written confirmation, which must be presented at the hostel upon your arrival. You can also reserve your space by contacting an American Youth Hostel in most major American cities, through the central hostel office in London, or with the individual hostels. Most hostels can also reserve ongoing reservations for you.

CENTRAL LONDON YOUTH HOSTELS

CITY OF LONDON YOUTH HOSTEL (11)
34 Carter Lane, The City, EC4
193 beds, no private facilities

This Victorian building is adjacent to St. Paul's Cathedral and was, until 1968, the school for St Paul's choirboys. It is the only London YHA hostel that has single rooms; most rooms hold four to six beds.

FACILITIES AND SERVICES: Central heat, public phones, TV in lounge, restaurant, money changing, theater booking, coin-operated laundry

TELEPHONE: 020-7236-4965
FAX: 020-7236-7681
EMAIL: city@yha.org.uk

INTERNET: YHACity@compuserve.com
TUBE: St. Paul's, Blackfriars
CREDIT CARDS: MC, V
RATES: All rates are per person. Single £26 over 18 years, £23 under 18 years; slightly lower rates in rooms with more beds; Continental or English breakfast included.

EARL'S COURT YOUTH HOSTEL (38)
38 Bolton Gardens, Earl's Court, SW5
154 beds, no private facilities

An old townhouse offering 154 beds with rooms packed full of up to a dozen snoozers. The area is a popular Cheap Sleep, and within a 15-minute journey to museums. There is no curfew, no lift or safe, no smoking allowed in the bedrooms.

FACILITIES AND SERVICES: Central heat, public phones, restaurant, coin-operated laundry, kitchen privileges, money changing, TV lounge, no lift
TELEPHONE: 020-7373-7083
FAX: 020-7835-2034
EMAIL: earlscourt@yha.org.uk
INTERNET: YHAEarlsCourt@compuserve.com
TUBE: Earl's Court, Gloucester Road
CREDIT CARDS: MC, V
RATES: All rates are per person. Single over 18 years £22, under 18 years £20; slightly lower rates as the beds increase in the room; English breakfast included.

HOLLAND HOUSE, KING GEORGE IV MEMORIAL YOUTH HOSTEL (40)
Holland Walk, Holland Park, W8
201 beds, no private facilities

This refurbished hostel is an old Jacobean mansion built in 1607 and situated in Holland Park. There are a few rooms with only six to eight beds, but most rooms hold twelve to twenty beds.

FACILITIES AND SERVICES: Central heat, public phones, restaurant, kitchen, TV lounge, money changing, coin-operated laundry
TELEPHONE: 020-7937-0748
FAX: 020-7376-0667
EMAIL: hollandhouse@yha.org.uk
INTERNET: YHAHollandHouse@compuserve.com
TUBE: Holland Park
CREDIT CARDS: MC, V

RATES: Prices are per person no matter how many beds are in one room. Single over 18 years £20, under 18 years £18; Continental or English breakfast included.

OXFORD STREET YOUTH HOSTEL (26)
14 Noel Street, Soho, W1
75 beds, no private facilities

The location, right in the heart of Soho, makes this the best choice for a short-term London stay. Room are shared between only two to four travelers.

FACILITIES AND SERVICES: Central heat, public phones, lift, TV/VCR in lounge, kitchen facilities, money changing (bad rates), theater booking

TELEPHONE: 020-7734-1618
FAX: 020-7734-1657
EMAIL: oxfordst@yha.org.uk
INTERNET: YHAOxfordStreet@compuserve.com
TUBE: Oxford Circus, Tottenham Court Road
CREDIT CARDS: MC, V
RATES: Prices are per person. Double rooms £22 regardless of age; slightly less for 3- and 4-bedded rooms; breakfast not included; Continental breakfast packed to take away £2.50.

ST. PANCRAS YOUTH HOSTEL (1)
Euston Road, Euston, NW1
150 beds, no private facilities

This is the newest YHA London hostel, with easy access to most attractions and transport links to the north.

FACILITIES AND SERVICES: Central heat, public phones, kitchen, TV lounge, coin-operated laundry, money exchange

TELEPHONE: 020-7388-9998
FAX: 020-7388-6766
EMAIL: stpancras@yha.org.uk
INTERNET: YHAStPancras@compuserve.com
TUBE: Euston, King's Cross, St. Pancras
CREDIT CARDS: MC, V
RATES: Prices are per person. Over 18 years £26, under 18 years £22; slightly less in rooms with more than two beds; Continental or English breakfast included.

Shopping: Cheap Chic

People who tell you money can't buy happiness don't know where to shop.
—Anonymous

London . . . a kind of Emporium for the whole Earth.
—Joseph Addison, Spectator, *no. 69, May 19, 1711*

According to the British Tourist Authority, shopping is the most popular tourist activity in London, outstripping visits to the Tower of London, Madame Tussaud's, the theater, the Changing of the Guard, and the Elgin Marbles. Whatever you need or want in this world-class shopping city, you can buy it, order it, or have it especially made for you. There are shops catering to everyone from the queen and the English gentry to East End Cockneys and those on the wild side of today's fashion. And don't forget the famous London food halls, specifically those at Harrods, where the feast for your senses will entice you to shop for a picnic or a full-blown meal, or to purchase worldwide gourmet items to bring home as gifts.

With inflation running in double digits, you probably won't come home with the bargain of a lifetime, but that's not the point. The great sport of London shopping lies in exploring different places, finding unusual things, and enjoying them once you are home. Despite everything you hear to the contrary, there are finds at the outdoor markets, as well as in china, woolens, and stylish clothing created by the young designers of tomorrow.

Discount shopping as we know and love it in the States, I am sorry to report, is not a strong shopping alternative in London. Sales are held in January and July, and these events attract buyers from around the globe. People wait all year for these few weeks, when prices are slashed from 30 to 70 percent on most goods. Some shopping lunatics camp out overnight before Harrods opens on the first day of its January sale. The less devoted will still snag some bargains if they can withstand the crowds, which seem to lose their usual sense of British decorum during the hunt.

Cheap Chic shoppers should pay close attention to the secondhand couture shops, which are called dress agencies. These are not smelly used-clothing shops hidden on dreary backstreets with fashion castoffs you wouldn't be caught dead wearing. Instead, they are some of the smartest shopping addresses in town. Here customers bring their gently worn designer clothing to sell on consignment. This means you can buy a Chanel suit for a fraction of retail and look like a million dollars. Other good sources of discount shopping are found in the *Evening Standard* newspaper and the weekly *Time Out* magazine, which run ads throughout the year for top designers who are having a one- or two-day sale in an empty storefront.

Besides the myriad shops and department stores, London is famous for street markets. But don't go to one of these huge outdoor circuses expecting to find hidden and valuable treasures for only a few pounds. Go instead for the overall experience, the great vibes, and the fun of just being there. These open-air bazaars are good places to find little gifts and mementos as well as kicky fashions that last a moment or two. Be careful, however, and don't get taken in by a glib dealer who will try to sell you the moon. If it smells like vinyl, it is not a rare leather product out of the Amazonian jungle, no matter what the dealer claims. If you remember that a bargain is only a bargain if you can afford it, and, more important, there are no *real* bargains left, just lucky purchases, you will do fine.

It is beyond the scope of *Cheap Sleeps in London* to detail the vast London shopping scene. To get you started, I have outlined the main shopping areas, and listed major department stores, indoor and outdoor markets, and a sampling of interesting shops that sell everything from buttons to umbrellas. The information about the shops and markets was correct at press time, but details do change. Some places will have closed, changed hands, or altered hours. If you are making a special trip, I urge you to call ahead and check the facts so you will not waste time on a false hope.

CHEAP CHIC SHOPPING TIPS

1. Know your prices at home so you will be able to spot a good buy when you see it in London.

2. If you like it, want it, can get it home, and can afford it, buy it when you see it. If you wait until later and tell yourself you will come back, you probably won't do it, and if you do, it won't be there, and you will kick yourself when you end up paying more for it someplace else.

3. Bring color swatches of anything you are trying to match; try on as much as possible; and if you are buying clothing for someone else, bring their measurements and a tape measure (in both inches and centimeters) to make sure the item will fit. Returns are seldom accepted.

4. Pack an empty, soft folding suitcase in your luggage so you can transport your treasures home with you without the extra hassle and expense of mailing and insuring your package. An extra suitcase over the airline limit of two, plus a carry-on, will cost you around $100, which is payable at check-in time. This is cheap when you consider the mailing and insurance costs and the worry that the box may not arrive or that it will be damaged en route.

5. Take time to fill out the paperwork for a VAT (value-added tax) refund, and remember to turn it in at the customs office at the

airport *before* you relinquish your luggage, but *after* you go through passport control. (For further details on the ins and outs of VAT, see page 243.)

6. If you are a committed shopaholic, consider a trip to London during the January or July sales. Check with the airlines and some of the higher-priced hotel chains in London. Many offer four- and five-day package deals around the sale time, especially in January when there are fewer tourists (see The Basil Street Hotel, page 138). The January sale at Harrods is both theater and legendary shopping. More than 350,000 shoppers surge through the store on the first sale day, and 2,000 temporary clerks are added to take care of them. At the height of the sale, £1 million are rung up per hour! Crowd control is handled by London bobbies out en masse. The bargains are good, but be careful of the bin merchandise, which has been brought in specifically for the sale and is of lesser quality than Harrods' regular goods.

7. Unless you are a big-time antiques dealer, buy for the pleasure an object will give you, not for long-term investment qualities the dealer may extoll. After all, if you like it, you won't want to part with it.

8. When buying from a street merchant or antiques dealer, remember: cash, not plastic, is king. For more strategies on indoor/outdoor London market shopping, see pages 288 and 290.

9. *Never* change money in a shop or at a money-changing booth at an outdoor flea market. The one exception to this rule is Marks & Spencer, which gives excellent rates and does not charge a commission. In the small shops, the rate will *never* be in your favor.

10. When returning to the United States, remember these points when going through customs:

    • You and every member of your family, regardless of age, can bring back $400 worth of purchases duty-free. Family members can pool their deductions.

    • Don't cheat, don't smuggle, and for heavens sake, don't do drugs.

    • Be nice.

    • See "Customs," page 245, for further pointers.

SHOPPING HOURS

Bette Midler said it all: "When it is 3 o'clock in New York, it is still 1938 in London." The good news is that all stores are legally able (not required) to stay open for six hours on Sunday. Finally, London merchants have gotten the message that consumers shop on their days off and spend money. Surprise, surprise! The frosting on the cake is that more and more shops and large department stores are staying open on bank holidays as well. Sunday and bank holiday hours are usually from 11 A.M. or noon until 5 or 6 P.M. During the week, large department stores open between 9:30 and 10 A.M. and close at about 6 P.M. The British idea of "late" shopping is that one night a week they stay open one hour longer. Many of the shops around Covent Garden stay open nightly until 7 or 8 P.M., some even later on the weekends and in summer.

WHAT SIZE IS THAT IN THE UNITED STATES?

British sizing can be very confusing if you don't have a head start on how to deal with it. Most manufacturers have their own cuts, and some even put smaller sizes on larger items to flatter those with a fuller figure.

Women's Clothing

American	8	10	12	14	16	18
British	10	12	14	16	18	20
Continental	38	40	42	44	46	48

Women's Shoes

American	5	6	7	8	9	10
British	4	5	6	7	8	9
Continental	36	37	38	39	40	41

Men's Suits

American	34	36	38	40	42	44
British	34	36	38	40	42	44
Continental	44	46	48	50	52	54

Men's Shirts

American	14½ 15	15½ 16	16½ 17	17½ 18
British	14½ 15	15½ 16	16½ 17	17½ 18
Continental	37	38	39	41	42	43	44	45

Men's Shoes

American	7	8	9	10	11	12	13
British	6	7	8	9	10	11	12
Continental	39½	41	42	43	44½	46	47

Children's Clothing

American	3	4	5	6	6X
British	18	20	22	24	26
Continental	98	104	110	116	122

Children's Shoes

American	8	9	10	11	12	13	1	2	3
British	7	8	9	10	11	12	13	1	2
Continental	24	25	27	28	29	30	32	33	34

The key to success, of course, is to try everything on. Because this isn't always possible, be sure to bring measurements for those not with you and carry a tape measure with both inches and centimeters. Watch out on men's shirts. The sleeve length is not mentioned, so you will have to measure them. Table and bed sizes are also different from ours, so be careful.

DO CHINA IN A DAY

When the brochure says "Do China in a Day," it is talking about Stoke-on-Trent, the china and pottery bargain capital of England. Here is where you can stock up on seconds, overruns, and pieces you never can find at home if your pattern happens to be English. You can take the train from Euston Station (156 miles, two hours) for around $100. Better yet, if there are at least two of you, or you plan to buy in bulk, rent a car and drive from London. The M6 motorway provides easy access; the potteries are off the M6 junction 15 from the south and junction 16 from the north. It is a long day trip, but the car makes life much easier once you arrive in Stoke. The trip is not worth the effort if you just want to browse and pick up a vase or two. But for brides and serious china shoppers, it is. For noncommitted Cheap Chic shoppers, there are factory tours on Monday through Friday, and interesting exhibits to fill their time while you are unearthing one bargain after another.

No matter how you get there, your first order of business is to go directly to the Pottery Centre next door to the train station. Here you can load up on information about whatever brand you are interested in, and from there, you can take a taxi or the bus that links many of the outlets. Forget about walking. Stoke-on-Trent is made up of six towns all blended together. From north to south they are: Tunstall, Burslem, Hanley (the city center), Stoke, Fenton, and Longton. The thirty-plus factory shops and ceramics museums are located throughout what is now called Stoke-on-Trent, and covers thirty-six miles.

What's here? Coalport, Johnson Brothers, Minton, Portmeirion, Royal Doulton, Royal Stafford, Spode, Staffordshire enamels and ceramics, Wedgwood, and much more. Shipping is possible, although some outlets do not mail seconds . . . but *you* can. For more information, contact the Tourist Information Centre: Quadrant Road, Hanley, Stoke-on-Trent, ST1 1RZ, tel: 01782-236000; email: stoke.tic@virgin.net; Internet: www.stoke.gov.uk/tourism. The center is open Monday–Saturday 9:15 A.M.–5:15 P.M., and although it is closed on Sundays, many factories are open.

SAVING MONEY AT LONDON'S MUSEUMS—THE WHITE CARD

London's museums offer a visual banquet of delights—from Goya at the Royal Academy of Arts to Fabergé at the Victoria and Albert. Now visitors can save significant money by purchasing a three- or seven-day pass, called the White Card or Go See. This great money-saving card (which can be bought either in London or in the States) allows admission to these two museums, plus more than a dozen others. With the average per person admission fee running between £6–8, it can save money, depending on how many places you intend to cram in. Once you begin using your card, you must visit museums on consecutive days and can use the card for going back to one place several times. And don't forget the best part, besides saving significant money, you won't have to stand in line to buy a ticket . . . you'll already have it.

Purchasing the White Card in the States: Ticket brokers Edwards and Edwards in New York City will sell you this pass, but their prices include an $8 per person booking fee that you won't pay if you purchase the card in London. A three-day single pass is $36 and a three-day family pass (two adults and four children aged sixteen and under) is $65. A seven-day single pass is $54, and a family pass is $97. Contact them at 1-800-223-6108, Monday–Saturday 9 A.M.–9 P.M., Sunday noon–7 P.M., all EST. Edwards and Edwards can also handle all your London theater and concert bookings for you.

Purchasing your card in London: You can buy your White Card/Go See tickets at London Tourist Offices or the museums themselves. A single three-day pass is £16, or £26 for seven days. Family tickets cost £32 for three days and £50 for seven.

The participating museums and galleries are: Apsley House, BBC Experience, Barbican Gallery, Courtauld Institute Galleries, Design Museum, Hayward Gallery, Imperial War Museum, London Transport Museum, Museum of London, Museum of the Moving Image, National Maritime Museum, Natural History Museum, Royal Observatory Greenwich (the Meridian Line in Greenwich), Royal Academy of Arts, Science Museum, Theatre Museum, Tower Bridge Experience, and the Victoria and Albert Museum.

London Tourist and Visitor Information Centers are in Victoria Station Forecourt, Greenwich, Gatwick and Heathrow Airports, and Waterloo International Terminal, Arrivals Hall.

NOTE: For a listing of museum shops, please see page 295.

SAVING MONEY AT LONDON'S THEATERS AND CONCERTS

Half-price tickets for theater performances and concerts (plus a service charge of £2 per ticket) are sold at the Half-Price Ticket Booth on the south corner of Leicester Square. What a deal, you think: All the top London shows and concerts for half price. *Wrong!* Yes, you can buy tickets for some of the hit shows and concerts, but not all on the top-ten hit parade by any means. Here is how the Half-Price Ticket Booth works. Drop by their kiosk on the south edge of the grassy part of Leicester Square and check out what's "on sale" for the day's matinee and evening shows. Tickets are sold in a limited number only for that day's performances and are restricted to four per person. There is a £2 service charge per ticket, you have no seat choice, no returns, and no use of your credit card. If you are willing to queue for up to an hour or more, pay cash, and hope for a good seat . . . good luck. Warning: Be wary of ticket touts around here who try to sell you front-row seats to Andrew Lloyd Webber's latest hit. These are bogus. The Half-Price Ticket Booth is on the south corner of Leicester Square; no telephone; tube: Leicester Square. It's open Tuesday–Saturday for matinees from noon to thirty minutes before the performance and for evening performances from 1 to 6:30 P.M.; Sunday it's open for matinees only from noon to 3:30 P.M.

If queuing for a theater ticket at the Half-Price Ticket Booth is not your idea of vacation fun, there are other ways to purchase theater and concert tickets. The easiest, and costliest, way is to book before leaving home through Keith Prowse, 234 West 44th Street, New York, NY 10036; tel: 212-398-1430 or 800-669-8687 (outside New York). Once in London, it is almost as expensive to buy tickets through a booking agent such as those in the basement of Harrods, or deal with your hotel concierge. Be forewarned that in addition to the full price of your ticket, agencies and concierges take a service charge, sometimes as high as 25 percent on *each* ticket, depending on the popularity of the show. Unless you are hell-bent on seeing a particular show and cost is no object, I suggest that you wait until you arrive in London and try your luck directly at the theater box office. This way you will at least save the booking fee. If you are being very frugal, and don't mind cutting it close, then you can take your chances by snagging a reduced standby ticket at the box office about an hour before curtain. If you have an International Student ID card, or are a senior citizen, you are also eligible to buy tickets at the box offices of most of the top shows at reduced prices. Not all theaters participate in this, and some do it only for matinees, so call first. If you are a senior citizen but don't look it, bring along your passport as proof of age. Free West End theater guides are distributed by tourist offices and kept in most hotels. You can also check the daily papers for what's on or look in the weekly magazine *Time Out.*

VAT REFUND

You *must* ask for the VAT refund; no one will volunteer it. The VAT refund is 17½ percent in theory, but not always in fact.

What Is It?

Value-added taxes (VAT) are taxes included in the price of goods and services, including hotel rooms, cars, books, jewelry, restaurant meals, and clothing. As a tourist, you cannot get a rebate for the hotel or restaurant VAT (some corporate businesses can, but it is involved and not applicable here), but you can get a rebate for your shopping purchases, unless you are buying from a flea market vendor. It is important to be aware that it is possible you may not get the full 17½ percent back, and you may have to pay the store a commission (up to £5) to do the paperwork. Hang in there . . . it can be worth it.

How Does It Work?

Visitors to Britain planning to leave within six months of arrival may claim back the VAT they spent on shopping purchases. When you are in a store, ask what their minimum expenditure is for you to claim the VAT refund. The amount varies, but all stores have a minimum purchase requirement, usually between £50–100, and some (Marks & Spencer) insist it be made in one branch, not in a combination of several. You do not have to buy everything all at once, but you must save your receipts and total them when you know you have finished shopping at that store. Most major department stores have VAT departments where they will help you with the paperwork, but if not, there are several ways to go: (1) the store gives you the paperwork and you fill it all out, (2) the store fills it out and charges you a fee for doing it, or (3) they offer you a discount to forget all about the VAT. My advice? Take the discount in a New York minute! *Important:* You must show your passport at the store granting you the VAT. Without it you won't get to first base. The store will always ask you how you want to take the VAT: refunded to your credit card, or mailed to you in a pounds sterling check. The best way, by far, is to have the refund put on your credit card. It not only provides you with a record of the transaction, and is faster than waiting for a check, but the credit will be in U.S. dollars, not a foreign check that will cost you time and money to convert at your bank . . . if they will convert it at all. If not, you can contact the Ruesch International, which converts VAT refund checks at current exchange rates for a $3 service charge per check. Endorse each of your VAT checks "Payable to Ruesch International," and mail to the Collections Department, 700 11th Street, NW, Washington, D.C. 20001; tel: 800-424-2923; fax: 202-408-1211. There are no limits on the number of checks they will convert, or on the amounts involved.

Turning in the Paperwork to Get Your VAT Refund

Before you leave England (and I assume that will be at either Heathrow or Gatwick airports), you *must* have all the forms completely filled out. Please do this before you leave your hotel for the airport, not standing in the queue waiting your turn. When you arrive at the airport, make this your first priority, and allow extra time. During peak travel seasons, lines are lethal. *After* you go through U.K. passport control, go directly to the customs official who deals with VAT. This is done *before* you clear U.K. customs or relinquish your luggage. By law, you are required to have your purchases with you. No one has ever asked to see mine, but agents have the right to inspect every item you are claiming for your VAT refund. The officer will stamp your papers and there will be a mailbox by the desk where you deposit the envelopes that the store should have given you along with the paperwork. Unless the envelope is already stamped by the store, you should stamp it before leaving for the airport, because the VAT customs people don't stock stamps. That is all there is to it. Now you have time to hit the duty-free shops in the airport before boarding your flight. The refund may take a while to arrive by check, or show up on your credit card, so be patient. Naturally, when you made your purchase, you got the name, address, telephone, and fax (if they have one) of the store. Claims are valid for a limited time, usually up to a year from the date of purchase. If you don't get your money in three months, contact the store before the time runs out.

CUSTOMS

Each person returning from abroad is allowed to bring back $400 worth of duty-free items. This allowance is per person and age doesn't matter. Everyone in your family with you on the trip, including a baby, is entitled to $400 worth of duty-free, meaning your purchases can be pooled. You pay a flat 10 percent duty on the next $1,000 worth of merchandise. Thereafter, duty is on a product basis and can get expensive. Have your receipts ready and make sure they coincide with what you filled out on the landing card. Don't cheat; don't lie . . . they will catch you and examine your luggage (and maybe your person) down to the last breath mint.

Any purchases worth *less* than $50 can be shipped back to the States as an unsolicited gift and is duty-free. It does *not* count in your $400 limit. If the value is more than $50, you will pay customs when the package arrives.

Important: Send one unsolicited gift per person for each mailing, and don't mail anything to yourself.

Antiques must be one hundred years old to be duty-free.

A work of art is duty-free and it doesn't matter when it was painted or who the artist was.

If you have expensive camera gear, lots of imported luggage, or watches, carry the receipts for them, or you could end up paying duty on them.

Finally, people who look like hippies get stopped and have their bags searched. So do bejeweled and bedecked women wrapped in full-length minks and carrying expensive luggage. For more information, send for the free brochure "Know Before You Go" available from the U.S. Customs Service, Box 7407, Washington, D.C. 20044; tel: 202-927-6724.

SHOPPING AREAS

Most shopping is concentrated along certain streets and in specific areas, making London an easy city in which to plan a shopping expedition. Each area is different, with its own character and atmosphere. Traditional men's clothing is found on Savile Row; both Old and New Bond streets are known for their fashionable boutiques, art galleries, and auction houses; while King's Road and High Street Kensington are the places for the latest word in new-wave fashions. Book-lovers will head for Foyles at 113–119 Charing Cross Road, and one-stop power shoppers will find everything they need, and generally overpay for it, at Harrods,

the famous Knightsbridge department store where you can buy everything from a tube of toothpaste to a ball gown, or arrange to sell your
house and its contents and move to the tropics.

The West End (W1)

The West End is the heart of London and one of the most important
shopping areas of the city. The big shopping streets are here: Oxford and
Regent streets, Savile Row, Jermyn Street, Old and New Bond streets,
and Piccadilly Circus, with the world's largest Tower Records store. Also
here is the beautiful and expensive Burlington Arcade, Aquascutum,
Hamley's toy store, Liberty, Selfridges, and much more. If you only have
time to window-shop for an hour or so, you will not forget your time
spent on New and Old Bond streets. The shops are magnificent; so are the
prices.

Knightsbridge (SW1, SW3)

After the West End, Knightsbridge has the largest concentration of
shops. The most important streets to remember are Brompton Road
(Harrods is here), Sloane Street (Harvey Nichols and designer boutiques),
Walton Street (glorious gift and clothing boutiques), and Beauchamp
Place (pronounced BEECH-um). This is a block-long strip of exclusive
shops where the late Princess Diana's favorite designer, Bruce Oldfield,
has a shop. Another of her favorites along here was Janet Reger, a
specialist in luxurious lingerie. Her most popular designs are in pure silk,
trimmed in handmade lace and in loads of colors. Prices run from £10 for
a garter to £350 for a silk dressing gown.

Kensington (W8)

When you get off at the High Street Kensington tube station, you will
be right in the middle of a wonderful shopping area concentrated along
Kensington High Street and Kensington Church Street. Kensington
High Street is one of London's hottest stomping grounds for style-
conscious fans chasing the latest craze. If you love far-out fashions, do not
miss Hype DF, and a look-see at the multiples such as Jigsaw, Next, and
Whistles. For the more traditionally minded, there is a Marks & Spencer,
House of Fraser, a branch of the British Home Stores (dull), and Laura
Ashley. Antiques lovers will enjoy strolling along Kensington Church
Street, where both sides of the street are lined with jewel-like shops
featuring museum-quality antiques and collectibles.

Chelsea (SW3, SW10)

Saturday is the best day to experience Chelsea. Take the tube to Sloane
Square and start with a quick look through The General Trading Com-
pany on Sloane Street, then hit the housewares and linens at Peter Jones
Department Store, forgoing their fashions, which are strictly from hunger.

Continue to work your way down both sides of King's Road. The shops along here come and go, but they all display every new trend the fashionites under-fortysomething are wearing. Once the home of punkers wearing skintight leather and spiked purple hair, the area has calmed down a bit because most of these fashion victims have moved on to Notting Hill Gate, or are hanging out at Covent Garden. You will probably see more Sloane Rangers (British yuppies) in their Ralph Lauren and Laura Ashley clothes, either behind the wheel of their Range Rover or pushing a magnificent pram holding a picture-perfect baby, than you will freaky dressers toward the Sloane Square end. The farther you go along King's Road toward Fulham, the more bizarre things get. Antiques buffs will want to save time for a look through the Antiquarius Gallery, and keep your eye on the notice board outside the Chelsea Town Hall for announcements of weekend antique shows.

While you are in Chelsea, please make a detour to one of my favorite neighborhood shopping areas, Chelsea Green. Allow time to window-shop and peek into these very upmarket and oh so English shops, which are dotted around the charming Chelsea Green. All the basic necessities of life are here. You can buy your daily newspapers, pick up some fresh fish for dinner, have your clothes cleaned in a choice of three cleaners, do your laundry, and have your hair done. If you are considering a permanent move to London, there are estate agencies to handle all the details of finding just the right flat for you and interior decorators to redo it. In addition you will find antique and dress shops; a perfume boutique; a framer; the best greengrocer in London; a tearoom and two doors away a sweet and savory pie shop; a smart bar and even smarter restaurant; a matchbox-size toy store that children of all ages love (see Traditional Toys, page 279); and down Elystan Street leading to Fulham Road, a French pastry shop; La Scala dress agency (see page 276); Elistano, a great Italian restaurant (see *Cheap Eats in London*); a wine shop; a shoe repairman; a meat market; and a corner pub where you can hoist a few while watching all the important sports events on their wide-screen televisions.

Here's how to find Chelsea Green: Coming from Sloane Square, walk along King's Road until you see the Safeway, turn right on Anderson (which becomes Sloane Avenue), and continue on to Whitehead's Grove. Turn left and after a block you will be at Chelsea Green. If you are coming from the other direction on King's Road, turn left on Markham or Jubilee Place, which are lined with mews houses, and you will walk straight into Chelsea Green. If you are coming from the South Kensington tube, exit on Pelham Street and cross over Brompton Road (you will see Sir Terence Conran's Bibendum Restaurant and Habitat store on your right) to Sloane Avenue. Walk about two blocks and turn right on Whitehead's Grove, just after you pass the Nell Gwynn block of flats on your left and a Europa convenience store on your right. Tube: Sloane Square or South Kensington.

Covent Garden (WC2)

The old flower and vegetable market has been turned into a complex of snazzy shops, market stalls, and boutiques that seem to come and go faster than you can say "Rex Harrison and Julie Andrews in *My Fair Lady*." It is an upbeat, vibrant part of London, jammed with clothing shops, arts and crafts markets, restaurants, pubs, and cafés where you can sit and watch the wild things go by. Outside Covent Garden itself, a carnival atmosphere prevails, with a show put on by sidewalk mimes, jugglers, magicians, and musicians. The whole area is a tourist attraction that is fun and boisterous night and day. You should not leave London without at least walking through it.

Store Listings by Postal Code

W1—THE WEST END (see map page 46)

Shops

Department Stores

THE BODY SHOP (18)
374 Oxford Street, W1

TELEPHONE: 020-7409-7868
TUBE: Bond Street
HOURS: Daily 10 A.M.–7 P.M.
CREDIT CARDS: AE, DC, MC, V
TYPE: Natural cosmetics and skin-care products

The Body Shop is Britain's largest skin- and hair-care retailer, specializing in natural products that are as pure as possible and *never* treated on animals. Some of their ingredients include cucumber, carrot, seaweed, strawberry, and grape, in addition to the usual aloe and vitamin-enriched creams and lotions. All shops are self-serve and each product has an explanation of what it can do for you. Several sizes are available, making it easy and inexpensive to experiment before making investments. The small sizes are great to tuck into a travel bag or to take home as little gifts. Prices are very reasonable, especially for the smallest sizes, many of which cost around a pound or two.

The Body Shop has branches throughout London (and in the United States now as well). There are too many to list, but here are a few of the more central locations:

    54 King's Road, SW3, tube: Sloane Square
    203 Kensington High Street, W8, tube: High Street Kensington
    The Market, Covent Garden, WC2, tube: Covent Garden
    15 Brompton Road, Knightsbridge, SW3, tube: Knightsbridge
    The London Pavillion, Piccadilly Circus, W1, tube: Piccadilly Circus

NOTE: The hours given above are basic. Many of the shops have a weekly late-night opening and except for the Oxford Street location, are open on Sunday from around midday until 5 or 6 P.M. Most are open bank holidays.

BOOTS (38)
44–46 Regent Street, W1

TELEPHONE: 020-7734-6126
TUBE: Piccadilly Circus
HOURS: Mon–Sat 8:30 A.M.–8 P.M.; Sun noon–6 P.M. The hours at the other locations vary, but are generally Mon–Sat 10 A.M.–6 P.M., with the larger ones open on Sunday. Most are open bank holidays.
CREDIT CARDS: AE, MC, V
TYPE: Drugstore with everything from a British point of view

I never have met a shopper who didn't love Boots, which is one of

England's best-known chemists (drugstores) with more than ninety locations in London and forty in the West End. Actually, most branches are more like mini-department stores, with sections devoted to children's needs, stationery, food, household items, cosmetics, and health-care products. They also dispense drugs. The prices are competitive and the supply and selection excellent. They stock my favorite French makeup brand, Bourjois (the prototype for Chanel). I also like their own brand No. 7, a takeoff on Chanel No. 5, and their fragrance- and additive-free brand of soaps and lotions called Simple. The Boots on Regent Street at Piccadilly Circus is listed here because it is one of the biggest stores, but you will never be too far away from a Boots because almost every neighborhood has at least one.

BROWN'S–LABELS FOR LESS (29)
50 South Molton Street, W1
TELEPHONE: 020-7514-0052
TUBE: Bond Street
HOURS: Mon–Sat 10:30 A.M.–6:30 P.M.
CREDIT CARDS: AE, MC, V
TYPE: Discounted designer clothing

All along South Molton Street are several Brown's boutiques, which are famous for discovering, encouraging, and featuring U.K. and international fashion talent. All but this one at 50 South Molton Street are beyond the pocketbooks of prudent Cheap Chic shoppers. At this address, however, you will find men's and women's designer clothing and accessories that did not sell in any of the other Brown's shops. The labels vary, but if you are lucky should include Chloe, DKNY, Montana, Moschino, Byblos, Comme des Garcons, and a host of others representing every major fashion trend currently in vogue. Service ranges from cool to downright frosty, but ignore these fashion snobs and do your thing.

THE BUTTON QUEEN (20)
19 Marylebone Lane, W1
TELEPHONE & FAX: 020-7935-1505
TUBE: Bond Street
HOURS: Mon–Wed 10 A.M.–5 P.M.; Thur–Fri 10 A.M.–6 P.M.; Sat 10 A.M.–4 P.M.
CREDIT CARDS: AE, MC, V
TYPE: Buttons of every description

Button, button, who has the button? The Button Queen does! For the definitive word in buttons, this is the place. Owners Martyn and Isabel Frith have an enormous supply of buttons in pearl, wood, glass, silver, and porcelain, as well as buttons for collectors, dress designers, military buffs, or anyone else wanting to have something different in the way of buttons. If you go around lunchtime, stop by Paul Rothe & Son at 35 Marylebone Lane for a great sandwich (see *Cheap Eats in London*).

CULPEPER (42)
21 Bruton Street, Berkeley Square, W1

TELEPHONE & FAX: 020-7629-4559
MAIL ORDER TELEPHONE: 01223-894-054
MAIL ORDER FAX: 01223-893-104
EMAIL: culpeper@dial.pipex.com
INTERNET: www.culpeper.co.uk
TUBE: Bond Street, Green Park
HOURS: Mon–Fri 9:30 A.M.–6 P.M.; Sat 10 A.M.–5 P.M.
CREDIT CARDS: AE, MC, V
TYPE: Pure essential oils and aromatherapy products

Culpeper products take their name from Nicholas Culpeper (1616–1654), who believed in the healing powers of herbs, pure food, and moderate exercise. The emphasis at Culpeper today has expanded from products made from only natural ingredients (free from chemicals or sprays of any kind, and never tested on animals) to include aromatherapy products and herbal preparations for health and beauty. The two shops stock soaps, lotions, remedies, a wide range of aromatherapy oils, herbs, spices, honeys, and herbal jellies. You can also buy more than seventy-five varieties of herb and wildflower seeds, herb mustards, herb fragrances, and books about herbs. The company has a reputation for quality, simple yet attractive packaging, and excellent value. If you are into this sort of way of life you will love shopping here. If you can't get to London, you can shop by mail order.

NOTE: There is a branch at 8 The Piazza, Covent Garden, WC2; tel: 020-7379-6698.

DAUNT BOOKS (2)
83 Marylebone High Street, W1

TELEPHONE: 020-7224-2295
FAX: 020-7224-6893
TUBE: Baker Street
HOURS: Mon–Sat 9 A.M.–7:30 P.M.; Sun 11 A.M.–6 P.M.
CREDIT CARDS: MC, V
TYPE: A bookshop known for its comprehensive travel section

The *Daily Telegraph* called Daunt Books "The most beautiful bookshop in London—designed for travellers who like reading." It is true! What a fabulous selection of more than 25,000 titles, new and secondhand, arranged into countries. Within the sections you will find not only guides, maps, and travelogues, but novels, histories, biographies, cookbooks . . . anything that will inform, stimulate, or amuse. They can also send you any title in stock on the day of order or find any book currently in print. The staff is well informed and very helpful. Of course, they do carry all the books in the *Cheap Eats* and *Cheap Sleeps* series.

DENNY'S (37)
55A Dean Street, W1

TELEPHONE & FAX: 020-7287-1239
MAIL ORDER HOT LINE: 01372-377904
EMAIL: dennys@btinternet.com
INTERNET: www.dennys.co.uk
TUBE: Leicester Square, Piccadilly Circus
HOURS: Mon–Fri 9:30 A.M.–6 P.M.; Sat 10 A.M.–4 P.M.
CREDIT CARDS: MC, V
TYPE: Cooking attire

It is a great place to shop if you are looking for serious and proper chef's attire to wear while whipping up gourmet meals. They have a catalog and will do mail order to the United States.

HAMLEY'S (34)
188–196 Regent Street, W1

TELEPHONE: 020-7734-3161
TUBE: Oxford Circus
HOURS: Mon–Wed, Fri 10 A.M.–7 P.M.; Thur 10 A.M.–8 P.M.; Sat 9:30 A.M.– 7 P.M.; Sun noon–6 P.M.
TYPE: Toys

The ultimate toy store on seven floors of pure fun and fantasy for everyone, no matter what age. Even if you have no children, or don't even *like* them, this famous store will captivate you on some level. Prices? Not cheap, but for some of the smaller items, certainly affordable.

JOHN BELL & CROYDEN (14)
50–54 Wigmore Street, W1

TELEPHONE: 020-7935-5555
FAX: 020-7935-9605
TUBE: Bond Street
HOURS: Mon–Fri 9 A.M.–6:30 P.M.; Sat 9 A.M.–5 P.M.
CREDIT CARDS: MC, V
TYPE: Dispensing chemist

The motto of John Bell & Croyden is, "Where excellence is an everyday word." This chemist shop certainly lives up to those words by operating the most amazing "drugstore" you will see in London, perhaps anywhere. Not only will they fill prescriptions for just us folks, they are the chemist for the queen, Prince Philip, and the Queen Mother. In addition to the pharmacy section, the shop stocks almost every health and beauty aid known to civilized man, and a vast array of products to aid the disabled, including canes and surgical appliances such as stockings and corsets. You will also find vitamins, health foods, aromatherapy products, perfume, soaps and shampoos, dental needs, even a one-hour film developing service. If you are worn out after doing London, make an appointment at their osteopathic and naturopathic clinic, which is open

Monday 9 A.M.–2:30 P.M., and Thursday 2–6 P.M. Even if you don't buy as much as a toothbrush, go just to see it.

LE CORDON BLEU (13)
114 Marylebone Lane, W1

TELEPHONE: 020-7935-3503, 800-457-CHEF (toll-free from the U.S.)
FAX: 020-7935-7621
TUBE: Bond Street
HOURS: Demonstrations Mon–Fri 9:30 A.M. and 1:30 P.M.
CREDIT CARDS: MC, V
TYPE: Cooking demonstrations, classes, gourmet goodies, and related items

If you love good food and/or just love to cook, spend a half day attending one of this world-famous cooking school's demonstrations. Reservations are required, at least one day in advance. If you go to the demonstration, plan on watching. If you want to get your hands into things, you will have to enroll in a course. There is also a Cordon Bleu boutique featuring their own gourmet goodies and related culinary items. What fun to go home with an apron or something else from here to give to your favorite chef. The cost of a demonstration is £15 and courses start at £145.

L'OCCITANE (32)
237 Regent Street, W1

TELEPHONE: 020-7290-1426
TUBE: Oxford Street, Piccadilly Circus
See page 261 for write-up.

LUSH (35)
40 Carnaby Street, W1

TELEPHONE: 020-7287-5874
TUBE: Oxford Circus
For more details on these natural, handmade cosmetics, see page 277.

PAST TIMES (41)
155 Regent Street, W1

TELEPHONE: 020-7734-3728
TUBE: Piccadilly Circus, Oxford Street
HOURS: Mon–Sat 9:30 A.M.–6 P.M.; Sun 11 A.M.–5 P.M.
CREDIT CARDS: AE, DC, MC, V
TYPE: Gifts inspired from Britain's past

Past Times is an exercise in nostalgia, showcasing replicas of crafts, toys, stationery, jewelry, and much more that cover Britain's history as far back as the Celts. The selection is excellent and the items make interesting gifts. At Christmastime the selection is particularly good. They do a color mail-order catalog that is nice for armchair travelers. To order by phone, call 01993-770440 (24 hours a day, seven days a week) or fax 01993-770477.

Other London locations:

Covent Garden: Central Arcade, The Piazza, WC2, tube: Covent Garden, tel: 020-7240-9265.

Kensington: 179–181 Kensington High Street, W8, tube: High Street Kensington, tel: 020-7795-6344.

Chelsea: 146 Brompton Road, SW3, tube: Knightsbridge, tel: 020-7581-7616.

NOTE: Hours may vary slightly in the other London locations.

REJECT CHINA SHOP (40)
71 Regent Street, W1

TELEPHONE: 020-7734-4915

INTERNET: www.chinacraft.co.uk

TUBE: Piccadilly Circus

HOURS: Mon–Sat 9 A.M.–6 P.M.; Thur until 8 P.M., Sun 11 A.M.–5 P.M.; bank holidays 10 A.M.–5:30 P.M.

CREDIT CARDS: AE, DC, MC, V

TYPE: China, crystal, silver, pottery, and gifts

Maybe the name fit at one time, but no longer. The stock offered is the same quality, and often the same price, you will find at Harrods. There are sales in January and June when you might hit a bargain; otherwise, it isn't likely unless you buy in bulk (i.e., six place settings of first quality will be 10 percent less), or find a second. I never can find any seconds and the staff was uncertain as to the discount on them. You can get the $17\frac{1}{2}$ percent VAT refunds after you spend £100. It will be automatically deducted from your total if you have them ship your purchase (you still pay the postage), or if you hand carry your items, you will pay the VAT and apply for a refund. In either case, the store will pack for you.

Other locations: 183 Brompton Road, corner Beauchamp Place, SW3, tel: 020-7581-0739, tube: Knightsbridge; The Piazza, Covent Garden, WC2, tel: 020-7379-8374, tube: Covent Garden.

SHELLY'S (25)
159 Oxford Street, W1

TELEPHONE: 020-7437-5842

TUBE: Oxford Circus

HOURS: Mon–Sat 9:30 A.M.–6:30 P.M.; Thur until 8 P.M.; Sun noon–6 P.M.; open most holidays during Sunday hours

CREDIT CARDS: AE, MC, V

TYPE: Shoes, shoes, shoes

If you have a young-at-heart mindset, and sturdy feet to match, shop at Shelly's for the hottest shoe fads at prices that won't leave you teetering as much as their eight-inch platform boots will.

Other locations: All over London, but some of the more central are at: 270–276 Regent Street, W1, tube: Oxford Circus; 44–45 Carnaby Street, W1, tube: Oxford Circus; 14 Neal Street, WC2, tube: Covent Garden; 40 Kensington High Street, W8, tube: Kensington High Street; 124 King's Road, SW3, tube: Sloane Square.

SOUTH MOLTON DRUG STORE (30)
64 South Molton Street, W1

TELEPHONE: 020-7493-4156
TUBE: Bond Street
HOURS: Mon–Fri 9 A.M.–6 P.M.; Thur until 6:30 P.M.; Sat 9:30 A.M.–6 P.M.
CREDIT CARDS: AE, MC, V for purchases over £5
TYPE: Discounted and discontinued cosmetic and skin-care products

If you can stand the terrible music and lethal lunchtime crowds of shop girls who swarm through looking for the latest cosmetic fad, you, too, will probably find a treasure or two. This shop carries discontinued and remaindered lines of Elizabeth Arden, Revlon, and Max Factor, all at low prices. Not all the popular brands are always available, and there are many offbeat ones you never heard of. Quality and quantity can be spotty. The shop also carries its own budget line of cosmetics with giveaway prices starting at £1.50. The turnover is enormous, so if at first you don't succeed, try, try again.

STANFORDS AT BRITISH AIRWAYS (39)
156 Regent Street, W1

TELEPHONE: 020-7434-4744
FAX: 020-7434-4636
EMAIL: sales@stanford.co.uk
TUBE: Piccadilly Circus, Oxford Circus
HOURS: Mon–Sat 9:30 A.M.–6 P.M.; Sat 10 A.M.–4 P.M.
CREDIT CARDS: MC, V
TYPE: Travel maps and books about Britain
For details on this wonderful travel book store, see page 272.

STANFORDS AT BRITISH VISITORS CENTER (44)
1 Lower Regent Street, W1

TELEPHONE & FAX: 020-7808-3891
EMAIL: sales@stanford.co.uk
TUBE: Piccadilly Circus
HOURS: Daily 9 A.M.–6 P.M.
CREDIT CARDS: MC, V
TYPE: Travel books and maps
This branch of Stanfords sells only maps and books on Britain.

YVES ROCHER (17)
7 Gees Court, W1

> **TELEPHONE:** 020-7409-2975
> **TUBE:** Bond Street
> **HOURS:** Mon–Sat 10 A.M.–6 P.M.
> **CREDIT CARDS:** MC, V
> **TYPE:** Beauty services and Yves Rocher products

There are six hundred Yves Rocher shops in France and only one in London. Be glad you know about this one because it is a great find. If you are not already familiar with the Yves Rocher line, it is a good one, based on natural ingredients and plants. Prices are very good, quality is high, and the staff is knowledgeable. In addition, they do reasonably priced facials, body wraps, waxing, and the cheapest and best manicures and pedicures I found in this part of London. Appointments are necessary. When you go, look for the different "specials" that are being featured for both skin-care products and beauty services.

W2—PADDINGTON AND BAYSWATER (see map page 58)
Shops

BAYSWATER ROAD ART EXHIBITION (36)
Clarendon Place until Queensway, W2

> **TELEPHONE:** None
> **TUBE:** Queensway, Lancaster Gate
> **HOURS:** Sat–Sun 8 A.M.–5 P.M.
> **CREDIT CARDS:** Depends on artist, but most will take MC or V
> **TYPE:** Original art and crafts

Smart shoppers arrive early, at least by 10 A.M., when the selection is best. The exhibition runs along the north side of Hyde Park and Kensington Gardens on Bayswater Road. More than 280 artists display their works, which are in all price and quality categories. You can select from modern to romantic, watercolor or oil, pen and ink, or handmade crafts. Most of the artists are present, so you can meet them and discuss the price. Many take plastic and can arrange shipping. If you don't want to ship and insure your new piece of art, which could cost more than the piece itself, go over to Whiteleys of Bayswater Shopping Center (see below) and buy another suitcase for carting home your extra purchase(s). Even if you have to pay an excess baggage fee to the airline (usually around $100) it will probably be less than shipping and insuring it and *much* less trouble . . . believe me.

PLANET ORGANIC (6)
42 Westbourne Grove, W2

TELEPHONE: 020-7221-7171

FAX: 020-7221-1923

TUBE: Bayswater

HOURS: Mon–Sat 9 A.M.–8 P.M.; Sun 11 A.M.–5 P.M.

CREDIT CARDS: MC, V

TYPE: Health foods and related items

When you are through shopping at Whiteleys, walk another few minutes to the top of Queensway, turn left, and enter the American-inspired world of Planet Organic, a natural foods supermarket with one of the largest supplies of organic products in England. Here, spread out over five thousand square feet, is the best selection of health foods and related products I found in London. In addition to the organic fruits and vegetables that could inspire a sudden conversion to healthiness, there is a complete range of organic meats and poultry, fresh fish, baked goods, frozen foods, vitamins, cosmetics, a full-service deli where you can buy healthy sandwiches and takeaway food, a cheese counter, juice and coffee bar, organic wines, fresh flowers, and food for your dog. If you are confused and don't know what to buy, there is a qualified nutritionist to help you. Wherever possible, products are without artificial additives, preservatives, refined sugar, or hydrogenated fat.

WHITELEYS OF BAYSWATER SHOPPING CENTER (11)
Queensway at Porchester Gardens, W2

TELEPHONE: 020-7229-8844

TUBE: Bayswater

HOURS: *Stores* Mon–Sat 10 A.M.–8 P.M.; Sun noon–6 P.M. *Restaurants* 10 A.M.–10 P.M. daily. *Cinemas* daily

CREDIT CARDS: Depends on shop

TYPE: Multilevel shopping complex

An indoor shopping complex with four floors of shops, restaurants, and cinemas, with Marks & Spencer, NEXT, the Body Shop, Esprit, book and toy stores, and much more. It is a good place to go with family because there is something for everyone to do while mom shops. If you are worn out, your feet hurt, and your back aches, please go directly to Reflexions on the ground floor, next to the Café Rapallo. In this small salon, trained therapists will do foot reflexology or massage your aching back in increments of fifteen minutes to an hour. Trust me . . . the foot reflexology session is worth its weight in gold, and you will feel like a million dollars after, especially if you get Fran to do you.

W8—KENSINGTON (see map page 58)

AMAZON (47)
1–22 Kensington Church Street, W8

TELEPHONE: 020-7937-4692
TUBE: High Street Kensington
HOURS: Mon–Fri 10 A.M.–6 P.M.; Sun noon–5 P.M.
CREDIT CARDS: AE, DC, MC, V
TYPE: Discounted designer clothing

Amazon, with its six shops all along one block, qualifies as the McDonald's of Cheap Chic retail. The total space adds up to eleven floors of discounted merchandise. Each shop has a slightly different emphasis, but the bottom line is always the same: to sell clothes, shoes, and accessories for men, women, and children at greatly reduced prices. Amazon buyers are always on the lookout for anything new and fresh that is a good deal. They buy in bulk and pass the discounts along to you. The quality is good and a few brands you can expect to see are the French Connection, Versace, Ralph Lauren, and Calvin Klein. The stock changes almost daily, the sales never stop, and the turnover is huge . . . never mind the bargain-hunting shoppers, who are advised to shop with care: there are absolutely and positively no refunds.

COCOON (45)
110 Kensington Church Street, W8

TELEPHONE: 020-7221-7000
EMAIL: cocoon@clara.net
INTERNET: www.home.clara.net/cocoon
TUBE: High Street Kensington
HOURS: Mon–Sat 10 A.M.–5 P.M.; closed between Christmas and New Year's and two weeks in mid-August
CREDIT CARDS: AE, DC, MC, V
TYPE: Custom-made raincoats, coats, and off-the-rack jackets for men and women

One satisfied customer writes: "My Cocoon raincoat has now been thoroughly tested in every kind of extreme situation (torrential rain, falling full length in the mud, seawater, and sunshine) and I thought you would like to know how much I love the coat, how comfortable I feel in it, and how efficient it is."

When Willie and Malla Macdonald began Cocoon in 1985, their aim was simple: to design the stylish, lightweight rainwear that would shrug off the rigors of Scottish weather without being heavy and cumbersome. Their coats are handmade in their workshop in Scotland near Loch Lomond, where craftsmanship and attention to detail are their top priorities. I can assure you that cocooning will take on a wonderful new meaning for you if you are lucky enough to own one of their coats.

Lightweight, breathable, and noncreasing, Cocoon coats are the perfect traveling companion, available in two types of fabric—showerproof and waterproof—come in several colors, and are lined in detachable Viyella wool, or unlined. The coats come in stock sizes or can be made to any size and length you desire at no additional cost. There are also matching hats and hoods. If you are lucky, you can purchase your Cocoon coat at one of their shops. However, if you don't see exactly what you want, your coat can be customized to your specifications and sent to you at any address on the planet. All this takes about four or five weeks. Finally, you can send for a catalog and order by mail. Once you have your coat, you will never cocoon another way.

Other locations: Cocoon, 28 Victoria Street, Edinburgh, EH1 2JW, Scotland, tel: 0131-226-2323; Factory, Mail Order and Shop, Lomond Industrial Estate, Alexandria, Dunbartonshire G83 OTL, Scotland, tel and fax: 01389-755511.

EHRMAN (46)
Lancer Square, off Kensington Church Street, W8

TELEPHONE: 020-7937-8123 (see phone listings below)
FAX: 020-7937-8552
INTERNET: ehrmankits@btinternet.com
TUBE: High Street Kensington
HOURS: Mon–Fri 9:30 A.M.–5:30 P.M.; Sat 10:30 A.M.–4:30 P.M.
CREDIT CARDS: MC, V
TYPE: Needlepoint (known as "tapestry" in England)

If you are a needlepoint enthusiast, know one, or just appreciate the art, visit this magnificent shop. I promise you will be very impressed, and probably inspired to buy a kit and take up this art form. The shop itself is a blaze of color. Here you will find all the beautiful designs featured in their catalogs plus many more, all done up so you can truly appreciate the vibrant colors, intricate patterns, and general scope of each piece. The only time these display items are available for purchase is during their January sale. The staff can sometimes be quite pleasant and helpful.

If you cannot go to the store, at least send for a catalog, which you can do from the toll-free U.S. number given below.

Lancer Square is a development at the bottom of Kensington Church Street. The best landmark to watch for is Café Rouge, as you come up from Kensington High Street.

Ordering Information:

Within the U.K.: 020-7937-4568 (general inquiries); 020-8573-4891 (ordering). To order a catalog, send £2 to the following address: Ehrman, Freepost, London, W8 4BR, United Kingdom.

From the U.S.: Ehrman Tapestry, 5300 Dorsey Hall Drive, Suite 110, Ellicott City, MD 21042; tel: 888-826-8600 (toll-free order line), 410-884-7944 (customer service); fax: 410-884-0598; email: usehrman@clark.net

HYPE DF (50)
48–52 Kensington High Street, W8

TELEPHONE: 020-7938-3801
TUBE: High Street Kensington
HOURS: Mon–Sat 10 A.M.– 6 P.M.; Thur until 8 P.M., Sun noon–6 P.M.
CREDIT CARDS: Depends on designer
TYPE: Ultra far-out fashions for both sexes

Take your teenagers and your camera to Hype DF (formerly Hyper-Hyper), the testing ground for avant-garde designers in London to display their talent in a supermarket of stalls showcasing fashion on the far, far side of sane and sensible. The designers may come and go, but they are all creating tomorrow's new-wave fashions for those not afraid to dress on the wild side today. In addition to the incredible clothes and accessories, there is a restaurant, hairdresser, and nail salon, money changer, and lots of loud music.

JIGSAW (53)
65 Kensington High Street, at intersection of Kensington Church Street, W8

TELEPHONE: 020-7937-3573
TUBE: High Street Kensington
HOURS: Mon–Fri 10:30 A.M.–7 P.M.; Sat 10 A.M–7 P.M.; Sun noon–6 P.M.
CREDIT CARDS: AE, MC, V
TYPE: Classic, youthful fashions for men and women

Lots of coordinated looks in classic clothes that still keep pace with the styles and colors of the moment are available at all branches of this better-than-average chain. There are at least a dozen branches throughout central London, so if this one doesn't work for you, there is bound to be one near you that does.

KENSINGTON MARKET (54)
49–53 Kensington High Street, W8

TELEPHONE: 020-7938-4343

TUBE: High Street Kensington

HOURS: Mon–Sat 10 A.M.–6 P.M., Sun noon–6 P.M.

CREDIT CARDS: Depends on stall

TYPE: Strange fashions considered by some to be de rigueur

Kids love it . . . parents go into catatonic arrest after one quick look at the merchandise sold in stalls named Spank, Hair by Fairy, Skin Flash, and Pink Fluffy. If you are into fringe, body piercing, lots of black leather, whips and chains, skintight jeans, bright pink and purple spiked hair (for men), or anything else in cult or weirdo-wear, then strap your cash to your body and venture forth at the Kensington Market. You *must* be tuned-in to this sort of attire and attitude to appreciate the place. In other words, if you like clothes from Talbots, Laura Ashley, or the Gap, you won't be a customer here.

NOTE: There have been rumors that the market may close or relocate, but nothing has been confirmed because it is considered such a London institution.

L'OCCITANE (49)
70 Kensington High Street, W8

TELEPHONE: 020-7938-4135

TUBE: High Street Kensington

HOURS: Mon–Sat 10 A.M.–7 P.M.; Sun noon–6 P.M.

CREDIT CARDS: AE, MC, V

TYPE: Essential oils, fragrances, bath and beauty care products from Provence

Purity and simplicity are the guiding principles behind the L'Occitane line. Based on essential oils, flower infusions, milk and honey, their lovely products are a joy to use. Try any of their shea butter–based soaps or creams, a bottle of their cinnamon orange aromatic bath gel, or a box of their fragrantly scented lavender candles, and you too will become a devotee.

Other locations in London: 237 Regent Street, W1, tel: 020-7290-1426; 67 King's Road, SW3, tel: 020-7823-4555.

NEXT (51)
54–60 Kensington High Street, W8

TELEPHONE: 020-7938-4211

TUBE: High Street Kensington

HOURS: Mon–Sat 10 A.M.–6:30 P.M.; Sun noon–6 P.M.; open late one night during the week

CREDIT CARDS: AE, DC, MC, V

TYPE: Conservative, traditional clothing for men, women, and children. Some stores carry their line of cosmetics and housewares.

NEXT shops are all over London, or as someone aptly put it, "Next to almost everything." These shops are popular and quite the British yuppie favorite for traditional yet stylish clothing and accessories. Prices are not cheap, but if you look hard, and check the seasonal sale racks, chances are you will pick up something you will wear and enjoy for years. I like their coordinated outfits, which have pants, skirts, blazers, and blouses you can mix and match to create several different looks. I also like their cosmetic line, especially the tubes of hand and nail cream. The Kensington High Street branch is one of the biggest, with departments for men, women, children, shoes, accessories, lingerie, and interiors.

NOTE: If the prices at the London NEXT shops are too high, consider trying your luck at NEXT to Nothing, their discount shop in Ealing, which is just on the edge of London. Stock consists of men's and women's clothing that has not sold in their London retail shops within the last six months. Prices are guaranteed to be at least 30 percent, and in most cases up to 50 percent, less than full price. If you have a morning to spare and are a NEXT shopper, this could be a worthwhile shopping safari. NEXT to Nothing, Unit 11, Arcadia Centre, Ealing, W5, tel: 020-8567-2747; tube: Ealing Broadway; hours: Mon–Sat 9:30 A.M.–6 P.M., Sun 11 A.M.– 5 P.M.

PAST TIMES (52)
179–181 Kensington High Street, W8
TELEPHONE: 020-7795-6344
TUBE: High Street Kensington
TYPE: Gifts inspired from Britain's past
For details, please see page 253.

PORTMEIRION GIFT SHOP (48)
13 Kensington Church Street, W8
TELEPHONE: 020-7938-1891
FAX: 020-7376-1770
TUBE: High Street Kensington
HOURS: Mon–Sat 10 A.M.–6 P.M.
CREDIT CARDS: AE, MC, V
TYPE: Nothing but Portmeirion pottery

Of course, everything is cheaper at their shop in Stoke-on-Trent (see "Do China in a Day," page 241), but for Portmeirion collectors limited to London, this shop offers the best selection of all their patterns. In January, June, and July there are sales, and all year there are some seconds. You can order any piece they make and have your purchases shipped worldwide. VAT kicks in after you spend £50.

Since Portmeirion Potteries was founded by Susan and Euan Cooper-Willis over thirty years ago, the company has developed into an internationally known business. People have always collected the pottery, but recently the market for collecting has grown, and many of their early designs are being bought and sold at prices above their original cost. In view of this, a Portmeirion Collectors' Club has been formed to help existing collectors and encourage new ones. If you are a tried-and-true Portmeirion lover, you may want to look into joining. Please contact the club secretary at 01782-743416.

W11—NOTTING HILL AND PORTOBELLO ROAD
(see map page 58)
Shops

BOOKS FOR COOKS (2)
4 Blenheim Crescent, W11

TELEPHONE: 020-7221-1992
FAX: 020-7221-1517
EMAIL: info@booksforcooks.com
TUBE: Ladbroke Grove
HOURS: *Store* Mon–Sat 9:30 A.M.–6 P.M. *Restaurant* Mon–Sat lunch 1–3:30 P.M., coffee and pastries all day
TYPE: Bookshop with small restaurant

Books for Cooks stocks the most comprehensive inventory of cookbooks in London. You name it . . . they have it or can order or find it for you and have it sent to your home address. Don't miss having lunch in their little restaurant, which features weekly changing gourmet vegetarian fare and luscious pastries (see *Cheap Eats in London* for more details).

CATH KIDSTON (28)
8 Clarendon Cross, W11

TELEPHONE: 020-7221-4000
FAX: 020-7229-1992
TUBE: Holland Park
HOURS: Mon–Fri 10 A.M.–6 P.M.; Sat 11 A.M.–6 P.M.
CREDIT CARDS: MC, V
TYPE: English floral fabrics on a wide selection of merchandise

Two floors of English rose and floral prints on fabrics, wallpaper, and wearing apparel to keep you enchanted for hours. Everything you see is made exclusively for the shop. All grandmothers are hereby forewarned about their captivating children's clothing . . . I defy you to leave without something! Also featured are small gifts in their own fabrics, perhaps padded hangers, ironing board covers, mother-child matching aprons, cushions, cosmetic bags, or a fabric-covered box tied with a satin ribbon. If you cannot get to the store, they have a mail-order catalog.

THE GARDEN BOOKSHOP (4)
11 Blenheim Crescent, W11
TELEPHONE: 020-7792-0777
FAX: 020-7792-1991
TUBE: Ladbroke Grove
HOURS: Mon–Sat 9 A.M.–6 P.M.
CREDIT CARDS: AE, MC, V
TYPE: Books on every aspect of gardening

"If it grows, we have something on it, or can get it for you." That is the promise of this shop, which stocks a vast selection of books devoted to all aspects of the art and pleasure of gardening. In addition, they stock an impressive number of books about design and architecture, flower arranging, botanical art, and interior decorating. If you are a gardener . . . would-be or otherwise, or know someone who is, this shop is a must. They have a catalog and will do mail order.

MARIBOU (31)
55 Pembridge Road (beginning of Portobello Road), W11
TELEPHONE: 020-7727-1166
TUBE: Notting Hill Gate
HOURS: Mon–Sat 10 A.M.–6 P.M., closed three to four days at Christmas
CREDIT CARDS: AE, MC, V
TYPE: Handmade clothing

Ginny De-Bell makes everything in her shop: the hats, bags, coats, jackets, skirts, and blouses. Her specialty is velvet- and tapestry-trimmed jackets. I bought one in red with black velvet appliqué and it is a sensation with either a cocktail skirt or a pair of jeans. New this time around were her luxurious reversible velvet scarves that are just the thing to keep the winter chill at bay on a London night out. Each item is unique, and uses old pieces of tapestry, velvet, and chiffon for decoration. Prices are very reasonable.

PORTOBELLO CHINA & WOOLLENS, LTD. (7)
89 Portobello Road, W11
TELEPHONE: 020-7727-3857
FAX: 020-8874-9353
TUBE: Notting Hill Gate
HOURS: Mon–Fri 10 A.M.–5 P.M.; Sat 9 A.M.–5 P.M.
CREDIT CARDS: AE, MC, V
TYPE: Discount china and woolens

If you think you are going to scoop up cashmere sweaters anywhere in the British Isles for a song, think again. You will do better to watch the sales at home. However, there are good buys in colors and styles you may not see elsewhere. For best prices in London, look no further: this is the place. Sweaters, scarves, robes, shawls, hats, and gloves in cashmere, lambswool, and blends are stacked in bins, boxes, and on shelves in this cluttered shop. Some are seconds; some have discrepancies you can barely detect; and some are big names like Jaeger, Peter Scott, and Robertson. A few have the labels removed. The shop also stocks first- and second-quality British china: Christmas Tree Spode, Johnston Brothers, Wedgwood, Royal Creamware, and more are always discounted. This place is an absolute zoo on Saturday mornings, when the Portobello Road market is in full swing. For best choice and ease of purchase, go during the week when you can have the store and the clerk to yourself.

SHEILA COOK TEXTILES (5)
184 Westbourne Grove, W11

TELEPHONE: 020-7792-8001
FAX: 020-7229-3855
EMAIL: sheila.cook@dial.pipex.com
INTERNET: www.sheilacook.co.uk
TUBE: Notting Hill Gate
HOURS: Mon–Sat 10 A.M.–6 P.M.
CREDIT CARDS: AE, MC, V
TYPE: Vintage clothing

If you are interested in textiles, costumes, and accessories dating from the late eighteenth century through Mary Quant and the 1970s, a visit to Sheila Cook should be on your London shopping list. All of her stock, which is selected for quality, condition, and design, is beautifully displayed and sold to fashion and interior designers, as well as to the public. Doll collectors buy her fabrics and trim to create authentic doll clothing; costume designers keep her name handy for hats, accessories, and shawls. If you saw *Evita,* the jewelry came from here, and in *Titanic,* the parasols and fans were from Sheila's treasure trove. When you arrive, just ring the bell and someone will let you in.

TRAVEL BOOKSHOP (3)
13–15 Blenheim Crescent, W11

TELEPHONE: 020-7229-5260
FAX: 020-7243-1552
INTERNET: www.thetravelbookshop.co.uk
TUBE: Ladbroke Grove
HOURS: Mon–Sat 10 A.M.–6 P.M.
CREDIT CARDS: AE, MC, V
TYPE: Travel books

Great selection of globe-trotting old and new travel books to interest every voyager, even if your trip is in your dreams from your armchair.

VIRGINIA (27)
98 Portland Road, W11
TELEPHONE: 020-7727-9908
FAX: 020-7229-2198
TUBE: Holland Park
HOURS: Mon–Sat 11 A.M.–6:30 P.M.
CREDIT CARDS: AE, MC, V
TYPE: Vintage clothing and costumes

Vintage vamps will be in heaven at Virginia's. If the style was worn between 1880 and 1930, chances are that Virginia has something to tempt you. Downstairs is a draped cave, festooned with lace, lingerie, and baubles. Throughout the rest of the store are displays of fans, feathers, gorgeous beaded bags, and vintage clothing to touch the romantic side of even the most stoic shopper.

WC1—BLOOMSBURY (see map page 88)

Shops

CREATIVITY–KNITTING AND NEEDLECRAFTS (39)
45 New Oxford Street, WC1
TELEPHONE: 020-7240-2945
FAX: 020-7240-6030
TUBE: Tottenham Court Road
HOURS: Mon–Sat 9:30 A.M.–6 P.M.
CREDIT CARDS: MC, V
TYPE: Knitting and needlecrafts

Peter and Sylvia Owen know their knitting and needlecrafts and are only too happy to assist you with yours. Their large, jam-packed shop is the last private independent needlecraft shop in London, and has been in this location for thirty years. Their stock is mind-boggling . . . if it has to do with knitting or needlecraft—especially needlepoint—this is mecca. They are happy to ship, but unfortunately do not have a catalog. However, if you called or faxed them with a request, I can't imagine they couldn't fill it.

JAMES SMITH & SONS (38)
Hazelwood House, 53 New Oxford Street, WC1

TELEPHONE: 020-7836-4731

FAX: 020-7836-4730

TUBE: Tottenham Court Road

HOURS: Mon–Fri 9:30 A.M.–5:25 P.M.; Sat 10 A.M.–5:25 P.M.

CREDIT CARDS: MC, V

TYPE: Umbrellas, walking sticks, and seat sticks

An umbrella, walking stick, or seat stick purchased from James Smith & Sons will not be cheap, but it will last your lifetime, and probably that of your heirs. Just be sure that what you are buying is made by them. They do sell some other brands, but you are not here for those . . . *only* the ones displaying the official James Smith & Sons insignia. If you are not in the market for a fine umbrella, please take a few minutes just to look at this fascinating shop, which is the oldest and biggest umbrella shop in Europe. Almost unaltered in a century of doing business in the same spot, the storefront is a perfect example of Victorian shop front design. Before Smith & Sons occupied it, the building housed a dairy. When you go inside, if you look closely, you can still see some of the original blue and white dairy floor tiles that date from 1857. While you think custom umbrellas may have a limited appeal, think again: seven hundred are sold and repaired here every month. Unless you bought your umbrella here, however, they are unable to repair it.

RENNIES AT FRENCH'S DAIRY (26)
13 Rugby Street, WC1

TELEPHONE: 020-7405-0220

TUBE: Russell Square

HOURS: Tues–Sat 10 A.M.–6 P.M.

CREDIT CARDS: None

TYPE: British collectibles from the twenties, thirties, and forties

I first noticed this great little shop as I was hurrying along Lamb's Conduit Street to check on the Lamb's Pub (see *Cheap Eats in London*). The colorful tiled front caught my eye, and I made a special trip back to see it. I have always been so glad I did.

The building has quite a history, but the most pertinent concerns the two dairy shops that preceded Rennies. The first dairyman tenant (Mr. French) moved in around the middle of the nineteenth century. His successor, John Davies, was responsible for the tiled facade you see today. Members of his family ran the dairy shop until 1994, when Paul and Karen Rennie, along with their cats, Ruby and Harris, restored the shop and opened Rennies at French's Dairy. No, they don't sell milk. They specialize in twentieth-century British art and design of the twenties, thirties, and forties . . . and the forms modernism took in Britain after World War II. While the furniture will be too big for your suitcase, or to mail, poke around and you are sure to find a must-have or two you can take home. I found a lovely early piece of Scottish Buchan pottery that I collect, several vintage scarves, and some adorable toys. Unfortunately, Ruby is no longer with us, but she is fondly remembered by her favorite customers. You will see her picture on a series of note cards sold in the shop.

Before you leave the area, please take a moment or two and walk down Lamb's Conduit Street to Coram's Fields, a seven-acre playground open to all children, and adults if accompanied by a child. The park has had a recent face-lift, making it even more appealing to all who love it.

WESTAWAY & WESTAWAY (35, 37)
64 Great Russell Street, and 92–93 Great Russell Street, WC1

TELEPHONE: 020-7405-4479 (first location), 020-7636-1718 (second location)

FAX: 020-7405-1070

TUBE: Holborn, Tottenham Court Road

HOURS: Mon–Sat 9 A.M.–5:30 P.M.; Sun 11 A.M.–6 P.M.

CREDIT CARDS: AE, DC, MC, V

TYPE: Scottish knitwear specialists

These two shops, one across and the other down the street from the British Museum, offer a vast selection of Scottish Highland dress and knitwear. They can make a kilt from over four hundred tartans, sell you a cashmere or lambswool sweater in a variety of colors and shades, outfit your children, and mail goods to your home address. While prices are not in the bargain-basement category, they are some of the best you will find in London. Be sure to check the bins in each department for tag ends that haven't sold, and remember their sales in January and late June.

WC2—CHARING CROSS, COVENT GARDEN, LEICESTER SQUARE, AND THE STRAND (see map page 88)
Shops

CULPEPER (50)
8 The Piazza, Covent Garden, WC2

TELEPHONE: 020-7379-6698
TUBE: Covent Garden
HOURS: Mon–Thur 10 A.M.–8 P.M.; Fri–Sat 9 A.M.– 8 P.M.; Sun 10 A.M.–6 P.M.; holiday hours vary

For more details about this natural-products shop, please see page 251.

DR. MARTENS DEPARTMENT STORE (51)
1–4 King Street, Covent Garden, WC2

TELEPHONE: 020-7497-1460
TUBE: Covent Garden
HOURS: Mon–Sat 10 A.M.–7 P.M.; Thur until 8 P.M.; Sun noon–6 P.M.
CREDIT CARDS: AE, MC, V
TYPE: Dr. Martens mega department and shoe store

If you don't have a teen in your life, you probably don't know or care about Dr. Martens shoes. (The name is correctly written as Dr. Martens, but pronounced Doc Martens.) The shoes originated unpretentiously fifty years ago in Germany when Dr. Klaus Marten designed air-cushion shoes to wear after suffering a skiing accident. Soon, the sturdy shoes were being worn by elderly ladies with foot problems. Over time, they found their way to Britain, where the young people transformed the clodhoppers into cult wear and fashion icons that have been spotted on everyone from Madonna to the pope.

Did someone mention shoes in this galvanized-steel, exposed-brick multistory mecca for Dr. Martens fans? Besides footware, which is somewhat cheaper here than in the United States, you can buy, or try to avoid buying, all the essential accessories, including bags, watches, and stationery your teen considers merchandise "to die for."

FOYLES (43)
113–119 Charing Cross Road, WC2

TELEPHONE: 020-7437-5660
FAX: 020-7437-1574
TUBE: Tottenham Court Road
HOURS: Mon–Sat 9 A.M.–6 P.M.; Thur until 7 P.M.
CREDIT CARDS: AE, DC, MC, V
TYPE: Books

Established in 1904, this is considered by many to be one of the world's greatest bookshops, where you can buy the latest best-seller, all the books in the Cheap Eats and Cheap Sleeps series, or browse the rows of rare and out-of-print titles.

HALF-PRICE TICKET BOOTH AT LEICESTER SQUARE (53)
South corner of Leicester Square, WC2
TELEPHONE: 020-7836-0971
TUBE: Leicester Square, Piccadilly Circus
HOURS: Tues–Sat matinees noon–30 minutes before performance; for nightly performances 1–6:30 P.M.; Sun: matinees only noon–3:30 P.M.
CREDIT CARDS: None, cash only
TYPE: Discount tickets for theater and concerts sold on day of performance only

For complete details, see "Saving Money at London's Theaters and Concerts," page 242.

LUSH (50)
Units 7 & 11, The Piazza, Covent Garden, WC2
TELEPHONE: 020-7240-4570
TUBE: Covent Garden
HOURS: Mon–Sat 10 A.M.–7 P.M., until 8 P.M. in summer; Sun noon–6 P.M.
Please see page 277 for information about these handmade cosmetics.

MUSEUM STORE (50)
37 The Piazza, Covent Garden, WC2
TELEPHONE & FAX: 020-7240-5760
TUBE: Covent Garden
HOURS: Mon–Sat 10:30 A.M.–6:30 P.M.; Sun 11 A.M.–5 P.M.
CREDIT CARDS: AE, DC, MC, V
TYPE: Selection of items sold in museum stores worldwide

If you can't get to the Metropolitan Museum of Art in New York, or your favorite major museum elsewhere, stop here and see what they have in their shop. Museum stores throughout the world are represented here and the stock is fascinating—everything from inexpensive posters to unusual jewelry and clever gifts.

NEAL'S YARD DAIRY (46)
17 Shorts Gardens, WC2
TELEPHONE: 020-7379-7647
FAX: 020-7240-2442 (for mail order)
EMAIL: mailorder@nydairy.co.uk
TUBE: Covent Garden
HOURS: Mon–Sat 10 A.M.–7 P.M.; Sun 10 A.M.–5 P.M.
CREDIT CARDS: MC, V
TYPE: Cheese from the British Isles

You can smell it as you round the corner . . . Neal's Yard Dairy, a tiny shop with cheese stacked floor to ceiling, offers the widest range of British and Irish cheese in the country. For cheese lovers, this is heaven. All the cheeses are from farms in Britain and Ireland, many of them matured in the dairy's cellars or on its farm in Kent, which also supplies the shop with yogurt and crème fraîche. The selection is seasonal. The staff is great, and sampling is encouraged. They also do mail order, but encourage you to first call them so they can tell you what's particularly good even if you can't come in for a taste.

Their warehouse is at Borough Market, 6 Park Street, London SE1 (see page 282 for details).

NEAL'S YARD REMEDIES (45)
15 Neal's Yard, WC2
TELEPHONE: 020-7379-7222
TUBE: Covent Garden
HOURS: Mon–Sat 10 A.M.–6 P.M.; Sun 11 A.M.–5 P.M.
CREDIT CARDS: MC, V
TYPE: Natural lotions and potions
Homeopathic remedies, supplements, teas, cosmetics, toiletries, bath and hair products, essential oils . . . if it is natural and geared to keeping you at your healthy best, it's here.

PAST TIMES (50)
Central Arcade, The Piazza, Covent Garden, WC2
TELEPHONE: 020-7240-9265
TUBE: Covent Garden
TYPE: Gifts inspired from Britain's past
For details, please see page 253.

PETER RABBIT & FRIENDS (50)
Unit 42, The Piazza, Covent Garden, WC2
TELEPHONE: 020-7497-1777 (shop); 01539-822888 (mail order)
EMAIL: info@lakefield.edi.co.uk
INTERNET: www.lakefield-marketing.co.uk
TUBE: Covent Garden
HOURS: Mon–Fri 10 A.M.–8 P.M.; Sun 10 A.M.–6 P.M.
CREDIT CARDS: AE, MC, V
TYPE: Peter Rabbit, Paddington Bear, and Winnie-the-Pooh
The world of Peter Rabbit, Paddington Bear, and Winnie-the-Pooh awaits you on two floors in Covent Garden.

REJECT CHINA SHOP (50)
The Piazza, Covent Garden, WC2
TELEPHONE: 020-7379-8374
TUBE: Covent Garden
For details, please see page 254.

THE SILVER VAULTS (42)
53–64 Chancery Lane (entrance is just past the address), WC2

TELEPHONE: 020-7242-3844 (general information)
TUBE: Chancery Lane
HOURS: Mon–Fri 9 A.M.–5:30 P.M. (no entry after 5:20 P.M.); Sat 9 A.M.–1 P.M. (no entry after 12:50 P.M.)
CREDIT CARDS: Depends on dealer
TYPE: Silver

No serious lover or collector of silver should miss the Silver Vaults. In the late 1800s the rich stored their valuables in private underground vaults in central London. These same vaults have been turned into more than forty shops for dealers of modern and antique silver. If it is silver, it is here, and in all price ranges.

STANFORDS (47)
12–14 Long Acre, WC2

TELEPHONE: 020-7836-1321
FAX: 020-7836-0189
EMAIL: sales@stanford.co.uk
TUBE: Covent Garden
HOURS: Mon–Fri 9 A.M.–7:30 P.M.; Sat 10 A.M.–7 P.M.
CREDIT CARDS: MC, V
TYPE: Travel books and maps

If it is a map of your neighborhood, the world, or the moon . . . or a travel guide on any destination on the planet, Stanfords has it. Amazing selection of books, maps, charts, globes; helpful staff; four locations. Other locations: Stanfords at Campus Travel, SW1 (see page 275), Stanfords at British Airways, W1 (see page 255), and at the British Visitors Center, W1 (see page 255).

VANELL (49)
Aldwych (no street number), next door to the Waldorf Hotel, WC2

TELEPHONE: 020-7497-0557
TUBE: Covent Garden
HOURS: Mon–Sat 9 A.M.–6 P.M.; Sun 10 A.M.–4 P.M.
CREDIT CARDS: AE, DC, MC, V
TYPE: Fake jewelry and accessories

It's fake, fun, gaudy, and priced to sell. If you need a necklace, pair of earrings, or other bauble to complete an outfit, or love wearing the current glitzy fad, Vanell no doubt carries just what you are looking for.

SW1—BELGRAVIA, KNIGHTSBRIDGE, PIMLICO, VICTORIA, WESTMINSTER, AND WHITEHALL (see map page 116)

Shops

THE BLEWCOAT SCHOOL GIFT SHOP AND INFORMATION CENTER–NATIONAL TRUST GIFT SHOP AND INFORMATION CENTER (9)
23 Caxton Street, SW1

TELEPHONE & FAX: 020-7222-2877
TUBE: St. James's Park
HOURS: Mon–Fri 10 A.M.–5:30 P.M.; Thurs until 7 P.M.
CREDIT CARDS: AE, MC, V
TYPE: Gifts, many exclusively sold by the National Trust

The National Trust is a charity founded to protect Britain's fine homes and beautiful countryside. This gift shop, located in the historic Blewcoat School, has china, glassware, pottery, kitchenware, books, stationery, spices, preserves, crafts, and knitwear, most of which are exclusive to the National Trust. By shopping here you are helping the National Trust's work of conserving and protecting over 560,000 acres of countryside, 200 houses and castles, 114 gardens, 59 villages, country parks, churches, and ancient monuments. As a charity, the National Trust is not run or funded by the government, and depends on the support and generosity of the public to continue its work.

NOTE: Blewcoat School was built for the education of poor children, and named for the color of the tunic worn by its pupils. There is a figure of a "Blewcoat Boy" in the niche above the entrance door.

THE EXCHANGE BELGRAVIA (13)
30 Elizabeth Street, SW1

TELEPHONE: 020-7730-3334
TUBE: Victoria
HOURS: Mon–Sat 10 A.M.–4 P.M.
CREDIT CARDS: MC, V
TYPE: Dress agency

Five percent of the profits from this dress agency (clothes on consignment) goes to the National Kidney Research Fund. The *bon-ton* location in Belgravia means the gently worn clothes must be as upmarket as the customers who often cruise by on a regular basis just to see what's been brought in the day before. While not worth a taxi ride across town, it is worth a browse if you are nearby . . . say en route to Buckingham Palace for tea.

GENERAL TRADING COMPANY (16)
144 Sloane Street, SW1

TELEPHONE: 020-7730-0411
FAX: 020-7823-4624
EMAIL: catalog@general-trading.co.uk
INTERNET: www.general-trading.co.uk
TUBE: Sloane Square
HOURS: Mon–Sat 9:30 A.M.–6 P.M.; Wed until 7 P.M.
CREDIT CARDS: AE, DC, MC, V
TYPE: Housewares and gifts

Unusual, unique, and always stylish living accessories displayed in a series of townhouse rooms that wind all over. As you weave your way upstairs, down narrow halls, in and out of rooms, you will be captivated by all you see: books, garden items, children's gifts, stationery, china, glassware, luggage, and a sensational tabletop department. This is all high-quality merchandise, reflected in the fact that Princess Diana registered here many moons ago. Breakfast and lunch are served in a garden café in the back, but I have always found it to be expensive and inconsistent.

ONE NIGHT STAND (23)
44 Pimlico Road, SW1

TELEPHONE: 020-7730-8708
FAX: 020-7730-2064
EMAIL: onenightstand@ndirect.co.uk
TUBE: Sloane Square
HOURS: By appointment Mon–Fri 10 A.M.–6:30 P.M.; Sat 10 A.M.–5 P.M.
CREDIT CARDS: AE, MC, V
TYPE: Fancy-dress rental

If you have been invited to a fancy-dress ball, to the cocktail party of the season, or to meet the queen and didn't pack a thing to wear, don't despair—call One Night Stand. This agency will come to your rescue with a fabulous selection of party dresses for hire (Britspeak for "rent"). You can hire your outfit and all the accessories, including a fur wrap, for up to three days. The clothes, all cleaned after wearing, are from top American and British fashion designers. If you fall in love with your outfit, you will have to be in town in January or July and August, the only times during the year they sell their stock. Appointments are preferred over walk-ins. Dress rental prices range from £70–90 for short dresses; £75–150 for long. A refundable security deposit (£350) or your credit card number is required in addition to the rental fee. Optional damage insurance (£8.50) is available and recommended. Sizes: U.S. 4–16.

Now that you have your drop-dead gorgeous outfit, what about the rest of you? One Night Stand recommends Pam Wrigley, who specializes in makeup, hair, and nails for special occasions. The great part is that she transforms you wherever you are . . . you don't have to go to her. Prices on request. Telephone: 020-8742-1994; fax: 020-8742-2780.

STANFORDS AT CAMPUS TRAVEL (10)
52 Grosvenor Gardens, SW1

    TELEPHONE: 020-7730-1314
    FAX: 020-7730-1354
    EMAIL: sales@stanford.co.uk
    TUBE: Victoria
    HOURS: Mon–Fri 9 A.M.–6 P.M.; Sat 10 A.M.–5 P.M.
    CREDIT CARDS: MC, V
    TYPE: Travel books and maps
    For details on this travel book store, see page 255.

SW3—CHELSEA (see map page 136)

ACCESSORIZE (11)
33-C King's Road, SW3
TELEPHONE: 020-7730-1295
TUBE: Sloane Square
HOURS: Mon–Sat 10 A.M.–6 P.M.; Sun noon–5 P.M.
CREDIT CARDS: AE, MC, V
TYPE: Accessories

These small stores all over London sell whatever is "hot" in color-coordinated accessories at very reasonable prices. They have hats, scarves, jewelry, hair ornaments, umbrellas, purses, belts . . . everything you need to pull together an outfit that is very "now."

THE CHELSEA GARDENER (16)
125 Sydney Street, SW3
TELEPHONE: 020-7352-5656
FAX: 020-7352-3301
TUBE: Sloane Square, then bus No. 11, 22, or 19
HOURS: Mon–Sat 10 A.M.–6 P.M.; Sun noon–6 P.M.
CREDIT CARDS: AE, MC, V
TYPE: Gardens and plants

The Chelsea Gardener is both a source and an inspiration for those seeking imaginative new ideas for their gardens. They offer help and advice on everything related to gardening and plants, whether yours is planted on a tiny balcony or a vast country estate. They also display a great selection of everything to help out your green thumb, from plants and pots to garden ornaments and furniture. Worth a visit if you love to dabble in dirt.

LA SCALA (7)
35–39 Elystan Street, SW3
TELEPHONE: 020-7589-2784
TUBE: South Kensington
HOURS: Mon–Sat 10 A.M.–5:30 P.M.
CREDIT CARDS: MC, V
TYPE: Dress agency (resale shop)

Who can afford Chanel off the rack, or even last season's leftovers? You can if you haunt the London dress agencies or resale shops. After one or two runs through designer boutiques, you will recover your acute case of "sticker shock" by becoming a resale addict, just as the most fashionable London women are . . . and I won't mention any names, but you would be surprised to find out who shops here! Of all the dress agencies in London, including the strip across the street and around the corner from Harrods, this one is head and shoulders above the rest. If you go to only one, let it be La Scala.

The shop has expanded and now carries treasures for men (Hermes ties for £22–30 and no spots), children (grandmothers beware), and women.

The stock is up-to-the-minute, in perfect condition, beautifully displayed according to type and size, and the staff, headed by owner Alexandra Reid, is very helpful. They carry U.S. sizes 6–16, with loads in size 8. Also available are shoes, bags, hats, jewelry, and other accessories. La Scala gets my highest recommendation.

LEVY AND FRIEND (9)
47 Sloane Avenue, SW3
TELEPHONE: 020-7589-9741
TUBE: South Kensington
HOURS: Tues–Sat 11 A.M.–5 P.M.
CREDIT CARDS: AE, DC, MC, V
TYPE: Dress agency (resale consignment shop)

If retail clothing prices keep rising, consignment dress agencies are going to be the wave of the future. For me, they offer the smart buys of today. More and more stylish Londoners are buying secondhand and not afraid to admit it. Wouldn't you love to find a pair of Ferragamo shoes for less than half price, a cashmere blazer for next to nothing, an assortment of Gucci, and a new (tags still on) suede jacket for about $50? I found these items and many more at Levy and Friend. The value is here, and I can recommend the shop strongly. The two ladies who run it, Carole Levy and Linda Friend, are very helpful; the stock is interesting and changes regularly; and the prices are definitely right.

L'OCCITANE (14)
67 King's Road, SW3
TELEPHONE: 020-7823-4555
TUBE: Sloane Square, then walk or take bus No. 11, 19, or 22

There are other locations on Regent Street and Kensington High Street. Please see page 261 for details.

LUSH (15)
123 King's Road, SW3
TELEPHONE & FAX: 020-7376-8348
TUBE: Sloane Square, then walk or take bus No. 11, 19, or 22
HOURS: Mon–Sat 10 A.M.–7 P.M.; Sun noon–6 P.M.
CREDIT CARDS: AE, MC, V
TYPE: Natural, handmade cosmetics

Lush must be short for luscious ... and that is exactly what these beauty products are. The company believes "in making our own fresh products by hand, printing our own labels and making our own fragrances. We believe in long candlelit baths, massage, filling the house with perfume, and in the right to make mistakes, lose everything, and start again. We also believe that our products should be good value, that we should make a profit and that the customer is always right."

The stores are set up to look like a deli, and all their soaps, creams, elixers, and lotions, which are handcrafted from natural plant-based ingredients, will not only take care of your hair, face, and body but your mind. Preservatives are used as little as possible, and all the products are marked by a sell-by date to ensure their freshness and potency. The imaginatively named products are displayed in bulk and cut and sold to order. Huge rounds of soaps can be sliced by the ounce; refrigerated face creams are dispensed from bowls. I can hardly pass one of their stores in London without darting in for a bar of their Red Rooster, Banana Moon, or Honey Waffle soap, a tub of Wow Wow face mask, the Angels on Bare Skin gentle facial scrub, or another bottle of their soothing Dreaming of Summer bath oil. For the ultimate massage, they recommend their "Massage a Trois" bars—Choco Lala, made with dark chocolate scented with violet; Mont Blanc, with orange flowers and white chocolate; and Cherie Ripe, a fruity bar with the smell of cherries and cassia buds. If you like really crazy, indulgent bath products, treat yourself to one of their Great Balls of Bicarb, which will liven up your bath with fizzing, frothy bath ballistics. Drop it in and watch it hurl and whirl itself around in the water, soothing, moisturizing, or stimulating as it goes. To be wide awake, buy the Slammer or Summer Blues; to stay awake, Waving not Drowning; for aching muscles it's Fizzy O'Therapy, and to soften everything, you will want a Butterball.

If you are traveling to Australia, Canada, Croatia, Scotland, Sweden, or to other cities in England, there are Lush locations. At press time there are three other Lush outlets in London: two in Covent Garden and another on Carnaby Street, but check when you are in London because more are in the pipeline. To order by mail, contact their Vancouver office. Telephone: 888-734-5874; fax: 01202-661-832, email: sales@lush.co.uk.

NOTE: Next door to the King's Road Lush is Starbucks, a perfect refueling stop for anyone in your group who wouldn't get a kick out of a shopping spree at Lush.

MONSOON (11)
33-D King's Road, SW3

TELEPHONE: 020-7730-7552
TUBE: Sloane Square
HOURS: Mon–Sat 10 A.M.–6 P.M.; Wed until 7:30 P.M.; Sun noon–6 P.M.
CREDIT CARDS: AE, DC, MC, V
TYPE: Fashions for the young at heart

Monsoon is an English chain with brightly colored clothing designed in England and made up in India, Thailand, and Hong Kong. These styles are young and light, with colors and prints coordinated for mixing and matching. Prices are affordable, especially when they have a sale. The price on the garments reflects the quality of the sewing, so check them over carefully before buying, as quality varies from piece to piece. Locations for Monsoon are all over London.

NURSERY WINDOW (6)
83 Walton Street, SW3
TELEPHONE: 020-7581-3358
FAX: 020-7823-8839
TUBE: South Kensington
HOURS: Mon–Sat 10 A.M.–5:30 P.M.; closed Dec 24–Jan 2
CREDIT CARDS: AE, MC, V
TYPE: Exclusive children's clothes and gifts

For the most adorable clothing, accessories, and equipment for the babies and children in your life, this shop is pure paradise. They offer all the beautiful clothing, accessories, and room decorations the well-dressed and -housed child will need from birth until the teen years. The owners have researched the market and have chosen the best and most practical items. The cottons are all 100 percent washable; the spotted voile and laces come from Switzerland and are also washable. All of their accessories are handmade in England. They stress that there may be cheaper products out there, but by your third child, theirs will look great and still be going strong. The have a mail-order catalog with all of their products attractively pictured and described.

PAST TIMES (2)
146 Brompton Road, SW3
TELEPHONE: 020-7581-7616
FAX: 020-7581-9016
TUBE: Knightsbridge
HOURS: Mon–Sat 9:30 A.M.–6 P.M.; 11 A.M.–5 P.M.
CREDIT CARDS: AE, DC, MC, V
TYPE: Gifts inspired from Britain's past
For further details, see write-up on page 253.

REJECT CHINA SHOP (3)
183 Brompton Road, SW3
TELEPHONE: 020-7581-0739/7225-1696
FAX: 020-7225-2283
TUBE: Knightsbridge
For details, please see page 254.

TRADITIONAL TOYS (12)
56 Godfrey Street, Chelsea Green, SW3
TELEPHONE: 020-7352-1718
FAX: 020-7349-9603
TUBE: Sloane Square, South Kensington
HOURS: Mon–Fri 10 A.M.–5:30 P.M.; Sat until 6 P.M.
CREDIT CARDS: AE, MC, V
TYPE: Toys

My London flat was just around the corner from Sarah Campos's enchanting toy store on Chelsea Green. Each day as I passed by I would see some new and adorable treasure in her windows . . . maybe a cuddly bear with a tartan bow, a funny little pink pig wearing ballerina shoes and a smile, a dolly's pram complete with a lace-trimmed blanket, or a doll that would fit perfectly into a little one's hand. I will admit it. I did most of my Christmas shopping here, and I mean for my own friends as well as the under-ten set. No matter what your price range, what age or gender you are shopping for, Sarah will have something to make you and the recipient very happy.

NOTE: If you are not in the market for toys, you should make time for a delightful shopping detour to Chelsea Green—an oasis in the middle of London (see page 247).

SW7—SOUTH KENSINGTON (see map page 144)
Shops

DRESS AGENCIES ON CHEVAL PLACE (CONSIGNMENT STORES) (11)
Cheval Place, SW7

TUBE: Knightsbridge
HOURS: Generally Mon–Sat 10 A.M.–6 P.M.
CREDIT CARDS: MC, V in all, AE, DC in some
TYPE: Consignment clothing with designer labels, all previously owned

For years, fashion-savvy women have brought their designer clothing to these shops to sell. The deal is this: The clothes are brought in (by appointment *only*), the shop accepts them (they must be clean), and puts a price tag on the items. The owner gets a percentage, as does the store. The shopper gets a good price and the chance to wear designer clothing when all we really can afford are Walmart fashions on special. U.S. sizes available are 6–16. If you don't see what you want in one store, just keep working the street. You can also accessorize your wardrobe with belts, bags, hats, jewelry, shoes, and scarves. Quality and choice varies greatly.

It isn't easy shopping, but it's fun if you love couturier clothing, but not the prices. Prices may *seem* high, but they are at *least* 50 to 60 percent below retail.

The Dress Box, 8 Cheval Place
Pandora, 16–22 Cheval Place (the biggest; a lot by Chanel and Hermes)
Renate, 4 Cheval Place
Salou, 6 Cheval Place
Strelios, 10 Cheval Place

THE LINEN MERCHANT (6)
11 Montpelier Street, SW7

TELEPHONE: 020-7584-3654
FAX: 020-7584-3671
TUBE: Knightsbridge
HOURS: Mon–Sat 9:30 A.M.–6 P.M.
CREDIT CARDS: AE, MC, V
TYPE: Linens

In today's world of polyester and drip-dry, many have forgotten all about the beauties and pleasures of magnificent linens. A walk by this lovely store will refresh your mind, and you will be inspired to buy something, even if it is only one of their unusual hankies. Grandmothers, don't say I didn't warn you . . . their baby clothes are captivating. Prices will reflect the quality. The personal attention given to each customer harkens back to an earlier era.

TIBOU (21)
19 Harrington Road, SW7

TELEPHONE & FAX: 020-7581-3432
TUBE: South Kensington
HOURS: Mon–Sat 10 A.M.–6 P.M.
CREDIT CARDS: AE, MC, V
TYPE: French children's clothes

This enclave around the South Kensington tube station is the heart of the *quartier française* in London. Everywhere you look there is something French, from patisseries and fast-food bistros to the French Lycée, with an enrollment of 2,700 students, and Tibou, which specializes in children's designer clothes. The shop, owned by Ratiba Tibou, stocks Baby Dior, Pomme Framboise, Mini Mode of Salzberg, pajamas by Arthur, and swimwear by Archimede for ages one to sixteen. The prices reflect the high quality, therefore the sales in January and July are eagerly awaited. The window displays, which showcase Mme. Tibou's artistic side, are wonderful.

SW10—FULHAM (see map page 144)
Shops

GANESHA (40)
6 Park Walk, SW10

TELEPHONE: 020-7352-8972
TUBE: South Kensington, plus a long walk
HOURS: Daily noon–6 P.M.
CREDIT CARDS: MC, V
TYPE: Gifts from the Orient

It is not worth a special trip from the West End, but if you are around Fulham Road or the far end of King's Road, take a quick detour on Park Walk and browse through this jam-packed Asian-style dime store that stocks something for every pocketbook. The tiny ground-level room is stuffed with trinkets and treasures from all over Asia and India. It is a good place to buy clever and cheap gifts. The downstairs room is devoted to large items—tables, chests, and so on—at reasonable prices. Usually the clerk is welcoming, but don't expect much from the aloof owner, who positions herself at the till behind the front counter and chain-smokes.

SE1—SOUTH BANK AND WATERLOO (see map page 170)
Shops

NEAL'S YARD DAIRY WAREHOUSE (4)
6 Park Street, Borough Market, SE1

TELEPHONE: 020-7407-1800
FAX: 020-7378-0400
EMAIL: mailorder@nydairy.co.uk
TUBE: London Bridge
HOURS: Mon–Fri 10 A.M.–6 P.M.
CREDIT CARDS: MC, V
TYPE: Warehouse for Neal's Yard cheeses

If you like their shop near Covent Garden, you will be mad about this warehouse, where the cheeses are stacked and the smells tantalizing. At both shops, sampling is encouraged and the staff very knowledgeable and friendly.

Department Stores

Whatever you need or want, or never imagined you should have, can be found in one of London's many department stores. These large emporiums make good shopping sense if you have only a few hours to shop. All of the stores are known for their January and July sales. Only people who have earned a black belt in shopping should attempt opening day at a Harrods sale. If you do brave this onslaught, you will need superhuman stamina and patience to withstand the merciless crowds clamoring and clawing for bargains that come only once or twice a year. Shopping hours have improved, at least from a British point of view. Most stores are open five or six hours on Sundays and bank holidays, and one so-called late night during the week. Late means they close one hour later at 7 or 8 P.M. on that night. Each area of London has a different late night, and most of the stores in it comply.

DEBENHAMS (21)
334–338 Oxford Street, W1 (see map page 46)
TELEPHONE: 020-7580-3000
INTERNET: www.debenhams.com
TUBE: Bond Street, Oxford Circus
HOURS: Basically Mon–Sat 10 A.M.–7 P.M.; Sun noon–6 P.M.
CREDIT CARDS: AE, DC, MC, V

The remodeling failed to remove its run-of-the mill atmosphere. This is one you can safely avoid with absolutely no regrets.

D. H. EVANS (22)
318 Oxford Street, W1 (see map page 46)
TELEPHONE: 020-7629-8800
TUBE: Bond Street, Oxford Circus
HOURS: Mon–Fri 10 A.M.–7 P.M.; Sat 9:30 A.M.–7 P.M.; Sun noon–6 P.M.; open most bank holidays

CREDIT CARDS: AE, DC, MC, V

In keeping with the times, there is a computer superstore on the fifth floor. Otherwise, it is a large, old-fashioned department store featuring good, sturdy stuff that will never find its way into the closets of fashion wildcats.

DICKENS & JONES (24)
244 Regent Street, W1 (see map page 46)
TELEPHONE: 020-7734-7070
TUBE: Oxford Circus
HOURS: Mon–Sat 10 A.M.–6:30 P.M.; Wed until 7 P.M.; Thur until 8 P.M.; Sun 11 A.M.–5 P.M.
CREDIT CARDS: AE, DC, MC, V

Part of the House of Fraser, aimed toward the working person who cannot afford bespoke clothing. The men's clothing is boring; women's varies. Best parts are the ground-level cosmetics department and the Mariage Freres concession, a French importer that sells the finest teas in the world.

FENWICK (31)
63 New Bond Street, W1 (see map page 46)
TELEPHONE: 020-7629-9161
TUBE: Bond Street
HOURS: Mon–Sat 9:30 A.M.–6 P.M.
CREDIT CARDS: AE, DC, MC, V

Affordable clothes nicely displayed over three floors. Say "Fennick," not Fenwick.

FORTNUM & MASON (46)
181 Piccadilly, W1 (see map page 46)
TELEPHONE: 020-7734-8040
EMAIL: info@fortnumandmason.co.uk
INTERNET: www.fortnumandmason.co.uk
TUBE: Green Park, Piccadilly Circus
HOURS: Mon–Sat 9:30 A.M.–6 P.M.
CREDIT CARDS: AE, DC, MC, V

Fortnum & Mason is famous for its grocery department with knowledgeable clerks ready to serve you. Where else would you be told which tea is best suited to the water in any particular city? It was opened in 1701, and a major part of its success came from providing expatriate Britishers living throughout the empire with products they otherwise would not have had. It still sells a huge variety of gourmet items, as well as its famous picnic hampers for the races at Ascot, and is a supplier to Buckingham Palace and the queen. There is a tableware department in the basement, a stationery and gift department on three, and a womens department on the first floor that stocks designer labels including Issey

Miyake and Missoni. There is also a tearoom/restaurant on the ground level that I no longer can recommend. Please be sure to look at the clock outside the front entrance on Piccadilly. It is as famous as the store itself.

HARRODS (4)
87–135 Brompton Road, SW1 (see map page 116)
TELEPHONE: 020-7730-1234
INTERNET: www.harrods.com
TUBE: Knightsbridge
HOURS: Mon–Sat 10 A.M.–6 P.M.; Wed and Fri until 7 P.M.
CREDIT CARDS: AE, DC, MC, V

The first stop on the yellow brick road of London shopping is Harrods. It is simply not to be missed. You will stand in awe of the sheer size and magnitude of this world-class department store that covers four and a half acres of land space and fifteen acres of prime shopping territory in Knightsbridge. If you are seriously shopping, get in training: Of the more than three hundred departments spread out over seven floors, there are more than sixty fashion departments alone. The mother of all English food halls covers 35,000 square feet with eighteen different departments filling seven elaborately decorated rooms and the necessary service personnel to wait on you properly. That is just the fresh food! A level below is the grocery department. Elegance and abundance has its price, but in January the sales are on and special police forces are stationed outside for mob control. Harrods boasts that it can take care of all of your needs from the cradle to the grave (they have a funeral department). Because it is a full-service department store, there just isn't much they don't have or can't arrange, including excellent half-day tours of London in their own air-conditioned buses with tea and cookies served after the tour. You can get either a morning or afternoon tour, both of which leave right in front of the main entrance.

Warning: There are rules and more rules:

1. There is a dress code for crossing the threshold, and armed guards to enforce it. You are not allowed in wearing shorts, vest tops with nothing underneath, backpacks, or torn jeans (no matter how much they cost).

2. You are not allowed to bring, let alone use, your camera; carry or leash your dog; smoke a cigarette; or eat outside of the restaurants. You can bring in your mobile telephone, but heaven forbid you use it.

3. You can forget about using the toilet unless you pay £1, or produce a paid receipt from one of their restaurants (no other department, even the food hall, qualifies) for a meal in excess of £8! This is outrageous. Harrods certainly doesn't need the extra money, and with armed guards at the entrances, certainly the riffraff will be kept out. No other store in London practices this sort of robbery. Harrods should know better.

HARVEY NICHOLS (3)
109–125 Knightsbridge, SW1 (see map page 116)
TELEPHONE: 020-7235-5000
TUBE: Knightsbridge
HOURS: Mon–Fri 10 A.M.–7 P.M.; Sat until 6 P.M.; Sun noon–6 P.M.
Restaurants open later (call to get hours).
CREDIT CARDS: AE, DC, MC, V

"Harvey Knicks," sometimes written as "Nics," is how you refer to this Knightsbridge shrine to the latest fashions, and without question the most luxurious department store in London (sorry, Harrods). If I could afford it, I would never shop anyplace else. All major designers are represented, including many from America. If you are in London during the January sales, your attendance is absolutely required. On the top floor is a very modern food hall selling every exotic piece of produce you ever heard of, and some you have not. Here also are cafés that have long lunch queues and a posh restaurant with understaffed and overworked waiters. To work off the calories you consume, make an appointment at the Aveda Spa. Designer labels and displays of every major style trend cover three more floors; cosmetics and perfumes yet another. If you love housewares, don't miss the fourth floor, a treasure trove of home fashion ideas ranging from the traditional and useful to the completely wacky.

JOHN LEWIS (23)
278–306 Oxford Street, W1 (see map page 46)
TELEPHONE: 020-7629-7711
INTERNET: www.johnlewis.co.uk
TUBE: Oxford Circus
HOURS: Basically Mon–Sat 9:30 A.M.–6 P.M.
CREDIT CARD: None, except their own card

Along with Peter Jones, Liberty, Selfridges, D. H. Evans, and Harrods, this is one of the stores in central London that carries the range of goods you would expect to find in a full-service department store. Hard to get excited about this one, however.

LIBERTY (33)
210–220 Regent Street, W1 (see map page 46)
TELEPHONE: 020-7734-1234
INTERNET: www.liberty-of-london.com
TUBE: Oxford Circus
HOURS: Mon–Sat 10 A.M.–6:30 P.M.; Thur until 7:30 P.M.
CREDIT CARDS: AE, DC, MC, V

Arthur Lasenby Liberty opened a shop at this address in 1875. The present faux-Tudor building was constructed in 1924 with the timber from two Royal Navy warships. It is easy to get lost in the maze of departments and boutiques that meander over two large buildings, but what a wonderful place to wander. To save yourself wasted shopping time, get a store map and study it before you strike out. Liberty is known worldwide for their fine Liberty print fabrics. A Liberty tie, scarf, covered bracelet, or even a hankie makes a perfect gift that even the most demanding person on your list will recognize and enjoy. There are no bargains here, but if you look carefully, you will find something. If you are in London during the January sales, come on the last day and you can save up to 70 percent on selected goods.

LILLYWHITE'S (1)
24–36 Lower Regent Street, SW1 (see map page 116)
TELEPHONE: 020-7930-3181
TUBE: Piccadilly Circus
HOURS: Basically Mon–Sat 9:30 A.M.–6 P.M.; Sun 11 A.M.–5 P.M.; open some bank holidays
CREDIT CARDS: AE, DC, MC, V
This is the largest sporting goods store in England, with few breathtaking savings unless you hit a sale, and even then it is still questionable. If you are a sportsperson, though, this is mecca . . . even if you don't buy a single golf ball. All brand names are represented, including American.

MARKS & SPENCER (15)
458 Oxford Street, W1 (see map page 46)
TELEPHONE: 020-7935-7954
INTERNET: www.marks-and-spencer.co.uk
TUBE: Bond Street, Marble Arch
HOURS: Mon–Fri 9 A.M.–8 P.M.; Sat until 7 P.M.; Sun noon–6 P.M.; open bank holidays
CREDIT CARDS: None. But the lady at the information booth told me, "Our cash machines take every card under the sun, including American ones I've never heard of." Good luck!
This information lady also told me something I already knew: Marks & Spencer has terrific lingerie, especially the little numbers in silk. There are hundreds of branches of this British shopping tradition in the U.K., where it is referred to as "Marks & Sparks." In addition to the silk underwear, best buys include sweaters, children's clothing, and the food in the basement. Forget the men's department, too high. To get your VAT refund, check with the Marks & Spencer you are in to be sure they participate. *All* of your purchases must add up to that store's required total before you get the refund. You cannot shop at several different branches and pool the receipts. There are numerous branches in London, including ones on Kensington High Street (W8, tube: High Street Kensington), King's Road (SW3, tube: Sloane Square), and Edgeware Road (W2, tube: Marble Arch). Hours may vary slightly.
NOTE: Cash is king at all the Marks & Spencer stores, but some of the best rates in London for changing money are at the M&S exchange offices . . . and they do not charge a commission. Such a deal.

PETER JONES (17)
Sloane Square, SW1 (see map page 116)
TELEPHONE: 020-7730-3434

EMAIL: peter-jones@john lewis.co.uk

TUBE: Sloane Square

HOURS: Mon–Sat 9:30 A.M.–6 P.M.; Wed until 7 P.M.

CREDIT CARDS: None, except for their own

I like Peter Jones for its fine linens, fabrics, china, and houseware departments. The clothing department is boring. Sloane Rangers (British yuppies) shop here in full force on Saturday mornings.

SELFRIDGES (16)
400 Oxford Street, W1 (see map page 46)
TELEPHONE: 020-7629-1234

INTERNET: www.selfridges.co.uk.

TUBE: Bond Street

HOURS: Mon–Sat 9:30 A.M.–7 P.M.; Thur and Fri until 8 P.M.; Sun and bank holidays noon–6 P.M.

CREDIT CARDS: AE, DC, MC, V

American businessman Henry Gordon Selfridge opened the doors of his store in 1901. It had London's first television sales department (1926) and always has fabulous window displays created by specially commissioned artists and designers. Today at Selfridges you will find a huge cosmetics and perfume department, a theater booking agent, wonderful food halls, good-looking fashions, a big household section, and a pleasing staff. Miss Selfridge on Duke Street (same telephone; tube: Bond Street) stocks trendy yet affordable fashions for anyone wanting to feel under thirty-five, even if that birthday is in the distant past.

Indoor Antiques Markets

Shopping Strategies for Indoor Antiques Markets

If you are a collector, try to save some time to wander through the mazes of stalls in these indoor London antiques markets. Whatever your fancy, from Art Deco jewelry to old buttons, teddy bears, dolls, boxes, handmade lace, or furniture, you are bound to find it here and in spades.

Bargaining is expected, but be realistic, the dealer has to make a living. Usually the higher the price, the more room to deal, but *please* don't try to bargain down something priced at £10. As in any market transaction, cash, not plastic, is king. A good phrase to use when dealing is "What is the trade on that?" which implies that you are in the antiques business. Always buy the best you can afford and don't settle for something cracked, chipped, or otherwise damaged, even if the dealer insists it won't matter. Of course it will, so move on to the next dealer . . . the competition is stiff.

ALFIES ANTIQUE MARKET
13–25 Church Street, NW8

TELEPHONE: 020-7723-6066
FAX: 020-7724-0929
EMAIL: alfies@clara.net
INTERNET: www.alfies.clara.net.com
TUBE: Edgware Road, Marylebone
HOURS: Tues–Sat 10 A.M.–6 P.M.
CREDIT CARDS: Depends on seller

I never miss a swing through Alfies, a sprawling collection of antique dealers selling at prices that (after you have bargained) are affordable. The location is not central, and it is not one of the mainstream tourist markets . . . so you are more inclined to find something of quality and value. It bills itself as the biggest permanent covered antiques market in Britain, with forty thousand square feet of space and 350 sellers tucked throughout the joined buildings, plus a greasy spoon café on the top floor.

NOTE: One of my favorite stalls is Stand G144, run by Stevie Pearce, who has the most amazing collection of costume jewelry on her side of the Atlantic Ocean. She also stocks bags and other accessories, but you are here to zero in on her jewels. When you see her corner, you will wonder how she keeps track of anything, but believe me she does. If you don't see what you are looking for, just ask and she is likely to pull it out of one of the boxes stacked on the floor and under her feet. She sells nothing over £15, and 90 percent of her stock is priced to sell at under £10. I found a handful of Parisian buttons and badges dating from the early 1900s to present day.

ANTIQUARIUS (13)
135 King's Road, SW3 (see map page 136)

TELEPHONE: 020-7351-5363
TUBE: Sloane Square, then take bus No. 11, 19, or 22 (if you don't want a long walk)
HOURS: Mon–Sat 10 A.M.–6 P.M.
CREDIT CARDS: Depends on dealer

There are over a hundred stalls selling everything from clocks and lace to porcelain and watches. Known for buttons, textiles, Art Deco, and collectibles like corkscrews, pipes, dolls, and teddy bears. It is across King's Road from the Waitrose supermarket and the Chelsea Cinema.

GREY'S ANTIQUE MARKETS (28)
58 Davies Street and 1–7 Davies Mews, W1 (see map page 46)
TELEPHONE: 020-7629-7034
TUBE: Bond Street
HOURS: Mon–Fri 10 A.M.–6 P.M.
CREDIT CARDS: Depends on stall
TYPE: Two antiques markets with a multitude of individual sellers

Called the biggest in the world, it is a good place to browse to get an idea of what's available. Prices are not in the bargain category, but you are not expected to pay sticker prices.

Outdoor Markets

Shopping Strategies for Outdoor Markets

London markets are entertaining and fun for everyone, even the die-hard couch potato whose idea of shopping is to thumb through a mail-order catalog and dial a toll-free 800 number. For serious antique or collectible shopping enthusiasts, a predawn visit to one of London's big outdoor flea markets is something you will never forget. While you probably will not unearth a rare Minton vase for a few pence, you will find something you want and have fun in the bargain.

At all the flea markets, bargaining is expected and part of the game. There are always two prices for everything, the "punter's" and the dealer's. You know who you are. There are two phrases to keep in mind when discussing price: "What is the best you can do?" and, when talking antiques, "What is the trade on that?" which means, what is the dealer price?

For most of these outdoor markets, Saturday and Sunday are the times to shop, and you *must* get there when the market opens . . . I am talking 5 A.M. for Bermondsey and 6 A.M. for Portobello Road. These are the times for hard-core bargaining and buying. I do not recommend the wee hours at Petticoat Lane; the neighborhood is just too dicey.

No matter which market you go to, it is better to travel in pairs for these early morning safaris. Dress simply. Dealers will charge what the market will bear, and if you are clad in designer togs and high-visibility jewelry, the prices will not go down. With the exception of Covent Garden and some of the dealers on Portobello Road, don't count on your credit cards because not all, and sometimes not many, sellers take them. Not only that, but credit cards just don't command the same discount attention as folding money does. Don't kid yourself . . . pickpockets work the outdoor markets and are fleet-footed pros who will snatch your wallet or purse before you know what hit you. *Wear a money belt* under your clothing, not strapped around your waist for all to see and dip into.

BERMONDSEY MARKET (ALSO CALLED NEW CALEDONIAN MARKET) (13)
Bermondsey Square, south of Tower Bridge, SE1 (see map page 170)

TUBE: Borough or London Bridge and walk south

HOURS: Fri 5:30 A.M.–1 P.M. (starts closing at noon)

Bermondsey Market—also called New Caledonian Market—is the most serious and professional antiques market. The sellers set up by 5:30 A.M., and by 9 A.M. the dealers have picked through. Across the street is a covered market called the Bermondsey Antiques Market and Warehouse. The real fun is outside, early in the morning, so get up early, take your flashlight, and keep your money in a money belt.

BERWICK STREET MARKET (36)
Berwick and Rupert Streets, W1 (see map page 46)

TUBE: Leicester Square, Piccadilly Circus

TYPE: Outdoor produce market

The West End's cheapest fruits and vegetables are hawked on Berwick Street from Monday to Saturday 8 A.M.–6 P.M. If it hasn't sold by 4 P.M. Saturday afternoon, the prices fall to the giveaway level. When you hit Rupert Street, quality goes downhill.

BRICK LANE MARKET (1)
Brick Lane, Cygnet Street, Sclater Street, E1 (see map page 166); Bacon Street, Cheshire Street, Chilton Street, E2

TUBE: Aldgate East, Shoreditch, Liverpool

HOURS: Sun 8 A.M.–1 P.M.

Few tourists come here, but the streets are full of locals out for a bargain. Brick Lane itself is the place to go for leather, junk jewelry, produce, and jellied eels. This is a rough-and-tumble market . . . be careful and don't go alone.

CAMDEN MARKETS
Camden Lock Place, off Chalk Farm Road, NW1

HOURS: Indoor stalls Tues–Sat 10 A.M.–6 P.M.; outdoor stalls Sat–Sun 10 A.M.–6 P.M.

STABLES YARD: Off Chalk Farm Road, opposite Hartland Road

Tourists have turned the Camden Markets into London's fourth biggest tourist attraction. This tells you not to expect the bargain of a shopping lifetime on a rare antique, but you *can* expect to have a good day's outing poking through all there is to see. Camden Lock, a cobbled courtyard leading to the canal, is where the crowds congregate to rifle through the stalls selling crafts and castoffs of various worth and artistic merit. There is a street-party atmosphere, with lots of funky young Londoners just hanging out. The Stables Yard is probably the best-value part, but not for the casual visitor, unless you are into furniture—from antique through the sixties—or lighting fixtures. There are some interesting ethnic Cheap Eats around here. The other three markets under the Camden Market umbrella are Camden Canal Market, Camden Market, and Electric Market, none of which are worth a special trip. When you have had enough of the markets, walk along the peaceful Regent's Canal, or hop on one of the boats that ply the canal. The tube for all the markets is Camden Town, and credit card policies vary with each seller.

CAMDEN PASSAGE
Upper High Street, N1

TUBE: Angel

HOURS: Tues–Sat 10 A.M.–5 P.M., market stalls Wed and Sat 8 A.M.–4 P.M.

Camden Passage is *not* to be confused with the Camden Markets listed above. They aren't even in the same postal code. On Wednesday and Saturday, the area is jammed with hundreds of stalls. The rest of the week, shops sell antiques along an alleyway. The focus is on small tchotchkes, and there are few bargains.

COVENT GARDEN MARKETS: APPLE, JUBILEE, OPERA (50)
Covent Garden, WC2 (see map page 88)

TUBE: Covent Garden

HOURS: Daily 10 A.M.–6 P.M.; may vary on holidays and in the summer

TYPE: Antiques, crafts, clothing, tourist kitsch

The original Covent Garden of Eliza Doolittle fame was a fruit and vegetable market, but now it is a mall of shops and restaurants. The little side streets that go off in every direction are filled with boutiques, coffeehouses, restaurants, and other shops. The whole area is great fun and should not be missed. In addition to the permanent shops in Covent Garden itself, there are three separate markets, which are hard to tell apart. Remember: Monday is antiques *only* at all three; otherwise Apple sells crafts, Jubilee sells junk, and Opera sells tourist items.

Apple: Apple Market is inside the Piazza, under the rooftops of Covent Garden in a courtyard between permanent shops. Monday, antiques; weekends, good British crafts; rest of the time, a mixture of the good, bad, and ugly.

Jubilee: Jubilee is in Jubilee Hall, off Southampton Street. Monday, antiques; other days, clothing, jewelry, crass tourist trash.

Opera: The entrance is off King Street. Monday, antiques; rest of the week, even worse than Jubilee when it comes to tourist items.

GREENWICH MARKET
Off College Approach, Stockwell Street, Greenwich High Road, and Greenwich Church Street, SE10

TRANSPORTATION: Greenwich Rail, or take the boat that leaves every half hour from Westminster Pier

HOURS: Sat–Sun 9 A.M.–5 P.M. (some stalls are open on Friday)

A Saturday or Sunday spent wandering through the Greenwich market stalls used to be a must-do for every serious flea market fan. The stands and merchandise on display have become a bit tackier and tattier lately, but a Sunday spent taking the boat to historic Greenwich is still great fun on your trip to London. To keep a focus on your shopping, remember that stalls in Bosun's Yard Market and the Central Market have somewhat better quality, but you can forget the Village and Greenwich markets, which concentrate on pure junk and greasy hawker food. Greenwich is not all shopping. In addition, you can tour the millennium dome, straddle the meridian line (thus standing simultaneously in the eastern and western hemispheres), wander through the park, or explore the three-masted *Cutty Sark* or *Gypsy Moth* sailing vessels.

OLD SPITALFIELDS MARKET (6)
Commercial Street between Lamb Street and Bushfield Street, E1 (see map page 166)

TUBE: Liverpool Street

HOURS: Sun 10 A.M.–5 P.M.

When I went to look at the Old Spitalfields Market two years ago, there were about three stalls selling tired veggies and a dog show for mutts going on in the center of the open-air building. Hardly the stuff of a write-up. This time around, people are talking about the Sunday market, which features quality organic produce. The emphasis on natural extends to crafts stalls and vendors just in from Tibet selling unbleached cotton clothing, wooden toys, and enough candles and scented soaps to keep you and your surroundings smelling sweetly for a year. Around the edge are various food stalls selling everything from coffee and doughnuts, to chili pickles and Oriental noodles. My favorite for a forbidden grease-out or a sugar fix is Fat Boy's Diner, where you can sit on a red leatherette stool at the counter and indulge in a hot dog and a malt, or order a burger and fries washed down by a cherry coke (see *Cheap Eats in London* for details). During the week the place is utter dullsville. The organic produce is gone and so are most of the market stalls. The center section is devoted to practice sessions for men's and women's soccer teams, whose shouts and whoops drown out everything else. Still, there are the same restaurants open as on Sundays.

PETTICOAT LANE (7)
Middlesex Street, Goulston Street, New Goulston Street, Toynbee Street, Wentworth Street, Bell Lane, Cobb Street, Old Castle Street, Cutler Street, E1 (see map page 166)

> **TUBE:** Liverpool, Aldgate
> **HOURS:** Sun 9 A.M.–2 P.M.

A morning spent at this famous East End market is an experience: a wild kaleidoscope of color, noises, and smells . . . including jellied eels sold from carts. Actually, there is no Petticoat Lane. Look for Middlesex Street and the others, where hundreds of stalls attract hordes of buyers and lookers. The best leather goods are found on New Goulston Street; the antiques section is called the New Cutler Street Market and is known for its scrap gold and silver, coins, medals, and stamps. Take cash, bargain like mad, and have fun.

PORTOBELLO ROAD (30)
Portobello Road off Pembridge Road, W11 (see map page 58)

> **TUBE:** Notting Hill Gate
> **HOURS:** Sat market 7 A.M.–4 P.M., but best until about 1 P.M. Shops Mon–Sat 10 A.M.–5 P.M.
> **TYPE:** Outdoor flea market

On Saturday, Portobello Road is one of Britain's most famous antiques and bric-a-brac markets. The rest of the week it is a quiet street lined with dealers selling antiques from their shops. The Saturday market has three sections. The first and most posh is a five-block strip from Chepstow Villas north, where the street is lined with stalls selling jewelry, lace, objets d'art, paintings, books, and antiques, or would-be antiques. Sellers along here can spot a tourist a mile away and are not above taking them for as much as possible. Be careful. The next section, near Lonsdale Road, is primarily fruit and vegetable hawkers, and from Tavistock Road to Goldborne Road cross streets is pure, unadulterated junk. *Beware of pickpockets at all times.*

Important: The people you see on Saturday with the stands and stalls are *not* extensions of the shops behind them.

Museum Shops

London has such an enormous variety of museums that entire books are devoted to their collections. In the present climate of reduced government grants, museums have had to reinvent themselves and in the process become more aggressively commercial. For shoppers, this is a bonus, because greater emphasis has been placed on luring the museum-goers into the museum shop. Most of London's major museums now have interesting shops that are definitely worth a look. They all sell reproductions from their own collections, and books about them, that you will not find anyplace else. Quality is high and the items are often unusual (and represent good value for money). In most of the museum stores, you can shop without having to pay admission to get into the museum itself. All the shops listed below take at least two major credit cards. *Tip:* If you have time for just one museum shop, do the Victoria and Albert.

For reduced admission fees to many London museums, please read about the White Card, page 253.

Bank of England Museum Shop, EC2	**296**
Bramah Tea & Coffee Museum Shop, SE1	**296**
British Museum Shop, WC1	**296**
Courtauld Gallery Shop, WC2	**297**
Design Museum Shop, SE1	**297**
Imperial War Museum Shop, SE1	**297**
Kensington Palace Shop, W8	**298**
London Transport Museum Shop, WC2	**298**
Museum of London Shop, EC2	**298**
Museum of the Moving Image Shop, SE1	**299**
National Gallery Museum Shop, WC2	**299**
Natural History Museum Shop, SW7	**299**
The Queen's Gallery and Shop at Buckingham Palace, SW1	**300**
The Royal Mews Shop, SW1	**300**
Royal Academy of Arts Shop, W1	**301**
St. Paul's Cathedral Gift Shop, EC4	**301**
Science Museum Shop, SW7	**301**
Tate Gallery Shop, SW1	**301**
Tower of London Shop, EC3	**302**
Victoria and Albert Museum Shop and Crafts Council Shop, SW7	**302**

BANK OF ENGLAND MUSEUM SHOP (9)
Threadneedle Street, entrance on Bartholomew Lane, EC2 (see map page 166)

TELEPHONE: 020-7601-5545
TUBE: Bank
HOURS: Mon–Fri 10 A.M.–5 P.M.
CREDIT CARDS: MC, V

The bank covers three acres, and its vaults hold the country's gold reserves. The only part open to the public is the Bank Museum and the shop, which sells postcards and the usual posters.

BRAMAH TEA & COFFEE MUSEUM SHOP (7)
1 Maguire Street (near the Design Center), SE1 (see map page 170)

TELEPHONE: 020-7378-0222
FAX: 020-7378-0219
TUBE: Tower Hill, and walk across the bridge
HOURS: Daily 10 A.M.–6 P.M.
CREDIT CARDS: AE, MC, V

Even if you never drink coffee or tea, this is a fascinating place. Located in the atmospheric old warehouse section known as Butler's Wharf, the museum tells the 350-year history of two of the world's most important commodities, tea and coffee, and displays Edward Bramah's stunning collection of tea and coffee artifacts. The Tea and Coffee Room offers . . . of course, tea and coffee. The small retail shop sells the Bramah teas and other related products, including lovely teapots, teacups, and coffeepots.

BRITISH MUSEUM SHOP (34)
Great Russell Street, WC1 (see map page 88)

TELEPHONE: 020-7580-1788 (recorded information); please see below
EMAIL: sales@bmco.co.uk (catalog sales)
TUBE: Russell Square
HOURS: Daily 10 A.M.–5 P.M.
CREDIT CARDS: AE, DC, MC, V
TYPE: Museum gifts

There are three separate shops selling unique gifts. The bookshop is a standout. You can request a free mail-order catalog be sent to you. From the U.S., tel: 011-44-1276-606088; fax: 011-44-1276-609102.

Gift Shop in the Forecourt: 020-7323-8175
Bookshop: 020-7323-8587
Children's Shop: 020-7323-8828/9

COURTAULD GALLERY SHOP (52)
Somerset House, The Strand (down from the Hotel Strand Continental), WC2 (see map page 88)

TELEPHONE: 020-7873-2579
FAX: 020-7873-2417
TUBE: Charing Cross, Aldwych
CREDIT CARDS: MC, V
HOURS: Mon–Sat 10 A.M.–6 P.M.; Sun noon–6 P.M.

The collection was founded in 1931 by industrialist and art patron Samuel Courtauld, and it features many of the most important Impressionist and Postimpressionist works in London. The small gift shop carries posters, stationery, cards, and books based on this and other collections.

DESIGN MUSEUM SHOP (8)
Butler's Wharf, 28 Shad Thames Street, SE1 (see map page 170)

TELEPHONE: 020-7403-6933
TUBE: Tower Hill
HOURS: Daily 11:30 A.M.–5:45 P.M.
CREDIT CARDS: AE, MC, V

The Design Museum is devoted to the study of design. The shop has a good selection of designer articles, including china mugs and socks. Many of the products featured in the museum are also sold in the shop. This area is part of the New London development along the River Thames.

NOTE: In order to get to the Design Museum and the Bramah Tea & Coffee Museum, walk along Shad Thames Street, which runs through Butler's Wharf. When it was built in 1871, it was the largest wharf along the River Thames. In 1984, largely due to the insight of Sir Terence Conran, the area slowly started to redevelop. It now consists of his restaurants (expensive), boutiques, art galleries, pubs and wine bars, and the usual sandwich shops.

IMPERIAL WAR MUSEUM SHOP (10)
Lambeth Road, SE1 (see map page 170)

TELEPHONE: 020-7416-5000
TUBE: Elephant & Castle, Waterloo
HOURS: Daily 10 A.M.–6 P.M.
CREDIT CARDS: MC, V

The national museum of twentieth-century warfare and Britain's memorial to the two world wars is housed in a former lunatic asylum that was once known as Bedlam. Some of it is dull, but not the re-creation of World War I trenches, London's Blitz Experience, or the exhibition on espionage. The shop sells model airplanes any boy would love.

KENSINGTON PALACE SHOP (44)
Kensington Gardens, W8 (see map page 58)
TELEPHONE: 020-7937-9561
TUBE: High Street Kensington, Queensway
HOURS: Daily palace 10 A.M.–4 P.M.; shop 10 A.M.–5 P.M.
CREDIT CARDS: MC, V

Kensington Palace will forever be remembered as the last home of Diana, Princess of Wales. The recently redone State Apartments, once the home of William and Mary and the birthplace of Queen Victoria, can be viewed on a special tour that includes the Royal Ceremonial Dress Collection, including dresses worn by the present queen, but none of Princess Diana's.

LONDON TRANSPORT MUSEUM SHOP (50)
The Piazza, Covent Garden, WC2 (see map page 88)
TELEPHONE: 020-7379-6344
TUBE: Covent Garden
HOURS: Daily 10 A.M.–6 P.M., last admission to museum at 5:15 P.M.
CREDIT CARDS: MC, V

The museum, housed in part of the old Victorian Flower Market in Covent Garden, tells the story of London's public transportation system, from the first horse and buggy to the latest space-age marvel. Kids adore it. They can sit in the driver's seat of a red double-decker bus or a tube train. The gift shop is super . . . loads of reproductions of the famous London Transport posters, plus all sorts of other fun things, including "Mind the Gap" paraphernalia that ranges from a pencil or a mug to boxer shorts . . . all with the Mind the Gap logo properly positioned for emphasis.

MUSEUM OF LONDON SHOP (8)
150 London Wall, EC2 (see map page 166)
TELEPHONE: 020-7600-3699
INTERNET: www.museumoflondon.org.uk
TUBE: Barbican, St. Paul's
HOURS: Mon–Sat 10 A.M.–5:50 P.M.; Sun and bank holidays noon–5:50 P.M.

The museum was built in the mid-seventies on the site of a Roman fort. The exhibits tell the story of London and Londoners from prehistoric times to the present. An illuminated model recounts the story of the Great Fire of London, complete with smoke and crackling noises. The shop has the typical postcards, replicas, and gifty stuff.

MUSEUM OF THE MOVING IMAGE SHOP (1)
South Bank, Waterloo Road, SE1 (see map page 170)
TELEPHONE: 020-7401-2636 (recorded information)
TUBE: Embankment, Waterloo
HOURS: Daily 10 A.M.–6 P.M., last entry 5 P.M.

This museum, which tells the story of film, television, and animation, is very popular with children. Forget the first section and head to the area of silent films. Kids can read the news and watch themselves on the monitor, make an animated strip, fly with Superman, or try the many working models. Great gift shop with books on movies, posters, masks, movie-theme gifts . . . even aprons.

NATIONAL GALLERY MUSEUM SHOP (55)
Trafalgar Square, WC2 (see map page 88)
TELEPHONE: 020-7747-2537; 020-7747-2870 (mail order)
FAX: 020-7747-5951
EMAIL: simon.sutton@ng-longon.org.uk
INTERNET: www.nationalgallery.org.uk
TUBE: Charing Cross, Leicester Square
CREDIT CARDS: AE, MC, V
HOURS: Daily 10 A.M.–5:45 P.M.; Wed until 8:45 P.M.

The National Gallery has more than two thousand paintings covering all the leading European schools from the thirteenth to the early twentieth centuries. There are two shops, one by the main entrance and a larger one in the Sainsbury Wing. Besides the usual posters and books, keep your eye out for their line of scarves, ceramic tiles, amusing T-shirts, and regal velvet slippers.

NATURAL HISTORY MUSEUM SHOP (18)
Cromwell Road, SW7 (see map page 144)
TELEPHONE: 020-7938-9062 (shop); 020-7938-9022 (bookshop)
TUBE: South Kensington (take the Museums exit)
HOURS: Mon–Sat 10 A.M.–5:50 P.M.; Sun 11 A.M.–5:50 P.M.
CREDIT CARDS: AE, MC, V

The Natural History Museum was the Visitor Attraction of the Year in 1998. I am not surprised if sheer numbers are the guiding measure of popularity. When I was there, the queue of excited young people waiting to get in to see an exhibition on bugs stretched for three blocks down Cromwell Road. You can go to the shops without paying to go to the museum. To do this, drop by the reception area, sign in, and wear the sticker that identifies you as a shopper only. Free entrance to the museum is between 4:30 and 5:30 P.M. on weekdays and 5 and 5:30 P.M. on weekends, but in that short time span, I don't know what you would be able to see. In addition to the gift and bookshops, near the exit of the dinosaur exhibit in Gallery 21 there is a Dino-store featuring everything you can imagine with a dinosaur motif, and a plethora of information about these prehistoric beasts. Your children will adore this shop . . . just a warning.

THE QUEEN'S GALLERY AND SHOP AT BUCKINGHAM PALACE (6) AND THE ROYAL MEWS SHOP (7)
Buckingham Palace Road, SW1 (see map page 116)
>**TELEPHONE:** 020-7839-1377
>**FAX:** 020-7930-9625
>**EMAIL:** information@royalcollection.org.uk
>**INTERNET:** www.royal.gov.uk
>**TUBE:** Victoria, St. James's Park
>**HOURS:** See below
>**CREDIT CARDS:** AE, MC, V
>**TYPE:** Memorabilia from Buckingham Palace and the Royal Mews

THE QUEEN'S GALLERY AND SHOP AT BUCKINGHAM PALACE
HOURS: Daily 9:30 A.M.–5 P.M., closed April 2, December 25–26

It used to be open only during the summer, which is when Buckingham Palace is open to visitors, but the royals are smart enough to know they have a cash cow here, so now you can spend money 362 days of the year in their Gallery Shop. The shop is very well done and has a tasteful selection of regal gifts that run the gamut from pens and playing cards marked with the Buckingham Palace insignia to halcyon boxes, with countless goodies way under £10. I like the Victorian lavender sachets, the packets of fudge wrapped in a Palace box with a red tassel on top, the little bags of hot toddy mix, and the exceptional variety of note cards, including boxed editions of Prince Charles' watercolors. There is even a bench for nonshoppers.

NOTE: Tours of Buckingham Palace take place daily from 9:30 A.M.–4:40 P.M. between the first week in August through the first week in October. Admission is around £10 and you must book ahead. You can do this using your credit card by telephoning 020-7321-2233, or in person from the Ticket Office in Green Park.

The Changing of the Guard takes place daily at 11:30 A.M. from April 1 until July 1, and on alternate days thereafter.

THE ROYAL MEWS SHOP
HOURS: The shop hours are the same as those for the Royal Mews. Mon–Thur noon–3:30 P.M.; in the summer when Buckingham Palace is open Mon–Thur 10:30 A.M.–4 P.M., closed on all royal occasions. This shop is open only to ticket bearers for the Royal Mews.

Please try to work your sight-seeing schedule to coincide with a time the Royal Mews is open. These are the working stables and garages that house the perfectly groomed horses and magnificent coaches and gilt-trimmed carriages you see in every royal procession. For my money, it is one of the must-sees for every London visitor.

ROYAL ACADEMY OF ARTS SHOP (45)
Burlington House, Piccadilly, W1 (see map page 46)
TELEPHONE: 020-7439-7438
TUBE: Piccadilly Circus, Green Park
HOURS: Daily 10 A.M.–5:45 P.M.
CREDIT CARDS: AE, DC, MC, V

Popular changing exhibits here do inspire crowds and long lines. Best time to avoid the crush is early Sunday or Monday mornings. Most of the merchandise in their shop is geared to whatever blockbuster show is on.

ST. PAUL'S CATHEDRAL GIFT SHOP (10)
St. Paul's Church Yard, EC4 (see map page 166)
TELEPHONE & FAX: 020-7329-2029
TUBE: St. Paul's
HOURS: Mon–Sat 9 A.M.–5 P.M.; Sun 10:30 A.M.–4 P.M.
CREDIT CARDS: AE, MC, V

Set in the arched basement of St. Paul's Cathedral, this large gift shop is definitely worthwhile. The selection covers everything from key rings and T-shirts to lovely illustrated books, church memorabilia, and British-made goods. It is all in good taste . . . even the key rings aren't corny. Enter on the side if you don't want to pay to tour the cathedral. Bonus: one of the best public bathrooms in London, and places to sit for your nonshopping tagalongs. There is also a café, but I recommend timing your visit to include lunch at The Place Below in the crypt at St. Mary-le-bow Church on Cheapside in The City, EC2 (see *Cheap Eats in London*).

SCIENCE MUSEUM SHOP (10)
Exhibition Road, SW7 (see map page 144)
TELEPHONE: 020-7938-8187
TUBE: South Kensington (take the Museums exit)
HOURS: daily 10 A.M.–6 P.M.
CREDIT CARDS: MC, V
TYPE: Science-related items

The Science Museum packs five floors full of discoveries and inventions, with explanations about how things work. The many hands-on exhibits make it a paradise for children of all ages. The bookstore is no exception.

TATE GALLERY SHOP (33)
Millbank, SW1 (see map page 116)
TELEPHONE: 020-7887-8876
TUBE: Pimlico
HOURS: daily 10 A.M.–5:40 P.M.
CREDIT CARDS: MC, V
TYPE: National collection of British and modern art

The Tate is well loved for its collections of international modern arts and British artists. Not to be missed are the Turner paintings in the Clore Gallery extension. In May 2000 the contemporary art is scheduled to be moved to the new Tate Gallery of Modern Art in the old Bankside Power Station. The Millbank building will then be the Tate Gallery of British Art. The gift shop is very good, featuring loads of gift books, boxes of stationery, and posters of their exhibitions. My favorite purchases are their umbrellas inspired by Monet, Miró, Matisse, and Braque.

TOWER OF LONDON SHOP (12)
Tower Hill, EC3 (see map page 166)
TELEPHONE: 020-7709-0765
TUBE: Tower Hill
HOURS: Winter (Nov–Feb) Tues–Sat 9 A.M.–4 P.M., Sun–Mon 10 A.M.– 4 P.M.; summer (Mar–Oct) Mon–Sat 9 A.M.–5 P.M., Sun 10 A.M.–5 P.M.
CREDIT CARDS: AE, MC, V

The Tower of London has been a castle, a palace, and a prison. Now it is a favorite tourist destination. One of the biggest attractions are the Crown Jewels, and while you may never wear the real thing, you can buy replicas of some of the pieces in the gift shop.

VICTORIA AND ALBERT MUSEUM SHOP AND
CRAFTS COUNCIL SHOP (19)
Cromwell Road, SW7 (see map page 144)
TELEPHONE: 020-7938-8438
FAX: 020-7938-8623
TUBE: South Kensington (take the Museums exit)
HOURS: Mon noon–5:45 P.M.; Tues–Sun 10 A.M.–5:45 P.M.
CREDIT CARDS: MC, V
TYPE: Best museum shop in London

The Victoria and Albert has the world's largest collection of decorative, fine, and applied arts, as well as the national sculpture collection. Its galleries cover seven miles and attract over one million visitors a year. The gift shop keeps pace . . . it is the best in London, especially the handmade items from Britain's leading craft artists.

Cheap Chic by Type

Glossary

America and Britain are two great nations divided by a common language.
—George Bernard Shaw

English	American
A	
all-in	all-inclusive
anorak	hooded jacket (parka)
B	
bank holiday	legal holiday
bathroom	a room with a bathtub in it
bedsit or bed-sitter	studio or one-room apartment
bespoke	custom-made clothing
bill	check (restaurant)
bobby	police officer
bonnet (car)	car hood
book (*v.*)	to reserve
boot	car trunk
braces	suspenders
briefs	jockey shorts
brolly or bumbershoot	umbrella
C	
call	visit, as in pay a visit or call into a shop
caravan	trailer, mobile home
car park	parking lot
carriage	railroad car
chemist	pharmacist
chemist shop	drugstore, pharmacy
coach	bus
cot crib	baby crib
cotton	thread
cotton wool	absorbent cotton
cupboard	closet
D	
directory inquiries	telephone information
double	hotel room with double bed
dual carriageway	divided highway
E	
eiderdown	comforter
en suite	hotel room with private toilet, shower, and/or bathtub

F

face flannel	washcloth
first floor	second floor
flat	apartment
flex	electric cord
fortnight	two weeks

G

ground floor	first floor

H

hair grip	bobby pin
hair slide	barrette
high street	main street
hire (*v.*)	to rent (as in rent a car)

I

ironmonger	hardware store

J

jumble sale	used clothing sale, as in rummage
jumper	cardigan sweater

K

knickers	underpants

L

ladder	pantyhose run
let (*v.*)	to lease, rent
lie in, have a lie in	to sleep in
lift	elevator
loo	toilet
lorry	truck
lower ground floor	below street level, basement level

M

mackintosh	raincoat
mate	pal

N

nappy	diaper
net curtain	sheer curtains
nought	zero

O

off-license/wine merchant	retail liquor store
off the peg	ready-made
one-off	onetime event or happening

P

pants	shorts (men's underwear)
partner	live-in boyfriend or girlfriend
personal call	person-to-person telephone call
petrol	gasoline
phone box or call box	telephone booth
point, power point	outlet, socket

post	mail
postal code	zip code
pram	baby buggy
public school	private school
push chair	stroller
push out the boat	spend beyond the limit

Q

queue	waiting line

R

reception (hotel)	front desk
return ticket	round-trip ticket
ring (v.)	to telephone
roundabout	traffic circle
rubber	eraser

S

schedule	same meaning, pronounced "shed-ule"
self-catering	accommodation with kitchen
self-drive	car rental
service flats	apartment hotel
single ticket	one-way ticket
stalls	orchestra seats in the theater
subway	underground passageway
suspender belt	garter belt
suspenders	garters
swing a cat ("You couldn't swing a cat in here.")	saying for describing size of a room

T

telly	television
tights	panty hose
torch	flashlight
trainers	sneakers, athletic shoes (e.g., Nike)
treble (room)	hotel room with three single beds

V

VAT (value-added tax)	sales tax
vest	man's undershirt

W

waistcoat	vest
wardrobe	closet
water closet (WC)	toilet
wellies	waterproof boots
windscreen	windshield

Z

zebra crossing	pedestrian crossing
zed (letter)	pronunciation of letter z

Index of Accommodations

Index of Cheap Chic

Readers' Comments

While every effort has been made to provide accurate information in this edition of *Cheap Sleeps in London,* the publisher and author cannot be held responsible for changes in any of the listings due to rate increases, inflation, currency fluctuations, the passage of time, management changes, or any losses thereby caused. The publisher and author also cannot be held responsible for the experiences of readers while traveling.

Cheap Sleeps in London is updated and revised on a regular basis. If you find a change before I do, or make an important discovery you want to pass along, please send me a note stating the name and address of the hotel or shop, the name of the people you dealt with, the date of your visit, and a description of your findings. As the hundreds of readers who have written to me know, your letters are very important to me; I investigate every complaint and pass on every compliment you send me, and I read and personally answer every letter. Because of this, I do not provide an email address, since the volume of mail it would generate would make it impossible to personally reply to each message. I hope you will understand and still take a few minutes to drop me an old-fashioned letter telling me about your Cheap Sleeps in London. Thank you in advance for taking the time to write.

Send your comments to Sandra A. Gustafson's *Cheap Sleeps in London,* c/o Chronicle Books, 85 Second Street, Sixth Floor, San Francisco, CA 94105.